LONG-VOWEL SHIFTS IN ENGLISH, *C.* 1050–1700

The English language has undergone many sound-changes in its long history. Some of these changes had a profound effect on the pronunciation of the language: a number of these significant instances of language evolution are generally grouped together and termed the 'Great Vowel Shift'. These changes are generally considered unrelated to other, similar long-vowel changes taking place a little earlier. This book assesses an extensive range of irregular Middle English spellings for all these changes, with a view to identifying the real course of events: the dates, the chronology, and the dialects that stand out as being innovative. Using empirical evidence to offer a fresh perspective and drawing new, convincing conclusions, Stenbrenden offers an interpretation of the history of the English language which may change our view of sound-change completely.

GJERTRUD FLERMOEN STENBRENDEN is Associate Professor of English Language at the University of Oslo.

STUDIES IN ENGLISH LANGUAGE

The aim of this series is to provide a framework for original studies of English, both present-day and past. All books are based securely on empirical research, and represent theoretical and descriptive contributions to our knowledge of national and international varieties of English, both written and spoken. The series covers a broad range of topics and approaches, including syntax, phonology, grammar, vocabulary, discourse, pragmatics, and sociolinguistics, and is aimed at an international readership.

Already published in this series:

Steven Jones, M. Lynne Murphy, Carita Paradis and Caroline Willners: *Antonyms in English: Construals, Constructions and Canonicity*
Christiane Meierkord: *Interactions across Englishes: Linguistic Choices in Local and International Contact Situations*
Haruko Momma: *From Philology to English Studies: Language and Culture in the Nineteenth Century*
Raymond Hickey (ed.): *Standards of English: Codified Varieties Around the World*
Benedikt Szmrecsanyi: *Grammatical Variation in British English Dialects: A Study in Corpus-Based Dialectometry*
Daniel Schreier and Marianne Hundt (eds.): *English as a Contact Language*
Bas Aarts, Joanne Close, Geoffrey Leech and Sean Wallis (eds.): *The Verb Phrase in English: Investigating Recent Language Change with Corpora*
Martin Hilpert: *Constructional Change in English: Developments in Allomorphy, Word Formation, and Syntax*
Jakob R. E. Leimgruber: *Singapore English: Structure, Variation and Usage*
Christoph Rühlemann: *Narrative in English Conversation*
Dagmar Deuber: *English in the Caribbean: Variation, Style and Standards in Jamaica and Trinidad*
Eva Berlage: *Noun Phrase Complexity in English*

Nicole Dehé: *Parentheticals in Spoken English: The Syntax-Prosody Relation*
Jock Onn Wong: *English in Singapore: A Cultural Analysis*
Anita Auer, Daniel Schreier and Richard J. Watts: *Letter Writing and Language Change*
Marianne Hundt: *Late Modern English Syntax*
Irma Taavitsainen, Merja Kyto, Claudia Claridge and Jeremy Smith: *Developments in English: Expanding Electronic Evidence*
Arne Lohmann: *English Co-ordinate Constructions: A Processing Perspective on Constituent Order*
John Flowerdew and Richard W. Forest: *Signalling Nouns in English: A Corpus-Based Discourse Approach*
Jeffrey P. Williams, Edgar W. Schneider, Peter Trudgill and Daniel Schreier: *Further Studies in the Lesser-Known Varieties of English*
Nuria Yáñez-Bouza: *Grammar, Rhetoric and Usage in English: Preposition Placement 1500–1900*
Jack Grieve: *Regional Variation in Written American English*
Douglas Biber and Bethany Gray: *Grammatical Complexity in Academic English: Linguistics Change in Writing*
Gjertrud Flermoen Stenbrenden: *Long-Vowel Shifts in English, c. 1050–1700: Evidence from Spelling*

Earlier titles not listed are also available

LONG-VOWEL SHIFTS IN ENGLISH, *C.* 1050–1700

Evidence from Spelling

GJERTRUD FLERMOEN STENBRENDEN

University of Oslo

CAMBRIDGE
UNIVERSITY PRESS

University Printing House, Cambridge CB2 8BS, United Kingdom

One Liberty Plaza, 20th Floor, New York, NY 10006, USA

477 Williamstown Road, Port Melbourne, VIC 3207, Australia

314-321, 3rd Floor, Plot 3, Splendor Forum, Jasola District Centre, New Delhi - 110025, India

79 Anson Road, #06-04/06, Singapore 079906

Cambridge University Press is part of the University of Cambridge.

It furthers the University's mission by disseminating knowledge in the pursuit of education, learning and research at the highest international levels of excellence.

www.cambridge.org
Information on this title: www.cambridge.org/9781107677517

First published 2016
First paperback edition 2018

A catalogue record for this publication is available from the British Library

Library of Congress Cataloging in Publication data
Stenbrenden, Gjertrud Flermoen, author.
Long-vowel shifts in English, c. 1050–1700 : evidence from spelling / Gjertrud Flermoen Stenbrenden.
pages cm. – (Studies in English language)
Includes bibliographical references and index.
ISBN 978-1-107-05575-9 (hardback)
1. English language–Middle English, 1100–1500–Vowels. 2. English language–Middle English, 1100–1500–Orthography and spelling. 3. English language–Old English, ca. 450–1100–Vowels. 4. English language–Old English, ca. 450–1100–Orthography and spelling. 5. English language–Pronunciation–History. 6. English language–Phonology, Historical. 7. English language–Grammar, Generative. 8. Lingusitic change–History. I. Title.
PE553.S74 2016
427′.02–dc23 2015028161

ISBN 978-1-107-05575-9 Hardback
ISBN 978-1-107-67751-7 Paperback

Contents

Abbreviations

acc.	accusative
AN	Anglo-Norman
Bck	Buckinghamshire
Bed	Bedfordshire
Brk	Berkshire
Cam	Cambridgeshire
CF	Central French
Chs	Cheshire
Cnw	Cornwall
Cu	Cumberland
Da	Danish
dat.	dative
Dby	Derbyshire
Dor	Dorset
Du	Dutch
Dur	Durham
Dvn	Devonshire
E	East(ern)
e	early
Ely	Isle of Ely
ERY	Yorkshire, East Riding
Ex	Essex
f[em].	feminine
Fr	French
G	German
GA	General American
Gael	Gaelic
gen.	genitive
Gl	Gloucestershire
Gmc	Germanic

Go	Gothic
Gr	Greek
GVS	Great Vowel Shift
Ha	Hampshire
Hrf	Herefordshire
Htf	Hertfordshire
Hu	Huntingdonshire
IE	Indo-European
imp.	imperative
ind.	indicative
inf.	infinitive
IOM	Isle of Man
Kt	Kent
L	Latin
l	late
La	Lancashire
Lei	Leicestershire
Li	Lincolnshire
Lon	London
LP	Linguistic Profile
m[asc].	masculine
ME	Middle English
MEOSL	Middle English Open Syllable Lengthening
Midl	Midland
ModE	Modern English
MS	manuscript
MSS	manuscripts
Mx	Middlesex
N	North(ern)
n[eut].	neuter
n	noun (in tables)
Nbld	Northumberland
NF	Norman French
Nfk	Norfolk
Nht	Northamptonshire
NME	Northern Middle English
nom.	nominative
Norw	Norwegian
NRY	Yorkshire, North Riding

Nt	Nottinghamshire
OE	Old English
OFr	Old French
OFris	Old Frisian
OHG	Old High German
OK	Old Kentish
OL	Old Latin
ON	Old Norse
ONbn	Old Northumbrian
OS	Old Saxon
OSL	Open Syllable Lengthening
Ox	Oxfordshire
PDE	Present-Day English
pers.	personal
Pet	Soke of Peterborough
pl.	plural
poss.	possessive
ppl.	participle
pres.	present
PrGmc	Proto-Germanic
PrIE	Primitive Indo-European
pt.	past tense
pron.	pronoun
RP	Received Pronunciation
Ru	Rutland
Run	Runic
S	South(ern)
Sal	Shropshire
sb.	noun (substantive)
SE	South-East(ern)
Sfk	Suffolk
sg.	singular
SHOCC	shortening of vowels before fortis consonant clusters
SME	Southern Middle English
Som	Somerset
StE	Standard English
Stf	Staffordshire
Sur	Surrey
Sw	Swedish

(2) and (3) in the concluding chapter, after I have assessed the spelling evidence for ME long-vowel shifts and determined the answers to question (1) in Chapters 2–8.

A fifth problem has to do with the theoretical frameworks used to provide the most suitable model for chain-shifts. For instance, Optimality Theory uses contraints rankings to determine the course of change, and the winning ranking is the one that gives the expected output; this is circular, however, in that the output is known *a priori* and is exactly what the constraints and the rankings are supposed to capture. A case in point is Łubowicz, who addresses 'the typology of chain shift mappings in the context of various theoretical proposals' (2011: 1718). Even if she allows diachronic drag-chains, she questions 'whether pull shifts are possible synchronically' because they 'are not admitted under any of the theoretical proposals' she examines (2011: 1720). This is putting the cart before the horse: Drag-chains and pull-chains are descriptive labels and open to empirical observation; if the theories cannot account for them, the conclusion is not that such changes cannot happen, but that there is something wrong with the theory. Łubowicz claims that *diachronic* drag-chains 'are different, as they can be seen as different processes that apply at different stages in the development of the language' (2011: 1728), but it is unclear why this cannot apply to synchronic drag-chains also.

1.2 Topics and aims

1.2.1 Middle English long-vowel change

This work is concerned with a number of changes in long-vowel pronunciation that took place between *c.* 1050 and 1700. There is general consensus among scholars as to the phonetic nature of the OE vowels (Quirk and Wrenn 1990; Mitchell and Robinson 1992: §§7–8; Sweet 1992: §2). A comparison between the OE realisations and that of their modern reflexes reveals great differences, especially regarding long vowels. In other words, it is clear that changes must have happened to the pronunciation of long vowels sometime between OE and PDE. Traditionally, these changes have been assigned to two separate groups.

The first group consists of four lOE or eME changes, namely (a) the unrounding and/or lowering of OE *ȳ* to [iː] or [eː]; (b) the monophthongisation and subsequent unrounding of OE *ēo* to [øː] > [eː]; (c) the backing, rounding, and raising of eME *ā* to [ɔː], which took place in the dialects south of the Humber; and (d) the fronting and raising of eME

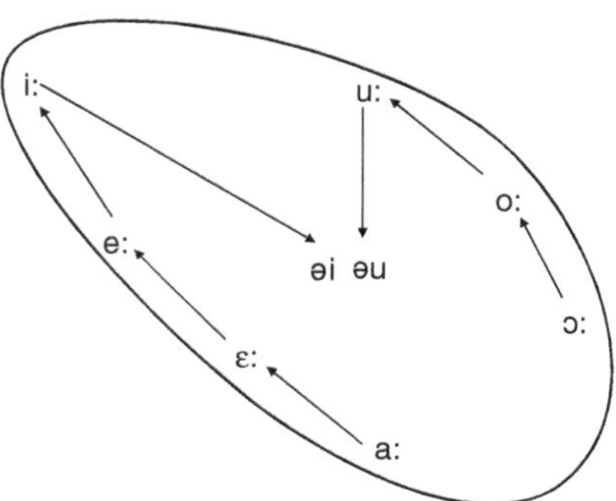

Figure 1.1 The 'Great Vowel Shift', early stage.

ǭ [o:] to [ʉ:], which took place north of the Humber.[1] Changes (c) and (d) are assumed to have been completed before 1350.

The second set of changes is usually collectively referred to as 'the Great Vowel Shift' (GVS), and denotes a vocalic restructuring whereby the eME non-close vowels *ē, ę̄, ō, ǭ* and lME *ā* were raised one height to [i:], [e:], [u:], [o:], [æ:] respectively, and the close vowels *ī* and *ū* were diphthongised, first to [ɪi] and [ʊu], later to [əi] and [əu]. Through later changes, the [e:] (< ME *ę̄*) was further raised to [i:] in most words in StE, but diphthongised to [eɪ] in a few words (*yea, break, steak, great*); the [æ:] (< lME *ā*) was raised to [e:] and then diphthongised to [eɪ]; and the [o:] (< ME *ǭ* < OE *ā*) was diphthongised to [oʊ] (and eventually to /əʊ/ in RP). The 'GVS' is generally held to have begun around 1400 and to have been completed *c.* 1750; the following vowel diagrams capture the stages of the 'GVS' (Figures 1.1 and 1.2); the shape of the articulatory vowel space follows Prokosch (1939: 97–98) and Labov (1994: 256–261).

Table 1.1 gives an overview of long-vowel changes in the ME and eModE periods. No attempt has been made to date the changes exactly or to indicate the internal chronology. The term 'eME *ī*' includes the reflexes of OE *ī, ȳ, ēog/ēoh, ēag/ēah, iht, yht, eoht, eaht*, and OE *i/y* in lengthening contexts; 'eME *ū*' includes the reflexes of OE *ū*, OE *u* in lengthening contexts, and OE *ōg/og*; 'eME *ę̄*' is generally the reflex of OE *ǣ*; 'eME *ǭ*' is generally the reflex of OE *ā* (south of the Humber); and 'ME *ā*' is the product of Middle English Open Syllable Lengthening (MEOSL). A dash indicates no further change.

Anglicists in the nineteenth century soon came to regard the changes of the second group as being somehow interrelated and interdependent, that is, they were part of a chain-shift. Most notable among these linguists

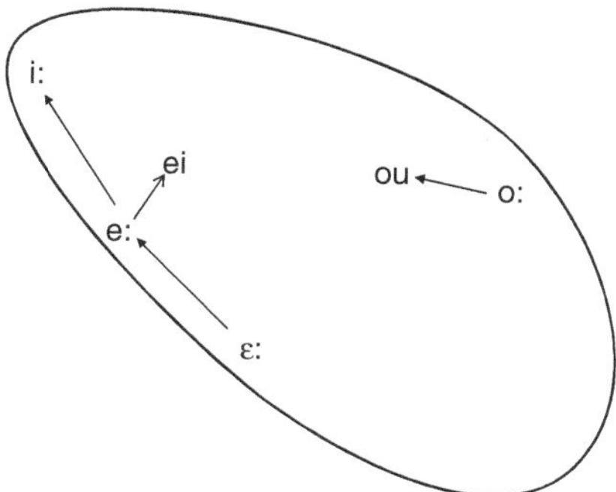

Figure 1.2 The 'Great Vowel Shift', late stage.

Table 1.1 *Middle English and Modern English long-vowel changes*

eME	ME	eModE	PDE	Examples
ī [i:]	[ɪi]	[əi]	/aɪ/	*white, sty, bind, night, bright*
ū [u:]	[ʊu]	[əu]	/aʊ/	*brown, pound, fowl, bough*
ē [e:]	[i:]	–	/i:/	*green, see, teeth*
ō [o:]	[u:]	–	/u:/	*tooth, tool, moon*
ę̄ [ɛ:]	[e:]	[i:] or [eɪ]	/i:/ or /eɪ/	*deal, sea; great, steak*
ǭ [ɔ:]	[o:]	[oʊ]	/əʊ/ (RP), /oʊ/ (GA)	*home, stone, boat*
ā [a:]	[æ:]	[ɛ:] → [eɪ]	/eɪ/	*lady, take*

are Jespersen and Luick. Jespersen named it 'die groβe Vokalverschiebung' (1909: 231). At first, he no doubt coined this phrase to serve as a conceptual map, or some kind of mental shorthand, which was useful as a way of organising the material and for getting a mental grip of the nature of these changes. The English translation of this phrase, 'the Great Vowel Shift', was soon adopted by other linguists. Jespersen also presented the changes in terms of a diagram (1909: 232; the raised dot is Jespersen's symbol for vowel-length) (see Figure 1.3).

However, although there may have been no idea of a process involved in this concept of 'the Great Vowel Shift' at first, it was soon reified: the concept itself acquired near-factual status. That is, the capitalised vowel shift was conceived of as a unitary event with its own inner coherence, which needed a special kind of explanation. The question soon turned to which vowel(s) moved first, and whether this initial change triggered a push-chain or drag-chain. What is more, the shift was considered unique

Figure 1.3 Jespersen's representation of the Great Vowel Shift (1909: 232).

to English. This view of the 'GVS' has been challenged, most notably by Stockwell since the early 1960s, and by Stockwell and Minkova (1988a, 1988b, 1997). It is the contention of this book, in agreement with Stockwell and Minkova and many other scholars, that the concept of a 'GVS' as a unitary event is illusory, that the changes started earlier than has been assumed, and that the changes of both the sets mentioned above took longer to be completed than most handbooks claim.

Evidence for these vocalic changes is found in (a) previous stages of English, (b) the sound system of PDE, (c) comparative material from other Gmc languages, (d) spellings, (e) rhymes, and (f) 'eyewitness' accounts by sixteenth- and seventeenth-century orthoepists. Each of these is treated below.

On the correspondences between spellings and phonetic value, Campbell observes that 'our knowledge of the sounds of a dead language can never be more than approximate' (1959: §31). Further (1959: §31),

> The following reconstruction of the phonetic system of Old English is based on the probable value of the symbols when they are used to write Latin of the same period, and upon reasonable deductions from the history of the sounds both in Germanic and in the later periods of English.

Thus, the sound correspondences of the OE vowel letters are relatively transparent. When these sound values are compared to the PDE vowels on an etymological basis, it is clear that the phonetic realisations of long vowels changed at some point in time. Further evidence for the initial sound value of OE vowel symbols is found in other Gmc languages: PrGmc *ī* is still realised as /iː/ in Danish and Norwegian (e.g. Norw. *hvit* /ʋiːt/ 'white'); PrGmc *ū* is still realised as /uː/ in Danish (e.g. *hus* /huːs/ 'house'); and PrGmc *ē* still has the sound value /eː/ in Norwegian, Danish, and Swedish (e.g. Norw. *se* /seː/ 'see').

Spellings and rhymes provide a different kind of evidence, especially when they depart from traditional orthography. Such evidence, along with its status as proof of sound-change, is treated in detail in Section 1.5. After the rise of StE in the fifteenth century and the introduction of the printing press in 1476, there arose a need for a uniform spelling. The press entailed mass production of texts, so that the variety of spelling shown by a manuscript (MS) corpus inevitably disappeared. But consistency within the typesetting was another matter. Consequently, from *c.* 1530 onwards, numerous orthoepistical works on the 'right' spelling and pronunciation were published. Much information about the pronunciation of English can be gleaned from such works, but they are generally too late to offer any insights on the initial stages of the 'GVS', and even less on the earlier set of changes; they do sometimes provide confirmation of changes that have already happened or are taking place in the authors' own dialects. Evidence from the early orthoepists has been used in this work to cast light on the later stages of the long-vowel shifts examined here.

1.2.2 *Previous research on the 'Great Vowel Shift'*

This section gives a brief survey of research on the 'GVS'; previous research on each individual vowel is dealt with in the relevant chapters. Following Luick (1896, 1899, 1901, 1912, 1914–40, 1932) and Jespersen (1909), who were among the first to see these changes as a set of interdependent changes, most handbooks present the 'GVS' as an event which needs to be explained (e.g. Algeo and Pyles 2005). According to Wolfe (1972), questions regarding the shift can be grouped into five categories: (1) *how* questions, (2) *what* questions, (3) *why* questions, (4) *where* questions, and (5) *when* questions.

What questions seek to establish exactly what happened at the phonetic or sub-phonemic level during the 'GVS'. For example, the diphthongs that developed from eME *ī* and *ū* pre-suppose that a glide vowel must have developed before the original vocalic nucleus, and there is general consensus that the first stage would have entailed the formation of minimal diphthongs, [ɪi] and [ʊu]. *What* questions then try to identify the later development of these minimal diphthongs, producing PDE [aɪ] and [aʊ]: for instance, the on-glide may have centralised to [ə] and then 'dropped down' in vocalic space, or the on-glide may have been front [e], which lowered along a front path. The answer to this may be crucial in determining why the diphthongised reflex of etymological *ī* did not merge with the etymological diphthong [ei].[2] Such 'near-mergers' have attracted attention from, for example, Kökeritz (1932), Orton (1933), Stockwell (1978), and Labov (1994).

How questions try to ascertain by what stages the 'GVS' came about; three basic views have been put forward. The first states that the close vowels diphthongised first, leaving a void in the close front and back position, and pulling the other long vowels up to fill consecutively vacant vowel slots, in a drag-chain process. The second position holds that the half-close vowels *ē* and *ō* moved first, forcing the close vowels *ī* and *ū* to diphthongise in order to avoid merger, in a push-chain process. The third suggests that all the 'GVS' changes were more or less simultaneous. Naturally, such questions are related to *when*-type questions (see following text). Luick was the first scholar to present arguments and evidence for a push-chain (although he did not invoke any such metaphor; Luick 1914–40: §479). An examination of the northern dialects of England provided his basis for concluding thus: in some northern dialects, eME *ū* did not diphthongise; in the same dialects, OE *ō* had previously been fronted and raised to *ǖ*; and eME *ī* seems to have diphthongised earlier than in the southern dialects. Luick clearly saw a causal relationship between these changes. His push-chain theory was rejected by Jespersen, who postulated a drag-chain, and claimed that the northern evidence could be interpreted the other way round (Jespersen 1909: 233):

> But the nexus may be equally well established the other way: after /i·/ and /u·/ had been diphthongized, there was nothing to hinder /e·/ and /o·/ from moving upwards and becoming /i·/ and /u·/; where /u·/ subsisted, /o·/ was not allowed to move upwards.

Strang (1970: §§101–4) offers arguments in favour of both views, whereas Western (1912) maintains that the changes of the 'GVS' were simultaneous. What these scholars have in common is that they all regard the changes as connected and systemic, and they see the 'GVS' as caused by language-internal factors, that is, by some 'drift' or tendency within the language itself (Luick 1914–40 II: 449). Crucial to any such 'conspiracy' view is the 'displacement theory' (so named by Stockwell and Minkova 1988a: 365), first presented by Luick (1932), which states that native speakers have a subconscious feel for the phonetic distance between phonemes, and that they tend to want to preserve that distance. In other words, if one phoneme were to move in phonological space, the other phonemes would move as well, in an attempt to (1) avoid merger and (2) 'remedy' the imbalance caused by the first change. It is claimed that since merger results in the loss of at least one distinctive phoneme and also in homonymy – which, it is assumed, is detrimental to communication – it is therefore avoided (Luick 1896: 315; but see Ringgaard 1982). Against such views it may be argued, (a) that merger between the reflexes of OE *ē* and *ǣ* in fact *did* take place in the 'GVS' itself; (b) that Strang (1980) has shown that the average number of meanings for any English word is roughly four, and that homonymy thus does not impair efficiency of communication; (c) that vowel systems are rarely symmetrical; and (d) if changes cause an 'imbalance' in the system, and must be remedied, it is difficult to understand why they happened in the first place.

Linguists who pose *why* questions attempt to find *explanations* or *causes* of vocalic chain-shifts of the type seen in the 'GVS', and in so doing, they have investigated (a) prosodic factors (Samuels 1972, Jordan 1968, Johnston 1992), (b) functional causes (Samuels 1972), (c) system-internal causes (Jespersen 1909, Luick 1914–40), (d) socio-linguistic factors (Labov 1994), and (e) typological issues (Donegan 1985, Donegan *unpubl.*). Tendencies discovered in related languages, as well as general principles of sound-change established by modern linguistics, are key in framing and finding answers to these questions. For instance, work carried out by Labov (1994) on chain-shifts of various kinds suggests that in Gmc languages, long vowels tend (1) to be raised, (2) to be fronted, and (3) to diphthongise, but not to be lowered or backed, except in combinative changes (i.e. changes conditioned by the phonetic context). It should be noted that such tendencies in themselves require an explanation. Samuels, believing suprasegmental variants are responsible for a number of sound-changes, points out that 'forceful styles may show a *higher* or *more fronted* tongue-position, whereas the less stressed variants of relaxed styles may show *lower, more centralised* or *retracted* tongue-positions' (1972: 21, his emphasis). If so, this goes a long way towards explaining why vowel shifts of the kind investigated here are a common feature of Gmc languages, which are stress-timed.

Where questions and *when* questions are somewhat different in nature. *Where* questions try to uncover the geographical dialect(s) in which the 'GVS' was initiated, and *when* questions try to identify more precise dates for the successive stages of the shift. Luick (1914–40: §§479 ff.) pays some attention to the geographical spread and distribution of the 'GVS' changes, whereas Kökeritz (1932), Orton (1933), and Johnston (1992) all devote part of their discussions to attempting to establish the dates for the stages of the 'GVS'. The aim of Boisson (1982) is to identify the internal chronology of the 'GVS' changes. The present work also attempts to answer *where* and *when* questions.

Finally, in more recent years, *who*-type questions have been posed by socio-linguists (e.g. Smith 1993, 2007; Labov 1994), and have been concerned with social variables such as gender, education, class, prestige, mobility, and types of social links as important factors involved in the adoption and spread of linguistic changes, including the 'GVS'.

1.2.3 What is wrong with the traditional account of the 'GVS'?

Most handbook accounts deal with the particular nature and outcome of the 'GVS' in *Standard* English only and disregard dialect evidence altogether. Yet, most non-standard dialects of English do not show the mostly symmetrical pattern of vowel-raising and diphthongisation seen in RP; this is evidenced by for example Dieth (1932, for Buchan), Kökeritz (1932, for Suffolk), Orton (1933, for Durham), and Widén (1949, for Dorset). In parts of the North, for instance, OE *ā* remained and was later fronted and diphthongised; OE *ō* was fronted and raised to [ʉ:]; and OE *ū* [u:] remains (Orton 1933). Moreover, the vowel systems of various PDE dialects may shed light on the stages of, for example, the diphthongisation of the close vowels in the 'GVS'. In Eastern Canadian English and Scots English, for example, OE *ū* is reflected as [əʊ], at least in certain contexts (e.g. in *out* and *about* in the former dialects, and in *down* and *pound* in the latter), which points to centralisation of the developing on-glide (cf. the *what* questions treated above). Smith (1993) has used dialect evidence in his treatment of the 'GVS'.

Furthermore, up until about thirty years ago (with a few notable exceptions), chain-shifts of the 'GVS' kind were treated as uniquely English and unique *within* English. However, it is now recognised that similar chain-shifts affecting the long vowels have taken place in most Gmc languages, except Danish. Thus, PrGmc *ī* and *ū* have diphthongised in German also, giving Modern High German /ai/ and /au/, for example in *Wein, weiss* and *Haus, braun*; a similar development can be traced for these vowels in Dutch, where, in addition, the etymological *ō* has been raised to /u:/ (Pelt 1980; Frankis 1986; van Reenen and Wijnands 1989; Peeters 1991); on the South-African chain-shift, see Lass and Wright (1985). Again, such changes are regarded as connected and systemic, as are diachronic long-vowel changes in Swedish and Norwegian, in which two etymological non-close back vowels were raised and the close back vowel was fronted: ON *á* > /o:/, *ó* > /u:/, *ū* > /ʉ:/ (Benediktsson 1970a, 1970b; Haugen 1970, 1976; Torp and Vikør 1993: 61–62; Eliasson 2010). Besides, Swedish /i:/ is now pronounced as a minimal diphthong /ij/ in some regions, and sporadic diphthongisation of SEN /ʉː/ is found in Norwegian dialects. However, neither the Swedish diphthongisation of /iː/ nor the Norwegian diphthongisation of /ʉː/ is seen as part of any systemic shift. Finally, chain-shifts affecting vowels have been going on and are going on in various PDE dialects, for example in Australian and Cockney English (Sivertsen 1960; Mitchell and Delbridge 1965; Wells 1982: 301–334) and eastern and southern American English (Labov, Yaeger, and Steiner 1972; Labov 1994, 2002).

Related to the view that vowel shifts like the 'GVS' are unique to English, is the view that the 'GVS' was a single, unified, coherent 'event', with a definite beginning and end, requiring its own explanation. The very fact that the name of the shift is usually capitalised bears witness to this attitude, which has been held by, for example, Algeo and Pyles (2005), Baugh and Cable (2002), Strang (1970), and notably by Lass (1976, 1980, 1987a, 1987b, 1988, 1990, 1992, 1997); in later years, however, Lass has abandoned the concept of a unitary 'GVS' (pers. comm.). Stockwell (1960, 1964, 1972, 1978) has always maintained that vowel shifting is nothing out of the ordinary in the history of English and the other Gmc languages, and has in fact been going on for the last 1500 years (Stockwell 1969: 93). Stockwell and Minkova (1988a, 1988b, 1990, 1997) elaborate this theory, which holds that the lOE mergers of *ī* and *īg/ig* and of *ū* and *ūg/ug* resulted in minimal diphthongs, and that this opened up for the further diphthongisation of etymological *ī* and *ū*. Stenbrenden (2010) finds in favour of their basic claims.

The dates postulated for the beginning of the 'GVS' provide another problem. Jespersen (1909) believed the shift must have started around 1500, and this is the date still indicated in many handbooks; Luick (1914–40: §§479ff.) postulated a somewhat earlier date. Attention has since been drawn to a short poem usually referred to as the 'Hymn to the Virgin', written around 1450 (Prins 1972); Dobson (1968: §§137, 156) dates the poem to the fifteenth century. This poem is written in English, but according to Welsh spelling conventions; and in it, etymological *ī* is spelt <ei>, etymological *ū* is spelt <ow>, etymological *ō* is spelt <w>, and etymological *ē* is spelt <i>. According to Welsh orthography of the time, <ei> and <ow> must represent diphthongs, <w> must represent a close back vowel, and <i> a close front vowel. In other words, this poem indicates very clearly that the vowel shift was well under way *c.* 1450; accordingly, the initial stages of the shift have been set to around 1400 by most recent scholars. Wyld (1927, 1936) and Kökeritz (1954) in fact date the early stages to the fourteenth century, but their views have been generally ignored.

A pilot study was carried out earlier (Stenbrenden 1996: 121–132), for which irregular spellings for historical long monophthongs were extracted from corpora of ME sources not previously available (*SMED* and *LALME*). This and later studies (Stenbrenden 2010, 2013) concluded that the incipient stages of the shift likely took place much earlier than 1400, in fact as early as the mid-thirteenth century (which conclusion is accepted by Minkova 2014: 253–254). Moreover, the ME spellings also indicated that the set of earlier changes took longer to be completed than was thought before, such that there appeared to be a lengthy temporal overlap between the two sets of changes. If this were the case, it would open up a number of new questions concerning the internal chronology of ME long-vowel changes; besides, there seemed no valid reason to treat the two sets of changes separately. These preliminary conclusions strongly suggest that a large-scale investigation of ME irregular spellings would be worthwhile in order to reassess some aspects of the history of English phonology.

1.2.4 The purpose and scope of this study

The present work analyses spelling evidence from the entire ME period, with a view to answering *when* and *where* questions concerning ME long-vowel change. Due to the lack of recorded ME speech, and the fact that early phonetic accounts of English do not start to appear until the sixteenth century, this book treats ME unorthodox written forms that are potential manifestations of the changes in question. More precisely, I attempt to determine which irregular spellings may be used as evidence of sound-change, to find out where and when such spellings appear first, and how they spread regionally and temporally, in order to see if any patterns emerge. Ultimately, the goal is to determine whether it is possible to establish an internal chronology of ME long-vowel changes and to see if there are any particular ME regions that stand out as loci of change.

Vastly more material is presented here, and on a much larger scale, than has been done hitherto. The irregular spellings extracted are *prima facie* evidence of sound-change, and the extent of such forms suggests that the case for postulating early vowel shift from occasional spellings is considerably stronger than has been assumed. However, simply listing irregular spellings for ME long vowels hardly proves anything; rather, each unconventional spelling ought to be assessed in terms of the entire orthographic system in which it occurs, that is the full range of spellings for that vowel (and other long vowels) in the scribal text in question, as far as the material allows. Likewise, spellings for one long vowel may be compared to those for other long vowels within the same system, thus revealing whether or not the scribe's orthography is irregular in general. In this context, two avenues present themselves: (1) all the irregular spellings extracted may be included and analysed; or (2) the most promising parts of the material may be presented, and the spelling *system* of each and every source of aberrant forms could be analysed in minute detail. The first avenue was chosen, simply to demonstrate the bulk of the material. The discussions and analyses contained in the individual chapters partly sift the material, and detailed examination of spellings systems has been provided in many cases. Such examination has shown that when the entire orthographic system of a particular source is assessed, the initial interpretation of the aberrant spellings and their phonetic correspondences may have to be reconsidered. For this reason, the second avenue must clearly be travelled too…

Thus, it is *not* the main objective of this work to treat the *how*, *what*, or *why* questions relating to the 'GVS', but to establish, so far as it is possible, a chronology of change. This will of course shed light on whether it makes sense to talk of a 'trigger' of change, or whether a push-chain or drag-chain mechanism was at work, or neither. Nor does this study find support in any current linguistic theory. The decision to leave theory out is a fully conscious one: firstly, it allows other linguists, regardless of theoretical orientation, to make use of the collections of ME data found herein and to interpret them how they see fit. Secondly, it is often the case that theoretical persuasion will influence both which data are included and also their interpretation: one's recognition of relevance itself often depends on a theoretical persuasion. Hence, this work simply offers a systematic compilation of ME occasional spellings for long vowels, and a discussion of what such spellings may imply about ME phonology. Rhyming evidence has not been systematically exploited, but occasional reference has been made to rhymes which may imply vowel shift.[3]

This study is an exercise in the art of the practicable: since the publication of *SMED* and *LALME*, and the relatively recent online publications of *LAEME* and *LALME*, there is now much more material easily accessible for analysis on a large scale than has ever been the case before, and the material contained in these sources is reliable, since it has been collated against MSS. However, the spellings collected in this book in no way exhaust the ME material: hence, it is certainly not the case that 'if it is not in the corpus, it is not in the language'. The existence of *LAEME*, *SMED*, and *LALME* facilitates the review of a very much wider range of attestations than has been attempted hitherto, with regard to both particular spellings and the dates at which they appear. The written record of eME is variously fragmentary, in respect both of time and particular places, but what there is can now be much more comprehensively surveyed than before. Thus, despite the limitations pointed out before, there is still enough material to determine whether the story of ME long-vowel shifts, as conventionally told, adds up or not.

1.3 Description of sources and method

1.3.1 Introduction and description of LALME

LALME covers the period 1350–1450 for most of English-speaking Britain, although some very late documents have been included as well, and the southern corpus contains some material from the late thirteenth and early fourteenth centuries. It includes documents that are localisable with respect to time and place, and uses wholly vernacular texts. Although its local documents are usually of known date, the literary manuscripts, most of which are copies at indeterminate remove from the original works, are generally datable only on palaeographical grounds. The data are organised on a regional basis, and can be looked up county by county. In addition, *LALME* provides maps with a very high density of attestation: there are *c.* 1200 survey points for the whole country (as compared to 300 in *SED*, Orton and Dieth 1962). The lME manuscripts examined for *LALME* are all listed in Volume I (*LALME*, I: 57–171).[4]

The material in *LALME* is organised mainly on a lexical basis, and was compiled by the use of questionnaires. These questionnaires record the orthographic variants occurring for a set number of items (i.e. a word or morpheme, and sometimes a phonological category), thus creating a linguistic profile (LP) for the text.[5] Since the same items were recorded for all the documents (with some differences between the northern and southern corpus, and always provided that the relevant items were actually found in the texts), their LPs constitute a good basis for cross-dialectal comparison, at least with respect to particular lexemes and their regionally based orthographic representations.[6] A list of all 280 items, with notes, is found in Volume III (pp. xviii, xx-xxii).

The aim of any dialect atlas of ME is two-fold: firstly, to determine the provenance of the writers of the various texts, and secondly, to use this information to 'elucidate the geographical distributions of the material' (*LALME*, I: 9). The main problem is that mediaeval scribes mostly remain anonymous, and so the dialectal provenance of their language must be determined on linguistic or extra-linguistic grounds. Now, if texts were to be localised *a priori* solely on linguistic principles, one could certainly run the risk of committing dialectal tautologies.[7] Therefore, there is a need for texts that can be localised on non-linguistic grounds, that is, texts which have definite affinities with given places or areas. Such texts are called 'anchor' texts, because they provide dialectal anchors or fixed points of reference; and the linguistic material they contain is plotted on maps (*LALME*, I: 9–10). Anchor texts are predominantly local documents, most of which are short texts with limited vocabulary. In order to compile a dependable dialect atlas for ME, one is therefore in need of longer texts with much larger vocabularies, which usually means literary texts. The problem with literary texts is that their language in most cases has not been localised. This is where the 'fit'-technique comes in (*LALME*, I: 10–12). Modern dialectology recognises that languages cannot be divided into neat and discrete dialects; rather, there is a dialect continuum, with 'non-random, orderly patterning [of linguistic features] over space' (*LALME*, I: 10). Since every lexical item (or phonological category) displays a unique 'non-random, orderly patterning over space', each regional dialect would also show a unique *combination* or *cluster* of linguistic features. Thus, given a sample ME text, it would be possible to localise the language of the said text within a restricted area, from an analysis of the *combined* set of orthographic linguistic features found in that text, using information from maps of plotted items from the anchor texts. Since for any dialect it is the *combination* of features which is unique, it is vital to plot as many features/items as possible on the maps. The more ME texts that are safely localised by the help of items maps, the more dependable the grid becomes, and the easier it will be to localise other texts.[8] Description of the 'fit'-technique is provided by McIntosh (1963) and Benskin (1991a). For critique of *LALME*, see Burton (1991), and Benskin's rejoinder (Benskin 1991b).

Most of the *LALME* categories are lexical. Nevertheless, much phonological evidence may be abstracted from it, and some categories of survey, particularly for the southern half of England, are overtly phonological. This phonological material is contained in the *Appendix of Southern Forms* (*LALME*, IV: 309–25). Irregular spellings were extracted from both the *Appendix of Southern Forms* and the *County Dictionary*.[9]

1.3.2 Introduction and description of SMED

The material contained in the *Survey of Middle English Dialects 1290–1350* (Kristensson 1967, 1987, 1995, 2001, 2002; henceforth *SMED*) covers all of England, and has been extracted from Lay Subsidy Rolls (LSR), or from comparable material when such rolls are lacking for a particular area. Where possible, *SMED* makes use of two Subsidy Rolls of diverse dates from each county to cover the area twice. The LSR are essentially Latin documents, but since they are records of tax-payers and their tax payments, recorded district by district, they contain a great deal of vernacular material on personal names and place-names. The Lay Subsidy was collected almost all over the country, at times fixed by parliamentary grant of such subsidies. Therefore the Rolls are precisely dated. Tax payments were often recorded by local officers (Kristensson 1967: xii); thus, the material is assumed to reveal the genuinely local pronunciation of the various names listed. The result of Kristensson's investigations is a delineation of the Northern, West Midland, East Midland, and Southern dialect areas, which delineation remains Kristensson's main objective. The forms presented are organised on a phonological basis; from the standpoint of the present study, this organisation is ideal. The lists of material from *SMED* are by intention exhaustive, unless otherwise indicated.

The material in *SMED* was collected on the assumption that the original tax assessment rolls were recorded by local people, and that the names therefore reflect local pronunciation. Serious reservations were voiced against this assumption after the publication of *SMED1*, notably by McClure, who pointed out that Kristensson's sources are in fact not the original local assessment rolls, but summaries of these 'copied out into "county" rolls by clerks of the chief taxers' (McClure 1973: 188). Nor does Kristensson record different hands. The linguistic trustworthiness of the rolls therefore depends on the 'probability of copying errors and [...] the possibility that scribal influence is interfering at two stages with the reliability of the forms' (1973: 188). McClure demonstrates that copying errors are not infrequent, that the 'county roll clerks were not especially familiar with the local nomenclature' (1973: 190), and that scribal influence is responsible for much of the spelling variations. Essentially (1973: 191),

> professionally trained scribes were among the more mobile members of medieval society [...] The fact that some of the chief taxers' clerks made elementary mistakes in local nomenclature should warn us not to assume too readily that the spellings in the subsidy rolls are wholly representative of local usage.

Kristensson's reply tries to refute McClure's most serious arguments, but he admits that some degree of scepticism is sound, and that a local assessment roll must be compared with 'the corresponding part of a county roll'

(1976: 52) to determine its reliability. This is what Kristensson does next, distinguishing three categories of spelling discrepancies: (a) scribal errors, (b) orthographic variants, and (c) normalised spellings 'which belonged to the county roll scribe's spelling conventions' (1976: 55). Kristensson states that categories (a) and (b) need not concern us, since they occur in all ME texts. As for normalised spellings, they are said to be a corrective (on the part of the county roll clerks) to the various forms found in the local rolls, which, he claims, were recorded by 'persons barely literate', who 'wrote what they "heard" or what they thought they "heard"' (1976: 56). But since the original assessment rolls are nearly all lacking, it is disturbing indeed if the surviving county rolls display standardised spellings (although appeal to standardisation is anachronistic at this date), because such spellings would obscure the 'local speech' that is supposed to be the very foundation of *SMED*. However, Kristensson and McClure agree that the spelling changes in the county rolls do not imply a different pronunciation of the names involved, and hence that 'their presence is unlikely to affect seriously any broad generalisations about the phonology of an area' (McClure 1973: 190). Kristensson (1976) concludes that spellings of onomastic material are a better and safer source of local pronunciation than literary texts, because (a) in onomastic material there would be no considerations of 'vulgarity' of form, and (b) onomastic material often appeared in a legal context, and had to reflect the pronunciation correctly in order to avoid having its authenticity called into question.

Hence, Kristensson regrettably seems to sweep the differences under the carpet. Moreover, when irregular spellings and their phonetic implications do not fit in with Kristensson's preconceived ideas of their regional distributions, they tend to be dismissed, either as scribal errors or as showing influence from neighbouring dialects (cf. Hudson 1969: 69). In other cases, Kristensson invokes 'influence' from non-local people who, it is claimed, had moved to the area in question; but evidence for such migration is thin on the ground.[10]

McClure's most critical argument, and one which Kristensson has never really refuted, is the fact that spellings for a given item – within the same county – *change with the scribe*. The example quoted (1973: 191–2) is the reflex of OE *hyll* HILL in Nottinghamshire: Nottinghamshire generally has <i> for OE *y*, but for *hyll*, <u> is dominant, although <i> appears also. On closer inspection of the 1327 roll, it turns out that the two hands in which the roll is written demonstrate different usage: hand A writes <Hill> or <–hill> (in compounds), hand B writes <Hull> or <–hull>. The 1332 roll is similarly written in two main hands, of which hand C uses <i>, and hand

D uses <u>. However, as the wapentakes for which each of the hands is responsible do not match those of hands A and B, the distribution of <i> vs. <u> in the 1332 roll differs from that of the 1327 roll.[11]

This is devastating for the view that the clerks just 'wrote what they "heard"' and that what they recorded was genuinely local pronunciation. Rather, it could be that they were scribes of unknown local origins who, when they were recording onomastic material, were transposing morphemes rather than phonemes. At least, it leaves open the possibility that a scribe or copyist, when listening to some name, might assimilate it to his native form when he recognised the lexeme. Kristensson's axiom, that the language of the LSR is by definition precisely localised, is simply not true. Their language may or may not be reliably localised, but that does not mean that material extracted from *SMED* is useless with regard to the general phonological history of English. The irregular spellings are there and need to be explained, regardless of local origin. If forms of regional dialect change in an orderly fashion across space – and the evidence is that for the most part they do – it is still possible to make informed guesses as to the provenance of such spellings, and to say something worthwhile about them.[12]

1.3.3 Introduction and description of LAEME

LAEME and its Corpus of Tagged Texts have been available online since 2008.[13] A brief introduction follows later; for a fuller description of the project, see Laing (1994, 1995 and 2008). *LAEME* covers the period *c.* 1150–1325 for all of England. *LAEME* and *LALME* therefore jointly cover almost the entire ME period, though there is very little evidence from the early twelfth century, and the period 1300–50 is largely ignored. The surviving eME material is, however, not evenly distributed across the country: MSS are relatively abundant from the SW Midlands and SE Midlands, less so from the Central Midlands and the South, and are hardly at all to be had from the North and the N Midlands. *LAEME* incorporates literary, legal, and administrative MSS alike, although documentary material is scarce, since Latin was the language of official records in the designated period. This makes the task of establishing so-called 'anchor texts' difficult (as described in 1.3.1). For *LALME*, such anchor texts were most often found in the legal and administrative material. The paucity of such data for eME is partly remedied by the fact that literary MSS from the same period often contain non-linguistic evidence that makes localisation possible. Such tentative localisation obviously needs testing against the later localised material found in *LALME*.

While *LALME* contains LPs with a fixed number of items, the *LAEME* corpus, in contrast, contains entire texts that have been transcribed, all from original manuscripts or facsimiles. Each word is tagged individually for lexico-grammatical information. This approach increases the number of recorded items enormously, and makes available the textual contexts of any given form. Thus, the *LAEME* corpus is eminently suitable for studies within the fields of historical dialectology and phonology, although the phonology may be inferred only after close analysis of the orthographic systems in which irregular spellings occur.

ME texts continue to be added to the Corpus of Tagged Texts, so the extracts from *LAEME* found in the present work represent what I had access to at the time I started collecting material systematically, and thus exclude some of the texts now online.[14] Since the texts are available in their entirety, it is possible to consider the irregular spellings within the orthographic *system* in which they occur. In a work on this scale, however, it is impossible to examine every such system, but some systems will be investigated for illustration, to see what difference such an approach makes to the interpretation of individual spellings. Such investigations may serve as a model and are representative of what may be done with the spellings collected in this book.

The *LAEME* material is not organised on a phonological basis, such that one can make quick and easy searches for phonological categories (or 'lexical sets', cf. Wells 1982: 127–68). Lists of words belonging to a lexical set were made by marking each relevant item in the tagged dictionary and generating a list of all the textual variants of the marked items. In other cases, only aberrant spellings (arranged according to text) were extracted. Since the texts have been assigned dates and localisations (in the form of National Grid references), it is possible to identify the date and provenance of the irregular spellings. Consequently, the chronology and possible spread of the occurrence of these spellings may also be determined.

Generally, only the *irregular* forms found in *LAEME* have been reproduced in my tables. They are grouped according to the traditional categories of English historical phonology, and it has been indicated in which texts the forms appear. It is therefore possible to assess each spelling in terms of the system to which it belongs by collating all the material for each text. *All* spellings have been collected for a high number of items with OE *ā*, *ǣ*, *ū*, and *ȳ*; these spellings have been counted, and dominant vs. secondary and minor forms have been indicated for each text, in tables where the texts are chronologically arranged. This was done in an attempt to chart (a) the ME spellings and phonetic correspondences of OE *ȳ*,

(b) the eME backing and rounding of OE *ā*, (c) the use of <ou>/<ow> vs. <u> for eME *ū*, and (d) the ME spellings for OE *ǣ*. The lists of material from *LAEME* are by intention exhaustive, but some items are certain to have been inadvertently overlooked.

The material from *LAEME* has proved invaluable: The fact that the material in general has hitherto not been accessible in print, and that it is now organised on a linguistic and dialectal basis, adds to the importance of its being examined systematically. Besides, given Stockwell and Minkova's early vowel-shift hypothesis, evidence from *early* ME is crucial in determining the date at which the various long-vowel changes started in the regional dialects of English.

1.3.4 Introduction and description of additional ME sources

The material extracted from 'additional sources' is not included in any of the surveys discussed earlier. I have not been able to ascertain whether all the editions are faithful printed versions of the original texts. The language in some has certainly been normalised; therefore, in so far as irregular spellings appear at all, they must be a feature of the original text. Most of the material is dated, albeit tentatively in some cases; a good portion of it has also been localised. Some of the texts are described by Laing (1993), yet have not been analysed for inclusion in *LAEME*; others appear in the Index of Sources for *LALME*, but have not been included in the maps or in the form of an LP. With regard to datings and localisations, I have used the editors' notes, as well as the information given by Laing (1993) and *LALME*. Whenever there has been disagreement between the editors' dates and/or localisations, and those of Laing (1993) or *LALME*, I have followed the latter two. In those instances where localisation has not previously been made, and where the linguistic evidence is not too scanty, an attempt has been made to arrive at probable placements with the aid of *LALME* maps. In cases where placing is impossible or too uncertain, I have indicated this, but still included any important evidence for vowel-change.

Bennett and Smithers (1966) provide eME literary material from the period *c.* 1175–1330. The material is dated, but only approximately in most cases, and localised, except for the shorter poems. Brown (1950) offers unpublished thirteenth-century ME lyrics, and Brown (1952) unpublished fourteenth-century religious lyrics. The material is mostly dated, but only very roughly, and some of it is localised, at least tentatively. Burrow (1992) provides ME verse from *c.* 1300–1500 (though some of the late MSS or early prints are later). The sources are mostly dated and localised, but it remains uncertain whether dating and localisation have been made with regard to the MSS/prints, or to the hands, or to the language of the texts. Three compendia from the fourteenth century contain over 1500 medical receipts; these collections are known as the *Rawlinson Compendium*, the *First Corpus Compendium*, and the *Second Corpus Compendium*, and they are written in Latin, Anglo-Norman, and English. Hunt and Benskin (2001) offer a printed version of these (see pp. 86–8 for editorial principles). Only the two Corpus compilations have any amount of text in English; Benskin's account (2001: 193–230) of the language of the receptaria thus covers these two, and relevant forms in my lists have also only been abstracted from these. Benskin's LPs of the two texts follow *LALME* conventions; he concludes (2001: 207) that the language belongs to W Norfolk/Ely, and he dates the hand to 1320–30.

1.3.5 The corpus approach

Linguistics is an empirical science, and traditionally, there are three ways of collecting the data submitted to analysis: by introspection, by eliciting anwers from informants, and by studying texts (Johannessen *et al.* 2003, McEnery and Wilson 2001). In historical linguistics, the informants are long since dead; the surviving texts themselves are therefore our witnesses. The use of corpora – bodies of texts – has been established as one of the most fruitful ways of excerpting and analysing considerable amounts of linguistic data, also within historical linguistics (Kytö *et al.* 1994; Hickey *et al.* 1997; Facchinetti and Rissanen 2006). Some of the advantages of the corpus methodology are listed in the following (McEnery and Wilson 2001: 13–20). Corpora consist of 'naturally occurring data', which are observable and verifiable, whereas introspective judgements are subjective and unobservable; in a digital corpus, linguistic structures (simple words, collocations, or longer structures) can be searched for with the aid of computers, which can retrieve all examples that fit the search, but also sort the material, and calculate frequencies and provide statistics, thereby ensuring a 'more systematic approach to the analysis of language' (McEnery and Wilson 2001: 15); corpora usually consist of large amounts of data, which potentially make conclusions drawn from them more statistically significant; corpora usually contain representative samples of text. Despite the obvious advantages of using corpora in linguistic research, it is important to recognise their limitations. In the words of Curzan and Palmer (2006: 21), 'Quantitative research [...] does little without context or interpretation. As they say in Helsinki [...]: "Research begins where counting ends"'. In other words, corpus data must be analysed and interpreted with the help of introspection and research intuition. Since corpora usually do not contain *all* historical texts of a given period, the linguist must avoid the temptation 'to extrapolate too far from the particular database/genre under analysis, since its examples tell us not about language generally and entirely but about language in that specific discourse or genre, in those available texts' (2006: 21). It is especially important to keep this in mind when one analyses early ME, for which the surviving evidence is patchy and incoherent, at least for parts of the country. McEnery and Wilson (2001: 19) share Curzan and Palmer's view:

> A corpus and an introspection-based approach to linguistics are not mutually exclusive. In a very real sense they can be gainfully viewed as being complementary. [...] Corpus linguistics is, and should be, a synthesis of introspective and observational procedures.

Of course, not all corpora are machine-readable, although the current definition of 'corpus' seems to suggest that such is the case (see e.g. Curzan and Palmer (2006: 18), who in fact argue that the definition of 'corpus' should be expanded). However, empirical linguists have always made use of data retrieved from 'bodies of texts'. On an abstract level, 'the corpus of historical English' may be defined as 'all surviving historical English texts combined'. On the concrete level, there is now a substantial number of corpora containing scanned, and sometimes tagged, historical English texts (cf. Kytö *et al.* 1994). Kytö and Rissanen (1997: 9) acknowledge the broader definition of a 'corpus' when they say that 'A historical linguist must therefore rely on a corpus, either in the old sense of the word, that is a text or a collection of texts yielding linguistic evidence on the phenomenon studied, or in the new sense of the word, that is the computerized version of the same'. Two of the corpora used here are digitial, that is, the online *LAEME* and *LALME*; *SMED*, although not machine-readable, is a corpus all the same.

1.4 Presentation of material, notation, and organisation

The material is presented chronologically: forms from *LAEME* are presented before the spellings from *SMED*, *LALME* and additional sources. The county abbreviations used in *LALME* are used throughout; see *LALME* (I: 562).

1.4.1 Material from LAEME

The provenance of the irregular spellings abstracted from *LAEME* is indicated by index number of sample text (see online *LAEME*). Where no localisation has been made, only the index number appears. The use of single and double round brackets, as found in *LALME* (see the following text), has been adopted for some of the material from *LAEME* also; additionally, triple parentheses have occasionally been used when a given spelling is extremely rare in the source in which it occurs.

1.4.2 Material from SMED

In the lists of spellings from *SMED*, (letters and) numbers refer to the (county and) date of the LSR in question, as this is uniquely defining for this material. There are no Subsidy Rolls for Durham or Cheshire, 'which in their capacity of palatinates were exempt from the Lay Subsidy' (Kristensson 1967: xiii). *SMED* therefore makes use of other sources of onomastic material from Durham and Cheshire.

For Durham, the following sources have yielded irregular spellings, with abbreviations in parentheses (Kristensson 1967: xv):

Account Rolls of the Durham Dean & Chapter Muniments (*AccR*),
Ecclesiastical Subsidy Roll 1294–97 (*ESR12*),
The Durham Roll of the Justices Itinerant 1301–1302 (*JustIt*),
Judgement Roll 1344 (*JR*),
Registrum Palatinum Dunelmense (*RPD*),
The Halmote Court Rolls 1296–1347 (*HCR*).

For Cheshire, the following sources show irregular spellings:

The Chartulary or Register of the Abbey of St. Werburgh Chester (*CRA*),
Ecclesiastical Subsidy Roll (*ESR*),
Selected Rolls of the Chester City Courts (*CCC*),
Talbot Deeds 1200–1682 (*TD*).

1.4.3 Material from LALME

In the lists of spellings from *LALME*, numbers refer to LP numbers. Round brackets are used in the following way. An unmarked form shows the dominant variant of a given item for that LP. If a variant occurs with a relative frequency of between one-third and two-thirds of that of the dominant form, the form is enclosed within single round brackets (secondary variants). Double parentheses are used when the registered form occurs with a relative frequency of less than 33% of that of the dominant variant (minor variants).

The *LALME* material for SE Wiltshire and Nottingham is here revised and supplemented by analyses from Benskin (pers. comm.). The material consists of the following MSS, of which (a)–(c) show Wiltshire language, and (d) shows Nottinghamshire language:

(a) Trowbridge, Wiltshire Record Office, D1/2/5, will of Sir John Dauntsye, Larkstock, 1390; cited as DTSY.
(b) British Library, Harley Charter 45 A 37, 1376, cited as WLTN.CT.
(c) Salisbury Cathedral Library, MS 39, the Gospel of Nicodemus, Hand A, 1452 or earlier (c. 1425–1450); this is part of *LALME* LP 5371. The *LALME* report of Wlt 5371 is inadequate (Professor Samuels was allowed only half an hour with the MS, and permission for microfilming was refused); it has been fully revised by Benskin, and represents Hand A only.[15] The language of Hand B, which is properly LP 5372, is mixed (E Midland and Wiltshire; see Section 6.2.3 for details).
(d) Nottinghamshire Record Office: CA 4448, Rental of the Commons of Nottingham, 1435; *LALME* LP 96.[16]

1.4.4 Material from additional ME sources

Irregular spellings have indeed been noted and discussed by scholars in the past (e.g. Zachrisson 1913, Whitehall 1935), but never been systematically compiled. Therefore, such spellings have also been included, and I address the scholars' interpretations of them.

1.4.5 Notation

Conventional philological notation will be used throughout. Angle brackets (< >) are used for actually attested written forms in ME text, irrespective of their phonetic or phonological status. Citation forms are italicised, and their respective glosses enclosed in single inverted commas. Italics are also used to indicate the inferred sound value of older linguistic forms, since their exact phonetic value remains unknown and their phonological status is often uncertain: here, the use of italics makes it clear that one is speaking the language of imprecision.

Square brackets ([ ]) enclose phonetic symbols. They are used whenever the exact phonetic output is either known, as in the case of modern languages, or inferred, as in the case of historical stages of language. For the latter category, the phonetic transcription is necessarily broad. Slant lines (/ /) enclose phonemes. A *phoneme* is here defined as the smallest contrastive linguistic unit that can bring about a change in meaning. The number and phonetic realisation(s) of such contrastive units depend on the language examined and on the date at which the language is examined. Therefore, slant lines will be used only in cases where the system of contrastive phonemes in a language has been properly investigated. Hence, I do *not* follow the practice of many handbooks on historical English, in which '/ /' merely means 'approximate phonetic value'.

Sometimes, however, the notation or symbols used have simply been taken over from my sources or the handbooks consulted. Symbols in square brackets are International Phonetic Alphabet (IPA) symbols, whereas symbols for historical forms are used according to traditional Germanic philology. Note in particular <ȝ> 'yogh', which is used for IPA [ɣ], and <þ> 'thorn', which is used for IPA [θ]. Further, in the fonts used, the 'insular *g*' is reproduced as <ᵹ>, and the 'wynn' as <ƿ>; however, <w> is usually used for MS 'wynn', and <ȝ> for the 'insular *g*'.

The PDE pronunciation of the place-names adduced as evidence from *SMED* has been gleaned from Forster (1981), unless otherwise stated. Present-day identities have been taken from *SMED* itself; cf. *SMED1* (Kristensson 1967: xviii–xix).

1.4.6 Organisation

The present work is organised in the following way. Chapter 1 introduces the topic and the sources of the material extracted, and also discusses to what extent orthographic material can be used to shed light on historical vowel-change. Chapters 2–8 treat each of the eME long vowels in turn, in alphabetical order. Chapter 9 offers conclusions and the view of ME long-vowel change that is suggested by the evidence.

The nature of the ME material to a large extent dictates the chapter organisation. Each chapter first outlines the development of the vowel in question, as presented in the handbooks; then follows a discussion of the extracted ME spellings and their status as evidence of long-vowel change.

1.5 On using spelling as evidence for sound change

This problem lies in the interface between spelling and pronunciation, and is crucial with regard to the *raison d'être* of this work. Put briefly, the questions posed are the following. To what extent is spelling phonetically based? And how can spellings be used as evidence for the pronunciation of a language at any given point in time? These are important questions, since 'it is *written* material of the late Middle English period itself which provides us with the bulk of what we believe we know about the spoken language of that time' (McIntosh 1956: 27; emphasis mine). This rests on the belief that there is a correlation 'between a given variety of the spoken language and the "equivalent" or "corresponding" variety of the written language' (1956: 27). Penzl (1957: 13–14) states that

> The relationship between symbol and sound, between the graphemic and the phonemic system is a basic problem in historical linguistics. Alphabetic writing itself in its inception used to involve a certain "phonemic" interpretation of the sounds on the part of the scribes.

That is, at the outset, alphabetic (and syllabic) writing involves phonetic and/or phonological analysis of the speech sounds of the language in question. It would nevertheless be a mistake to view the early written forms of a language as phonetic transcript. The initially transparent sound-letter relationships are frequently obscured by later sound changes. The users of the language often solve this discordance by changing the written norm so as to bring it closer to the spoken language. There is commonly a time gap between the first stages of a sound change and the point at which it is 'noticed' by native speakers as bringing about a discrepancy between the spoken and written forms of the language (Samuels 1972: 4–6). Not infrequently, however, spelling 'freezes' and becomes standardised. In such cases, spelling fails to mirror the phonetic make-up of words; instead, spelling becomes the norm-regulated recording of letters in sequences (i.e. 'words'), which sequences *symbolise meaning* and merely *indicate*, to a greater or lesser degree, their phonetic/phonological basis. According to Wrenn (1943: 14),

> On the one hand our spelling seems to be static, but on the other it tends to become ideographic – or rather the written "words" tend to become group-symbols of group-sounds, that is a group of letters symbolizes collectively a group of noises expressive of an idea or thing with no consciousness of any relationship between individual letter-symbol and individual noise.

Besides, the conventions of written language 'were never intended [...] to reveal facts about its spoken equivalent to the uninitiated' (McIntosh

1956: 39). Some information (as, for example, phonetic details) is taken for granted and thus not expressed, exactly because the scribe was writing for those to whom the system was known and sufficient. It may hence be argued that letters are merely symbolic units, in so far as sounds are concerned, in much the same way that words are symbolic units representing meaning.[17]

These observations seem to imply that the relationship between letter and sound is haphazard and hence cannot be subjected to analysis in any consistent and fruitful way, particularly for older stages of the language, whose spoken forms remain largely unattested. This is fortunately far from the truth. The mediaeval concept of *littera* is worth mentioning in this context. *Littera* is an abstract term, roughly corresponding to the PDE 'letter'. Firstly, this term was seen as a three-faceted entity, one of the facets being the *nomen*, or name, by which the *littera* could be referred to. Greek 'beta' and Norwegian 'be' are thus different *nomines* for the same *littera*. (The name concept as a reference is more transparent for the classical alphabets, which were pictographic in origin: 'aleph', for instance, is the Semittic article *al* plus *eph* 'the strong one', referring to the elephant or ox.) Secondly, the *littera* manifests itself physically on parchment or paper in different shapes; for the *littera* 'b', such shapes could include <b>, <ß>, and <B>. These manifestations were referred to as *figurae*, and their number and exact shape vary, depending on the language used, the time of recording, the context, etc. Finally, the *littera* had a certain *potestas* ('power'), a certain sound quality, or range of sound qualities, attached to it. The *littera* 'b' may thus have the *potestates* [be:], [bi:], [b], [ß], [b^{h}], etc., depending on the language analysed.

The important thing to note here, however, is that, notwithstanding the sometimes wide range of *potestates* attached to a certain *littera*, there are sound qualities that could not by any stretch of imagination belong to the same *littera*. To use an example from PDE: the *littera* 'a' has the name 'a' /eɪ/, the *figurae* <A>, <a>, and <ɑ> (in print), and the following *potestates*: /eɪ/ (*make*), /ɑ:/ (*dance*), /æ/ (*hand*), /ə/ (*about*), /ɪ/ (*manage*), /eə/ (*mare*), /ɔ:/ (*ball*), /ɒ/ (*yacht*). Yet there are sound qualities that would never be attached to English 'a', for example, /u:/, /əʊ/, /k/, or /str/. It is this fact that makes it at all valid to use spelling as evidence for sound values: on the evidence of rhymes, of early orthoepists' statements, and of the known previous and later history of sounds, it is possible to determine *within limits* the range of *potestates* which could possibly be attached to a *littera* at any given point in time, and similarly which could in all likelihood be ruled out. In the words of McIntosh (1956: 30), a given written form

> carries with it then certain definite reservations as to the legitimate phonetic range of spoken equivalents. The main reason for this is that any given letter has [...] similar (though not [...] identical) phonetic implications in each and every variety of the written language.

That is, 'only by understanding the limitations of the correlation [between the spoken and written language] can we [...] make proper use of the available written material as evidence about the spoken language' (McIntosh 1956: 28). Written forms do not give any precise information about their corresponding spoken forms in terms of exact phonetic values or allophones, but at 'the same time there are signs of some sort of *systemic* correlation' (1956: 29). As the earlier PDE example clearly illustrates, the range of probable *potestates* can be rather wide; it is exactly the narrowing down of these limits that is part of the purpose of the present work. The *littera* concept has in fact never been completely abandoned; for example, Peacock (1869: 12) makes explicit reference to the 'power' of letters. In more recent years, however, the concept has been revived: see, for instance, Benskin (1982a), *LALME* (III: Introduction), Laing (1999: 941).

When spelling departs from conventional and well-established orthography, this in itself begs an explanation. According to Penzl (1957: 14),

> the use and distribution of graphemes is important evidence in synchronic analysis. The known derivation of the symbols and their original values can be used for general phonetic identifications [...] Diachronic interpretations are facilitated by the observation of changes in the orthographic system, of internal orthographic fluctuation or of a modern discrepancy between symbol and pronunciation. Not every change in spelling implies a change in pronunciation [...]. Not only the analysis of orthographic systems, but also the study of deviations from them, namely of occasional spellings ('naive spellings'), provides evidence. Their synchronic analysis reveals the discrepancy between the traditional orthography and the phonemic system of its user.

This book is concerned with ME spellings and their interpretation in terms of phonetic correspondences, with regard to vowels. Part of the challenge lies in interpreting certain digraph spellings for historical diphthongs and monophthongs. The problem of interpretation becomes particularly acute when these digraph spellings occur in front of letters historically corresponding to a fricative (i.e. <ȝ>, <ȝt>, <gh>,

<ght>, <ht>). The range of possible readings is illustrated in the schematised diagram that follows.

How are digraph spellings to be interpreted in terms of phonetic values?
I As genuine diphthongs, in which case the question is whether the diphthongs are either

(A) historical/etymological diphthongs; or
(B) diphthongised historical monophthongs, which are either
  (i) historically long monophthongs (*white* type < OE *hwīt*); or
  (ii) historically short monophthongs lengthened in 'lengthening environment' (*child* type < OE *cild*); or
  (iii) historically long monophthongs followed by a fricative which is vocalised (*sty* type < OE *stīg*); or
  (iv) historically short monophthongs followed by a fricative which is vocalised (*night* type < OE *niht*), in which case the sound value of the vocalised fricative
    (a) shows a minimal contrast to the preceding vowel, producing a minimal diphthong (as in Stockwell and Minkova's interpretation, i.e. [ɪi] or [ij] for *night*); or
    (b) is the same as the sound value of the preceding vowel, producing a long monophthong (i.e. [ii] or [i:]), thus belonging properly under II that follow, though in this case, the digraph spellings consist of a vowel letter and a consonant letter, not two vowel letters.

II As monophthongs, in which case the first element of the digraph indicates vowel quality, the second is merely a diacritic device; the diacritic second element of the digraph then indicates either

(A) quantity, that is, a long vowel; or
(B) quality, that is, a raised/lowered vowel; or
(C) both quantity and quality, that is, a long raised/lowered vowel.

Due to the process described under I B iv b, not just vowel graphemes, but also graphemes traditionally symbolising a fricative may come to be used as length diacritics in non-historical contexts (e.g. <fyȝnd> FIND), or they are used in combination with digraphs of two vowel letters (e.g. <leyȝt> LIGHT, <heyȝ> HIGH), that is, they are back spellings. The logic behind this seems to be the following: If <ȝ> is nothing but a historical remnant, though usefully indicating the length of the preceding vowel, then why not use it to indicate vowel length in other words, whose vowel is not historically long either, but has come to be so? It may be of interest to note that although <ei>/<ey> abound for historical ī, there are extremely few such spellings with <ȝ> following the digraphs; in other words, <ȝ> is rarely used as a length diacritic in words whose vowel has always been long. For WHITE, for example, <weyte> is found, but no *<weyȝte>.[18]

It is particularly with close vowels and diphthongised (originally close) vowels that problems of interpretation arise, though not exclusively. There are, for instance, also potential problems associated with the interpretation of <ou>/<ow> for historical ō (originally spelt <o(o)>): these spellings are modelled on the much older use of <ou> for historical ū, which habit was in turn adopted from French, where [ou] had monophthongised to [u] at an earlier stage. The later history of ME ō shows that eventually raising occurred, and so it is assumed that the innovative <ou>/<ow> forms for original ō, for example, <goud> GOOD, testify to vowel raising. As will appear from the earlier schematic overview, this may not be so, since the <u> in this context may equally well have been used as a diacritic indicating vowel quantity. However, this latter interpretation seems unlikely, *unless* <u> *is used elsewhere* to indicate vowel length in the same orthographic system.

Thus, if any interpretation of the digraph spellings in terms of phonetic values is to be made credible, the following considerations, which have been merely touched on in the preceding, should be taken into account: the previous, as well as the later, history of the vowel sounds in question; the notion of back spellings; the dialect areas to which the spellings belong; the conventional orthography in these areas; and the spelling system(s) of the relevant text(s). This is strongly stressed by Wrenn (1943), who warns against what he calls the 'exaggerated belief in […] the significance of the evidential value of spelling', when he says that spellings 'as a guide to pronunciation should only be accepted as evidence when corroborated by other kinds of evidence' (1943: 16–17). Further, as diachronic linguists, we must, 'before using the orthography of a document as evidence, be sure that we know that its scribe is likely to be a reliable witness. We must also compare it fully with all the available evidences of other kinds' (1943: 26). And in conclusion (1943: 39),

> What I would chiefly stress is that philologists, while being fully sensitive to the possibilities and advantages of both the phonetic and the ideographic and symbolic attitudes to orthography – ready to explore and take advantage of both methods of sound-symbol relationship, – while being conscious also of the inevitable time-lag between the pronunciation of a language at a given moment and its graphic expression in a way of

> orthography, should, in handling spelling as evidence, explore always all the concomitant related factors.

McIntosh concludes the same (1956: 54), and Penzl expresses similar concerns when he states that diachronic linguists cannot expect to find a wide selection of evidence for each and every phonological change that has taken place within the lifespan of a language (Penzl 1957: 22–3):

> It is necessary, however, to make use of all available evidence and to correlate its data. Interpretation and even speculation has often taken the place of the missing data. It is imperative that the description of each assumed phonemic change should contain a discussion of the evidence, its type, scope, and conclusiveness.

At this stage, it is necessary to define the terms 'occasional/naive' and 'back/analogical' spellings. These terms appear in virtually all discussions of irregular spellings, and the latter are often used to preclude certain spellings from being used as evidence of vowel-change. Of occasional spellings, Penzl (1957: 14) says that 'the term [...] suggests a minority-type of orthography which occurs together with the majority-type in identical or contemporaneous texts'. While realising that they may be errors or orthographic variants, he seems more optimistic than Wrenn in his view of the possible usefulness of occasional spellings (1957: 14):

> They may reveal historical or dialectal variants for individual words [...] Synchronic analysis has to screen these spellings carefully within a given text and separate them from spellings that reveal the writer's or scribe's phonemic distribution or phonemic changes [...] Diachronic analysis centers on the relevant differences between the conventional orthography and the observed individual deviations.

That is, occasional spellings may point to both combinative and isolative changes as well as mergers, dialectally as well as in the standard variety, and may do so before the orthography changes generally (if it does at all). In this sense, all 'reverse spellings are really occasional at first' (1957: 14).

Back spellings (also called 'analogical' or 'inverted spellings') are best illustrated by an example provided by Penzl (1957: 18). In some High German dialects in the mid-twelfth century, the rounded front (*i*-mutated) vowels /ö/ and /ü/ merged with their unrounded counterparts /e/ and /i/. Hence, <e> and <i> are written for the historical umlauts <ö> and <ü>: <werter> for historically correct *Wörter* 'words'; <unglick> for historical *Unglück* 'misfortune'. On the basis of this *phonetic* and *phonological*

Table 1.2 *The logic behind analogical spellings*

Stage	Change	Rationale
1	[ø]/[y] <ö>/<ü> → [e]/[i]	phonetic/phonological change: merger between [ø] and [e] at /e/, and between [y] and [i] at /i/
2	<ö>/<ü> → <e>/<i>	occasional spellings indicating phonological change; even <ö>/<ü> = <e>/<i> to the historically unconscious writer, for they represent the same reality, i.e. the sound values /e/ and /i/
3	[e]/[i] <e>/<i> → <ö>/<ü>	analogy; reverse/back spellings

merger, there are also reverse spellings with <ö> and <ü> for historical <e> and <i>, not because the reflexes of /e/ and /i/ have rounded, but because <ö> and <e>, and <ü> and <i>, have come to be mere graphemic variants of the same sound. Examples are <bösser> for *besser* 'better' and <kürche> for *Kirche* 'church' (which were never rounded). The logic is as given in Table 1.2.

Hence, it seems that the very foundation for back spellings lies in phonetic facts, that is, a coalescence between hitherto separate phonemes: 'Reverse or inverse spellings [...] always indicate a phonemic coalescence' (Penzl 1957: 16). It will be shown in Chapter 5, however, that at least some analogical spellings may be due rather to graphemic extension.

Hence, the authorities all warn against *indiscriminate* use of spellings as evidence for sound change, date, dialect, etc. However, they all also agree that when spellings are treated with due caution, and are considered together with other available evidence, they play a crucial role in the study of past stages of language. In the words of Penzl (1957: 21):

> Thus modern pronunciations confirm the assumed terminal values of phonemic changes, while sometimes their relation to the modern orthographic symbols or an internal phonemic alternation throws light on earlier or initial values [...] The modern areal distribution can also sometimes indicate which values are [...] archaic and which innovations. This modern dialectal diffusion and differentiation has been used to postulate intermediate stages of a sound-change, but this seems more of a problem of historical reconstruction.

It is often implied that irregular spellings represent the scribes' more or less conscious attempts at rendering their speech faithfully by means of the Roman alphabet. It may be that this way of writing about the relation between speech and spelling puts the cart before the horse, as if the target of writing were a segmental *reconstruction* of speech; spelling is rather a product of variously imperfect *analyses* of speech, having in part its own rationale; and the speech analysed may be variously out of date. Adequate word-recognition is the functional criterion: there is every reason to believe that writing is logographic rather than phonetic (Benskin, pers. comm.). That is, writers do not generally attempt to reproduce their speech when they write; instead, they have learned that a certain sequence of letters represents a given word. The fluent reader does not reconstruct each word segment by segment, and it is far from clear that (all) fluent writers write in consciously apprehended segments – they write the word, that is, 'the written "words" tend to become group-symbols of group-sounds' (Wrenn 1943: 14; cf. *LALME I*, Section 1.4). ME scribes were performing within certain conventions, and these conventions may be disrupted by various factors, perhaps chiefly analogy. In this view, irregular spellings represent subconscious *interference* from speech habits. In the case of merger, once the same sound value has been attained for two previously separate phonemes, the previously separate spellings become interchangeable. This is indeed the rationale behind analogical or back spellings: if a given sound is spelt a certain way in one context, it can be spelt the same way in another. In Winters's words, analogy 'involves the more or less conscious workings of the human mind' and 'is based in the mental process by which speakers perceive certain linguistic units as related because of some shared feature(s) of their structure or meaning' (Winters 1997: 360). Hence, analogical change 'cannot be predicted a priori', but 'the analogical functioning of the brain […] creates a potential for such change at any time' (1997: 361).

Notes

1 The symbol '*ō*' will be used for traditional eME *ǭ*, and '*ē*' for traditional eME *ę̄*. They refer to the reflexes of OE *ē* (and of OE *ēo* in parts of the country) and OE *ō* respectively.

2 However, if the diphthong contours of these diphthongs differed, such a difference may have been enough to keep their reflexes apart (cf. Peeters 1991).

3 For some indication as to the controversy that may attend the interpretation of such material, consider Dobson's review (Dobson 1961) of Stanley's edition of the *Owl and the Nightingale* (Stanley 1960), and Stanley's rejoinder in his preface to the second edition (Stanley 1972).

4 Not all the MSS are actually included in the *LALME* corpus in the form of an LP or in the dot maps: some MSS contain genuinely mixed language and are therefore hard to localise; the language of others is too late or not dialectal enough to be included in a linguistic atlas for that period.

5 *LALME* (III: ix) states that the 'linguistic profiles [...] are the completed copies of a standard survey questionnaire. Each LP is an inventory, for some specified sample of text, of the forms observed which correspond to the test-items on the questionnaire'.

6 Meurman-Solin (1997) demonstrates that solely using pre-selected linguistic features in dialectal and other classification of historical texts may lead the linguist astray; entire tagged texts (which have been tagged for not only linguistic features, but also for genre, time period, and other variables) can offer a more correct picture with respect to 'conclusions about a particular language variety' (1997: 211) and to comparison between varieties.

7 The result would be a spatial classification or ordering, conceivably tidier than the natural/real dialect map, but still useful. How far this construct reflects the real map, if at all, rests on the observation (from modern dialect maps) that regional dialect changes, for the most part, in an orderly fashion across space. Even without anchor texts, the sequences and limits of the 'real' map would be reproduced. The construct would be analytic, not synthetic, but it would be tautological only in the way that mathematics can be considered tautological.

8 The 'fit'-technique is entirely uncontroversial to most Norwegians: students of Norwegian in upper secondary school are taught how to localise any spoken dialect sample of Norwegian with the aid of maps showing the regional spread of a variety of linguistic features. On a map of Norway they then cross out areas which do not show the features of the spoken sample, feature by feature, until they are left with a small blank area, to which the dialect most probably belongs. The only difference is that for ME, the material is written, not spoken. The value and dependability of the 'fit'-technique for the localisation of ME text has, however, been demonstrated in repeated tests, cf. *LALME* (I: Sections 2.3.3–2.3.6), and McIntosh (1963). Border-areas of course constitute a special problem, which is treated in *LALME* I: Section 2.3.5.

9 There is in fact some overlap between the forms recorded in the *Appendix of Southern Forms* and the forms recorded in the *County Dictionary* (cf. the lists from the *County Dictionary*); for an explanation of this, see *LALME* IV: 311.

10 Kristensson excludes Christian names, since (a) they were used all over the country, and were therefore often standardised, and (b) they were commonly abbreviated (1967: xviii, footnote 25). This raises the question, Do convention and standardisation stop at Christian names? It seems unlikely.

11 Hudson (1989: 104) points out that *SMED2* (W Midlands) includes material from the counties of Derbyshire, Leicestershire, and Nottinghamshire, which are traditionally held to be part of the E Midlands. Kristensson's reason for doing so is clear from map 9, which shows that <u> in HILL (indicating a retained rounded vowel) is found in these three counties as well as in the traditional W Midland counties. Kristensson's demarcation of dialect boundaries thus (at least partly) hinges on spellings for the reflex of OE *hyll*; McClure's demonstration that <i>/<y> *vs.* <u> in HILL changes with the hand therefore renders vacuous the entire foundation on which Kristensson

bases his claims. Hudson also finds the *SMED* maps crude in comparison with those of *LALME*, since Kristensson's maps do not indicate 'relative commonness' or the relative frequency of one form over another (*ibid.*). Hudson (1969: 69) hopes that subsequent studies 'may make clearer the relationship between the extant Rolls and the original returns', and makes the point that the scribes' choice between two spelling variants may very well have been based on something other than pronunciation.

12 For a more supportive review of *SMED*, see Nevanlinna (1999). McIntosh suggests that a more fitting title for *SMED* would be *A Survey of Middle English Phonology*, and that more could 'have been made of lexical contrasts within the northern area itself' (1969: 211). Moreover, since Kristensson's concerns are phonological, he does not distinguish variant spellings which he believes did not correspond to phonetic differences. Yet, such information would be invaluable, since different parts of the country show 'distinct preferences' regarding these spelling variants (1969: 213), and the distributional patterns of such regional preferences would add to our knowledge of ME dialects. Like McClure, McIntosh calls into question the local character of the language of the LSR (1969: 216), but does not appear as sceptical as McClure, since he states that Kristensson has 'established much interesting and indubitably reliable information about variations in pronunciation between one area and another' (1969: 212). The onomastic material from *SMED* should ideally be linked up with PDE onomastic material, and with the material provided by *SED*. Besides, there is a wealth of onomastic material and other English embedded in documents written otherwise in Latin (e.g. inventories and wills), some of which have been published by local record societies and archaeological societies, and whose language is solidly local. Unpublished material is found for instance in local record offices and in the collections of charters at the British Library. Likewise, the onomastic material contained in the volumes edited by the English Place-Name Society could be exploited. In short, there is a great wealth of material which Anglicists in general have hitherto ignored (Wright 1996 and Majocha 2005 being exceptions), and which is not subject to the kind of criticism with which *SMED* was met. Such material could shed light on (the lexical diffusion of) sound-changes, and could corroborate or refute the conclusions drawn by e.g. Wyld (1913–14a, 1913–14b), Sundby (1963), and Kristensson (*SMED*).

13 The URL address is: www.lel.ed.ac.uk/ihd/laeme1/laeme1.html. For more details on the source texts, see Laing (1993).

14 Additionally, there have been some changes made to three of the combined sets in the online *LAEME*. The texts which were first amalgamated into no. 1500 have now been separated into nos. 133, 134 and 135, because they are written in different hands; they are still entered in Huntingdonshire. For the same reason, no. 2003 has been separated into nos. 185 and 186; they are still both mapped in Thorney, Isle of Ely. No. 1900, which comprised three texts by the 'tremulus hand of Worcester', nos. 171, 172 and 173, has been separated 'because two of them are copied from what are somewhat different kinds of

OE source (the Worcester Fragments and Aelfric Grammar and Gloss) while the little Nicene creed text appears to be from a Middle English original' (Laing, e-mail dated 25.10.2010); nos. 171–3 are still entered in Worcestershire. Thus, since the mapping of the individual texts is still the same as for the combined sets, and since changing all references to these texts in the present work would be too time-consuming, I have chosen to use the old index nos. 1500, 1900 and 2003 respectively.

15 Hand A has copied from 129v12 to the end of 139v, and from the top of 143r to 146v; Hand B has copied from 140r to the foot of 142v; Hand C has copied 15 lines on 147r. Hand C is that of Thomas Cyrcetur, canon residentiary of Salisbury, who died in 1452. An inscription in his hand, recording the bequest of the book to Salisbury, appears on the same folio.

16 Additional information from the source is drawn from Benskin's analysis.

17 For instance, the English word *book* denotes 'a written or printed work of some length, especially on consecutive sheets of paper fastened or bound together in a volume' (*Webster's Unabridged Encyclopedic Dictionary of the English Language*), but the fact that this meaning is represented by the word *book*, and not, say, **xip*, is purely arbitrary (though historical and conventional). There is nothing in the word itself, or in its phonetic make-up, that makes it especially fit to characterise the type of object in question, and this is indeed why 'a written or printed work of some length [. . .]' is represented by *book* in English, by *bok* in Norwegian, and by *livre* in French.

18 *LAEME* does, however, contain the spellings <dreiȝ> for OE *drī* DRY in no. 229 (Gloucestershire; and similar spellings in other sources), and <seiȝeð> for OE *sīon* 'to strain, filter' (1.pl.pres.) in no. 64 (Essex). However, *drī* is probably a variant of *drȳge*, which would explain the use of <ȝ>; and *sīon* seems to be a variant of *sēon*, which is a contracted verb (which preserved the original medial consonant in the plural forms).

CHAPTER 2

The development of OE ā

2.1 Introduction

Spellings for the reflex of OE *ā* change in SME from OE <a> to <o>, <oa>, <oo>. Such innovative spellings started appearing around 1150, and are believed to indicate a change in the realisation of the reflex of OE *ā*, that is, backing, rounding, and raising of [ɑ:] to [ɔ:]. Most handbooks claim that this change had been completed in the dialects south of the Humber by around 1225. North of the Humber, OE *ā* remained, but was later fronted and raised during ME; the stage [ɛ:] is believed to have been reached before 1400 (Sweet 1888: §§666–8; Luick 1914–40: §§369–71; Dobson 1968: §98; Jordan 1968: §44). The later development of SME [ɔ:] shows raising to [o:] and diphthongisation to [ou] (whence /əʊ/ in RP), both in evidence from the sixteenth century (Zachrisson 1913: 153, 223; Dobson 1968: 673, Note 1). This chapter assesses ME spellings for the reflex of OE *ā* in an attempt to establish their most likely phonetic correspondences, and thus to determine the course of change.

2.2 On the nature of OE *ā*

First, certain hypotheses regarding the nature of OE *ā* are worth considering, namely that OE *ā* did not change in lOE or eME. One claim (Stockwell, pers. comm.) states that OE *ā* was always a back and rounded vowel, <a> representing [ɒ:] or [ɔ:]. If so, the new spellings emerging in ME were just that – new *spellings* – and not indicative of a change in pronunciation. The other view (Pilch 1997) holds that OE *ā* was phonetically [ɑ:], and that its value did not change in ME, despite the new spellings. A brief review will be given later of the arguments put forward.

Stockwell's arguments for thinking OE *ā* was [ɔ:] are as follows. (1) PrGmc is believed to have had three long vowel phonemes, /a: i: u:/. In WGmc, /i:/ split into /i: e:/, and /u:/ into /u: o:/; in OE, the last phoneme

/a:/ had also split into two phonemes /a: æ:/, <a>, and <æ>. Stockwell claims that the phonetic realisations of these are uncertain, but that the sound corresponding to <æ> may be inferred from its later development as front and half-open. Correspondingly, he states, the sound indicated by <a> may be inferred only from its later development, which is to /ɔ:/ > /ɔu/ > /əʊ/. Thus, <a> represented a back and rounded vowel in OE, and the scribes used <a> simply because <o> was already taken. (2) The asymmetry of the OE long-vowel phonemic system would be repaired if OE *ā* really was back and rounded. (3) Vowels are rarely rounded isolatively, whereas unrounding seems quite common.

Against Stockwell's (1), there are four counter-arguments. Firstly, each letter in the Roman alphabet had a traditional sound correspondence; the sound-value of <a> was /a(:)/. Although it is true that <o> was already taken for /o(:)/, AS scribes could have used a new or modified (*fuþorc*) symbol for a vowel-sound which was perceived to be different from either <a> or <o>, much the same way they used <y>, <ø>, and <æ> for sounds which were not part of the Latin vowel system. Secondly, the source of OE *ā* was partly Gmc *ai*,[1] whose reflex was a front vowel or diphthong in the other Gmc languages.[2] Northern English dialects, in which OE *ā* did not become [ɔ:] in ME, today have either still [a:] or a *front* raised vowel (monophthong or diphthong). Thirdly, NGmc shows an exact parallel to the sound change under consideration: NGmc also had an *ā*, which was backed, rounded, and raised to /ɔ:/, where it remains to the present day, for example, Norse *bát*, Norw. *båt* /bɔ:t/ 'boat'. Parallels are of course not evidence that it happened thus in OE, but they do shed light on what paths of development sounds often take in related languages. Finally, OE short *a* [a], and the shortened product of OE *ā*, later fall in with the reflex of OE *æ*; the phonetic realisation of these vacillates between [a] and [æ] throughout the history of English, both diachronically and synchronically. The other OE vowels form corresponding pairs of long and short vowels, for example, <e> [e] and [e:], <i> [i] and [i:]; if OE short *a* was *front*, it seems illogical to claim that OE *ā* was back and rounded.

These points together indicate that OE *ā* originally most likely had a central quality, and was unrounded. It is nonetheless likely that its allophones varied between being front, central, and back according to phonetic context; the fact that it ends up as [ɔ:] > [ɔu] is itself proof that it drifted to the back at some point. Also, it is physically more difficult for the tongue to move along the horizontal dimension in the low area of the vowel space, and so it is harder to distinguish different degrees of frontness or backness there than in the mid or high area; this is indeed indicated by the shape of the standard vowel chart.

Against Stockwell's (2) there are three counter-arguments. First, typological arguments ought to be treated with scepticism: though it may be true that some languages have symmetric vowel-systems, it is certainly not the case for all vowel-systems. Even if it were the case that the great majority of vowel-systems are symmetric, that fact would require its own explanation; to say that something is the case *for* typological *reasons*, constitutes a tautology. Second, the fact that Northern accents have a strong imbalance in the long-vowel system (i.e. more front vowels than back) tells in favour of the traditional view, as there still seems to be no systemic 'pressure' from this over-full front series. Besides, one might ask whether symmetry is a necessary condition for vowel systems to function. The answer to this is clearly in the negative: if it were, asymmetric systems would not develop in the first place. Third, it also seems reasonable to ask why the spelling would change at all if there was no change in pronunciation, as there would be no reason for scribes to depart from a well-established convention. Orthographic discontinuities attendant on the Norman Conquest are well-known: traditional <cw> was abandoned for <qu>, <þ> for <th>, etc. On the other hand, the fact that AN scribes started to write <o> for OE *ā* could in fact support Stockwell's claim that OE *ā* was [ɔ:]: The scribes would simply have abandoned the spelling <a> if they thought it was a poor match to the pronunciation of the words in which it occurred. However, Liebl (2006) finds that <o> for OE *ā* occurs *before* the Norman Conquest (cf. 2.6).

There are no really good arguments against Stockwell's (3), because it seems to be true. There are many examples of vowels becoming rounded in English, but rounding in these cases seems most commonly to be combinative, that is, due to the presence of a neighbouring rounded, nasal, or velar(ised) sound. Interestingly, this opens up the possibility that the change to OE *ā* was a combinative change, which is a line of thought that will be pursued throughout this work.

Like Stockwell, Pilch dismisses the new spellings <o(o)> as indicative of a phonetic change, and in fact denies the change OE *ā* > [ɔ:] altogether for structural reasons (1997: 437, 441–2). Unlike Stockwell, however, Pilch thinks [ɑ:] always remained, and the ME long-vowel system is hence presented as unchanged from OE to ME.[3] In his discussion of ME <stoon> STONE, Pilch claims that the vowel 'was [...] the most extreme "long-low-back" vowel of the inventory. Consequently, it must have been "low-back" /ɑ:/ in terms of distinctive features' (1997: 441). Apart from constituting a tautology, this definition disregards the distinctive feature of lip rounding entirely. Moreover, his account loses sight of the fact that when the vowel shortens in OE, the output is *a* (PDE /æ/), but when it shortens in southern ME, the output is *o* (PDE /ɒ/). Pilch's dismissal of spelling evidence also leaves the following question unanswered: If the realisation of OE *ā* did not change, what could have motivated the scribes to use a new symbol <o(o)> for it – a symbol, moreover, which had thus far been reserved for etymological back mid rounded /o(:)/?[4] Most importantly, Pilch's account does not explain how and when the southern accents of English ended up with a back and rounded reflex of OE *ā*, as evidenced by its PDE reflex, if there was never a process of rounding and backing.

Pilch admits that the phonetic realisation may have been different from what one would assume from his phonemic transcription. Thus, he states that the vowel of <stoon> 'must have been "low-back" lax in terms of distinctive features (we have no way of assigning it phonometric parameters' (1997: 441); and on the vowel of <deel> for OE *dǣl* DEAL, 'it must have been "low-front" /æ·/ (whatever its spelling or its narrow transcription)' (1997: 441). Such a disclaimer seems defeatist, especially when the title of Pilch's paper includes the word 'phonetics'; it ought perhaps to be changed to 'phonology'.

On East Saxon *ā* for WS *ǣ*^{2} (<WGmc *ā*), Kitson observes that Huntingdonshire, Bedfordshire, Buckinghamshire, and E Middlesex had *ā*, and that this *ā*, which was 'disappearing *c.*1400 is a retreating relic of it, just as many features of "Kentish" Old English are [relics of East Saxon]. As would be expected of such an origin, it is actually evidenced south of the Thames as well as north' (1998: 174). However, south of the Thames this *ā* merged with ordinary *ā*. Thus, OE *ǣ* did *not* develop into East Saxon *ā*, according to Kitson; rather, East Saxon and Kentish had *ā* for WS *ǣ*^{2} from the beginning. From this it follows that the early <a> and later <o> for the reflex of WGmc *ā* (WS *ǣ*^{2}) in Kentish and parts of the East Saxon area should be taken to indicate backing and rounding of *ā* to [ɔ:].

On the strength of the earlier arguments it seems certain that there was indeed a sound change in eME, south of the Humber, affecting etymological *ā*, the result of which was a back and rounded (and slightly raised) vowel.

2.3 Handbooks on the development of OE *ā*

The handbooks are mostly in agreement regarding the **dating** of the change under consideration. Wyld concludes that the change must have begun well before the mid-twelfth century, though it was not 'consistently nor universally expressed by the spelling' until the early thirteenth century (1927: §156; cf. Jordan 1968: §44). Luick puts the incipient stages of the change to the eleventh century in certain places (1914–40: §369), and suggests that the stage [ɔ:] was reached in these innovative areas in the course of the twelfth century, and that it had been reached all over the affected area in the course of the fifteenth. He thus acknowledges that the change might have taken some 500 years to reach completion. Wright and Wright believe the change had been effected by 1225 in all dialects south of the Humber (1928: §51), which is Prins's claim also (1972: §3.20). Strang treats the change in her period 970–1170 (1970: §164). Prins states that OE ***ā*** **after** ***w*** was rounded and raised to *ǭ* in all dialects, due to 'over-rounding', starting in the thirteenth century in the Midlands (1972: §3.22). This claim is worth bearing in mind in the discussion of the material later.

Concerning the **loci** of the change, Wyld believes it started in the South-East, whereas the South-West was 'slightly behind' (1927: §156). Luick states that the change took place first in the WS area, Worcestershire, and Kent (as does Jordan 1968: §44), starting in the eleventh century. The area south of the Thames and the S Midlands followed suit; here, [ɔ:] had been reached by the end of the thirteenth century. The N Midlands and Shropshire were even later. S Yorkshire still had an *a*-sound in the first half of the fourteenth century, but in the course of the fifteenth century, [ɔ:] had been reached all over the affected area, which included the greater part of Lancashire, S Yorkshire, and all of Lincolnshire (1914–40: §369). Luick also notes that in the North, there are frequent loans with southern [ɔ:], mostly in literary works. Strang's treatment names the South and the Midlands as the loci of change (1970: §164).

As far as the **spelling evidence** is concerned, some of the handbooks point out that the change was 'slow to be reflected in spelling' (Strang 1970: §164), and that the first <o>-type spellings appear in the mid-twelfth century in E Midlands texts. The following spellings are adduced by Wyld (1927) and by Prins (1972): <more> MORE in the *Peterborough Chronicle* (1154, Lincolnshire), <oʒe> and <oʒen> OWN in the *Kentish Homilies* (before 1150). In addition, there are a few <nohht> NOT in the *Ormulum* (1175, Lincolnshire). Wyld points out that other texts from the South or S Midlands of about the same period have <o> occasionally, dominantly, or exclusively,[5] whereas some southern texts have no <o> at all.[6] Spellings with <oa> are termed occasional (1927: §156). Luick states that the resulting sound was written <o>, sometimes <oa> in some texts in the thirteenth century, and later often <oo> in coda position and in closed syllables (1914–40: §369). Wright and Wright claim that the new sound was sometimes written <oa> or <ao> and 'from the fourteenth century onwards it was very often written **oo** in closed syllables and when final' (1928: §51).[7] Jordan agrees that the sound resulting from *ā* > [ɔ:] was spelt <o>, but also <oa> in the thirteenth century; later <oo> is found, especially in closed syllables and when final; <oa> appears towards the end of the fifteenth century (1968: §44). Prins comments that the spelling <oa> was used in eME to represent the new sound [ɔ:], but that it 'fell into disuse after 1200. It was reintroduced after c. 1420' (1972: §3.21).

The change under consideration is also believed to include OE *ā* from earlier *a* in the Anglian combination ***ald*** > ***āld***. Forms like <cold>, <holden>, <bold> appear in texts from the Midlands and even from the South (which is supposed to have been WS territory) from the mid-twelfth century. These <o> forms eventually oust the native forms of the South-Western dialects, even those of Kentish.

In the **North**, OE *ā* was fronted to [æ:] quite early, and subsequently raised to [ɛ:] > [e:]. Wyld finds it impossible to say exactly when this fronting began, since northern texts only start appearing from the end of the thirteenth and beginning of the fourteenth centuries. However, fourteenth-century Scottish rhymes indicate complete fronting to [e:] (Wyld 1927: §157). In early NME texts, the reflexes of OE *ā*, Norman French *ā*, and OE *a* in open syllables are levelled under the same sound. Scottish texts from Barbour's *Bruce* (1375) onwards consistently show <ai>/<ay>. Dobson states that in 'the North ME *ā* had perhaps already been fronted as far as [ɛ:] before 1400, for by this date we find evidence that NME *ā* had become identical with the monophthong developed from ME *ai*' (1968: §98). Wright and Wright date the early stages of the fronting to long open *ę̄* to the late thirteenth century. This fronting was not commonly reflected in spelling, and from Barbour onwards the reflex of OE *ā* is mostly spelt <ai>/<ay> (1928: §51). Prins asserts that eME *ā* remained in the North until *c.* 1300, whence it was fronted and raised successively to [a:] > [æ:] > [ɛ:], which stage was reached around 1400; it was later further raised to [e:] (1972: §3.23).

2.4 Discussion

2.4.1 On <o(o)> as evidence of change

As pointed out in the introductory chapter, innovative spellings may be unreliable as 'evidence' for historical phonology, since mediaeval writing is not phonemic transcript. Writing is taught behaviour, ruled to a large extent by convention. It is likely therefore that mediaeval scribes would remain faithful to the orthography they had been taught, unless they perceived a very marked discrepancy between what they had learnt and what they heard or spoke themselves. Besides, the same scribe could be a *literatim* copyist when recording a legal document, but be innovative when copying a piece of prose text or poetry; McIntosh (1963) and Benskin and Laing (1981) give accounts of different types of scribal behaviour.

Essentially, <a>-type and <o>-type spellings may be interpreted in various ways. Early <o> is a genuine innovation and a departure from the norm. Departures from the norm seem *a priori* to be indicative of 'something', usually change. The later, known history of the sound in question also suggests that the innovative spellings do indicate a new backed, rounded, and raised vowel. Thus, <o> may be taken at face value. Northern <o> is likely to be due to southern influence, but it is uncertain whether that means that northern scribes just *wrote* <o> (in words which according to their own observation were written with <o> in the South), or whether northern *speech* was somewhat influenced too.

The <a> spellings, on the other hand, are conventional, and may represent retained traditional /ɑ:/. However, they may correspond to new /ɔ:/, at least if all lexemes with OE *ā* changed simultaneously, such that the spelling <a> was seen to correspond to the sound /ɔ:/; that is, there was merely a difference in phonetic *realisation* (i.e. the *potestas* of the *littera* had changed). This may not, however, be very likely, for two reasons. (1) If the implementation of sound change is gradual and slow, at least in the initial stages, then at any given point in time, some words in some contexts will have [ɑ:], others [ɔ:], or the speaker may choose between co-existing variants [ɑ:] and [ɔ:] for the same words.[8] (2) Short *a* still existed in native words as well as in French loans, and this *a* was later lengthened to /a:/ in MEOSL (cf. Malsch and Fulcher 1975). The existence of this short *a* lessens the probability of the scribes linking the spelling <a> with the sound [ɔ:], although it may be noted in this context that NME retained <o> for [ü:], in face of <o> for [ɔ]. Therefore, it seems safe to take (late) <a> spellings at face value also, at least in texts where <a> and <o> are co-variants for the same phoneme, etymologically. The case may be different for texts with <a> only; here, there are two interpretations available: (1) the scribe could have been faithful to conventional orthography, or (2) the scribal dialect may not have seen the change under consideration. As long as *convention* rules orthography, lack of *evidence* for a change need not entail *no change*.[9]

It is also worth noting that the sound change itself could have been gradual, such that the reflex of old /ɑ:/ would slowly drift backwards and upwards, while undergoing rounding (such a gradual shift in phonetic realisation must be assumed for /ʌ;/, which started out as close, back, and unrounded, and is now open, central-to-front and unrounded in RP). Alternatively, backed and rounded allophonic variants could have been conditioned by the phonetic context, and these variants would catch on or spread, from context to context. Somewhere along this continuum, it must have been hard for the scribes to decide whether the vowel they were pronouncing was [ɑ:] or [ɒ:] or [ɔ:]. It may be impossible to know, but it seems at least probable that this difficulty in interpreting a new sound could be the direct reason why so many texts have both <a> and <o>, and also why quite a few texts feature <ao> or <oa>. Incidentally, <ao>/<au>/<oa> spellings may demonstrate the phonetic development behind *ā* > [ɔ:], especially if it can be shown that this change started with OE *ā* preceding or following bilabial *w*, velar *ȝ*, or nasal *n*: A rounded glide may have developed, or – metrically speaking – one of the morae of the long vowel may have become rounded in assimilation to the neighbouring consonant, and the rounding subsequently spread to the other mora as well.

To sum up, there are good reasons to take both ME <a> and ME <o> spellings for OE *ā* at face value, and to interpret them as representing an [ɑ:]-like sound and an [ɔ:]-like sound respectively.

2.4.2 *On French loans and MEOSL*

One further point needs mentioning, that is, that of chronology. The majority of the handbooks state that it is uncertain exactly when OE *ā* started to round and raise, but that it must have happened before MEOSL was effected; otherwise, words with OE *a* in open syllables (e.g. *make, name*) would have taken part in the change as well (cf. Wright and Wright 1928: §51). Strang states that the change must have happened **after** the late OE lengthening of *a* before certain consonant groups (since e.g. OE *cald* COLD is included in the change), but **before** the borrowing of French loanwords (1970: §164). In Note 1, Prins states that the resulting sound was probably *wider* (by which he probably means 'laxer') than the result of MEOSL of *o*, since Chaucer does not rhyme them (and Prins infers a contrast from non-identity), though they later merged in the standard language (1972: §3.20). MEOSL is supposed to have begun in the first half of the thirteenth century, so the reflex of OE *ā* must have started to change before this date (cf. Wright and Wright 1928: §§77–85; but see also Luick 1914–40, §392). This point is of course logically valid. Besides, most of the words adduced by Wright and Wright seem to have had a short vowel at the time they were borrowed, and that it was lengthened in MEOSL.

But if so, how is it possible for the rounding and raising of OE *ā* to have taken so long – as we will see – and still exclude the result of MEOSL of short *a*? In the course of eME, the reflexes of OE *æ* and OE *a* fell together; it is likely that the resulting sound had a distinctly front quality, which was preserved when the sound was lengthened, that is, [a:]. The reflex of OE *ā*, on the other hand, had started to be backed, rounded, and raised before 1150. Thus, the two reflexes would have been sufficiently different when MEOSL began to be kept apart (cf. Malsch and Fulcher 1975). As Wyld puts it, the reflex of OE *ā* 'must have undergone some slight rounding before these foreign words [i.e. Norman-French loans] got into the language, otherwise [...] it must have involved them as well' (1927: §156).

2.5 Discussion of material for OE *ā*

After extracting written forms for items with etymological OE *ā* from the three sources, I made separate tables for each. Hence, the use and frequency of <a> versus <o>, as well as the temporal and areal spread of <o>, are charted. Separate tables indicate forms other than <a>, and <o>, that is, <ao>/<oa>, and <oo>/<oi>, and <ae>, <æ>, <e>, <ea>, <eo>, respectively. All tables are found at the end of this chapter.

Since the *LAEME* material is coded for date, it is possible to make the tables roughly chronological, showing the changing proportions of variant spellings over time. The tables can be used with a view to answering questions of the following kind: Are changing spellings or changing proportions concomitant with the changes in pronunciation as postulated by the handbooks? Further, do the changing proportions coincide with the traditional dates given to the various ME long-vowel changes? And do any particular dates and loci stand out in terms of changed spellings or changes in proportions?

As might be expected, the ME material does not generally present neat and clear patterns regarding the development of OE *ā*. The material from each of the three sources is discussed later. The discussion is not well served by treating *LAEME*, *SMED*, and *LALME* material separately: the parts of these surveys that treat the same issue, and so cast light on each other, should be brought together. However, for reasons of chronology and consistency throughout the present work, the material from each survey will be discussed separately in this and subsequent chapters, but the concluding sections will attempt to tie all the relevant parts together.

2.5.1 Discussion of LAEME *material*

LAEME has a rich lexical yield for OE *ā*, and provides much documentation for both <a> and <o> for its reflexes; it should therefore be possible to track the initiation and spread of the change OE *ā* > *ǭ*. Preliminary conclusions are as follows, and are based on the spellings in Table 2.1.

With regard to the inception of change, there is no marked difference of spelling between (1) words in which OE *ā* was preceded or followed by a rounded sound, and (2) words in which OE *ā* was not preceded or followed by a rounded sound: the change seems to have happened at the same time with both categories. There is, however, a marked difference in frequency of <a> versus <o> spellings for the two categories, in that <o> spellings are *less* frequent for OE (*w*+)*ā*(+*w*) than for OE *ā* alone in the early stages. It does seem, however, that innovative <o> is more frequent in words with OE *w*+*ā* than in those with OE *ā*+*w*, in which <a> is retained long after other OE *ā* > *ǭ*, in many late ME MSS, cf. Prins's claims in Section 2.3.

If the change was combinative and did start in one single word, a likely candidate is OE *nāwiht* NOT, since even some sources with dominant <a> (or virtually only <a>) show <o> for NOTHING, NOT (and despite the statement in (a) earlier). Two other items, OE *ān* ONE and *swā* SO, also regularly appear with innovative spellings (cf. Liebl 2006).

There is no clear pattern of <a> *vs.* <o> with regard to the North-South distinction in the early stages of the shift, though in the thirteenth and fourteenth centuries, northern texts show dominant <a>, while southern texts show <a> or <o>. Perhaps the most surprising fact to emerge, at least if it is true that change is gradual and that OE *ā* > *ǭ* started in the eME period, is the fact that <o> spellings appear to be dominant over <a> in very early *LAEME* texts from Berkshire, Essex, and Suffolk (1150–99). However, <o> for OE *ā* is found even in OE texts, which suggests that the change started earlier than has been assumed (Liebl 2006); if so, <o> in eME texts does not preclude gradual change in the years before these texts were written.

Moreover, the change may not have started in the far South, but perhaps rather in East Anglia, since early <o> is reported in the *Peterborough*

Chronicle (1154) and in the *Ormulum* (1175, SW Lincolnshire), as well as in Essex and Suffolk, but also in the South-East (Kent, Sussex, London), and independently in the W Midlands (Gloucestershire, Staffordshire, Berkshire, and Oxfordshire).

The change had *not* been completed by 1225 in all the southern dialects, as claimed in some of the handbooks (e.g. Wright and Wright 1928), at least if the spellings are to be taken at face value. Nor is it true that the *ā* remained unchanged in all the dialects north of the Humber until the late thirteenth century: early <o> is found in northern texts as well as southern ones, as indeed noted by Luick (1914–40, §369). From *c.* 1250, <o> becomes dominant in SME.

Table 2.2 shows the distribution of <oa> and <ao>, and allows the following conclusions: forms with <ao> are rare, but are found from the early thirteenth century in Essex, Herefordshire, and Worcestershire. Spellings with <oa> are more common, and are found from *c.* 1200 in the Essex, the W Midlands, and London; they are particularly frequent in Worcestershire and Essex. Two texts from the Chancery (the 'Proclamation of King Henry III', 1258) show dominant <oa>, as do two texts from Norfolk and Cheshire (both 1250–99). Thus, Prins is wrong in stating that <oa> fell into disuse after 1200: on the contrary, it is **after** 1200 that these spellings become common.

The following observations may be made from Table 2.3, which records less frequent spellings, e.g. <oo>, <oe>, <u>. (1) <oo> starts appearing from the early thirteenth century onwards in Worcestershire, then (later in the same century and in the early fourteenth century) in Cheshire, Essex, and Kent, the SW Midlands, and the NE Midlands. (2) <oe> appears in the SW Midlands in the late thirteenth and early fourteenth centuries; <oi> is found once in Herefordshire in the same period; the same text has <ouw> twice and <uo> once. (3) <ou> appears in Gloucestershire (1275–99) and in Oxfordshire (*c.* 1300). (4) <u> is found a few times, in the E Midlands from the late twelfth century, and in the W Midlands from *c.* 1200 onwards. Sweet (1888: §666) remarks on <wumme> for 'woe (is) me!' in *St. Juliana* (which otherwise shows consistent <a>)[10] that it 'presupposes the rounded vowel, and makes it probable that the *a* is a traditional spelling, and in *so* by the side of *swa* the *o* is fully established'.

Forms with <æ>, <ai>, <e>, <ea>, <ei>, <eo> are reproduced in Table 2.4. They are quite frequent, and occur from the latter half of the twelfth century. The following may also be observed. (1) Interestingly, the earliest <æ>/<e>-type spellings do *not* appear in northern texts, of which there are few anyway, but in Berkshire, Essex, Suffolk, and Worcestershire from the latter half of the twelfth century. They then appear in other parts of the W Midlands and Kent from the early thirteenth century; in Somerset and Cheshire and some northern texts (Lancashire and Cumberland) from the mid-thirteenth century, and in the E Midlands from the late thirteenth century onwards. (2) Certain words seem to occur with <e>-type spellings more often than others: these are OE *ān* ONE, *nān* NONE (and compounds with *nā*), *þā* THEN, *swā* SO (and compounds with *swā*). (3) It is possible that some of these spellings are due to lack of stress, at least those which occur in compounds or in words of more than one syllable, for example, <alse> for OE *als swā*, <welle>/<weile> for OE *weilā*, but most of these irregular spellings occur in stressed syllables. Another reason for the high number of such spellings could be that the words in which they occur are very frequent. (4) Forms with <e> for the vowel of GOAT may have Scandinavian etymology, at least in text nos. 118 from Cheshire, and 159 from Lincolnshire; ON etymology is hardly behind similar forms appearing in Essex, Suffolk, Worcestershire, and Gloucestershire.

When <a> appears in compounds in texts with dominant <o>, it is possible that <a> here is due to shortening of *ā* to [a]. Examples are <halidai> HOLIDAY in text no. 1700, and <haliweie> 'holy way' in text no. 150 (both from Norfolk). Shortening may also be responsible for <a> in closed monosyllables, especially when MEOSL was under way.

2.5.2 Discussion of SMED *material*

The *SMED* material suggests a similar development as that indicated by the *LAEME* spellings.

OE ā *in general*

For the **northern** counties and **Lincolnshire**, *SMED1* has quite a few <o> for the reflex of OE *ā* in Lincolnshire, Lancashire, and the West Riding of Yorkshire, from the early part of the fourteenth century (Table 2.5); one or two <o> also appear in the North Riding of Yorkshire (1301), Northumberland (1316), and Durham (1344). Hence, the reflex of OE *ā* was starting to round and raise even north of the Humber from the beginning of the fourteenth century at the latest. This has been demonstrated by earlier research for southern parts of Lancashire, the West Riding of Yorkshire, and parts of Lincolnshire (Kesteven and Holland); *vide* Kristensson 1967 (pp. 30–8) for a discussion of the boundary and of earlier research. However, it is likely that rounded and raised variants of the reflex of OE *ā* spread to the other northern counties also by the fourteenth century.

The **W Midland** counties report a substantial number of forms with <a> for OE *ā*; these are mostly to be explained as due to shortening of *ā* before backing and rounding took place (cf. Kristensson 1987: 27). Names in which the <a> could be due to shortening have not been included in my lists or tables; nor have forms containing the element HOLY, as they all have <a>. The forms with <a> included in my lists thus cannot be explained as due to shortening. Kristensson explains some of them as 'probably names of persons who hailed from the north' (1987: 27), which may be the case for a few names; still, forms with <a> are quite numerous. Even Kristensson finds some of these 'remarkable', but claims they may be traditional spellings or due to scribal confusion (1987: 28). The power of tradition should of course not be underestimated, and may be behind some of the <a> forms in question. However, such forms are so numerous that it seems at least probable that the southern change of OE *ā* to *ǭ* had not yet been completed all over the area or in all words by the early fourteenth century. Names with <a> for OE *ā* are found all over the W Midlands except in Derbyshire.

Material from the **E Midlands** reports mostly forms with <o> for OE and eME *ā*, but also frequent <a> (especially in Norfolk, Northamptonshire, and Essex). Kristensson draws the conclusion that '[t]here is no doubt that OE *ā* had become /ɔ:/ in the whole area examined' (Kristensson 1995: 14); it seems less than certain, however, that the change had been completed, if the spellings are anything to go by.

Material from the **South** shows some conventional <a> for OE *ā* (e.g. <Ake> from OE *āc* OAK in Somerset (1333), present-day *Oake*). Such spellings occur in Berkshire, Dorset, Somerset, Kent, Sussex, and Wiltshire; they seem most numerous in Wiltshire, Somerset, and Kent. Kristensson's view is that some of these <a> forms 'may be due to influence from compounds in which /ɑ:/ had been shortened. [...] But we must also reckon with the possibility that /ɑ:/ lingered on in some localities or some ideolects [*sic*]' (Kristensson 2001: 26). The latter alternative seems the more probable for the forms included in my lists; this is borne out by the fact that those places referred to, of which it has been possible to ascertain the modern identity, have present-day <oa> /əʊ/.

OE ā+w

For the reflexes of OE *ā+w*, the following may be concluded from *SMED*. In the **North**, forms with <o> for OE *ā+w* form essentially the same pattern as forms with <o> for *ā*: they appear first in the East Riding of Yorshire (1297), then in Durham (1311–38), in Lincolnshire and Lancashire (1327 and 1332), and in the West Riding of Yorkshire (1346). The only exception is SW Lancashire (which is normally an *ǭ*-area), where forms such as <Lauton> and <Lawe> suggest that OE *ā+w* remained as *ā* (Kristensson 1967: 37).

In the rest of the country, conventional <a> for OE *ā+w* is rather more interesting. In the **W Midlands**, it is found in Cheshire in the period 1250–1300, which is not surprising, but also in Derbyshire, Leicestershire, Nottingham, and Oxfordshire in the period 1300–50. In Kristensson's opinion, these <au>/<aw> correspond to /au/, 'are probably due to early shortening of OE *ā*', and – together with similar spellings from southern Lancashire – they 'suggest [...] that OE *āw* appeared as ME /au/ in an indefinite part of the North-West Midland area' (Kristensson 1987: 29). If this were the case, judging from the evidence, it seems that the NE Midlands may also have had /au/ for OE *ā+w* up until the beginning of the fourteenth century.

For the reflexes of OE *ā+w* in the **E Midlands**, Kristensson points out that '[s]ix out of seven <aw> forms pertain to Essex, and probably illustrate the development /ɔu/>/au/ which is well attested in Kentish' (1995: 15). True, many conventional <aw> are found in Essex, but they are also found in Bedfordshire, Buckinghamshire, Cambridgeshire, and Huntingdonshire, which is left out of Kristensson's discussion.

The **southern** counties also report some <au>/<aw> for OE *ā+w*, in Dorset, Hampshire, Kent, Surrey, and Sussex; they are particularly frequent in Dorset and Kent. These forms are discussed in *SMED5*, where it is stated that OE *ā+w* 'generally gives /ɔu/, written <ow/ou>' (Kristensson 2002: 242); further (2002: 242),

> Forms with <au> in place-names may be due to *a* having been shortened (in trisyllabic forms), so that <au> represents /au/ from OE *a* + *w*. The same may be true of <aw> in trisyllabic words like *le Blawere* [...] Forms like *Crawe* (p) K 1332, *ate Lawe* (p) S[u]r 1332 [...] cannot be due to shortening of the diphthong but probably represent a development /ɔu/>/au/ in Kent and Do[r] (v. Jordan § 105 *Remark*).

Such a development is however not postulated for Surrey. It may be worthwhile collating the material from the South with the material from the southern parts of the Midlands. It will be remembered that there are a few forms with <au>/<aw> for OE *ā+w* in the E Midlands, especially in Essex, and it was commented that they 'probably illustrate the development /ɔu/>/au/ which is well attested in Kentish' (Kristensson 1995: 15). As noted earlier, such spellings are indeed more frequent in Kent and Dorset than in the other southern counties, so Kristensson may very well be right. Still, the forms from Dorset would require a different explanation insofar as they seem isolated from similar forms in the W Midlands, though they form a continuum with other <au>/<aw> in Hampshire, Sussex, Surrey, and Kent. To resolve this issue, the evidence for the 'well-attested' development of /ɔu/ > /au/ in Kentish would need a more thorough examination than has been feasible for the present work.

With regard to OE *ā+ʒ*, names with <o> for OE *ā+ʒ* appear in the West Riding of Yorkshire (1327), and in Lancashire (1332). Cubbin (1981) examines onomastic ME material for southern Lancashire; he is particularly concerned with the development of OE *ȳ* in this area, but cites spellings indicating OE *ā* > [ɔ:] as supporting evidence. Forms with <o> for the vowel of OE *hār* 'grey' are found in Lancashire from *c.* 1275 onwards, whereas a Kentish name *Maidstone* appears with <o> about fifty years earlier, also in Lancashire material (Cubbin 1981: 99). This is taken to indicate that Kentish had [ɔ:] for OE *ā* from *c.* 1220–25.

Summary of SMED *material*

The following conclusions may be drawn from the *SMED* material for OE *ā*.

1. In the South, <o> had *not* ousted <a> all over the area even by 1325 – indeed, <Stanes>, <Raa> and <Ake> are found in Middlesex, Kent, and Somerset in Rolls as late as the 1330s. By this time, however, it must be said that <o> is clearly dominant south of the Humber, whereas <a> is dominant north of it.
2. One might expect the use of <o> to be a little more frequent for OE *ā* before the rounding glides *w/ʒ*, but this is generally not the case: for example, <Blawere> appears in Kent in 1327, and <Lawe> in Surrey in 1332.
3. Forms with <o> appear in the North from the early fourteenth century onwards, except in Cumberland, Westmoreland, and the East Riding of Yorkshire; they are most frequent in Lancashire, the West Riding of Yorkshire, and Lincolnshire, that is, in counties in direct contact with more southerly dialects.
4. Forms with <e> are extremely rare, but one appears in Gloucestershire (1312) and another in Somerset (1327); the Lincolnshire Roll from 1327 has one <e> and one <ae>. In other words, such spellings are *not* found in the North.

5. Forms with <oo> are found in Lancashire as well as all over the E Midlands, and in large parts of the W Midlands; virtually all of them appear in open syllables.[11] They appear first in Hertfordshire (1307), Bedfordshire (1309), and Cambridgeshire (1312); the latest forms are from 1332.
6. <ouw> is recorded in Nottinghamshire (1327), Wiltshire (1327), and Devon (1329 and 1332).

2.5.3 Discussion of LALME *material*

It should be noted first that all *LALME*'s sources are generally dated from 1350 to 1450, although there are earlier and later exceptions, expecially in the North, where post-1450 MSS are often used. Therefore, no dates have been indicated for LPs in the tables for *LALME*. The following conclusions may be drawn from this material.[12]

Even at this late stage, <o> spellings have not completely ousted <a> for etymological *ā* in the South. Sporadic <a> is reported in Buckinghamshire, Cambridgeshire, Devon, Ely, Essex, Herefordshire, Middlesex, Northamptonshire, Rutland, Suffolk, Somerset, Surrey, Wiltshire, Worcestershire, and Warwickshire; <a> is rather frequent in source texts from Cheshire, Derbyshire, Leicestershire, Lincolnshire, Norfolk, and Nottinghamshire.[13] These forms may reflect variant pronunciations, and indicate that [ɑ:] in some cases was retained south of the Humber as late as 1450, and as far south as Devon and Surrey. The dot maps in *LALME* I show that <nat>-type spellings for NOT surprisingly cluster in the southern area of survey. On the other hand, forms with <a> for the vowel of BOTH are recorded in NME only, and for OWN, forms with <a> greatly preponderate in the North, though scattered examples are found in the southern area of survey also. For the stressed vowel of TWO and HOLY, <a> is attested only north of a line going from the Ribble in the west and along the ERY-Lincolnshire border in the east. For the vowel of KNOW, forms with <a> are also to be found in the N Central Midlands and the NE Midlands; the same is true for the vowel of SOUL. Given the *ā*/*ǭ*–line identified in *SMED*, this in fact seems to indicate that the *ǭ* area had receded in the late fourteenth and fifteenth centuries. Of course, the <a> in *LALME* could simply be conventional, or there may have been variant pronunciations in the border areas for a lengthy period of time.

Forms with <e>/<ae> for OE *ā* are few and far between, though the West Riding of Yorkshire boasts a few such forms for HOLY (ON etymology may be behind these) and OLD, and one Yorkshire source also has one for OLD. Spellings with <e> for SORROW do not appear in the North, but in Warwickshire and Norfolk; a Shropshire text has the form <neo> NOT. The form <gayt> GO 3.pers.sg. appears in Essex (LP 6290), and the <y> here is not used for the letter *thorn*.

Forms with <oo> are very common and appear all over the country, except in Sussex, Cumberland, and the East Riding of Yorkshire. These spellings are found in open and closed syllables alike (e.g. <too> TWO, <oown*e*> OWN). There are also <oi>/<oy> for OE *ā*, in the South, the W Midlands, and the North. Forms with <ouw>, <uo>, etc. appear in Lancashire, Lincolnshire, Norfolk, Warwickshire, Suffolk, Berkshire, Oxfordshire, Cambridgeshire, Devon, Somerset, Surrey, Kent, and Sussex.

2.5.4 *OE* w+ā

The incidence of OE *w+ā* is rather small, but Prins does not seem right in saying this *ā* was backed, rounded, and raised in *all* dialects, starting in the early thirteenth century. Rather, OE *w+ā* seems to have largely had the same development as OE *ā* in general (except in TWO and WHO).

For OE *swā*, forms with <o> are dominant in the *LAEME* material. There are, however, numerous forms with <a> in sources from Peterborough, Suffolk, Hampshire, and Worcestershire (1150–99), Essex, Herefordshire, Shropshire, and Cheshire (1200–24), Surrey and Cumberland (thirteenth century), and Lancashire, the East Riding of Yorkshire, and Huntingdonshire (1300–24).

For OE *twā*, <twa> appears in the *LAEME* material in Worcestershire (1250–99). In *SMED*, most forms with reflexes of OE *w+ā* have <a>: so in the East Riding of Yorkshire (1297), and in Lincolnshire, Durham, Gloucestershire, and Hertfordshire (1300–50). Some of these forms may be due to shortening of the vowel. Forms with <o> appear in Bedfordshire.

2.5.5 *OE* –eald, –ald

In OE, the Saxon and Kentish dialects had so-called 'fractured' *ea* before *ld*, whereas the Anglian dialects had *a*. Both OE *a* and *ea* are reflected as ME *a* /a/ in Anglian. Before *ld*, this vowel was lengthened to eME *ā*, which in turn took part in the development to *ǭ*.[14] Therefore, reflexes of OE *ā* and reflexes of OE *ald* should be spelt similarly in ME in supposedly Anglian dialects. Kristensson attempts to establish the divide between Saxon *eald* and Anglian *ald.* He concludes that Bedfordshire, Buckinghamshire, and Hertfordshire 'certainly belonged to the OE Saxon area' (1997: 275), and so did Huntingdonshire, Cambridgeshire, and SE Northamptonshire, although the spellings from the last three counties are mixed. His Map 2 (1997: 278) shows the demarcation line between Anglian and Saxon 'linguistic territory', where NW Northamptonshire and Rutland are Anglian areas, and the rest is Saxon.

The following is suggested by the *LAEME* material for OE *ea/a+ld* (Table 2.6).

1. The **northern** dialects no doubt had OE *a+ld,* though source text 132 from Cumberland (13th century) has only <ea>, and source text 122 from Cheshire (1240–50) has <e> once.
2. In the **W Midlands**, there is generally <a> in the early stages, and <o>, <a> later, but there are also <ea>, <e>, <eo> all over the area. The only source texts from the W Midlands with dominant <ea>, <e> are nos. 6 and 7 from Worcestershire (1200–49), no. 146 from Staffordshire (1225–49), and no. 10 from Gloucestershire (1275–1324); no. 1600 from Oxfordshire (1275–1324) also has some <e> spellings. It therefore seems uncertain which areas had Saxon *eald* and which had Anglian *ald.*
3. In the **E Midlands**, there is a mixture of <o>, <a>, <e>, <ea>. Dominant <ea>/<e> are found in Essex, Suffolk, London, Northamptonshire, Norfolk, and Ely; <e> is also found in Huntingdonshire. It thus seems reasonable to suppose that Saxon *eald* extended far into E Midland territory; alternatively, the form *eald* may not have been exclusively Saxon. On the whole, there is general agreement between spellings for OE *ā* and OE *a+ld* in texts from the north, and from the Midlands.
4. The **south** as expected stands out in that source texts from this area have contrastive spellings for OE *ā* and OE *ea+ld.* Devon, Somerset, Dorset, Hampshire, Surrey, and Kent all have dominant or only <e>, <ea>, <ia> for OE *ea+ld,* though a later source from Kent has dominant <a>, <o>, <ia>. Wiltshire has dominant <o>, but the earlier source text (no. 280, 1250–74) shows <a>, <e>, <eo>, <u> as well. Sussex surprisingly has only <o> (there is, however, only one form with OE *ea+ld* in the text in question, no. 67). There can nevertheless be little doubt that the southern, Saxon, dialects had OE *ea+ld.* For Kent, the evidence is somewhat more complex. Kentish is supposed to have had original *ea+ld,* but may have been influenced by neighbouring dialects; the problem is that the neighbouring area is Saxon territory and may

therefore be supposed to have had OE *ea+ld* as well. However, as noted earlier, Sussex also shows <o> in the first half of the thirteenth century.

The *SMED* spellings suggest the following points.

1. The material for the **north** and **Lincolnshire** shows forms with <o> for OE *a/ea+ld* in Northumberland, Lancashire, Lincolnshire, and the West Riding of Yorkshire, in the period 1316–46 (Table 2.9); they thus follow the general pattern found for OE *ā*. Besides, in those cases where the vowel was preceded by OE <c>, the northern material has <c>, not <ch>, indicating that the following vowel was back/central, and not front. These two facts clearly demonstrate that the northern dialects had OE *a*, not fractured *ea*, in these words (Kristensson 1967: 141). This agrees with the findings in *LAEME*.
2. The **W Midlands** material shows that OE *a+ld* normally appears with <o>. Expected <o> spellings are found all over the area, and are taken to 'represent Anglian forms. But this does not mean that they were indigenous in the areas where they occurred in ME speech' (Kristensson 1987: 118). Kristensson finds that Gloucestershire, Oxfordshire, and most of Worcestershire originally were *ea*-areas, even though these were not Saxon settlements. These areas thus ought not to have <o> spellings for OE *ea+ld*, but should have <e>. Such is not the case: both <a> and <o> are found, though a few <e> forms appear in Gloucestershire and Oxfordshire. Kristensson concludes that at 'an early period (probably even in late OE) Anglian unfractured forms supplanted fractured ones, and in the early fourteenth century were current in the whole area under examination' (Kristensson 1987: 119). This seems the only logical conclusion.
3. In the **W Midlands** material, <a> and <o> seem about equally frequent for OE *a+ld*. Some of the <a> spellings are no doubt due to vowel shortening, which means that the original long vowel must have been *ā*. But quite a few forms are not likely to have had a short vowel; these forms with <a> appear for OLD, BOLD, COLD, FOLD, OE **Healding, Halding*, and OE *weald, wald* in Cheshire, Derbyshire, Gloucestershire, Leicestershire, Nottinghamshire, Oxfordshire, Shropshire, Staffordshire, Warwickshire, and Worcestershire.

   In the entire area, <a> and <o> are found side by side, which indicates that the change of *ā* > *ǭ* must have started, but had not been completed by the early fourteenth century. Again, some of the <a> may of course correspond to a short vowel, but that is hardly the case for all of them.

4. The **E Midlands** material shows that both <a> and <o> are frequent for OE *ea/a+ld*; some forms with <e> also appear. Forms with <a> which are not likely to have had a short vowel occur in Bedfordshire, Cambridgeshire, Essex, Hertfordshire, Huntingdonshire, Middlesex, Northamptonshire, Norfolk, Rutland, and Suffolk.[15]
5. Spellings with <e> are particularly frequent in Essex, but also appear in Bedfordshire, Hertfordshire, and Suffolk. <Chalke-> is found in Huntingdonshire and is anomalous. These forms all indicate an original fractured OE *ea* before *lC*, and they therefore bear out 'Ekwall's supposition that these counties [i.e. Hu, Bed, Htf, Ex] belonged to Saxon territory' (Kristensson 1995: 91), but this statement is true only if 'Saxon' guarantees political and linguistic identity; Essex is not in question (as being Saxon politically), but the remainder were Anglian. Kristensson does not draw the same conclusion for Suffolk, although <e> appears there as well. However, since <a> and <o> spellings are dominant, Kristensson seems right in stating that the original, fractured, forms had probably been ousted by Anglian ones by the time the LSRs examined for *SMED* were recorded.
6. Collation of the *SMED* material with the *LAEME* material suggests that Kristensson may be justified in stating that Gloucestershire and Worcestershire may have been originally Saxon territory; however, all it really amounts to is that a characteristically Saxon *linguistic* trait is found in what politically was Anglian territory, and in company with other linguistic features that are characteristically Anglian, not Saxon. 'Characteristically' is not the same as 'exclusively'. Oxfordshire may also have been Saxon territory, according to Kristensson. Yet, the evidence from *LAEME* text no. 146 would lead one to suggest the same for Staffordshire, and that seems improbable. Kristensson also seems right in saying that Essex and Huntingdonshire may have been Saxon territory with fractured *ea*; but the *LAEME* evidence is just as convincing for London, Suffolk, Norfolk, Northamptonshire, and Ely.
7. The **southern** *SMED5* material shows that the dominant spelling for the reflex of OE *ea/a+ld* is <a>. Quite a few items with OE *ea/a + lC* have only <a> for the vowel; the material for these is not printed (Kristensson 2002: 149). Only <a> is found for: ALDERMAN (Wiltshire, Berkshire, and Kent); OE **scald/sceald* (Wiltshire, Berkshire, Surrey, and Hampshire); OE *Wealdhere* (Sussex). Only <e> is found for OE *hald, heald* 'sloping' (Sussex), and for OE **wealdisc* 'belonging to the Weald' (Kent). For other words with OE *ea/a+ld*, a variety of spellings are recorded, <o>, <ea>, <ei>, <ie>, <i>/<y>, etc.

8. Thus, in the south, <a> for the reflex of OE *a/ea* before *ld* is about twice as frequent as <o> and <e>/<ea>/eo>/<ei>, which is a little surprising for an area which is assumed to have been Saxon. It therefore seems that original OE *–eald* had been supplanted by Anglian *–ald*, which must have been lengthened and subsequently had the same development as etymological *ā*. In Kristensson's words, forms 'in <o> are Anglian and corroborate Ekwall's view [...] that unfractured forms spread southward, probably even in late Old English' (2002: 173). Kristensson believes that the <a> forms 'are due to early shortening' (2002: 173), which may be correct, but then the underlying long vowel must have had the quality [ɑ:]. Forms with <e>, <ea>, <eo>, <ei> are just as frequent as those with <o>, and are found in Somerset, Wiltshire, Berkshire, Kent, Surrey, Devon, Hampshire, Dorset, and Sussex, that is, the entire area. Devon has <ea> and Kent has both <ea> and <e>, despite Kristensson's explicit claim to the contrary (2002: 173). Devon has, however, no <a> for the reflex of OE *a/ea+ld*, but numerous <o>, which suggests early [a]/[ɑ] > [ɑ:] > [ɔ:]. Alternatively, since <yo> appears for initial *ea* in many instances, these <o> (and two <eo>) indicate 'a development *ēa>eā̭>ẹā̭>i̯ā̭>i̯ō* [>*jō*]' (2002: 173), that is, a shift of stress from the first element of the diphthong to the second, and then backing and rounding of the stressed [ɑ:] to [ɔ:]. The case for this development is strengthened by the forms <Choldewill> and <Chollewill>, with a palatalised initial consonant. The digraph <ea>, found in Kent and Devon, seems difficult to interpret; it has been suggested by Gradon (1979: 34ff.) that it implies /ɛ:/, with which Kristensson disagrees, since there are no examples in *SMED* of <ea> representing /ɛ:/. He therefore thinks the digraph indicates a diphthong, 'probably [e(:)ə] in Kent' (2002: 174). Regarding minor <ie> and <i>/<y> in Dorset and Hampshire, Kristensson states that such spellings 'are well-established in place-names, and are taken to reflect a change OE *ēa>īe>ī*' (2002: 217). It has, however, also been suggested that <i> for the reflex of OE *ēa* was 'used (by the side of <e>) to express a raised quality of the first el[ement] of the diphthong' (2002: 217), which may point to early vowel shift.
9. When the *SMED* material for the south is collated with that from *LAEME*, it is clear that Anglian *–ald* had already supplanted or was in the process of supplanting indigenous Saxon *–eald*. This process may have begun in lOE.

In *LALME*, forms with <a> for the vowel of OLD appear in Cambridgeshire, Norfolk, and Staffordshire. For the reflex of OE *–ald* in general, <-ald> and <-old> are about equally frequent, and both seem to occur throughout; there are no forms with <e> for the vowel. Forms with <a> for the vowel appear in the NW Midlands and the E Midlands. Thus, Anglian *–ald* had completely ousted Saxon *–eald* by lME, but the *–ald* of suffixes may not have been lengthened, since it seems not to share the general development of OE *ā*.

2.6 Summary and conclusions

The following conclusions may be drawn from the ME material here considered. It seems safe to assume that OE *ā* was beginning to be backed, rounded, and raised in the first half of the twelfth century at the very latest, but an even earlier date is suggested by Kitson (pers. comm.) and Liebl (2006), whose findings are dealt with in the following text.

The earliest <o> spellings are found in 1154 (the *Peterborough Chronicle*), in <onne>, <noht>, <na*m*mor(e)>. However, Peter Kitson has pointed out two <ston-> STONE, as well as <swo> SO in Dorset S938, which 'must be assigned to the second half of the eleventh century at the earliest' (pers. comm.).[16] It is interesting that these very early <o> spellings occur next to <n> and <w>, cf. the following paragraph.

Three items in particular fluctuate between having <a> and <o> in many sources: OE *ān* ONE, OE *nāwiht* NOT, and OE *swā* SO. Although the change of OE *ā* to *ǭ* has been assumed to be an isolative change, it seems possible that it may have started as a combinative change in words where the *ā* occurred next to /n/ and /w/, since such lexemes show early <o>. This is to be expected, at least in contexts where *ā* appears before or after *w*: assimilation or co-articulation would simply ensure that the lip-rounding for [w] is anticipated, or maintained, for the neighbouring vowel as well. Besides, it is important to bear in mind that some OE and ME dialects show rounding of short *a+n* to [o] <o>, for example, <mon> MAN, <hond> HAND; such backing and rounding could have acted as a 'bridge' for the long *ā* to be backed and rounded before a nasal as well. It should also be noted that in Anglo-Frisian fronting, *a* > *æ*, *except* before nasals, where it either remained or became *o*; and that WGmc *ā* > WS *ǣ*[1] (Anglian *ē*), *except* before nasals, where *ā* > *ō* (Campbell 1959: §127). WGmc *a* (long and short) therefore seems to have always developed differently (i.e. been rounded) before nasals than before other sounds.

This raises the question whether nasals may have similar formant frequencies as rounded vowels; the semi-vowel /w/ certainly has. Hajek (1997) makes interesting observations in this regard: although he seeks to establish universals in the processes of *nasalisation*, his findings may throw light on the current topic. He initially states that the 'premise that all sound change is in origin phonetically gradual is not incompatible with sound change as phonetically abrupt, that is, Lexical Diffusion, if [...] the two types of sound change can be seen to operate at different levels of the grammar' (1997: 13). With regard to proponents of Lexical Phonology, he states that (1997: 13)

> They also claim that the two types of sound change are diachronically related: the originally phonetically gradual and lexically abrupt nature of Neogrammarian-type change, consistent with the view expressed previously that all sound change is phonetic in origin, may be transformed over time into Lexical Diffusion through progressive percolation of the former into the deeper, more abstract regions of linguistic structure.

Hajek finds the almost exclusive focus on articulation *re* sound change unfortunate, as it has been suggested that 'sound change is generally perceptual in nature, since it is dependent on the listener's ability to deal with the ambiguous nature of the speech signal' (1997: 18). Such ambiguity is due to articulatory and/or acoustic constraints in the vocal tract, which cause significant and constant variation in the output. Hajek hence claims that 'constant synchronic variation in speech, the result of articulatory, acoustic and perceptual constraints, is considered to provide the source and phonetic basis of sound change' (1997: 24). Crucial in this context is the assumption that there is a non-random correlation between a certain sound change and its contexts, such that it is possible to place contexts from most likely to least likely 'along an implicational scale or parameter' (1997: 5). With regard to nasalisation, the features to consider are stress, vowel length and height. However, 'the acoustic cue for nasality was affected by lowering the intensity of the first formant' (1997: 90–1). Still, it remains to be seen whether surrounding nasals could cause rounding of a vowel due to similarities in the formants in nasals and rounded vowels. Hajek does not provide the answer to this, and the research he examines seems to point in different directions. However, some of the results indicate that low vowels may be pronounced with a lowered velum (=nasal airflow) even in oral contexts (1997: 125). In any event, this approach seems promising, in so far as nasality clearly correlates with vowel length and openness, although it remains to be seen whether nasals are also conducive to rounding of neighbouring vowels. An acoustic experiment carried out by Professor Inger Moen for me was inconclusive, but it seemed that the *third* formant of [ɑ:] was closer to that of [ɔ:] before a nasal than it was when [ɑ:] was final.[17]

In the material there seem to be no particular differences between OE *ā*, OE *w+ā*, or OE *ā+w/ʒ* as far as the *inception* of the change is concerned. There are, however, marked differences in the *frequencies* of <a>, <o>, and <e> for the various categories. Most notably, <o> is *less* frequent for *ā* in *w+ā* and in *ā+w/ʒ* in the early stages than for *ā* without a neighbouring labial, though <o> seems more frequent for *ā* in *w+ā* than in *ā+w*. It is possible that if *w+ā* > [wɔ:] early, it was only where [ɔ:] was not predictable contextually that the spelling needed to change, and so <a> instead of <o> for OE *ā* after <w> may simply be a conservative spelling.

The areas which show dominant <o> at a very early stage are: Suffolk, Essex, London, Kent, and Sussex; Berkshire, Oxfordshire; Gloucestershire, Worcestershire, and Staffordshire. Thus, OE *ā* > [ɔ:] may have started in these areas, that is, the South-East, the (S)W Midlands, and the SE Midlands. Forms with <o> are in fact found in most early ME texts, southern as well as northern, and there is a mixture of <a>-type, <o>-type, and <e>-type spellings all through the eME period.

SMED shows that the use of <a> continued throughout the period 1290–1350, as far south as in Somerset, Kent, and Middlesex, cf. Tables 2.7 and 2.8. *LALME* confirms this: <a> is used in the lME period, as far south as in Devon, Somerset, Middlesex, Essex, and Surrey.

In the North, <o> is also used throughout the ME period, though <a> is dominant. It is not true that the northern dialects remained totally unaffected by the SME change; they must have been somewhat influenced by their southern neighbours, in which the change was taking place, at least in the early stages of the change, and at least in the *written* language (cf. Luick 1914–40). Judging by the *LALME* material, however, such southern influence is still seen in the northern dialects in the mid-fifteenth century, as both <a> and <o> are found in the North up until that period.[18]

Forms with <oa> start appearing *c.* 1200 in Worcestershire, and are used throughout the thirteenth and early fourteenth centuries; for the later period, such forms appear in Norfolk. Texts localised as far apart as London, Cheshire, and Norfolk show dominant <oa>. Neither *SMED* nor *LALME* has any <ao> or <oa> spellings, so they must have fallen out of use in the early fourteenth century, and not immediately after 1200, as claimed by Prins (1972).

Forms with <oo> start appearing in the first half of the thirteenth century in Worcestershire, but do not really become common until the last quarter of the same century; they occur in the North-West (Cheshire), in the W Midlands (Worcestershire, Herefordshire, and Wiltshire), in the South-East (Kent and Essex), and in the NE Midlands (Norfolk and Ely). *SMED* shows <oo> in Lancashire, all over the E Midlands, and in Gloucestershire, Shropshire, and Staffordshire. In *LALME*, <oo> appears all over the country, *except* Sussex, Cumberland, and the East Riding of Yorkshire. *LAEME* and *LALME* report <oo> in open and closed syllables alike, so there are no apparent restrictions on its distribution in terms of syllable structure. In *SMED*, however, such spellings are restriced to open syllables, the only exception being <delook>. The spelling <oo> is conventional for the reflex of OE *ō*, so <oo> for OE *ā* indicates that the new *o*-quality of previous /ɑ:/ must be quite prominent.

Forms with <ae>, <æ>, <ai>/<ay>, <e>, <ea>, <eo>, <ei>/<ey> do not appear in the North until the mid-thirteenth century. They start occurring in the West, Central, and SE Midlands before 1200, and spread westwards, southwards, and northwards in the course of the thirteenth and early fourteenth centuries. In *SMED*, <e> spellings are extremely rare, but the 1312 LSR from Gloucestershire and the 1332 LSR from Somerset have one such form each, and the 1327 Roll from Lincolnshire has one <e> and one <ae>. In *LALME*, such spellings are few and far between, though texts from the West Riding of Yorkshire show a few such forms, and a Yorkshire text shows one.[19] The paucity of <ae>, <e> in the middle and late ME material suggests either that OE *ā* was not fronted and raised as early in NME as hitherto believed, or that <a> was kept as a conventional spelling regardless of change. The almost complete lack of <ae>, <e> in the *SMED* material for the North is particularly striking, and the *LAEME* material would lead one to suggest that the fronting and raising of OE *ā* started in the Essex-Suffolk and Worcestershire-Herefordshire-Shropshire area, which seems unlikely.

Regarding the NME development of OE *ā*, Smith (1994) draws attention to Chaucer's *Reeve's Tale*, whose narrative includes two students who speak a northern dialect, and whose language Chaucer tries to convey. There are a few spellings in the orthographic rendering of their speech that may imply northern vowel shift of OE *ā* to [e:]/[ɛ:]. These spellings are (1994: 434): <heem> HOME, <geen> GO pt.ppl., <neen> NONE. These indicate the early date of the northern shift, which 'was limited to the front series of long vowels', and 'was arguably the result of the fronting of back vowels and subsequent dissimilation which is a characteristics of that region possibly deriving from contact with Norse, and which seems to have taken place in the late twelfth/thirteenth century' (1994: 435). Given that the shift was earlier in the north (but only if the traditional dates for the 'GVS' are maintained), southern spellings would not have indicated the northern pronunciations, hence in these words the innovative <ee> for a fronted and raised reflex of OE ā (1994: 436):

> In the South, the spelling <ee>, pre-Shift, seems usually to have represented either /e:/ or /ɛ:/; since the Northern post-Shift pronunciation of <aCe>, <ai> was a mid-front vowel, then <ee> would have been an appropriate pre-Shift Southern way of indicating a post-Shift Northern pronunciation.

The sporadic nature of the spellings may suggest that the shift had just begun in the north and was undergoing lexical diffusion (1994: 436), or that Chaucer wanted to provide dialectal flavour without overdoing it.

Forms with <ouw>, <uo>, <u>, <w> started appearing in Herefordshire in the late thirteenth century (*LAEME*); they are then attested in Nottinghamshire, Wiltshire, and Devon (*SMED*); and finally in the South-West (Devon and Somerset), the South-East (Sussex, Kent, and Surrey), the E Midlands (Lincolnshire, Norfolk, Cambridgeshire, and Suffolk), the Central Midlands (Oxfordshire, Warwickshire, and Berkshire), and in Lancashire (*LALME*). They seem to indicate vowel-raising as far as close back [u:]. However, although such spellings are most frequent for TWO and WHO in *LALME*, they also appear for OLD and BOTH, which poses a problem for this interpretation. Samuels (1971) claims that some <uo> for OE ō in ME texts from Kent indicate a rising diphthong, and it is possible that the same is true of the <uo> here considered.

The change of OE ā > ǭ thus seems to have started simultaneously in different areas: in the SE Midlands and the South(-East), and in the (S) W Midlands. The change may have started in the latter half of the eleventh century. It appears *not* to be the case, however, that the change was complete by 1225 in all the southern dialects, but that it was a slow process which had not been completed even in the late fifteenth century. This conclusion seems to hold even if some of the <a> examined may be for [a] (as a result of shortening), and not for retained [ɑ:].

If the earlier conclusions are correct, there are further implications. The most important is that there must have been a considerable temporal overlap between the eME change of OE ā to ǭ on the one hand, and the 'GVS'-changes on the other, chiefly because the evidence for ō > [u:] (and other vowel-shift changes) is much earlier than previously allowed, as will be seen in subsequent chapters. The conclusions reached here concerning the change of OE ā > ǭ seem to be true of northern eME ọ̄ to ṻ;

also (Chapter 6): that is, the implementation of this change also appears to have taken more time than hitherto assumed. At any rate, it seems increasingly arbitrary and artificial to keep the so-called earlier changes separate from the vowel shift. Logically, they ought to be included in a 'Great Vowel Shift', if such there were. Further implications will be discussed in the concluding chapter.

Regarding the areal delimitations of retained *ā* vs. new *ǭ*, it seems evident that the Humber does not constitute an absolute boundary. The <o> spellings in *SMED1* seem to cluster: they appear in Lancashire south of the river Ribble; in the West Riding of Yorkshire, south of the river Wharfe, and west of the river Ouse; and in southern Lincolnshire (Kesteven and Holland). There are a very few <o> spellings from the North Riding of Yorkshire, Durham, and Northumberland. They are recorded first in the North Riding (1301), then in Northumberland (1316), and Durham (1344). They are also found in Lincolnshire, Lancashire, and in the West Riding of Yorkshire (1327–46). It is of course possible that <o> spellings would have been found earlier in these three counties if earlier LSRs were available from these areas.[20] The only counties in which <o> forms for OE *ā* do not occur at all, are Cumberland and Westmorland. Kristensson admits that there must have been a fairly large area where both <a> and <o> were used. He further states that the ME material strongly favours Luick's delimitation of the *ā* vs. *ǭ* area, which was made on modern evidence (Luick 1914–40, § 369, Anm. 1). Kristensson concludes that, for the time of his survey, the *ā*/*ǭ*-divide cut across the middle of Lancashire, the middle of the West Riding of Yorkshire, and the middle of Lincolnshire, from the Ribble in the west to the North Sea in the east (1967: 36). But isophones shift over time, so the *ā*/*ǭ*-divide in the early fourteenth century was different from that in the fifteenth century, as indicated by the *LALME* material.

Relatively recent work by Liebl throws light on the earliest stages of OE *ā* > [ɔ:], and supplements the analysis provided in the present chapter,[21] since the material he exploits covers OE as well as eME. He remarks by way of introduction that nobody has examined the 'origins and early geographical diffusion' of OE/eME *ā* > /ɔ:/ (2006: 19), and that he aims to 'review and supplement the accounts in the standard textbooks', using early onomastic material and spelling evidence from literary texts, documents and glosses (2006: 20). As a preliminary conclusion, Liebl states that the evidence supports those who maintain that the change started in the eleventh century. He urges caution, however, in that not all <a> spellings imply retained [ɑ:], but could be due to vowel shortening, especially in compounds. Likewise, not all <o> are instances of OE *ā* > [ɔ:], but may be the result of reduced stress, giving <o> (2006: 20–1). The arguments offered for the latter claim seem unsatisfactory, in that they do not explain why the shortened product of *ā* would be <o>.

Liebl refers to Klaeber (1902), who examined OE <o> for etymological *ā* and interprets these 'as phonetic spellings and evidence for incipient rounding of OE /ɑ:/' (2006: 21). Liebl compares Klaeber's adduced spellings with his own. Interestingly, there is a preponderance of early <o> for OE *ā* in the vicinity of a nasal, even as early as the ninth century, which is in agreement with my own findings. *Domesday Book* spellings make Liebl state that the presence of /w/ 'appears to have been highly conducive to the raising and rounding of /ɑ:/' (2006: 24), which goes counter to my findings; he finds that the liquids /l/ and /r/ may also have provided favourable environments for the change. From the adduced evidence, Liebl seems justified in saying that the change may have started before the twelfth century.

Forms with <o> for OE *ā* in the *Domesday Book* are recorded in place-names in Cornwall, Devon, Somerset, Wiltshire, Berkshire, Kent, Suffolk, Leicestershire, Northamptonshire, Hertfordshire, Buckinghamshire, Cheshire, and the West Riding of Yorkshire. Luick (1914–40: §369) claimed that the changes to OE *ā* originated in the WS area, Worcestershire, and Kent, beginning in the eleventh century. However, Liebl finds the evidence wanting, especially for Worcestershire (2006: 25–6). The fact that <o> is found in the West Riding of Yorkshire in the *Domesday Book* goes unnoticed, even though the implications are of great interest, especially when such early <o> is compared to the later and comparable onomastic material in *SMED*.

Liebl provides tables comparing <a> and <o> for OE *ā* in twelfth-century onomastic and textual material. The South, the E Midlands, and London clearly show the highest number of innovative <o>. Dorset, Sussex, Norfolk, London, Hertfordshire, Rutland, Cheshire, and Oxfordshire have the highest percentages of <o>, ranging from 15% to 33%. Somewhat surprisingly, Liebl still includes Kent in the 'counties of the South(-East) and East Midlands' which 'spearheaded the change' (2006: 29), although Dorset and Sussex both have higher percentages of <o> than Kent. In the W Midlands, Oxfordshire and Cheshire stand out, with 20% and 16% innovative <o> respectively. Thus, '/ɑ:/ > /ɔ:/, rather than spreading from the South to the North, might have started in Late Old English more or less simultaneously in several counties in the South as well as the E Midlands and W Midlands and radiated from there' (2006: 30). This conclusion tallies well with my own, not only for OE *ā* > [ɔ:], but for several 'GVS' changes. This observation is indeed commented on by Liebl for eME *ī*, referring to

Ogura, Wang, and Cavalli-Sforza (1991). Finally, Liebl expresses agreement with Lutz (2004) that OE *ā* > [ɔ:] and OE *ǣ* > [ɛ:] were roughly simultaneous and may have been early instantiations of a tendency to raise long vowels. In this context, the vacillation between *a/o* before nasals in (non-Mercian) OE should be borne in mind, as should the effect of lengthening before homorganic consonant clusters (e.g. before a nasal+C), which may well have destabilised the old *ā* vs. *ō* contrast.

The *LAEME* material for OE *ā* shows the following pattern: <o> suddenly becomes very frequent in the period 1175–99; in the period 1200–24, it becomes less frequent; then there is an increase in frequency throughout the period 1225–99, after which <o> again becomes less frequent, and traditional <a> takes over. Such a pattern may suggest that the change (like many linguistic changes, cf. Denison 1999), was slow at first, then 'exploded' through lexical diffusion (cp. Phillips 2006a, McMahon 1994: 47–55), to the extent that it became noticable to the scribes and therefore recorded in writing. However, since the change was purely realisational and did not lead to phonemic merger, the traditional spelling <a> was reverted to for a short time; the fact that the new spellings <o(o)> failed to distinguish between the reflexes of OE *ā* and OE *ō* may have played a role. But since the realisations [ɑ:] and [ɔ:] are quite different, the new, more phonetic <o>-type spellings became increasingly frequent and were eventually established for the reflex of OE *ā*.

2.7 Tables of ME material

2.7.1 *Material from* LAEME

Table 2.1 *<a> vs. <o> for OE* ā (LAEME)

County	No.	Date	Spellings
Peterborough	149	1154	a (((o)))
Essex	4	1150–99	o ((a))
Berkshire	63	1150–99	o ((a)) (((e)))
Essex	1200	1150–99	o ((a)) (((e)))
Suffolk	1300	1150–99	o ((a)) (((e, u)))
Hampshire	143	1175–99	a
Worcestershire	170	1175–99	a (((o, e)))
Worcestershire	5	c.1200	a (((o, e)))
Worcestershire	2000	c.1200	a ((o, oa, e, ea, eo, u))
Worcestershire	2001	c.1200	a ((o)) (((e, u)))
Oxfordshire	232	1175–1224	o ((a))
Lancashire	16	1200–24	a
Essex	64	1200–24	a (o) ((au)) (((æ, oa)))

(continued)

Table 2.1 (*cont.*)

County	No.	Date	Spellings
Essex	65	1200–24	a ((o, oa)) (((e)))
Essex	183	1200–24	a
Herefordshire	189	1200–24	a (o) (((ao, e)))
Gloucestershire	234	1200–24	o
Unlocalised	236	1200–24	o (((e)))
Shropshire	260	1200–24	a ((o)) (((u)))
Shropshire	261	1200–24	a ((o)) (((u)))
Shropshire	262	1200–24	a (((o, oa, ea, eo, u)))
Shropshire	1000	1200–24	a (((o, e, ea, u)))
Worcestershire	6	1200–49	a ((o)) (((e)))
Worcestershire	7	1200–49	o ((a)) (((e)))
Kent	8	1200–49	o ((a)) (((e, eu)))
Northamptonshire	66	1200–49	o (((a)))
Sussex	67	1200–49	o
Unlocalised	68	1200–49	o
Unlocalised	237	1200–49	o, oi
Worcestershire	1900	1200–49	o ((a, oa, oo, eo, ea, e, æ))
London	138	1225–49	o
Staffordshire	146	1225–49	o (((a)))
Worcestershire	245	1225–49	o ((a, oa, ea, e, eo))
Shropshire	272	1225–49	a (((o, e, ea)))
Herefordshire	273	1225–49	a (((o, e)))
Shropshire	275	1225–49	a (((e)))
Worcestershire	1800	1225–49	o (((a, oa, ea, e)))
Somerset	156	c.1240	o, a
Somerset	157	c.1240	a (o) ((e))
Cheshire	118	1240–50	a (((o, e, ea)))
Unlocalised	119	1240–50	a (((o, e)))
Unlocalised	120	1240–50	a (((o, e, ea, u)))
Unlocalised	121	1240–50	a (((o, e, ea)))
Cheshire	122	1240–50	a (((o, ea)))
Unlocalised	123	1240–50	a (((o, e, ea)))
Unlocalised	14	13th c.	o
Cumberland	132	13th c.	a, ea
Unlocalised	139	13th c.	o (a, e)
Surrey	184	13th c.	a ((o))
Unlocalised	265	13th c.	o ((a))
Huntingdonshire	266	13th c.	o ((a))
Unlocalised	267	13th c.	o
Unlocalised	268	13th c.	o ((a))
Unlocalised	17	1225–74	o
Unlocalised	176	1225–74	o
West Riding, Yks	231	1225–74	a ((e))
Unlocalised	235	1225–74	o
Unlocalised	13	1225–99	ey
Essex	11	1258	oa (o)
London	12	1258	oa ((o))

County	No.	Date	Spellings
Cheshire	124	1250–74	oa, a, o
Gloucestershire	158	1250–74	o (((ai, e)))
Worcestershire	276	1250–74	a ((o, e, ea, eo))
Worcestershire	277	1250–74	a ((æ, ai, e, o, oa, ao))
Worcestershire	278	1250–74	a ((æ, ai, e, o, eo))
Wiltshire	280	1250–74	o ((a))
Lincolnshire	130	1270	o
Lincolnshire	15	1250–99	o
Unlocalised	228	1250–99	o
Wiltshire	258	1250–99	o
Gloucestershire	271	1250–99	o (((a, e)))
Dorset	279	1250–99	o ((a))
Worcestershire	2	1275–99	o (((a, oo, ei)))
Worcestershire	3	1275–99	o ((a)) (((eo)))
Norfolk	131	1275–99	a
Cheshire	136	1275–99	o ((a, óó))
Cambridgeshire	137	1275–99	o (((a, e)))
Unlocalised	141	1275–99	o ((a, e))
Kent	142	1275–99	o ((a, oo, óó))
Devon	147	1275–99	o ((a))
Devon	148	1275–99	a, o
Norfolk	150	1275–99	o (((a, ei, u)))
Lancashire	151	1275–99	o
Essex	160	1275–99	o ((a)) (((oo)))
Gloucestershire	161	1275–99	o ((a))
Norfolk	175	1275–99	oa, o
Unlocalised	178	1275–99	o (((oe, e, u)))
Unlocalised	179	1275–99	o, a
Unlocalised	180	1275–99	o (a)
Unlocalised	181	1275–99	o
Unlocalised	227	1275–99	o (a)
Gloucestershire	229	1275–99	o
Unlocalised	233	1275–99	o, oe, oo, e
Unlocalised	238	1275–99	o
Unlocalised	239	1275–99	o
Unlocalised	240	1275–99	o
Unlocalised	241	1275–99	o ((a))
Unlocalised	242	1275–99	o ((a)) (((e)))
Unlocalised	243	1275–99	o
Unlocalised	244	1275–99	o ((a))
Herefordshire	246	1275–99	o ((a, o(o)i, ouw, e))
Herefordshire	247	1275–99	o (((a, oe)))
Herefordshire	248	1275–99	o (a) (((e)))
Herefordshire	249	1275–99	o (((a, e)))
Wiltshire	263	1275–99	o (((oo)))
Unlocalised	274	1275–99	?o
Herefordshire	1100	1275–99	o ((a)) (((e, ei, eo, ó)))
Norfolk	1400	1275–99	o ((a))(((oo, ae, ai, e)))

(*continued*)

Table 2.1 (*cont.*)

County	No.	Date	Spellings
Gloucestershire	2002	1275–99	o ((a)) (((ou, e)))
Norfolk	1700	1284–89	o ((a)) (((e)))
Lincolnshire	128	c.1300	o (ai)
Lincolnshire	129	1300	a ((o))
Lincolnshire	159	c.1300	o ((a)) (((ay)))
Unlocalised	174	c.1300	o, ou
Leicestershire	177	c.1300	a, o
Lincolnshire	182	c.1300	o ((a))
Gloucestershire	10	1275–1324	o ((a))
Unlocalised	18	1275–1324	o
Essex	162	1275–1324	o (a)
Somerset	163	1275–1324	o
West Riding, Yks	256	1275–1324	?a
West Riding, Yks	257	1275–1324	a
Unlocalised	259	1275–1324	o
Gloucestershire	264	1275–1324	o
Norfolk	269	1275–1324	o
Norfolk	270	1275–1324	o
Ely	282	1275–1324	o ((a)) (((oo, e)))
Oxfordshire	1600	1275–1324	o ((a)) (((e, ou)))
Unlocalised	19	1300–24	o
Herefordshire	125	1300–24	o, a
Wiltshire	140	1300–24	o (a) ((oe, oo))
Norfolk	155	1300–24	o ((a, oa, oo, e, u))
Durham	188	1300–49	a (o) (((ae)))
East Riding, Yks	230	1300–49	a, o
Huntingdonshire	1500	1300–49	a ((o))
Ely	2003	1300–49	a, o
Lincolnshire	169	1325–49	o ((a)) (((e)))

Table 2.2 *<oa>, <ao> for OE* ā (LAEME)

County	No.	Date	Spellings
Worcestershire	2000	c.1200	((oa))
Essex	64	1200–24	((oa,?ao))
Essex	65	1200–24	((oa))
Herefordshire	189	1200–24	((ao))
Shropshire	262	1200–24	((oa))
Worcestershire	1900	1200–49	((oa))
Worcestershire	245	1225–49	((oa))
Worcestershire	1800	1225–49	((oa))
Essex	11	1258	oa
London	12	1258	oa
Cheshire	124	1250–74	oa
Worcestershire	277	1250–74	((oa, ao))
Norfolk	175	1275–99	oa
Norfolk	155	1300–24	((oa))

Table 2.3 *<oo>, <oi>, <u> for OE* ā (LAEME)

County	No.	Date	Spellings
Suffolk	1300	1150–99	(((u)))
Worcestershire	2001	c.1200	(((u)))
Shropshire	260	1200–24	(((u)))
Shropshire	261	1200–24	(((u)))
Shropshire	262	1200–24	(((u)))
Shropshire	1000	1200–24	(((u)))
Unlocalised	237	1200–49	oi
Worcestershire	1900	1200–49	(((oo)))
Unlocalised	120	1240–50	(((u)))
Worcestershire	2	1275–99	(((oo)))
Cheshire	136	1275–99	((óó))
Kent	142	1275–99	((oo, óó))
Norfolk	150	1275–99	(((u)))
Essex	160	1275–99	(((oo)))
Unlocalised	178	1275–99	(((u)))
Unlocalised	233	1275–99	oo
Herefordshire	246	1275–99	((oo, oi, ou, uo))
Herefordshire	247	1275–99	(((oe)))
Wiltshire	263	1275–99	((oo))
Norfolk	1400	1275–99	((oo))
Gloucestershire	2002	1275–99	(((ou)))
Unlocalised	174	c.1300	ou
Ely	282	1275–1324	(((oo)))
Oxfordshire	1600	1275–1324	(((ou)))
Wiltshire	140	1300–24	((oo, oe))
Norfolk	155	1300–24	((oo, u))

Table 2.4 *<ae>, <æ>, <ai>, <e>, <ea>, <ei>, <eo> etc. for OE* ā (LAEME)

County	No.	Date	Spellings
Berkshire	63	1150–99	(((e)))
Essex	1200	1150–99	(((e)))
Suffolk	1300	1150–99	(((e)))
Worcestershire	170	1175–99	(((e)))
Worcestershire	5	c.1200	(((e)))
Worcestershire	2000	c.1200	((e, ea, eo))
Worcestershire	2001	c.1200	(((e)))
Essex	64	1200–24	(((æ, e)))
Essex	65	1200–24	(((e)))
Herefordshire	189	1200–24	(((e)))
Unlocalised	236	1200–24	(((e)))
Shropshire	262	1200–24	((ea, eo))
Shropshire	1000	1200–24	(((e, ea)))
Worcestershire	6	1200–49	(((e)))

(*continued*)

Table 2.4 (*cont.*)

County	No.	Date	Spellings
Worcestershire	7	1200–49	(((e)))
Kent	8	1200–49	(((e, eu)))
Worcestershire	1900	1200–49	((e, ea, eo, æ))
Worcestershire	245	1225–49	((e, ea, eo))
Shropshire	272	1225–49	(((ea, e)))
Herefordshire	273	1225–49	(((e)))
Shropshire	275	1225–49	(((e)))
Worcestershire	1800	1225–49	((ea, e))
Somerset	157	c.1240	((e))
Cheshire	118	1240–50	(((e, ea)))
Unlocalised	119	1240–50	(((e)))
Unlocalised	120	1240–50	(((e, ea)))
Unlocalised	121	1240–50	(((e, ea)))
Cheshire	122	1240–50	(((ea)))
Unlocalised	123	1240–50	(((e, ea)))
Cumberland	132	13th c.	ea
Unlocalised	139	13th c.	(e)
West Riding, Yks	231	1225–74	((e))
Unlocalised	13	1225–99	ey
Gloucestershire	158	1250–74	(((ai, e)))
Worcestershire	276	1250–74	((e, ea, eo))
Worcestershire	277	1250–74	((æ, ai, e, ea, ei, eo))
Worcestershire	278	1250–74	((æ, ai, e, eo))
Wiltshire	280	1250–74	(((eo)))
Gloucestershire	271	1250–99	(((e)))
Worcestershire	2	1275–99	(((ei)))
Worcestershire	3	1275–99	(((eo)))
Cambridgeshire	137	1275–99	(((e)))
Unlocalised	141	1275–99	((e))
Norfolk	150	1275–99	(((ei)))
Unlocalised	178	1275–99	(((e)))
Unlocalised	233	1275–99	e
Unlocalised	242	1275–99	(((e)))
Herefordshire	246	1275–99	((e))
Herefordshire	248	1275–99	(((e)))
Herefordshire	249	1275–99	(((e)))
Herefordshire	1100	1275–99	(((e, ei, eo)))
Norfolk	1400	1275–99	(((ae, ai, e)))
Gloucestershire	2002	1275–99	(((e)))
Norfolk	1700	1284–89	(((e)))
Lincolnshire	128	c.1300	(ai)
Lincolnshire	159	c.1300	(((ay)))
Ely	282	1275–1324	(((e)))
Oxfordshire	1600	1275–1324	(((e)))
Norfolk	155	1300–24	((e))
Durham	188	1300–49	(((ae)))
Lincolnshire	169	1325–49	(((e)))

Table 2.5 *Spellings for OE* -ēald, -eald *(Anglian* -ald > -āld*)* (LAEME)

County	No.	Date	Spelling(s)
Peterborough	149	1154	a
Essex	4	1150–99	ea (e) ((a, o))
Essex	1200	1150–99	ea ((o, a, e))
Suffolk	1300	1150–99	o, e (a) ((eo))
Hampshire	143	1175–99	ea
Worcestershire	5	c.1200	a, e
Worcestershire	2000	c.1200	a ((ea, o, e))
Worcestershire	2001	c.1200	a ((e))
Essex	64	1200–24	ea ((e, a, o, æ))
Essex	65	1200–24	ea ((e, a))
Herefordshire	189	1200–24	a, o
Gloucestershire	234	1200–24	o
Shropshire	260	1200–24	a ((o, e))
Shropshire	261	1200–24	a ((o, ea))
Shropshire	262	1200–24	a
Shropshire	1000	1200–24	a ((o, e))
Worcestershire	6	1200–49	ea ((e, a, u))
Worcestershire	7	1200–49	ea, e ((u, a))
Kent	8	1200–49	ea, ia, e (a)
Northamptonshire	66	1200–49	e
Sussex	67	1200–49	o
Worcestershire	1900	1200–49	o ((e, ea, eo, a))
Staffordshire	146	1225–49	o, e
Worcestershire	245	1225–49	o ((a))
Shropshire	272	1225–49	a
Herefordshire	273	1225–49	a ((o))
Shropshire	275	1225–49	a
Worcestershire	1800	1225–49	o ((a))
Somerset	156	c.1240	ea, e
Somerset	157	c.1240	ea
Cheshire	118	1240–50	a
Cheshire	122	1240–50	a ((o, e))
Cumberland	132	13th c.	ea
Surrey	184	13th c.	e
Essex	11	1258	ea, a, o
London	12	1258	ea (o)
Gloucestershire	158	1250–74	o ((e, a))
Worcestershire	276	1250–74	a ((o, ea, e, eo))
Worcestershire	277	1250–74	a (o) ((æ, e, eo))
Worcestershire	278	1250–74	a ((o, e, æ, ai))
Wiltshire	280	1250–74	o ((eo, a, e, u))
Lincolnshire	15	1250–99	o
Gloucestershire	271	1250–99	o (a) ((e))
Dorset	279	1250–99	ea
Worcestershire	2	1275–99	o ((a))

Table 2.5 (*cont.*)

County	No.	Date	Spelling(s)
Worcestershire	3	1275–99	o (a) ((e))
Cheshire	136	1275–99	o
Cambridgeshire	137	1275–99	?e
Kent	142	1275–99	a, o, ia
Devon	148	1275–99	ea
Norfolk	150	1275–99	o ((a))
Essex	160	1275–99	o
Gloucestershire	161	1275–99	o, a, i
Gloucestershire	229	1275–99	o
Herefordshire	246	1275–99	o
Herefordshire	247	1275–99	o
Herefordshire	248	1275–99	o ((a, e))
Herefordshire	249	1275–99	o ((a, e))
Herefordshire	1100	1275–99	o ((e, a))
Norfolk	1400	1275–99	e (ea) ((o))
Gloucestershire	2002	1275–99	o ((e, a))
Norfolk	1700	1284–89	o
Lincolnshire	159	c.1300	a
Lincolnshire	182	c.1300	o
Gloucestershire	10	1275–1324	e ((ie, a))
West Riding, Yks	256	1275–1324	au
Norfolk	269	1275–1324	o
Ely	282	1275–1324	o
Oxfordshire	1600	1275–1324	o ((e, a))
Herefordshire	125	1300–24	o
Wiltshire	140	1300–24	o
Norfolk	155	1300–24	o ((a))
Durham	188	1300–49	a
East Riding, Yks	230	1300–49	a
Huntingdonshire	1500	1300–49	o ((a, ea))
Ely	2003	1300–49	e, ea, o
Lincolnshire	169	1325–49	a (o)

2.7.2 *Material from SMED*

Table 2.6 *<o> for OE* ā *in NME* (SMED)

County	Date
North Riding, Yks	1301
Northumberland	1316
Lancashire	1327, 1332
Lincolnshire	1327, 1332
West Riding, Yks	1327, 1332, 1346
Durham	1344

Table 2.7 *<a> for OE* ā *south of the Humber* (SMED)

County	Date
Bedfordshire	1309
Berkshire	1332
Cambridgeshire	1330
Cheshire	1265–91, 1317, 1324, 1340, 1307–09
Dorset	1332
Essex	1327, 1332
Gloucestershire	1312, 1327
Herefordshire	1292
Hertfordshire	1307
Kent	1327, 1332
Leicestershire	1327, 1333
Middlesex	1334
Norfolk	1327, 1332
Northamptonshire	1332
Nottinghamshire	1327
Oxfordshire	1316, 1327
Rutland	1296
Shropshire	1327, 1332
Somerset	1327, 1333
Staffordshire	1327, 1332
Suffolk	1327
Sussex	1327, 1332
Warwickshire	1327, 1332
Wiltshire	1327, 1332
Worcestershire	1327, 1332

Table 2.8 *<a> for OE* ā+w/ȝ *south of the Humber* (SMED)

County	Date
Bedfordshire	1309
Buckinghamshire	1332
Cambridgeshire	1330
Cheshire	1265–91, 1269–91, 1291
Derbyshire	1327
Dorset	1327, 1332
Essex	1327, 1332
Hampshire	1327, 1333
Huntingdonshire	1332
Kent	1327, 1332
Leicestershire	1327, 1333
Nottinghamshire	1332
Oxfordshire	1316, 1327
Surrey	1332
Sussex	1327
Wiltshire	1332

Table 2.9 *<o> for non-WS* –āld *in NME and Lincolnshire* (SMED)

County	Date
Northumberland	1316
Lancashire	1327, 1332
Lincolnshire	1327, 1332
West Riding, Yks	1327, 1332, 1346

Table 2.10 *<o> for OE* ā+w/ȝ *in NME and Lincolnshire* (SMED)

County	Date
East Riding, Yks	1297
Durham	1311, 1337–8
Lancashire	1327, 1332
Lincolnshire	1327, 1332
West Riding, Yks	1327, 1346

Table 2.11 *<oo> for OE* ā (SMED)

County	Date
Hertfordshire	1307
Bedfordshire	1309, 1332
Cambridgeshire	1312, 1330
Essex	1327, 1332
Gloucestershire	1327
Huntingdonshire	1327, 1332
Lancashire	1332
Leicestershire	1327
Lincolnshire	1332
Staffordshire	1327

Notes

1 Another source of OE *ā* was the so-called Anglo-Frisian brightening, by which *ā* was fronted except in certain environments.

2 Some Norwegian dialects still have a front diphthong [ei] or [æi] (e.g. *bein* 'bone', *stein* 'stone') in these words; the other Norwegian dialects have a half-close or mid front long monophthong [e:] (*ben*, *sten*).

3 Still, Pilch includes a new sound in ME, i.e. /ɨ;·/ < OE /ew/, OFr. /ü/ (1997: 441); since this /ɨ;·/ seems not to derive from OE *ȳ*, the latter is somehow absent from the OE system presented (*ibid.*).

4 Interestingly, Pilch does invoke spellings as evidence of 'Orm's system' in note 2 (1997: 464).

5 The *Poema Morale* (Egerton MS, before 1200) has <o> and <a>; the *Ancrene Riwle* (1225) has only <o>. Regarding early Midlands texts, *Layamon* (SW Midlands, early MS *c.* 1205) has occasional <o> and (later MS *c.* 1250) general <o>; *Genesis and Exodus* and *Bestiary* (E Midlands, 1250) have regular <o>.

6 The *Holy Rood Tree* (1170), *Trinity Homilies* (before 1200), *Lambeth Homilies* (before 1200), the prose *Life of St. Julianne* (1210), *Wooing of Our Lord* (1210).

7 It may be noted that the sound resulting from rounding and raising of OE *ā* is said to have been probably a 'low-back-narrow-round vowel like the **a** in NE. **all**' (1928: §51; Wright and Wright's emphasis) whereas the sound resulting from MEOSL of *o* is said to have been a 'mid-back-wide-round' vowel. In current terminology, the sound resulting from the rounding and raising of OE *ā* would be called an open back rounded long tense vowel, whereas the product of MEOSL of OE *o* would be labelled as a half-open (or mid) back rounded long lax vowel (the terms 'narrow' and 'wide' probably correspond to 'tense' and 'lax', i.e. they describe the muscular quality of the tongue itself). The two sounds later coalesced, though they are still kept apart in North Midland dialects.

8 Denison (1999) points out that various types of linguistic change (phonological, morphological, and syntactic) frequently show the same pattern of change: new variants are infrequent at first and seem to spread very slowly; they then pick up momentum and become the dominant variant relatively quickly, before they seem to come to a halt, often before they have been implemented in all the available lexicon. This gives a characteristic S-shaped curve of diachronic change and accounts for apparent exceptions to otherwise general sound-changes; McMahon (1994) and Phillips (2006a) report similar findings.

9 This point is eminently illustrated by the language of the source text for *LAEME* no. 278 from Worcestershire (1250–74), which shows dominant <a> for OE *ā*: admittedly, this text also shows *occasional* <o> (e.g. <also> and <two>), but the back spelling <bac> BOOK indicates that the change of OE *ā* > *ǭ* has gone further in the language of the scribe than his orthography might suggest. One other *LAEME* text, i.e. no. 246 (Herefordshire, 1275–99), shows a back spelling <a> for OE *ō*, in the form <wawe> for OE *wōh*; but this text has dominant <o> for OE *ā*.

10 The *St. Juliana* text is found in two MSS: Oxford, Bodleian Library, Bodley 34, and London, British Library, Royal 17A xxvii. The texts are edited by S.R.T.O. d'Ardenne (1961). *LAEME* enters Bodley 34 in SE Shropshire, and dates it to the late 1230s or early 1240s; it is part of no. 1000. Royal 17A xxvii is dated to c. 1220–30, and the language is entered in SE Shropshire as part of no. 260.

11 *SMED4* does not record <oo> spellings, but states that they are exceptional (Kristensson 2001: 25).

12 The item NOT has *not* been included in the tables, since no distinction has been made in *LALME* between the adverb form and the noun ('naught'). For NOT, forms with <o> are clearly dominant, but forms with <a> are legion, and appear all over the South (e.g. in Kent, Sussex, and Cornwall).

13 The 'A, O' item shows clearly that forms with <o> dominate both in the North and in the South.

14 OE *a* was lengthened before other voiced homorganic consonant clusters also, but discussion here is restricted to OE *a+ld*.

15 For COLD, two forms with <o> are found in Northamptonshire and Norfolk; in the Essex Rolls, the one name containing COLD appears as <Chaldewell(e)>, and has been identified as present-day *Chadwell*; these two facts indicate that the lexeme originally had fractured OE *ea*. For OE *hald/heald*, one form with <o> is found in Essex. For OE *wald/weald*, <o> is found in Bedfordshire, Cambridgeshire, Essex, Huntingdonshire, Norfolk, and Northamptonshire; <e> occurs in Essex.

16 This is what Kitson says of the survey, which is 'extant in the twelfth-century Winchester cartulary': 'S938 is in a purported charter of Æthelred, with no explicit date and with dating-indications pointing (Keynes 1980:268) to mutually contradictory parts of his reign. Reduction of OE endings is substantially greater than in any genuine text of the mid-tenth century; ME

o- appears for OE *a-* in *ston(-)* x 2 (which occurs nowhere else in texts preserved in earlier than thirteenth-century manuscripts) and *swo* besides *swa*' (Kitson, letter dated 3 November 2003).

17 The experiment was carried out 25 November 2010. F3 in [ɑ:] was 2814 Hz in final position, and 2900 Hz before [n]; F3 in [ɔ:] was 3126 Hz in final position, and 2865 Hz before [n]. Thus, the third formant was very similar in [ɑ:] and [ɔ:] when they occurred before [n]. Lip-rounding lowers the frequency of all the three formants (Ladefoged 1962: 102–5; 2005: 176–80), but it is uncertain whether this played a role in the development of OE *ā*. This obviously needs more testing. Inger Moen suggests that it may not be the fact that [n] is *nasal* which influenced the *ā*, but rather its place of articulation: after alveolar or dental consonants, the closure between the upper and lower articulators may not be opened entirely, so that low vowels do not become as open as after labial or velar consonants.

18 The definitions of 'northern' ME and 'the North' are not clear; it has been suggested that the Humber-Ribble line should rather be the Humber-Lune line, at least for later ME (Samuels 1985).

19 However, ONbn *hǣlig* may be the etymon for <e> and <ae> for the vowel of HOLY. For OLD, the comparative and superlative forms were <eld-> (so also in ON), and ON lacked the positive <eald> or <ald> (but instead had *gamal*); thus, paradigmatic levelling may not be ruled out.

20 The LSRs are far from the only source for vernacular onomastic material in Latin administrative texts, and the *local* documents (of which there are thousands for the North) are a much more reliable source of local linguistic information than the existing LSRs. These documents are less convenient for dialect survey, because they are (relative to the LSRs) scattered in many collections and archives, and they are mostly far less concentrated records of vernacular material (Benskin, pers. comm.). Philologists have largely ignored them, but that is not to say that evidence cannot be had.

21 Some of Liebl's later material overlaps with the *LAEME* material extracted for the work in hand: this is the case for the *Trinity Homilies*, the oldest version of the *Poema Morale*, and the Final Continuation of the *Peterborough Chronicle* (2006: 29–30).

CHAPTER 3

The development of OE ǣ

3.1 Introduction

OE had *ǣ* from two main sources. OE *ǣ*^{1} (*i*-umlauted WGmc *ai*) was generally retained as distinct from OE *ǣ*^{2} in all dialects (Sievers and Cook 1968: §§57, 62, 90; Campbell 1959: §197), except in Kent and before dentals, before which *ǣ*^{1} was raised north of the Humber (cf. Luick 1914–40: §§187–8; Jordan 1968: §48, Anm.2). The *SMED* spellings confirm 'the time-honoured view that PrGerm *ai* + *i*, *i̯* was *ǣ* in Saxon and *ē* in Kentish, and lived on as ME /ɛ:/ and ME /e:/ respectively' (Kristensson 2001: 40). Kristensson finds no evidence of raising of *ǣ*^{1} before dentals south of the Humber (1987: 47; 1995: 24; 2001: 40).

OE *ǣ*^{2} is the reflex of WGmc *ā* (< PrGmc *ǣ*; Wright and Wright 1925: §119; Sievers/Cook 1968: §57). 'The distribution of OE *ē* and *ǣ* [...] is an important dialect criterion', in that *ē* is found in Anglian and Kentish, and *ǣ* in the Saxon dialects (Kristensson 1967: 56). Campbell regards the *ǣ*/*ē* split as dating from the Continental phase (1959: § 257). OE *ē* and *ǣ* are reflected as ME *ẹ̄* and *ę̄* respectively, but they are both spelt <e(e)>. To determine the quality of the vowel corresponding to <e(e)>, it is therefore necessary to look at forms with a shortened vowel, since shortened OE *ǣ* is <a>, and shortened OE *ē* is <e>. According to Brandl (quoted in Kristensson 1967), the dividing line between areas with and without OE *ǣ*^{2} 'passes along the western border of Ca[m] and Hu, the northern border of B[e]d, B[c]k, and O[x], and cuts across southern W[rk] and middlemost Wo[r] to the Severn' (Kristensson 1967: 57). The dialects south and west of this line had OE *ǣ*^{2}. In shortened forms, <a> is found all over the South, except in Dorset, Surrey, and Kent; but Kristensson concludes that 'there is nothing to contradict the view that D[or] and S[u]r were *ǣ*-areas and Kent an *ē*-area' (2001: 44).

Kristensson establishes a somewhat different isogloss from the material in *SMED2* (1987: 51–2, Map 6) and *SMED3* (1995: 28–32, Map 4). The line runs across the north-western tip of Gloucestershire, follows the eastern border of Herefordshire, cuts across Worcestershire, and Warwickshire in a south-easterly direction to the northern-most part of Oxfordshire, then cuts across Northamptonshire in a north-easterly direction, follows the southern border of Peterborough, and the northern border of Ely to Norfolk. North of this line, there was Anglian *ē*; south of it, there was Saxon *ǣ* (for *ǣ*²). Due to a large Saxon population, East Anglia – which would have had OE *ē* – had *ǣ* also (Kristensson 2001: 44). Moreover, East Saxon is supposed to have had *ā* corresponding to WS *ǣ*²: OE *ǣ* 'developed into /a:/ in East Saxon', that is, Essex, Hertfordshire, Bedfordshire, (most of) Cambridgeshire, Huntingdonshire, and Middlesex (Kristensson 1995: 31). There is nothing in the *SMED* material to contradict Kristensson's conclusions.

Kristensson (1997) gives in effect a summary of *SMED3*, at least as far as OE *ǣ*² vs. *ē* is concerned, and draws on onomastic material from *SMED3* as well as on other place-name evidence. Kristensson concludes that Bedfordshire, Buckinghamshire, and Hertfordshire 'certainly belonged to the OE Saxon area' (1997: 275), and so did Huntingdonshire, Cambridgeshire, and south-eastern Northamptonshire, in Kristensson's opinion, although the spellings from these are mixed, and it is unclear whether these areas are thought to have been Saxon linguistically or politically. As noted in Chapter 2, all it may amount to is the presence of a *characteristically* Saxon linguistic feature in an area which was Anglian politically. Kristensson's Map 2 (1997: 278) shows the demarcation line between Anglian and Saxon 'linguistic territory', where north-western Rutland and Northamptonshire are marked as Anglian areas, whereas the rest is Saxon.[1]

OE *ǣ* raised to ME /ɛ:/, which supposedly remained in eModE and became [e:] in the late 1600s (Dobson 1968: 607), although both Zachrisson (1913: 204) and Dobson (1968: 610) find that [i:] is in evidence from the sixteenth century in non-standard language; Zachrisson believes [i:] was generally adopted in the late seventeenth century (1968: 610).

This chapter presents ME spellings for eME *ǣ*, with a view to establishing its phonetic correspondences regionally and temporally, and to determining the course of change in ME and eModE. From the foregoing, it is clear that ME <i>/<y> for *ǣ* in texts now recognised as from areas with OE *ǣ* or OE *ē* may be used as evidence of raising. Since East Saxon and Kentish had *ā* for WS *ǣ*², forms with <a> and later <o> from these areas should be used as evidence for the development of OE *ā*, and not of OE *ǣ*.[2]

3.2 Discussion

3.2.1 Discussion of LAEME *material*

To recapitulate, all OE dialects are believed to have had [æ:] for OE ǣ^{1} (<WGmc *ai+i*), whereas only Saxon dialects had [æ:] for OE ǣ^{2} (<WGmc *ā*), for which Kentish and Anglian had [e:]. To determine whether the *LAEME* material confirms this account, spellings extracted for OE ǣ were divided into the traditional ME dialect areas, and reflexes of OE ǣ^{1} and ǣ^{2} were counted separately. The numbers are reproduced in Tables 3.1 and 3.2 (since <a>, <æ>, and <ea> presumably all correspond to [æ:], numbers for these have also been amalgamated in the tables).[3]

It should be kept in mind that the surviving material is unevenly distributed: for Suffolk, for instance, only one source is represented in the tables, and this text is from the late twelfth century; the Northern texts, on the other hand, are all dated to the period 1275–1350; the South is poorly represented in general, etc. Conclusions must therefore be tentative. The extracted spellings point in various directions: the reflexes of the two ǣ's do not seem to be kept apart in any systematic way. It is an open question whether this indicates that the two reflexes had merged – which they should have in (West) Saxon dialects anyway, since the vowel was [æ:] in both cases. It probably also points to raising of OE ǣ to [ɛ:], which quality would be difficult to reflect in writing.

In the E Midlands, there is in fact a higher number of <a>/<æ>/<ea> for OE ǣ^{2} (31.29%) than for ǣ^{1} (19.66%), which partly goes counter to the traditional assumption; it likely shows the East Saxon retraction of ǣ^{2} to [a:] (and the 'Saxon area' may have extended further north than has been assumed, cf. Kristensson's claim (1995: 28–32) that East Anglia had a large Saxon population). In the W Midlands, however, the spellings seem to confirm the conventional account, with twice as many <a>/<æ>/<ea> for OE ǣ^{1} (30.36%) than for OE ǣ^{2} (14.63%). Essex clearly stands out with a very high number of <a> for both ǣ's: this must be taken as relatively solid evidence for the postulated East Saxon development ǣ^{2} > *ā*, which may in fact have affected the reflex of OE ǣ^{1} also. However, there is little evidence for this change in other supposedly East Saxon areas. Essex is the only county with dominant <a>/<æ>/<ea> for ǣ^{2}, but other counties also have some such spellings: Lincolnshire, Cambridgeshire, Surrey, Hampshire, Wiltshire, Worcestershire, and Shropshire. Certainly, the relatively high number of such spellings in Shropshire, Worcestershire, and Lincolnshire seems not to lend support to the traditional delineation of the Saxon vs. non-Saxon areas.

Table 3.1 LAEME *spellings for OE* $\bar{\ae}^{1}$ *and OE* $\bar{\ae}^{2}$

Area	$\bar{\ae}^{1}$ <WGmc *ai+i*			$\bar{\ae}^{2}$ <WGmc $\bar{a}$		
	no.	%	<a/æ/ea>	no.	%	<a/æ/ea>
NORTH	1 <a>	0.92		9 <a>	7.63	
	97 <e>	88.99		107 <e>	90.68	
	11 <ai/ei>	10.09		2 <ai/ei>	1.69	
	Total: 109 tokens			Total: 118 tokens		
East Midlands 1150–1250	45 <a>	16.92	70 tokens 26.32%	65 <a>	35.91	98 tokens 54.14%
	23 <æ>	8.65		33 <æ>	18.23	
	2 <ea>	0.75		82 <e>	45.3	
	196 <e>	73.68		1 <ai>	0.55	
	Total: 266 tokens			Total: 181 tokens		
East Midlands 1250–1350	1 <æ>	1.05		4 <a>	2.76	
	92 <e>	96.84		140 <e>	96.55	
	1 <ei>	1.05		1 <o>	0.69	
	1 <y>	1.05				
	Total: 95 tokens			Total: 145 tokens		
EAST MIDLANDS TOTAL	45 <a>	12.46	71 tokens 19.66%	69 <a>	21.17	102 tokens 31.29%
	24 <æ>	6.65		33 <æ>	10.12	
	2 <ea>	0.55		222 <e>	68.09	
	288 <e>	79.78		1 <ai>	0.31	
	1 <ei>	0.28		1 <o>	0.31	
	1 <y>	0.28				
	Total: 361 tokens			Total: 326 tokens		
SOUTH-WEST	1 <a>	25	2 tokens 50%	1 <æ>	16.67	
	1 <æ>	25		5 <e>	83.33	
	2 <e>	50				
	Total: 4 tokens			Total: 6 tokens		

(continued)

Table 3.1 (*cont.*)

Area	ǣ^{1} <WGmc *ai+i*			ǣ^{2} <WGmc *ā*		
	no.	%	<a/æ/ea>	no.	%	<a/æ/ea>
SOUTH-EAST	2 <æ>	3.64		2 <a>	2.94	
	53 <e>	96.36		66 <e>	97.06	
	Total: 55 tokens			Total: 68 tokens		
West Midlands 1150–1250	1 <a>	0.32	138 tokens 44.37%	1 <a>	0.2	55 tokens1 1.07%
	19 <æ>	6.11		17 <æ>	3.42	
	118 <ea>	37.94		37 <ea>	7.45	
	173 <e>	55.63		424 <e>	85.31	
				14 <eo>	2.82	
				3 <ai/ei>	0.6	
				1 <ia>	0.2	
	Total: 311 tokens			Total: 497 tokens		
West Midlands 1250–1350	5 <a>	1.39	66 tokens 18.28%	10 <a>	2.05	89 tokens 18.27%
	42 <æ>	11.63		40 <æ>	8.21	
	19 <ea>	5.26		39 <ea>	8.01	
	290 <e>	80.33		391 <e>	80.29	
	3 <eo>	0.83		3 <eo>	0.62	
	2 <æi/ei>	0.55		2 <ei>	0.41	
				2 <i>	0.41	
	Total: 361 tokens			Total: 487 tokens		
WEST MIDLANDS TOTAL	6 <a>	0.89	204 tokens 30.36%	11 <a>	1.12	144 tokens 14.63%
	61 <æ>	9.08		57 <æ>	5.79	
	137 <ea>	20.39		76 <ea>	7.72	
	463 <e>	68.9		815 <e>	82.83	
	3 <eo>	0.44		17 <eo>	1.73	
	2 <æi/ei>	0.3		5 <ai/ei>	0.51	
				2 <i>	0.2	
				1 <ia>	0.1	
	Total: 672 tokens			Total: 984 tokens		
	Total ǣ^{1}: 1201 tokens			**Total ǣ^{2}: 1502 tokens**		

Table 3.2 LAEME *spellings for OE* ǣ^{1} *and OE* ǣ^{2}, *by county*

Area	ǣ^{1} <WGmc *ai+i*	ǣ^{2} <WGmc *ā*
NORTH		
Durham	3 e	1 a, 2 e
East Riding, Yks	1 a, 23 e, 1 ee	4 a, 27 e, 1 ai
Lancashire		4 e
North Riding, Yks	42 e, 2 ay	4 a, 27 e, 1 ee, 1 ay
West Riding, Yks	9 e, 3 ee, 1 ei	23 e
York	15 e, 1 ee, 6 ai, 2 ei	23 e
EAST MIDLANDS		
Cambridgeshire	4 e	1 a, 2 e
Ely	2 e	11 e
Essex	45 a, 5 æ, 2 ea, 37 e	65 a, 21 æ, 20 e
Leicestershire		1 e
Lincolnshire	6 æ, 44 e, 1 y	11 æ, 21 e, 1 é
Norfolk	1 æ, 59 e, 1 ee, 1 ei	3 a, 100 e, 5 ee, 10
Northamptonshire	4 e	8 e
Peterborough	5 æ, 1 e	1 æ, 3 e
Suffolk	7 æ, 136 e	50 e, 1 ai
SOUTH-EAST		
Kent	2 ae, 49 e, 2 éé	64 e
Sussex	1 e	2 e
Surrey	1 e	2 a
SOUTH-WEST		
Hampshire	1 æ, 2 e	1 æ, 5 e
Somerset	1 a	
WEST MIDLANDS		
Berkshire	1 a, 95 e, 1 eo	46 e
Cheshire	1 a, 17 ea	1 ea, 57 e, 1 eo, 1 ai, 2 ei
Gloucestershire	42 e, 1 eo	1 a, 74 e, 4 ee
Herefordshire	12 ea, 68 e, 1 éé	3 ea, 176 e, 2 é, 1 eo, 1 ei, 1 i
Oxfordshire	51 e	5 a, 52 e
Shropshire	74 ea, 18 e	30 ea, 104 e, 2 é, 13 eo
Staffordshire	1 e	1 e
Wiltshire	1 a, 6 e, 10 éé, 1 ee, 1 eo	24 ea, 29 e
Worcestershire	3 a, 61 æ, 34 ea, 158 e, 7 é(é), 5 ee, 2 æi/ei	5 a, 57 æ, 18 ea, 268 e, 2 eo, 1 æi, 1 i

The Ormulum (text no. 301), by virtue of its consistent orthography, is worth considering in more detail in this regard. For the items extracted from all *LAEME* sources, it has 6 <æ> and 19 <e> for OE ǣ^{1}, and 11 <æ>-type spellings and 2 <e>-type forms for ǣ^{2}. As it represents the language of S Lincolnshire *c.* 1175, it is supposed to have had [æ:] for the former, and [e:] for the latter; but the spellings indicate the opposite, with more <æ> for *ǣ*^{2}. Of course, percentages might change if all forms going back to the two *ǣ*'s were extracted and counted separately, which I did next for the portion tagged for *LAEME* (the Dedication and Preface, and a portion of the Introduction and Homilies). For OE *ǣ*^{1}, 107 tokens were counted, of which 3 have <a> (items ANY, NE+ANY, LADY), 68 have <æ>, and 36 have <e>. For OE *ǣ*^{2}, 166 tokens were counted, of which 9 have <a>, 141 have <æ> (including the highly frequent THERE), and 16 have <e>.[4] Clearly, <æ> is the most frequent spelling for both *ǣ*'s, which strongly suggests that even in non-Saxon dialects, the phonetic correspondence of OE *ǣ*^{2} must have been open [ɛ:], or indeed [æ:]. Of course, orthographic influence from standard late WS may not be ruled out entirely, but this is rarely invoked to account for Orm's other idiosyncracies…

The digraphs <eo> and <ea> are W Midlands innovations, and seem to be used to indicate [æ:]; the problem is that <ea>/<a>/<æ> are quite frequent for OE *ǣ*^{2} also (and are attested as far north as Worcestershire and Shropshire), for which Mercian is thought to have had [e:]. Again, it indicates that the reflex of OE *ǣ*^{2} had a half-open quality [ɛ:], perhaps even in OE. The <æi>/<ei> are more difficult to interpret, though the <i> may have been used as a diacritic to indicate a closer quality, for example, [ɛ:].

In order to see whether similar results would be obtained for some highly frequent words, I extracted forms for THERE, WHERE, HAIR (with OE *ǣ*^{2}), and EVER, NEVER (with OE *ǣ*^{1}), all with somewhat idiosyncratic ME and eModE developments, as well as for assorted words going back to OE *ǣ*. Table 3.3 shows raw figures and percentages of these 8474 spellings.[5]

The non-committal <e> is the most frequent spelling for all OE *ǣ* words combined in the earliest period covered by *LAEME*, but for some reason starts losing ground to <a> and <æ>, and above all to <ea>, in the period 1200–50. Around 1250, <ea> and <e> are about equally frequent; in the next 25-year period, <ea> sees a rapid decrease, and <a> is re-introduced as the second most frequent spelling for OE *ǣ*. In the later periods, <e> remains the most frequent spelling, and there is a steady decline in <a> forms. The last time period (1325–50) comprises only Northern and North-Eastern sources, which may explain the high percentage of <a> in this period (40.65%), because otherwise <a> is on the decline from 1250; it is probably also due to the idiosyncratic development of the vowel in HAIR, THERE, WHERE. One text, no. 155 (Norfolk, 1300–24), may also skew the percentages of <o> in the period 1300–24: it has no less than 119 <o> for THERE, WHERE, which may demonstrate the East Saxon development to [a:] (although Norfolk was supposedly not East Saxon), or of ON *á*,

Table 3.3 LAEME *spellings for OE* ǣ *(all words combined)*

Dates	Spgs	<a>	<æ>	<ea>	<e>	<eo>	<ai/ei>	<o>w	<i(e)>	Total
1150–1199	no.	165	126	2	634		1		1	929
	%	**17.76**	**13.56**	**0.22**	**68.25**		**0.11**		**0.11**	**100%**
	no.	<a/æ/ea> 293								
	%	<a/æ/ea> **31.54**								
1200–1224	no.	220	174	130	613	8		1		1146
	%	**19.2**	**15.18**	**11.34**	**53.49**	**0.7**		**0.09**		**100%**
	no.	<a/æ/ea> 524								
	%	<a/æ/ea> **45.72**								
1225–1249	no.	34	3	620	633	12	3			1305
	%	**2.61**	**0.23**	**47.51**	**48.5**	**0.92**	**0.23**			**100%**
	no.	<a/æ/ea> 657								
	%	<a/æ/ea> **50.35**								
1250–1274	no.	193	74	82	475	2	1	2		829
	%	**23.28**	**8.93**	**9.89**	**57.3**	**0.24**	**0.12**	**0.24**		**100%**
	no.	<a/æ/ea> 349								
	%	<a/æ/ea> **42.1**								
1275–1299	no.	213	2	23	1256	1	5	14	1	1515
	%	**14.06**	**0.13**	**1.52**	**82.9**	**0.07**	**0.33**	**0.92**	**0.07**	**100%**
	no.	<a/æ/ea> 238								
	%	<a/æ/ea> **15.71**								
1300–1324	no.	291			1186			144		1621
	%	**17.95**			**73.17**			**8.88**		**100%**
1325–1350	no.	459	2		652		13	3		1129
	%	**40.65**	**0.18**		**57.75**		**1.15**	**0.27**		**100%**
	no.	<a/æ/ea> 461								
	%	<a/æ/ea> **40.83**								
8474 tokens										

and should ideally not be included here (cf. 3.1). However, <o> in other time periods have also been included.

Numbers come out a little different when the material is sorted. EVER and NEVER end up with a short PDE vowel; it is unclear when the shortening occurred, but it may have been in the ME quantity adjustment period, which is thought to have started around 1225. Although their etymology is supposedly uncertain, they most likely had OE *ǣ*^{1}. Two other highly frequent words, THERE and WHERE, as well as HAIR, go back to OE *ǣ*^{2}, but have PDE /eə/.[6] For these reasons, it seems sensible to look at numbers for these words separately. Table 3.4 shows the numbers for THERE, WHERE and HAIR; Table 3.5 shows numbers for EVER and NEVER.

Two marked differences stand out when the numbers for all OE *ǣ* words combined are compared to those for OE *ǣ*^{2} (presumably [æ:] in Saxon dialects, and [e:] elsewhere): (1) there is in fact a huge *increase* in <e> after 1200 for the latter category, which may be indicative of raising to [ɛ:] or [e:] in those areas which had OE [æ:]; and (2) the digraph <ea> never catches on for OE *ǣ*^{2} before /r/ (though Table 3.1 shows that ME <ea> is common for OE *ǣ*^{2} in other words). If the dominance of <e> suggests raising to [e:], this raising seems to have started in the period *c.* 1200–50. It is also evident that there is 'lexical specificity' in the spellings for OE *ǣ*, as pointed out by Lass and Laing (2005: 281) for the reflexes of OE *ȳ*: <o> is virtually only attested for THERE and WHERE, which likely shows the development of OE/ON *ā*.

Forms with <a>/<æ>/<ea> become ever more frequent from the earliest period until 1250, when percentages drop dramatically; they are almost halved in the period 1250–74 (as compared to the preceding period), then all but disappear. The case is consequently the reverse for <e>: from being by far the most common form in the earliest period, numbers drop substantially in the period 1200–24, after which there is a steady increase, and in the last three time periods, numbers for <e> vary between 95% and 100%. This probably indicates that [e(:)] or [ɛ(:)] had become established in these two words from the mid-thirteenth century.

The same spellings for OE *ǣ* have been divided into dialect areas in the following tables (Tables 3.6, 3.7, 3.8, 3.9).

Generally, <a>-type spellings are much more frequent in Table 3.7 than in Table 3.1, due in all likelihood to the different development of the vowel in HAIR, THERE, WHERE than in the words with *ǣ*^{2} included in Table 3.1. In the North, <a> reigns supreme for the reflex of OE *ǣ*^{2} in the three items counted, which goes counter to the findings in Table 3.1, for the reason outlined earlier. Retraction to [æ:] or [a:], whether due to an OE variant

Table 3.4 LAEME *spellings for OE /æ:r/ in* THERE, WHERE, HAIR *(<OE $\bar{æ}^2$)*

Dates	Spgs	<a>	<æ>	<ea>	<e>	<eo>	<ai/ei>	<o>	<i(e)>	Total
1150–1199	no.	110	95		186		1		1	393
	%	**28**	**24.17**		**47.33**		**0.25**		**0.25**	**100**
	no.	<a/æ/ea> 205								
	%	<a/æ/ea> **52.17**								
1200–1224	no.	94	13	2	329	1		1		440
	%	**21.36**	**2.95**	**0.46**	**74.77**	**0.23**		**0.23**		**100**
	no.	<a/æ/ea> 109								
	%	<a/æ/ea> **24.77**								
1225–1249	no.	32	3	12	325		3			375
	%	**8.53**	**0.8**	**3.2**	**86.67**		**0.8**			**100**
	no.	<a/æ/ea> 47								
	%	<a/æ/ea> **12.53**								
1250–1274	no.	163	16	1	307			2		489
	%	**33.33**	**3.27**	**0.21**	**62.78**			**0.41**		**100**
	no.	<a/æ/ea> 180								
	%	<a/æ/ea> **36.81**								
1275–1299	no.	207	1	2	454		1	13		678
	%	**30.53**	**0.15**	**0.29**	**66.96**		**0.15**	**1.92**		**100**
	no.	<a/æ/ea> 210								
	%	<a/æ/ea> **30.97**								
1300–1324	no.	282			464			144		890
	%	**31.69**			**52.13**			**16.18**		**100**
1325–1350	no.	435	2		203		2	3		645
	%	**67.44**	**0.31**		**31.47**		**0.31**	**0.47**		**100**
	no.	<a/æ/ea> 437								
	%	<a/æ/ea> **67.75**								
3910 tokens										

Table 3.5 LAEME *spellings for OE /æ:/ in* EVER, NEVER *(<OE ǣ[1])*

Dates	Spgs	<a>	<æ>	<ea>	<e>	<eo>	<o>	Total
1150–1199	no.	37	22	1	154			214
	%	**17.29**	**10.28**	**0.47**	**71.96**			**100**
	no.	<a/æ/ea> 60						
	%	<a/æ/ea> **28.04**						
1200–1224	no.	65	124	71	182			442
	%	**14.71**	**28.05**	**16.06**	**41.18**			**100**
	no.	<a/æ/ea> 260						
	%	<a/æ/ea> **58.82**						
1225–1249	no.			455	178			633
	%			**71.88**	**28.12**			**100**
1250–1274	no.	21	20	33	103	1		178
	%	**11.8**	**11.23**	**18.54**	**57.87**	**0.56**		**100**
	no.	<a/æ/ea> 74						
	%	<a/æ/ea> **41.57**						
1275–1299	no.	5		19	533		1	558
	%	**0.89**		**3.41**	**95.52**		**0.18**	**100**
	no.	<a/æ/ea> 24						
	%	<a/æ/ea> **4.3**						
1300–1324	no.				481			481
	%				**100**			**100**
1325–1350	no.	12			258			270
	%	**4.44**			**95.56**			**100**
2776 tokens								

Table 3.6 *Spellings for OE ǣ in* LAEME *(all words combined), by dialect area*

Dates	Spgs	<a>	<æ>	<ea>	<e>	<eo>	<ai/ei>	<o>	<i(e)>	Total
North	no.	439			350		13			802
	%	**54.74**			**43.64**		**1.62**			**100%**
E Midl(early)	no.	346	225	3	317		1		1	893
	%	**38.74**	**25.2**	**0.34**	**35.5**		**0.11**		**0.11**	**100%**
		574 (**68.28%**)								
E Midl(late)	no.	68	5		586			153		812
	%	**8.37**	**0.62**		**72.17**			**18.84**		**100%**
		73 (**8.99%**)								
E Midl(total)	no.	414	230	3	903		1	153	1	1705
	%	**24.28**	**13.49**	**0.18**	**52.96**		**0.06**	**8.97**	**0.06**	**100%**
		647 (**37.95%**)								
S-E	no.	9			417					426
	%	**2.11**			**97.89**					**100%**
S-W	no.	10	6		12					28
	%	**35.71**	**21.43**		**42.86**					**100%**
		16 (**57.14%**)								
W Midl(early)	no.	60	72	530	1314	15	3	1		1995
	%	**3.01**	**3.61**	**26.57**	**65.86**	**0.75**	**0.15**	**0.05**		**100%**
		662 (**33.19%**)								
W Midl(late)	no.	632	73	98	2130	3	6	7		2949
	%	**21.43**	**2.48**	**3.32**	**72.23**	**0.1**	**0.2**	**0.24**		**100%**
		803 (**27.23%**)								
W Midl(total)	no.	692	145	628	3444	18	9	8		4944
	%	**14**	**2.93**	**12.7**	**69.66**	**0.36**	**0.18**	**0.16**		**100%**
		1465 (**29.63%**)								
8474 tokens										

Table 3.7 LAEME *spellings for OE* $\bar{æ}^2$ *in* HAIR, THERE, WHERE, *by dialect area*

Dates	Spgs	<a>	<æ>	<ea>	<e>	<eo>	<ai/ei>	<o>	<i(e)>	Total
North	no.	427			6		2			435
	%	**98.16**			**1.38**		**0.46**			**100**
E Midl(early)	no.	171	97		63		1		1	333
	%	**51.35**	**29.13**		**18.92**		**0.3**		**0.3**	**100**
		268 (**80.48%**)								
E Midl(late)	no.	52	3		214			153		422
	%	**12.32**	**0.71**		**50.71**			**36.26**		**100**
		55 (**13.03%**)								
E Midl(total)	no.	223	100		277		1	153	1	755
	%	**29.54**	**13.25**		**36.69**		**0.13**	**20.26**	**0.13**	**100**
		323 (**42.79%**)								
S-E	no.	6			259					265
	%	**2.26**			**97.74**					**100**
S-W	no.	9	3		6					18
	%	**50**	**16.67**		**33.33**					**100**
		12 (**66.67%**)								
W Midl(early)	no.	53	11	10	607	1	3	1		686
	%	**7.72**	**1.6**	**1.46**	**88.48**	**0.15**	**0.44**	**0.15**		**100**
		74 (**10.78%**)								
W Midl(late)	no.	594	16	3	929		1	6		1549
	%	**38.35**	**1.03**	**0.19**	**59.97**		**0.07**	**0.39**		**100**
		613 (**39.57%**)								
W Midl(total)	no.	647	27	13	1536	1	4	7		2235
	%	**28.95**	**1.21**	**0.58**	**68.72**	**0.05**	**0.18**	**0.31**		**100**
		687 (**30.74%**)								
3708 tokens										

Table 3.8 LAEME *spellings for OE ǣ[1] in* EVER, NEVER, *by dialect area*

Dates	Spgs	<a>	<æ>	<ea>	<e>	<eo>	<o>	Total
North	no.				221			221
	%				**100**			**100**
E Midl(early)	no.	101	98	1	59			259
	%	**39**	**37.83**	**0.39**	**22.78**			**100**
		200 (**77.22%**)						
E Midl(late)	no.	12	1		241			254
	%	**4.72**	**0.39**		**94.88**			**100**
		13 (**5.11%**)						
E Midl(total)	no.	113	99	1	300			513
	%	**22.03**	**19.3**	**0.19**	**58.48**			**100**
		213 (**41.52%**)						
S-E	no.	1			59			60
	%	**1.67**			**98.33**			**100**
S-W	no.		2		4			6
	%		**33.33**		**66.67**			**100**
W Mid(learly)	no.	1	46	373	422			842
	%	**0.12**	**5.46**	**44.3**	**50.12**			**100**
		420 (**49.88%**)						
W Midl(late)	no.	25	19	45	805	1	1	896
	%	**2.79**	**2.12**	**5.02**	**89.84**	**0.11**	**0.11**	**100**
		89 (**9.93%**)						
W Midl(total)	no.	26	65	418	1227	1	1	1738
	%	**1.49**	**3.74**	**24.05**	**70.6**	**0.06**	**0.06**	**100**
		509 (**29.28%**)						
2538 tokens								

Table 3.9 LAEME *spellings for OE* ǣ *(various items), by county*

Area	NEVER, EVER (OE $\bar{æ}^1$)	HAIR, THERE, WHERE (OE $\bar{æ}^2$)
North		
Cumberland		2 a
Durham	8 e	11 a, 1 e
East Riding, Yks	99 e	111 a, 1 ai
Lancashire	1 e	
North Riding, Yks	35 e	132 a, 1 ai
West Riding, Yks	49 e	61 a, 3 e
York	29 e	110 a, 2 e
East Midlands		
Cambridgeshire	5 e	8 a, 1 e
Ely	17 e	1 a, 2 æ, 21 e, 3 o
Essex	101 a, 80 æ, 1 ea, 23 e	155 a, 2 æ, 16 e, 1 ie
Huntingdonshire	12 a, 6 e	4 a, 14 e
Lincolnshire	8 æ, 13 e	20 a, 92 æ, 4 e, 3 o
Norfolk	191 e	19 a, 1 æ, 164 e, 147 o
Northamptshire	15 e	1 e
Peterborough	11 æ, 4 e	8 a, 3 æ, 4 e
Suffolk	26 e	8 a, 52 e, 1 ai
South-East		
Kent	1 a, 57 e	2 a, 257 e
London		1 a, 1 e
Surrey		1 e
Sussex	2 e	3 a
South-West		
Devon	2 e	5 a
Hampshire	2 æ, 1 e	6 e
Somerset	1 e	4 a, 3 æ
West Midlands		
Berkshire	2 a, 143 e	37 a, 220 e
Cheshire	79 ea, 2 e	60 e, 3 ai/ei
Gloucestershire	4 a, 162 e	70 a, 173 e, 1 o
Herefordshire	61 ea, 241 e, 1 o	95 a, 6 ea, 210 e, 1 ei
Oxfordshire	127 e	165 a, 106 e, 5 o
Shropshire	231 ea, 52 e	1 a, 5 ea, 191 e
Staffordshire	4 e	2 e
Warwickshire		2 e
Wiltshire	47 e	105 a, 19 e
Worcestershire	20 a, 65 æ, 47 ea, 449 e, 1 eo	174 a, 27 æ, 2 ea, 553 e, 1 eo, 1 o

with *ā* or to ON influence, is clearly in evidence, and it is supported by later ME spellings with <a> or <o>. In the E Midlands also, forms indicating an open vowel are dominant by far in the early period, but see a dramatic decrease in numbers in the late period, which suggests raising. The preponderance of <a>-type spellings in these three items probably reflect an OE open vowel or influence from ON. As noted earlier, numbers for <o> are skewed, due to a very high number of <o> for THERE, WHERE in one Norfolk source. In the W Midlands, <e> remains the most frequent orthographic representation of OE ǣ^{2}, although <a>/<æ>/<ea> in fact become much more frequent in the late period. Whether this is the result of scribes' desire to represent [e:] and [ɛ:] differently is a question that eludes an answer. In the South-East, <e> clearly dominates, which is unsurprising, given that most of the spellings are attested in Kentish sources. In the South-West, which tends to go with the W Midlands, the figures are low, but spellings suggesting an open vowel outnumber <e>, which is the opposite of the figures in Table 3.1. The numbers for the South-West and the W Midlands thus confirm the conventional account that Saxon dialects had [æ:] for the reflex of WGmc *ā* > OE ǣ^{2}.

There is no way of knowing whether any of the extracted spellings in fact represent a shortened OE ǣ^{1}, but the possibility should be kept in mind. In the North, 100% of the forms have <e>, which is even higher than in Table 3.1, possibly indicating raising to [ɛ:] or [e:]; as most of the Northern sources are relatively late, raising to [e:] is not at all unlikely. In the E Midlands, the same picture emerges as for OE ǣ^{2}: <a>/<æ>/<ea> dominate (77.22%) in the early period (whereas Table 3.1 has 26.32% <a>/<æ>/<ea> in the early period for the E Midlands), and have been reduced to 5.11% in the late period; the same is true of the W Midlands. Again, figures are low for the South, especially the western part; <e> appears in 98.33% of the forms in the South-East. Given the diverging developments of the words included in Tables 3.7 and 3.8, the figures in Table 3.1 almost certainly present a more accurate picture of the reflexes of both ǣ's in ME.

In the E Midlands, and for the entire period covered by *LAEME*, Lincolnshire and Essex stand out, reporting a very high number of spellings which indicate an open vowel for OE ǣ^{2}. This corroborates the postulated East Saxon development of ǣ^{2}. Essex sources also indicate an open vowel for ǣ^{1}. Throughout the W Midlands area, there are numerous <a>/<æ>/<ea> for both ǣ's: there are however slightly higher numbers for ǣ^{2}, and not just in the southern areas, which historically were WS. Tables 3.2 and 3.9, with numbers for each county, thus show similar figures for the two ǣ's, except that there are more <a>-type spellings for ǣ^{2} in Table 3.9; as pointed out before, this demonstrates the different development of the vowel of the three words counted here. Hence, the numbers in Table 3.2 probably reflect the (proportions of) spellings for OE ǣ^{2} in eME more accurately.

The following potential vowel-shift spellings are found (Table 3.10).

Table 3.10 *Potential vowel-shift spellings for OE* ǣ *in* LAEME

County	No.	Date	Spelling
Essex	4	1150–99	<þier> THERE
Essex	64	1200–24	<sliep> SLEEP *3.sg.pt.*
Worcestershire	7	1200–49	<liache> LEECH
Worcestershire	278	1250–74	<spiche> SPEECH
Herefordshire	246	1275–99	<heit> HEATH <reid> *rǣd*
Herefordshire	249	1275–99	<liche> LEECH
Mixed (NE&SW)	214	1275–99	<silly> SǢLIG
Lincolnshire	159	c.1300	<lydy> LEAD *1.sg.ps.*
Norfolk	155	1300–24	<leiste> LEAST

The two forms for LEECH 'physician' seem to indicate raising, but OE also had forms with *ē* and *ȳ*; <þier> and <sliep> in nos. 4 and 64 could be AN spellings for [e:], which would still indicate raising of ME /ɛ:/ to /e:/, since both words stem from OE *ǣ*^{2}, Saxon [æ:]. Of the rest, <spiche> and <silly> (<OE *ǣ*^{2}, so probably non-Saxon *ē*) and <lydy> (<OE *ǣ*^{1}) certainly suggest raising all the way to [i(:)] from the mid-thirteenth century onwards, in the NE Midlands, and the (S)W Midlands. The two <ei> in no. 246 are difficult to interpret, but they are found in a text with a number of such digraphs for etymological long monophthongs, so the <i> may be a marker of length.

Forms with <ei>, <æi>, <ai/ay> are found in some quantity and are hard to interpret: the <i> may be a marker of length or of a closer vowel quality.[7]

3.2.2 Discussion of SMED *material*

The domains of the phonetic correspondences of OE *ǣ*^{1} and *ǣ*^{2} in ME dialects, based on analysis of *SMED* spellings, were established in Section 3.1.

Only a handful of *SMED* spellings indicate vowel shift. For OE *ǣ*^{1}, <Minskip> from the West Riding of Yorkshire (1327) indicates raising of /æ:/. For OE *ǣ*^{2}, <Silyman> (with SILLY) from Lincolnshire (1327) suggests raising of non-Saxon /e:/, as does <Silly> from Huntingdonshire (1327), whereas <Rydelingfeld> (with OE *Rǣdel/Rēdel*) from Suffolk (1327), <Brych> (with OE *Brǣc/Brēc*) from Somerset (1333), and <Ridelyngton> (with OE *Rǣda/Rēda*) from Dorset (1327) all testify to raising of Saxon /æ:/. Kristensson also believes the last two indicate raising

(2001: 44): the first one is thought to have raised because of the following /tʃ/; for the last one, two possible paths are suggested, either /æ:/ > /e:/ > /e/ > /i/, or /æ:/ > /e:/ > /i:/. The second path is the more likely. The Yorkshire-Lincolnshire-Huntingdonshire area and the Somerset-Dorset area therefore stand out.

3.2.3 Discussion of LALME *material*

LALME items with OE *ǣ*^{1} are ANY, EACH, ERE, FLESH, LADY, NEVER; items with OE *ǣ*^{2} are DREAD, READ, THERE, WHERE, and possibly WERE.

In ANY, <a> for the stressed vowel is found across the country. Numerous <o> are reported, which is not surprising, given OE forms like <ony>, showing vacillation between <a> and <o> before a nasal – the vowel must therefore have had co-varying [æ:] and [a:] in OE, and the <o> forms indicate the development of the latter; this is indeed the reason why tokens for ANY have not been included in the *LAEME* tables. In ERE too, <a> is attested everywhere, whereas in EACH, <a> is reported only in Essex and Sussex, and <ea> in Kent; for the vowel of FLESH, <ay> appears in a source from Cornwall. In LADY, <a> is the dominant spelling for the stressed vowel, which demonstrates the eME shortening to [æ] and merger with [a], which gave ME [a:] after MEOSL; this is the reason why LADY was left out in the *LAEME* material. In NEVER, <a> is attested in Lancashire, and <ea> in Durham, so by this stage, the vowel had certainly been shortened and was [e] in most of the area of survey. Thus, the *LALME* material for *ǣ*^{1} has dominant <e>, which indicates that its reflex had certainly been raised to [ɛ:], and even to [e:], in lME. ERE is the exception: although it shows dominant <e>, there are frequent <a> throughout the country; but since there are numerous <o> also, the vowel may have undergone retraction, possibly before /r/.

In DREAD, recorded for the southern area of survey only, <a> is found throughout, from Devon to Kent in the South, and from Shropshire to Norfolk in the N Midlands. In READ, also recorded exclusively for the southern half of England, <a> is attested in sources from the entire area. In THERE, the digraphs <ai> and <ei> are reported in the North only, whereas <a> is rather frequent across the country, which is true of <a> for WHERE also. Scattered <o> in THERE is found above all in Lincolnshire, but also in Nottinghamshire, and the North; exactly the same pattern appears for WHERE, though with attestations in Norfolk and Worcestershire also. Clearly, these items had OE/ME *ā* in this area, and the vowel participated in the eME backing and rounding to [ɔ:]. In WERE, whose ancestry seems

Table 3.11 *Potential vowel-shift spellings for OE* ǣ *in* LALME

Item	Spelling	Text
THERE	<thier>	Hrf 7400
	<thir/thyr>	Sx 5920
	<þire->	Ex 6190
	<þyr>	Bck 6630, Htf 6620
FLESH	<flich(e)>	Li, 588, Yk 1002
	<fliesche>	Hu 541
	<flych(e)>	Dvn 5040, Li 588, Nt 507 (x2), Sfk 8440, ERY 476
	<flysch(e)>	Dvn 9400, ERY 476 (x2)
	<flyse>	Nt 507
	<flyshe>	Dvn 5040
	<flyssh>	Dvn 5040

uncertain and which is recorded only for the northern half of survey, <ae> and <ai> are attested in the West Riding of Yorkshire; <o> appears in much the same area as <o> for THERE and WHERE (which may be due to ON influence or retraction before /r/); <a> is common throughout.

Summing up, <a> seems much more common for the reflex of *ǣ*^{2} than for *ǣ*^{1} in the *LALME* material, which is counter to expectations, and which in certain regards corroborates my findings for the early period, at least for the E Midlands. However, the picture may be distorted by the fact that three out of the five *LALME* items with *ǣ*^{2} have post-vocalic /r/ and show both early and late ME retraction to [a:] for whatever reason (East Saxon [æ:] > [a:], influence from ON in three highly frequent words, or lowering and backing before /r/). However, one should not lose sight of the fact that <e> is indeed the dominant orthographic representation for the reflexes of both *ǣ*'s in *LALME* sources.

Table 3.11 shows *LALME* spellings which might indicate raising of OE *ǣ*. However, as neither THERE nor FLESH has PDE /i:/, the vowel-shift status of these forms remains uncertain.

3.2.4 Discussion of material from additional sources

The texts edited by Hunt and Benskin (2001) have been localised linguistically to Ely and W Norfolk; the language therefore is Mercian and should have had OE [æ:] for *ǣ*^{1} and [e:] for *ǣ*^{2}. In the *First Corpus Compendium*, <a>/<ay> are attested for the stressed vocoid of ANY, and <e>/<ey> are found in FLESH (both with *ǣ*^{1}); <e> is reported in WERE, THERE, WHERE, and <a> and <e> in LET (all *ǣ*^{2}). ERE (*ǣ*^{1}) has <e> and <o>; the latter is consistent with the regional attestation of <o> (for OE *ǣ*) in both *LAEME* and *LALME*. In the *Second Corpus Compendium*, ANY appears with <a>, ERE with <o>, FLESH and NEVER with <e> (*ǣ*^{1}); WERE, THERE and LET (*ǣ*^{2}) have both <a> and <e>. The reflexes of *ǣ*^{1} and *ǣ*^{2} thus do not seem to be kept apart systematically, and <e> is of course non-committal regarding its phonetic correspondence(s).

Zachrisson concludes that since the reflex of eME *ē* is kept strictly apart from that of eME *ę̄*, and only the former is sometimes spelt <i(e)> in his sources (from London, Essex, and Norfolk), the value of the latter was [e:] in the sixteenth and early seventeenth centuries (1913: 68, 126, 150). The realisation [i:] is, however, in evidence (in the statements of the orthoepists) from the mid-sixteenth century (1913: 204); by the late seventeenth century, [i:] had been generally adopted (1913: 204, 223).

Dobson more conservatively believes [ɛ:] remained until the end of the seventeenth century, when it became [e:] in some speech (1968: 607), though it may have remained until the end of the eighteenth century (1968: 609). Still, 'during the whole of the sixteenth and seventeenth centuries there is evidence of [i:] pronunciations', indicating that there were (dialectal) co-variants [e:] and [i:], and the latter replaced the former (1968: 610). Dobson claims that this [i:] was not a sound-change at all, but went back to ME variants with close [e:], perhaps due to differences in Anglian and Saxon dialects (1968: 611–12), which seems somewhat far-fetched for all the reported cases.

3.3 Summary and conclusions

Firstly, the material suggests that OE *ǣ* raised to [ɛ:] in very early ME, and may have raised to [e:] in given areas, or in given words, at least in the mid-thirteenth century. Indeed, [i:] is in evidence in Worcestershire, Lincolnshire, and a source with mixed language (SW and NE Midlands) in the period 1250–1300. *SMED* also reports a few <i>/<y> from the North and the NE Midlands (West Riding of Yorkshire, Lincolnshire, and Huntingdonshire) as well as from Suffolk, Somerset, and Dorset. Not many later spellings indicate raising to [i:] – indeed, it is remarkable that none of Zachrisson's fifteenth-century primary sources has <i> for the reflexes of ME *ǣ*; his orthoepistical evidence, on the other hand, suggests raising to [i:] in the sixteenth century. The early <i> forms and their absence in lME and eModE indicate strongly that co-variants existed from relatively early ME and far into the eModE period; otherwise, it would be difficult to account for the fact that although most ME [ɛ:] words joined ranks with ME [e:] to give PDE /i:/, a few such words merged with the reflexes of ME *ai/ei* and [a:], producing PDE /eɪ/.

Secondly, the extracted material demonstrates that the two OE *ǣ*'s are not kept apart systematically at any time during the ME period. To be true, in the *LAEME* material from the W Midlands, there is a higher number of <a>/<æ>/<ea> for *ǣ*^{1} than for *ǣ*^{2}, which is as expected, but similar findings are conspicuously absent in the rest of the country; and in the E Midlands, the reverse is the case, especially for the period 1150–1250. This could be due to the fact that (a) *ǣ*^{2} retracted to [a:] in East Saxon, and (b) a high proportion of the spellings from the E Midlands are found in sources whose language has been entered in the East Saxon linguistic domain. There is little reason, however, to doubt the traditional wisdom that *ǣ*^{1} was OE [æ:] in all OE dialects, and that *ǣ*^{2} was [æ:] in Saxon dialects and [e:] elsewhere – the nature of the evidence is such that no hard and fast conclusions may be drawn. It should nevertheless be noted that <a>/<æ>/<ea> for *ǣ*^{2} is frequent enough in non-Saxon areas also to suggest that it may have corresponded to an open-mid rather than mid front vowel, that is, [ɛ:], even in Anglian.

With regard to the early raising of OE *ǣ* to [ɛ:], the arguments put forward by Lutz (2004) are of interest. Lutz argues that the OE quantitative distinction between vowels gave way, sometime during ME, to a new tense *vs.* lax distinction (2004: 213–14), which can be seen when spellings of (1) the original vowel and (2) the lengthened or shortened product (in lOE/eME) are compared. MEOSL demonstrates, Lutz claims, that the long–short distinction had been replaced by a tense-lax distinction: 'we have to assume a shift of aperture correspondences between short vowels and long vowels to have occurred at some time' in ME (2004: 213–14).

Such a shift of aperture correspondences may be due to '(a) lowering of the short vowels, (b) simultaneous raising of the long vowels and lowering of the short ones, (c) raising of the long vowels' (2004: 214). Traditional accounts have adhered to alternative (a), whereas Lutz states that a variant of alternative '(b) close to (c)' may capture facts better (2004: 215). Lutz's arguments are based on ME spelling evidence, which is 'notoriously unspecific' (2004: 215) regarding the quantity of vowels and the aperture distinction between the two front mid long vowels and the two back mid long vowels. Whereas the quantity of vowels has never been systematically reflected in spelling, the failure to distinguish, by orthographic means, the half-close vowels from the half-open ones 'arose in early Middle English [...] due to the raising of the two [OE] long open vowels /æ:/ and /ɑ:/' (2004: 216), which 'change of spelling in [eME] suggests a parallel raising development of the two most open long vowels' (2004: 216). However, the Roman alphabet did not provide the means by which to keep half-open vowels apart from half-close ones, which is why Anglo-Saxon scribes used <æ> to indicate a vowel whose quality lay between [e] and [a]. When the use of <æ> was discontinued, there were no distinct letters available to represent the half-open vowels; hence our difficulty in knowing the phonetic values of the reflexes of these vowels. The W Midland innovation <ea> for OE *ǣ* is interesting in this regard: the same thought process may have been at work here as that behind the use of the ligature/digraph <ae>/<æ> in OE – it is only the ordering of the two parts that is different. The abandonment of <æ> matters greatly in this discussion, but it is not treated at all by Lutz; nor is the use of futhorc letters or diacritics.

In Lutz's interpretation, OE had only one open short monophthong, variously pronounced [æ ɑ ɒ] and variously spelt <æ>, <a> and <a/o> respectively. ME, however, spells all of these as <a>, indicating a low central-to-back vowel (2004: 216–17); thus the allophonic variation of OE <a/æ> [a, æ] was lost in ME, in Lutz's opinion. Therefore, the open area of vowel space was sparsely inhabited, perhaps making the reflexes of OE /i, u, e, o/ (originally close and half-close) become more open (2004: 217), though this is a *non sequitur*. Lutz observes (note 17) that such a scenario also seems to be suggested by Luick (1914–40: §378) when he states that OE *e* went from 'mid-front-narrow' to 'mid-front-wide', and OE *o* went from 'mid-back-narrow' to 'mid-back-wide'. However, the terms 'narrow' and 'wide' are used to refer to the shape and quality of the tongue muscle, 'narrow' corresponding more to 'tense' than to 'close', and 'wide' corresponding more to 'lax' than to 'open'. Perhaps more to the point, ME scribes treat the reflexes of the OE open short vowel and open long vowels differently, as <a> and <e>/<o> respectively (Lutz 2004: 218). In Luick's terminology (1914–40: §361), the raising of OE *ǣ* involved a 'raising development from "low-front-wide" to "low-front-narrow"' (1914–40: §361). This implies, however, that only the *quality* of the tongue changed, from being lax to being tense, as 'wide' and 'narrow' do not usually refer to vowel height. Still, Lutz explicitly states that there was a simultaneous raising of the tongue (2004: 219), with concomitant natural rounding to [ɔ:].

With regard to the dating of this parallel raising, Lutz cites Luick (1914–40: §§361, 369), Schlemilch (1914: 16–21), and Jordan (1968: §§44,

47–8), who dated them to 'the eleventh century but pointed out that both <e>- and <o>-spellings are rare before the beginning of the twelfth century (but see Section 3.2.1). Their spelling evidence thus speaks for a parallel, simultaneous development of the two long open vowels' (2004: 219), which goes against the development suggested in the *Cambridge History of the English Language*, which assumes 'an asymmetrical stage of development, with OE /æ:/ changing to /ɛ:/ earlier than OE /ɑ:/ changing to /ɔ:/' (2004: 219).

Finally, the shift from 'syllable quantity to syllable cuts [...] which entails tenseness for vowels in smoothly cut syllables' could have caused the parallel raising of OE *ǣ* and *ā*, since '[p]honetically, tenseness is most difficult to sustain for open vowels.[8] Therefore, in the process of tensing, we should expect speakers of a stress-accent language to raise the most open vowels of such a system first' (2004: 220). Lutz calls this 'the First Push' or 'a prelude to the Great Vowel Shift' because – in a push chain (which is assumed) – the new raised vowels would have 'encroached upon the vowel space of close /e:/ and /o:/ and pushed them further up' (2004: 220), although spelling evidence for this is hard to come by. It is in MEOSL that the new aperture correspondence system is revealed, according to Lutz, where lengthened /ɪ/ results in [e:], etc. (2004: 221) – although it may be more correct to say that lengthened [ɪ] resulted in <e>, etc. And it was this new system of seven long tense vowels 'with four degrees of aperture which was subsequently raised further' in the 'GVS' (2004: 221).

However, if the 'GVS' was already under way during MEOSL or before it, as suggested by Stockwell (1985), many of Lutz' arguments lose their explanatory power, since it is the interplay between the raising of low tense vowels, MEOSL (and subsequent changes in vowel spellings), and the 'GVS' that is at the heart of her line of reasoning. Ritt's (1994) hypothesis concerning MEOSL and the 'GVS' also rests on the assumption that a tense-lax opposition arose in ME. Ritt's hypothesis will not be discussed further here, but in Section 4.1.

Liebl (2006) agrees with Lutz that the raising of the two eME open vowels /ɑ:/ and /æ:/ may have been roughly simultaneous and provided the 'first push', initiating the 'GVS'. If, however, the vocalisation of post-vocalic <g> in lOE is included in our account of long-vowel shifts, as Stockwell and Minkova (1988a, 1988b) argue it should, we are back to a 'drag-chain'. The vocalisation of <g> and its possible consequences are discussed in detail in Chapter 5.

Notes

1 Kitson (1998) finds Kristensson's account of WS *ǣ*^{2} vs. non-WS *ē* in *SMED3* too simplified, to the extent that Kristensson's demarcation of the two sounds does not indicate the 'divide between the settlement of the Angles and the Saxons in Old English times', but rather the 'smoothing out of earlier local distinctions once something like stable peace was established and people's speech no longer reflected in principle their personal continental ancestry but had come to conform to prevalent usage among their neighbours' (1998: 176).

2 Jordan (1968: §50) in fact claims that Essex, Hertfordshire, Bedfordshire, Huntingdonshire and part of Cambridgeshire had this *ā* for WS *ǣ*^{2}; see Section 2.1 for details.

3 For OE *ǣ*^{1} (<WGmc *ai+i*), the following items were counted: CLEAN aj., DEAL v., GLEAM n. and v., *hǣlend*, HEAL v., HEAT, HEATHEN aj. and n., LEAD v., TEACH, WHEAT. For OE *ǣ*^{2} (<WGmc *ā*), the following items were counted: GREEDY, LET, *rǣd* n., *rǣdan*, READ v., HAIR, LEECH 'physician', (*un*)*sǣlig*, SLEEP v. and n., SPEECH, STREET. For verbs, forms for the infinitive, imperative, indicative plural, and 1. singular present indicative were extracted.

4 Some items whose etymology is uncertain were left out, but these also have mostly <æ>, and a few <e>.

5 The 'assorted' items counted are CLEAN, DEAL V., GLEAM, GREED, HEAL, HEAT, HEATHEN, LEAN ('become lean'), REACH, READ, TEACH; OE *hǣlend*, *lǣnan*, *lǣtan*, *rǣd*, *rǣdan* (from both *ǣ* 's).

6 The *OED's* entry for HAIR states the following: **Forms:** α;. OE **hǽr**, **hér**, ME **hær**, ME **her**, ME–15 **heer**, ME–15 **heere**, **here**, (ME **herre**), 15 **hear(e**. β. ME **har**, **hare**, ME **hor**, ME **hore**, ME **haar(e**. γ;. ME–15 **heyr(e**, ME–16 **haire**, **hayre**, **heir(e**, 15– **hair**. **Etymology:** Common Germanic, Old English *hǽr*, *hér* = Old Frisian *hêr*, Old Saxon *hâr* (Middle Dutch *haer*, Dutch *haar*), Old High German *hâr*, (German *haar*), Old Norse *hár* (Swedish *hår*, Danish *haar*) < Germanic *hǣro^{m}*; not known in Gothic. The α; forms are native, < Old English, West Saxon *hǽr*, Anglian *hér*; the β forms are immed. from Old Norse *hár*, which gave in Middle English *hâr* in northern, and *hôr* in some north midland dialects. The later *heyr*, *heire*, *hayre*, *hair*, is not a normal repr. of Middle English *hêr*, *heer*, the modern English form of which would be (as in 16th cent.) *hear* or *here*; it seems to be partly a northern spelling, but mainly due to assimilation to haire n. The entry for THERE states the following: **Etymology:** Old English *þǽr*, *þár*, *þér*, cognate with Old Saxon *thâr*, Old Frisian *thêr*, *dêr*, Middle Low German *dār*, Middle Dutch *daer*, Dutch *daar*, Old High German *dâr* (Middle High German *dâr*, *dâ*, German *da*); compare also Gothic *þar*, Old Norse *þar* (Swedish, Danish *der*); all derivatives of the demonstrative stem *þa-*, pre-Germanic *to-* [...] Besides *þǽr*, etc., Old English had also a rare form *þāra*, probably an emphatic derivative, like Old High German *dāra*, *dāre*, and not cognate with Old High German *dara*, Middle High German *dare*, *dar*, 'thither'. In Middle English all the variants *þār*, *þǣr*, *þêr*, *þôr* appear also with final *-e*, perhaps taken from the adverbial *-e* in *inne*, *uppe*, *úte*, *fore*, etc. The later forms

thare and *there* may represent Middle English *þāre*, *þêre*, or the final *e* may merely indicate the long vowel.

7 No. 118 has three such forms in HAIR; 297 and 298 have <ai/ay> in HAIR, and no. 298 has two <ai/ay> in other words; no. 2 has <ei> once in CLEAN; no. 246 has <ei> twice; no. 295 has <ei> once; no. 278 has <æi> once; no. 296 has 8 <ai/ay> (in HEATHEN); no. 2002 has <ai/ay> once.

8 It may be argued here that if tenseness in open vowels is so hard to sustain, it would not have developed in the first place.

CHAPTER 4

The development of OE ē *and* ēo

4.1 Introduction

We learn from the handbooks that OE *ēo* monophthongised to front rounded [ø:] in all dialects in lOE. This [ø:] was unrounded to [e:] in the twelfth century in the North, the East, and the South Midlands; in certain dialects of the W Midlands, it remained until the late fourteenth century, when it unrounded there also. Late OE and ME forms like <horte>, <hurte>, and <huerte> OE *heorte* HEART are supposed to correspond to a front rounded [ø(:)] < *eo/ēo*. The reflex of OE *ēo* thus eventually fell in with the reflex of OE *ē* in ME. In Old Kentish, *ēo* was raised to *īo*, which in eME became *īe*; this *īe* in turn became a rising diphthong, which monophthongised to long close *ē* in the fourteenth century.[1] Hence, OE *ēo* > *ē* in all dialects, although later in Kentish and in the W Midlands than in the rest of the country. Therefore, spellings that indicate a front rounded vowel for OE *ēo* must be expected from the entire ME period, at least in texts written in the dialects of the W Midlands (Wright and Wright 1928: §§58–67; Luick 1914–40: §§259–64; Jordan 1968: §§66–7, 84–5; Campbell 1959: §§293–301, 329; Prins 1972: §§3.27–35; but see Gradon 1979).[2] OE *ēo* before *w* had a different development (Gradon 1979; Phillips 1997), and will not be treated here.

The reflex of OE *ē* was beginning to be raised to [i:] in the fourteenth century in some areas; this process had certainly begun in the early fifteenth century (Prins 1972: §4.7). Wright and Wright (1924: §71) and Ekwall (1975: §59) give a later date. In the 'Hymn to the Virgin', etymological *ē* is spelt <i>, corresponding to [i:] (Dobson 1968: §132). This /i:/ remains to the present day in RP and GA, but has been diphthongised to [ɪi] in some dialects, starting in the nineteenth century, and is reflected as [əi] in Cockney (Sivertsen 1960: 49; Wells 1982).

There is another source of ME *ē* than OE *ē* and *ēo*. MEOSL started in some dialects in the first part of the thirteenth century, earlier north of the Humber than south of it (Wright and Wright 1928: §§77–85; Luick 1914–40: §392). The traditional account states that the early stage affected the three non-close vowels *e o a*, and was more general in its operation; *i u* were affected half a century later (in East Anglia almost a century later), and not equally in all dialects. Contrary to Wright and Wright (1928: §84), it is often assumed that the products of MEOSL were articulatorily more open than the etymological short vowels that gave rise to them; an example is eME *ivel* > ME *ēvel* EVIL. That is, post-MEOSL spellings for OE *i* suggest that the lengthened product was [e:] rather than [i:]; the further development of the lengthened vowel suggests the same.[3] Stockwell, however, has argued that if the 'GVS' was early, etymological *ē* had reached [i:] by the time MEOSL set in (Stockwell 1960, 1972, 1978, 1985). Therefore, when etymological short *i* was lengthened, it did not correspond in quality to etymological *ī*, which had diphthongised, but rather to ME *ē* > [i:]. In this interpretation, the whole problem of putative raising of half-close vowels when shortened (e.g. eME *sēk* > ME *sick* SICK) and lowering of short close vowels when lengthened (e.g. eME *ivel* > ME *ēvel* EVIL) is a pseudo-problem: they are related processes, and they are easily and logically accounted for under the early vowel-shift hypothesis (Stockwell 1985: 310–11).

Ritt (1994), partly in response to Minkova (1982, 1985), argues that (1) lengthening of short vowels before homorganic voiced consonant clusters, (2) shortening of long vowels before voiceless consonant clusters (SHOCC), (3) MEOSL, and (4) trisyllabic vowel shortening (TRISH) are all products of one tendency, that is, eME quantity adjustment. This quantity adjustment tendency, typical of languages with isochronous stress, is found to have depended on a number of supra-segmental and segmental variables, including syllable weight, the weight of the foot, the quality of the affected vowel, and the quality of the consonant(s) coming after it.[4] The 'ultimate' syllable weight is found to be the target of this quantity adjustment, and the (in)stability of the second syllable[5] to have been decisive for its operation. Ritt's theory is relevant here in that it gives an account of the apparent lowering of short vowels in MEOSL, that is, that MEOSL seems not only to entail lengthening, but also lowering.

This fact may be accounted for in three ways (1994: 77; cf. Lutz 2004): (1) either MEOSL induced simultaneous lengthening and lowering; or (2) there were two separate changes, namely, lengthening and lowering; or (3) MEOSL only caused lengthening, but the long vowels were already raising, and so the lengthened product merged with the raised (but etymologically lower) long vowel. Alternative (3) is Stockwell's hypothesis (1985). However, there is nothing to suggest, in Ritt's view, that the long vowels were already raising when MEOSL took place; besides, MEOSL was triggered by the prosodic factors listed earlier. Therefore, since lowering of vowels cannot be directly linked to suprasegmental features, the 'lengthening and lowering' hypothesis is not supported by the material (1994: 78). However, 'an explanation of the mergers offers itself that depends neither on the assumption that the Great Vowel Shift started 250 years earlier than has ever before been assumed nor on the rather *ad hoc* introduction of a lowering process' (1994: 78–9). This explanation rests on the assumption that a 'tense-lax distinction had come to be introduced into the phonology of Middle English in such a way that all short vowels were systematically laxer than their long counterparts and long vowels tenser than their lax [i.e. short] counterparts' (1994: 79). Ritt formulates a rule which made all ME long vowels tense, but does not give an explanation for the rise of the tense-lax opposition.[6] Tense vowels are more peripheral in the vowel space: the tongue is raised and pushed further forward for [e:] than for [e]. Since the inputs to MEOSL were short/lax vowels, the output was probably lax as well. Thus, MEOSL of [ɪ] produced [ɪ:]. Further (1992),

> Therefore, a long /ɪ:/, for example, may easily have been interpreted as going back to a long vowel that was tensed rather than a short vowel that was lengthened. The long vowel that could have been the input of a tensing rule whose output was /ɪ:/ was a close /e:/. And this is exactly what lengthened /ɪ/ came to be re-interpreted as.

The last sentence contains a circular conclusion, for it is known *a priori* that the MEOSL output of *i* merged with etymological *ē* – indeed, it is this fact that made Ritt formulate the tensing rule in the first place. The rest of Ritt's argument, however, is sound. The difference between Stockwell's and Ritt's accounts is that 'Stockwell does not make the distinction between synchronic processes and their historical implementation' (1994: 80), which is an important distinction. Although the vowel-shift seems to have started much earlier than traditional accounts allow, the spelling evidence does not suggest that it was earlier than MEOSL; Ritt's hypothesis therefore squares better with the available evidence than Stockwell's theory.[7]

The important demarcation between WS *ǣ*^{2} and non-Saxon *ē* (< WGmc *ā*) was established in Chapter 3: *ē* was found in Anglian and Kentish, and *ǣ* in Saxon (Kristensson 1967: 56).[8] Thus, ME <i>/<y> for WS *ǣ*^{2} in texts now recognised as from Anglian areas or Kent may be used as evidence of the raising of *ē*.

For the sake of convenience, the reflexes of OE *ē*, OE *ēo*, and the MEOSL product of eME *i* will all be referred to as 'eME *ē*'. This chapter examines ME material for eME *ē*, with a view to determining the course of change for OE *ē(o)*, and to seeing whether irregular ME spellings may be taken to indicate early vowel shift of eME *ē* to [iː].

4.2 Discussion

4.2.1 Discussion of LAEME *material*

Old English ē

The material shows some irregular <æi>, <i>/<ii>, <y(e)>, and quite a few <ei>/<ey>, and <ie>; <ei>, and especially <ie> are the most frequent irregular spellings. It is difficult to interpret <ei>, but <i(e)> and <y(e)> seem to indicate raising of ME *ẹ̄* to [iː]. However, <ie>/<ye> are also known as AN spellings for [eː], which is reason for setting very early such spellings aside for the moment, as indeterminate evidence for raising. Innovative spellings which may indicate vowel shift are discussed in the following; it should be borne in mind that the forms extracted here and in subsequent chapters are irregular and, for the most part, occasional – they are therefore not statistically significant.

Table 4.10 at the end of this chapter contains all irregular spellings for eME *ē* in *LAEME*, even those that are questionable as evidence of vowel shift: readers may arrive at their own conclusions. Forms with <ie>/<ye> appear as indicated in Table 4.1 (for the recorded forms, see Table 4.10; forms whose vowel-shift status is uncertain are preceded by a question mark; PDE lexemes are given in small capitals; OE etyma are italicised, as is grammatical information).

Since <ie> in the earliest texts from Essex (nos. 4, 1200, 64, 65), Suffolk (no. 1300), and Kent (no. 8) may be AN spellings for [eː], the source texts are preceded by a question mark in the table. However, Gradon assesses various explanations put forward to account for Kentish <ie>/<ye> for etymological *ē*; these explanations range from seeing <ie>/<ye> as mere spelling-devices, to suggesting that they indicate sound change. In Gradon's view, 'it is likely that the spellings such as *hyer* represent a sporadic glide development' (1979: 27); the same is implied by <uo>/<wo> for etymological *ō* (cf. Chapter 6, Section 6.2.2). Gradon concludes that there is 'no doubt that the language of the *Ayenbite* shows both palatal and labial glides before the vowels *ē* and *ō*' (1979: 29). The adduced <ie>/<ye> for *ē* in *LAEME* sources from Kent (nos. 8 and 142) might

Table 4.1 *Incidence of <ie>/<ye> for eME* ē *(< OE* ē *and* ēo*)* (LAEME)

County	No.	Date
Essex	?4, 1200	1150–99
	?64, 65	1200–24
Suffolk	?1300	1150–99
Oxfordshire	?232	1175–1224
	1600	1275–1324
Sussex	?67	1200–49
Worcestershire	?5	*c.* 1200
	?6	1200–49
	245	1225–49
	277	1250–74
Kent	?8	1200–49
	142	1275–99
Wiltshire	280	1250–74
Cambridgeshire	137	1275–99
Gloucestershire	161, 2002	1275–99
Norfolk	1400	1275–99
	155	1300–24
Lincolnshire	159	*c.* 1300
Unlocalised	233	1275–99

therefore indicate the development of a palatal glide before *ē*. It is still possible that the glide development involved the raising of the first mora of [ee] to [ie], in which case it is difficult to distinguish between this process and early vowel-raising in Kent. Dobson (1968: 657, Note 2) thinks spellings like <clier>, <clyer> and <clyre> for CLEAR in the *Ayenbite* suggest raising of ME *ē* to [i:]. If <ie> in sources from the mid-thirteenth century onwards are indeed indicative of vowel shift, then parts of the W Midlands (Oxfordshire, Worcestershire, Gloucestershire, and Wiltshire), parts of the NE Midlands (Cambridgeshire, Norfolk, and Lincolnshire), and Kent stand out as loci of change.

The following discussion is limited to forms with <i>/<y> (Table 4.2), since <ie>/<ye> have already been dealt with. A single <ii> in HE appears in Wiltshire (no. 280). Quite a few <i>/<y> are recorded, first in Hampshire and parts of the W Midlands (Worcestershire, Shropshire, Wiltshire, and Gloucestershire), the E Midlands (Essex, Cambridgeshire, Norfolk, and Lincolnshire), and Kent. The (S)W Midlands, the South-West, and the E Midlands thus seem to have undergone early vowel shift of eME *ē*, along with Kent. Similar conclusions were reached from the <ie>/<ye> spellings.[9] It thus appears that the vowel shift started in different areas of the country at about the same time.

Table 4.2 *Incidence of <i>/<y>, and late <ie>/<ye> for eME* ē *(< OE* ē*)* (LAEME)

County	No.	Date	Spellings
Hampshire	143	1175–99	<hi> HE
Worcestershire	2000	c. 1200	<hi> HE
			<icwime> CWĒME
	2001	c. 1200	<g[i]kisce> GREEK
	1900	1200–49	<grigcis> GREEK
	277	1250–74	<fiede> FĒGAN *pt.*
			<gric-> GREEK
	278	1250–74	<hir> HERE
	2	1275–99	?<mi> ME
			<hire> HERE
			<fliʒ> FLEE *imp.*
			<hi> HE
Essex	64	1200–24	<sliep> SLEEP *pt.*
	65	1200–24	<ʒesiʒen> SEE *ppl.*
Kent	8	1200–49	<hi> HE
			<si> SĒ
	142	1275–99	<si> SE
			<i-bye> BE *ppl.*
			<hie/hye> YE
Shropshire	260	1200–24	<liðerede> LĒÞRAN
Wiltshire	280	1250–74	<bieres> BĒRE
			<grickes> GREEK
			<hi/hii> HE
Gloucestershire	161	1275–99	<hir/hier*e*> HERE
	229	1275–99	<hire> HERE
	2002	1275–99	<drie> DRĒGE
Cambridgeshire	137	1275–99	<hier> HERE
Norfolk	1700	1284–89	<hire> HERE
Lincolnshire	159	c. 1300	<suyt/suythe> SWEET
			<syen> SEE *ppl.*
Oxfordshire	1600	1275–1324	<i-fielde> FEEL *pt.*
			<fier> FĒRE
			<pier> PEER
			<quiene> QUEEN
Unlocalised	123	1240–50	<liðerede> LĒÞRAN

Forms with <ei>/<ey> (Table 4.3) are difficult to assess, but should nonetheless be included. They may indicate a sound somewhere in-between [i:] and [e:], or testify to the raising of the second mora of the etymological long monophthong; ditto the form <fæit> FEET, which appears in Worcestershire (no. 278, 1250–74). Kristensson in fact interprets similar *SMED* spellings as indicative of vowel shift, cf. Section 4.2.2.[10]

Table 4.3 *Incidence of <ei>/<ey> for eME* ē *(< OE* ē *and* ēo*)* (LAEME)

County	No.	Date	Spellings
Worcestershire	2000	*c.* 1200	<greite> GREET
	1900	1200–49	<forseiȝen-> FORESEEN
	245	1225–49	<iseien> see *ppl.*
			<iseie> see *1.sg.pt.sj.*
	3	1275–99	?<breist> BREED
Essex	65	1200–24	<beiete> BĒTAN
West Riding, Yks	231	1250–74	?<leise/leyse> LĒSAN
Herefordshire	246	1275–99	<feid/feit> FEET
			<bein> BE *inf.*
			<beit> BĒTAN
			<heir(e)> HERE
			<teit> TEETH
			<seine> SEE *inf.*
			<þeif> THIEF
	1100	1275–99	<aweydeþ> AWĒDAN
Gloucestershire	2002	1275–99	<i-seien> SEE *pl.ps.sj.*
			<i-seiene> SEEN *ppl.*
Unlocalised	179	1275–99	<leys-> LĒSAN
Lincolnshire	182	c. 1300	<leyse> LĒSAN
			<steide> STEAD
Unlocalised	174	c. 1300	<vn-seiþe> SEE *ppl.*
Ely	282	1275–1324	<seyn> SEE *ppl.*

In summary, the aberrant spellings for OE *ē* start appearing in the second half of the twelfth century, and occur throughout the period covered by *LAEME*. They are recorded first in Hampshire, Kent, the E Midlands, and the W Midlands. Although the early <ie> forms may be AN spellings for [e:], such forms from the later period may be adduced as evidence for the early vowel-shift hypothesis.

Old English ēo

Forms with <ei>/<ey> appear in Worcestershire (nos. 245 and 1900), in Gloucestershire (no. 2002), in Herefordshire (no. 246), in Ely (no. 282), and in an unlocalised text (no. 174). Forms with <i>/<y> occur as indicated in Table 4.4, and those with <ie> as shown in Table 4.5.

The lexemes SEE and WRĒON appear several times, and so may have been leaders in the raising of eME *ē*.[11] Sources from Suffolk, Essex, and Kent show <i>/<y> at an early date, and so do source texts from Lancashire, Cheshire, Shropshire, Worcestershire, Herefordshire, and Wiltshire. That is, the entire western and south-eastern regions likely were loci of change.

Table 4.4 *Incidence of <i>/<y> for OE* ēo (LAEME)

County	No.	Date	Spellings
Suffolk	1300	1150–99	<-tigi(n)g> TĒON *vn.*
Essex	64	1200–24	<life> LĒOF
	65	1200–24	<cnyle> KNEEL
Lancashire	16	1200–24	<lires> HLĒOR
Shropshire	261	1200–24	<bi-sih> BESEE *imp.*
	1000	1200–24	<bisih> BESEE *imp.*
	275	1200–49	<wrihen> WRĒON *inf.*
Kent	8	1200–49	<bi> BE *inf.*
	142	1275–99	<bi> BE *inf.*
Worcestershire	1900	1200–49	<twinunge> TWĒONIAN
	1800	1225–49	<vnwrih> WRĒON *imp.*
Cheshire	122	1240–50	<wrihe> WRĒON *inf.*
Unlocalised	121	1240–50	<bisih> BESEE *imp.*
Wiltshire	263	1275–99	<by-sy> BESEE *imp.*
Herefordshire	1100	1275–99	<bi-syh> BESEE *imp.*
Unlocalised	233	1275–99	<si> see *1.sg.ps.*
Unlocalised	239	1275–99	<bi-sih> BESEE *imp.*

Table 4.5 *Incidence of <ie> for OE* ēo (LAEME)

County	No.	Date	Spellings
Essex	4	1150–99	*see* table 4.10
	1200	1150–99	
	64	1200–24	
	65	1200–24	
Suffolk	1300	1150–99	*see* table 4.10
Kent	8	1200–49	*see* table 4.10
	142	1275–99	
Worcestershire	5	c. 1200	<bi-flien> BEFLĒON
	6	1200–49	<lief> LĒOF
	245	1225–49	<wrien> WRĒON *inf.*
Norfolk	1400	1275–99	<frie> FREE *3.sg.sj.*
	155	1300–24	<diep> DEEP
Unlocalised	233	1275–99	<trie> TREE

Again, the <ie> in the early sources from Essex, Suffolk, and Kent may be AN spellings for [eː].[12] However, as indicated in the discussion of Kentish <ie>/<ye> for etymological *ē*, Gradon suggests that such spellings in Middle Kentish sources imply a palatal glide before *ē* (Gradon 1979: 29). With respect to OK *īo*/*ēo*, she also examines the development of rising diphthongs from falling diphthongs in Middle Kentish. The traditional view since Luick is that OK did not have *ēo*, but that *ēo* had merged with *īo*. This assumption is unnecessary, since the Kentish 'text which shows least evidence of contamination, the Kentish Glosses, is the text which shows most examples of the graph *eo* for the long diphthong' (1979: 30). Besides, the normal reflex of *ēo* in Kentish place-names is *e*.[13] Gradon therefore proposes the following line of development (1979: 34).

The OK diphthong *ēo/īo*

(i) merged with /e:/
(ii) then developed to a rising diphthong [i̯e:]
(iii) merged with /i:/ in final position (and possibly in other cases)
(iv) developed to [ɛu] before *w*

It is at least possible that some of the <ie> in *LAEME* sources from Kent correspond to rising diphthongs. Later <ie>/<ye> for *ē* and *ēo* in sources from Kent are discussed in Section 4.2.2. Forms with <y> appear in Essex, Herefordshire, and in Wiltshire; <ye> occurs in Kent and Lincolnshire; cf. Table 4.10.

If these spellings testify to the raising of ME *ẹ̄*, the change seems to have started in Essex, Suffolk, Norfolk, and Kent, and independently in the western area, in Worcestershire, Herefordshire, Shropshire, Cheshire, and Lancashire.

4.2.2 *Discussion of* SMED *material*

Old English ē

Tables 4.6 and 4.7 indicate irregular spellings in *SMED*.

Kristensson does not rule out vowel-raising in the two irregular spellings for OE *brǣc* (Somerset; Kristensson 2001: 44), in <Ridelyngton> (Dorset), in <Minskip> (West Riding of Yorkshire), but seems to believe that raising was due to the following /n/ or /tʃ/. A postulated development /e:/ > /e/ > /i/ is believed to be behind the forms <Silly> OE *sǣlig/sēlig* (Huntingdonshire), <Ridliswrth> (Norfolk), and <Silyman> (Lincolnshire; Kristensson 1995: 31, 42; 1967: 57; cf. Jordan 1968: §34.1). No dates are given for this change, and the development could also have been (/æ:/ >) /e:/ > /i:/ > /i/; that is, 'Great Vowel Shift' and later shortening of the vowel in a polysyllabic word.

There are a few <i>/<y> for OE *ē* in the material from the North, W Midlands, E Midlands, and South. Some of these (<Ruyeton>, <Firyngford>, <Fyringford>, <Grynton(')>) are explained as due to the

Table 4.6 *Incidence of <i>/<y> etc. for WS* ǣ, *Anglian* ē (SMED)

County	Date	Spellings
Dorset	1327	?<Ridelyngton> OE **Rǣda*, **Rēda*
Huntingdonshire	1327	<Silly> SILLY
Lincolnshire	1327	<Silyman> SILLY
Somerset	1333	<Breich>, <Brych> OE *brǣc, brēc*
West Riding of Yorkshire	1327	<Minskip> OE *(ge)mǣnscipe*
	1346	<Minskip> OE *(ge)mǣnscipe*

Table 4.7 *Incidence of <i>/<y> etc. for OE* ē (SMED)

County	Date	Spellings
Bedfordshire	1332	<Sherryue> SHERIFF
Lincolnshire	1327	<Schirrif'>, <Shirif'> SHERIFF
		<Swyt'> SWEET
	1332	<Schirif'>, <Schiryf'>, <Shirryf'> SHERIFF
Norfolk	1327	<Ridliswrth> *OE* HRĒÞEL
North Riding of Yorkshire	1301	<Grynton(')> GREEN
	1332	<Grynton(')> GREEN
Nottinghamshire	1327	<Ryueton> REEVE
Oxfordshire	1316	<Fyringford> OE **Fēringas*
	1327	<Firyngford> OE **Fēringas*
		<Scherryue> SHERIFF
Somerset	1327	<Swyte> SWEET
Warwickshire	1332	<Swyte> SWEET

development /eː/ (> /e/) > /i/ (1987: 59; 1967: 62). With respect to the Lincolnshire forms for SHERIFF, Kristensson claims that they may have more than one explanation. 'Influence from ME *bailif(f)* may have played a part […], or *ē* may have been shortened in unstressed position and subsequently raised' (1967: 61); the same explanations presumably hold for similar forms in Bedfordshire and Oxfordshire.

The Lincolnshire form <Swyt> SWEET is 'isolated and is certainly not related to the great vowel-shift' (1967: 62), though one wonders why it could not be. A similar form <Swyte> appears in Warwickshire 1332 (Kristensson 1987). <Swyte> appears in the South also (Somerset). By the time Kristensson published *SMED4* (2001), he had obviously changed his mind with regard to such spellings, for he asserts that this form 'illustrates the raising of OE /eː/ to /iː/' (Kristensson 2001: 57). There are also numerous <ei>/<ey> forms for OE *ē* in the south. These appear for OE

KEEN, GREEN, REEVE, STEED, SWEET, and OE *sēfte* 'soft', in Hampshire (with the highest number of forms), Berkshire, Dorset, Sussex, Somerset, and Wiltshire. Since OE *ō* is very frequently spelt <ou>/<ow>, even <u>, in the same area (i.e. in Dorset, Hampshire, Wiltshire, Berkshire, Sussex, and Somerset), Kristensson draws the conclusion that although the proportion of <ei>/<ey> forms for OE *ē* is lower than that of <ou>/<ow> for OE *ō*, the fact that these irregular spellings appear in exactly the same area cannot be accidental. The view that <ei>/<ey> could denote /e:/ is discarded on the grounds that such spellings have been 'safely attested only in the North' (Kristensson 2001: 79).[14] Thus, 'seeing that <ey/ei> could stand for /i:/ I think that the above spellings denote /i:/, i.e. that ME /e:/ had been, or was being raised to /i:/' (2001: 79). This view is corroborated by the forms <Brych> and <Swyte> from Somerset.

Old English ēo

It may be recalled that OE *ēo* is supposed to have monophthongised to something like a front rounded [ø:] in the eleventh century, and to have been unrounded to [e:] in the North and the E Midlands in the twelfth century. For the North, the *SMED1* material generally corroborates the postulated develoment. Kristensson quotes Moore, Meech and Whitehall (1935), who stated that it would seem logical that the boundary for the retention of OE *y/ȳ* would coincide with that of [ø(:)] from OE *eo/ēo*. He finds however that the *SMED* material does not support their theory, as a number of <e> in Lancashire suggest unrounding there also, even south of the Ribble (Kristensson 1967: 181).[15] All of the North therefore appears to be a solid *e*-area, although there is a sprinkling of <u> or <o> in Lincolnshire,[16] the West Riding of Yorkshire,[17] and Northumberland.[18]

The W Midland counties are supposed to have retained [ø(:)] from OE *ēo* until the fourteenth or fifteenth centuries. Kristensson concludes in *SMED2* that in the northern parts of the W Midlands, that is, in Cheshire, Derbyshire, Leicestershire, Nottinghamshire, Shropshire, Staffordshire, Warwickshire, and probably Worcestershire, [ø] from OE *eo* had been unrounded, and was [e] in the early fourteenth century (Kristensson 1987: 127). Evidence for Herefordshire is lacking; for Gloucestershire and Oxfordshire, the case is not straightforward, since <eo>, <u> and <e> co-vary. Parts of both Gloucestershire and Oxfordshire were Saxon areas; Kristensson therefore thinks it probable that these two counties still had rounded [ø] in the early fourteenth century, although this is a *non sequitur*: it is not inconceivable that 'Saxon' admitted internal variation.[19] The case may, however, be different for the long vowel: the reflexes of OE *ēo* are usually spelt <e(e)>, but there are some <eo>, <eu>, <ue>, <u>, <uy> in Staffordshire, Shropshire, Herefordshire, Worcestershire, Warwickshire, Gloucestershire, and Oxfordshire. Since there are no <eo> spellings for OE *ēo* in Derbyshire, Nottinghamshire, and Leicestershire, it is 'almost certain that OE *ēo* had become /e:/ in these counties. The material for Ch[eshire] is too scanty for any conclusions to be drawn' (Kristensson 1987: 158).

Kristensson therefore draws the conclusion that [ø:] from *ēo* was being unrounded to [e:] in the beginning of the fourteenth century, in Oxfordshire, Gloucestershire, Warwickshire, Worcestershire, Herefordshire, Shropshire, and Staffordshire, but that [ø:] and [e:] continued to be used side by side, at least in given words or given areas or by given speakers (1987: 159). Map 13 in *SMED2* draws the boundary between retained [ø:] and [e:] across the northern parts of Shropshire and Staffordshire, which seems somewhat arbitrary. Material from the south-west and south may resolve the issue (see the following text). The relevance of this lengthy account is that if OE *ēo* had unrounded to [e:] in the area in question, forms with <i>/<y> may indicate vowel shift.

In *SMED3*, providing material from the E Midlands, Kristensson finds no evidence that runs counter to the postulated development that [ø:] here was unrounded early (Kristensson 1995: 122).

However, in Kent, the reflex of OE *ēo* > *īo* > *īe* quite early on, but see Gradon's conclusions (Section 4.2.1). Ek (1972) examines the development of OE *ēo* (and OE *ȳ*) in south-eastern ME, making use of onomastic material that partly overlaps with the *SMED* material. He concludes that not only Kentish, but also the dialects of London, Middlesex, Essex, Hertfordshire, and Cambridgeshire originally shared in the same development; Ek therefore claims that all of these counties had *īe* < OE *ēo c.* 1300 (1972: 122).

Kristensson maintains that the *SMED* material refutes Ek's claim: 'After all, Ek's investigation yielded only 10,6% [*sic*] *i*-forms (280 *i*-forms as against 2,375 *e*-forms), and many of the *i*-forms are questionable' (Kristensson 1995: 123, n.92). 10.6% is the figure for non-Kentish areas for the period 1100–1500, whereas the corresponding figure for Kent is 15.7% (Ek 1972: 94). In fact, Ek admits that <i> for OE *ēo* was replaced by <e> 'in the course of the ME period' (1972: 95), since there are more <i> in the period 1100–1300 both in Kent and counties other than Kent (which are treated together) than in the period 1300–1500. For Kent, the proportion for 1100–1300 is 21.7%, against 7% for 1300–1500; for the other counties, the percentage for 1100–1300 is 18%, against 5.5% for 1300–1500. Still, Ek may be right that some of the areas surrounding Kent also saw the development OE *ēo* > *īo* > *īe*, as it would be difficult to account for the 18% <i>-forms in the period 1100–1300 otherwise. However, Kristensson's material seems to indicate just as clearly that *īe* was recessive and its domain was considerably smaller by *c.* 1300 than Ek suggests. The same conclusion is reached by Martín, who examines Kentish place-names in ME documents. She concludes that (2002: 64):

> Our results do coincide with Ek's table, and therefore also contradict in part his own conclusion, since in our analysis [...] the *e*-variants predominate over the *i*-variants. The only coincidence here lies in the fact that the *i*-variant appears with a higher frequency in the 12th c. than in the 14th c., a fact that is directly connected with the peculiar development observed for the place-name forms compounded by OE *neowe*.

The fact that NEW appears as *nīwe* as well as *nēowe* in OE seems to have been overlooked. Accordingly, the proportion of <i> variants may be even lower than is claimed. The validity of the postulated change PrOE *ēo* > OK *īo* is therefore in question. What seems certain is (a) that <i>/<y> for WS *ēo*, whether in the form of digraphs or not, are more common in Kent than in other dialects, even from lOE; and (b) that such spellings reach a climax in the twelfth (or possibly thirteenth) century, after which they become less frequent. It remains an open question whether this implies that OK always had realisational variants for the sound corresponding to WS *ēo*, some with a close and some with a half-close first element, and that the variants with a half-close first element gradually ousted the others in the course of the ME period. If so, influence from the surrounding *ēo* area may have played a role.

In parts of the South, [ø:] is supposed to have been retained, in other parts it unrounded to [e:], and in Kent, the development was different (cf. the account earlier). Kristensson concludes from the *SMED5* material that the rounded reflex of OE *ēo* had probably unrounded to [e:] in all of the South in the early fourteenth century. However, as <u> or <eo>/<eu>/<oe> appear sporadically in all counties except Kent and Sussex, he thinks a rounded reflex lingered on (2002: 230). Interestingly, the minor variants indicating a rounded reflex pattern in an interesting way: <u> appears in Devon, W Somerset, Hampshire, W Surrey, Berkshire, Wiltshire, Oxfordshire, and Warwickshire, whereas <eo>/<eu> and <oe> are found in the intervening area comprising Dorset, Wiltshire, Gloucestershire, Worcestershire, and Shropshire; there are few relevant forms attested in Herefordshire and Cheshire (Kristensson 1987: Map 13; Kristensson

Table 4.8 *Incidence of <i>/<y> etc. for OE* ēo (SMED)

County	Date	Spellings
Bedfordshire	1309	<Flittewyk>, <Flytt'>, <Flyttewyk> OE FLĒOT
	1332	<Flitwyk> OE FLĒOT
Cambridgeshire	1330	<Gritton> OE GRĒOT
Essex	1327	<Lief> OE LĒOF
Hampshire	1327	<Chil(e)bolton>, <Chylebolton> OE CĒOL(A)
Kent	1327	<Try> TREE
	1332	<Lyef> OE LĒOF
Lincolnshire	1327	?<Dyrington> DEER
	1332	?<Dirington> DEER
Norfolk	1332	<Lyf'> OE LĒOF
North Riding of Yorkshire	1301	<Libreston> OE *Lēodbeorht*
Somerset	1327	<Lif>, <Lyf> OE LĒOF
	1333	<Lyf> OE LĒOF
Suffolk	1327	<Lyf> OE LĒOF
Surrey	1332	<Rydebrok'> REED
Warwickshire	1332	?<Lywyng> OE *Lēofing, Lȳfing*
Worcestershire	1327	<Dyring'> DEER <Ridmaleye>, <Ridmarleye> REED
	1332	<Dyring'> DEER <Rydmerley> REED

2002: Maps 19 and 20). Kristensson therefore believes a minor variant [ø:] remained, spelt <eo>/<eu>, <oe>, in parts of the W Midlands and South, whereas [ø:] > [y:], spelt <u>, in the South-West and parts of the South.[20]

Kristensson denies that the Kentish spellings <ie>/ye> indicate a diphthong or a glide, and agrees with Wyld (1927) that they 'are mainly spelling devices for monophthongs' and are 'just AN spellings for /e:/' (Kristensson 2002: 231); Gradon (1979) concludes otherwise (cf. Section 4.2.1).

Potential vowel-shift spellings in *SMED* are indicated in Table 4.8.[21]

Many of these may be explained as due to variant OE forms, but the northern form with <i> for OE *ēo*, <Libreston> (North Riding of Yorkshire) may indicate vowel-shift; Kristensson assumes shortening before raising to *i* (Kristensson 1967: 176), though it could have been the other way round; shortening is predictable in a trisyllabic (originally quadrisyllabic) compound.[22] Regarding the W Midlands forms with REED (Worcestershire, both Rolls), Kristensson maintains that they are due to shortening of ME [e:], not of [ø:] (Kristensson 1987: 158), which may be the case. But again, early raising of ME /e:/ may have taken place before shortening occurred. The forms with DEER and OE *Lēofing/Lȳfing*, in

Worcestershsire and Warwickshire, 'are reflexes of WSax forms with OE *īe*, later *ī, ȳ* ' (Kristensson 1987: 162). This may be the case, at least for the forms appearing in Worcestershire, but it seems less certain for the spellings found in Warwickshire. They could also be Anglian, given the geographical situation of both counties. Kristensson's compartmentalised view of 'WS', 'Saxon', 'Anglian', etc. as sharply bounded entities is regrettable, as it entails that what is characteristic in one is held to be exclusively its property, so that if it is found in another, it must have been artificially imported.

Continuing the discussion of the E Midlands forms regarding the general development of OE *ēo*, the irregular <i>/<y> and <ie> which do appear can hardly be said to be just continuations of a putative south-eastern change OE *ēo* > *īo* > *īe*, as they appear in Norfolk, Suffolk, and Bedfordshire. However, there are a very few <i(e)> in Cambridgeshire and Essex also, and the status of these remains more uncertain. The Bedfordshire forms with OE *flēot* may indicate either shortening (with prior raising) or vowel-shift raising of eME *ē* (< OE *ēo*). Kristensson invokes various explanations to account for the <i>/<y>: AN spellings habits, or immigrants 'from the Kentish dialect area' (1995: 122), or unattested forms with OE *īe* (1995: 123). Kristensson's method of postulating unattested OE forms seems a strange way of disproving a postulated vowel change. It is at least possible that the <i> and <y> spellings indicate early vowel shift of [eː(ə)] to [iː], and subsequent shortening to [i].

In his discussion of the Southern material, Kristensson states that the Hampshire forms with <Chil–> and <Chyl–> (OE *cēol* 'ship'), and <Rydebrok> (with REED) in Surrey, indicate [eː] > [i] (Kristensson 2002: 231). He claims that the same could be true of <Lif>, <Lyf>, <Lyef> OE *lēof*, but this seems far less certain, given that <i> and <y> here appear in monosyllabic names. The form <Try> TREE in Kent makes Kristensson conclude that although OE *ēo* was [eː] in Kent at the time, this vowel could raise to [iː] word-finally (2002: 231), which is in agreement with Gradon's claims (1979: 34).

4.2.3 Discussion of LALME *material*

Old English ē *and ME* ē *from MEOSL*

The *LALME* material extracted shows <ei>, <ey>, <i>, <ie>, <ij>, <y>, <ye> for eME *ē/ēo*.

For BEEN, <ey> for the vowel is attested in the North (Durham, the East and West Ridings of Yorkshire, and Westmoreland), and in the East

Midlands (Leicestershire and Lincolnshire). Forms with <ie> are recorded in sources categorised as 'NME', and localised sources from the North (Cheshire, Lancashire, Durham, and the West Riding of Yorkshire), as well as from the NE Midlands (Cambridgeshire and Lincolnshire); <ye> occurs in Lancashire; <y> appears in Cheshire, Lancashire, the West Riding of Yorkshire, Leicestershire, Norfolk, Rutland, and Staffordshire. In other words, potential vowel-shift spellings cluster in the North and in the NE Midlands.[23]

For the preterit of LET (< OE *lēt*, *lēton*), there is a single <liet> from Oxfordshire. For SHE, there are a few <i>, <ij>, <y>, and <ye> for the vowel. The form <hi> appears in Essex and Kent; <hij> is recorded in Middlesex; <hy> is found in Gloucestershire, Herefordshire, Kent, and Sussex; <hye> is attested in Kent and Middlesex; <i–> appears in Gloucestershire. For HE, <hy> is found in Wiltshire (LP 5371). These forms may all indicate raising of [e:]. For the past participle of SEE, there is one <syn> from Norfolk. For SEEK, <sike> occurs in Warwickshire, and <–syche> in the West Riding of Yorkshire. For THEE, <þi> is found once in a source from Wiltshire. For the pronoun YE (OE *gē*), <ie> for the vowel is found in Yorkshire sources and texts from the West Riding of Yorkshire. It is difficult to know whether <i> is just a glide after the palatal semi-vowel or indicates raising.

The Appendix of Southern Forms has some <i>/<y>, as well as <ie>/<ye> and <ei>/<ey>, for the reflexes of OE *ē* and *ēo*; individual words are unspecified in the LPs. Forms with <i>/<y> for the vowel of HE appear in Herefordshire (LP 7400) and Hampshire (LP 5511); for the vowel of THE in Kent (LP 6050); for the vowel of HERE in Devon, Essex, Hampshire, Norfolk, Shropshire, Suffolk, Surrey, and Worcestershire. Interestingly, there are quite a few other irregular spellings (<ie>/<ye>) for OE *ē* before /r/, which seems to suggest that *ē* may have first raised to [i:] before /r/ (cf. Dobson 1968: 655–8, 760ff.; also 636–9, 643–6). As for OE *ēo*, there appear <by(n)> BE in the South (Cornwall, Hampshire, Surrey, Sussex, Middlesex, and Kent), the (S)W Midlands (Wiltshire, Herefordshire, and Worcestershire), and the E Midlands (Cambridgeshire, Norfolk, Suffolk, and Essex). These could be unstressed variants with a shortened vowel (cf. PDE /bɪn/), but it is still an open question whether shortening preceded or followed raising of the vowel. That is, by lME, there is substantial evidence to back up the claim that vowel shift of the reflex of OE *ē*/*ēo* was well under way.

Old English ēo

LALME spellings that indicate retention of a rounded reflex of OE *ēo/eo* are found above all in Shropshire, but also in Herefordshire, Warwickshire, Derbyshire, Cheshire, Lancashire, Norfolk, Staffordshire, the West Riding of Yorkshire, and Somerset. The distribution of <eo>, <u> etc. for OE *ēo/eo* is thus not surprising, except perhaps for Norfolk and the West Riding.[24]

4.2.4 Discussion of material from additional sources

Zachrisson cites <i>/<y> for eME *ē* in fifteenth-century private letters and documents, which spellings are interpreted as indicating *ē* > [iː] (1913: 69–71, 223); the following are some of the adduced forms.

<besyche> BESEECH (Rymer's *Fœdera*)
<agryed> AGREED (Paston Letters, Norfolk)
<appyr> APPEAR (Paston Letters)
<belyve> BELIEVE (Paston Letters)
<besyking> BESEECHING (Paston Letters)
<dymeth> DEEMETH (Paston Letters)

Whitehall finds the following forms for eME *ē* in *The Records of the Borough of Nottingham* (1935: 69).[25]

<kyp> KEEP (Vol.II, no. 1, dated 1435)
<þyse> THESE (Vol.II, no. 17, dated 1483)
<thyse> THESE (Vol.I, no. 15, not dated in paper)
<wye> WE (Vol.I, no. 13, not dated in paper)

Strangely enough, these are deemed 'too ambiguous to be taken as evidence for the raising of ME *ē* to [iː]' (1935: 69). An explanation as to why they are 'ambiguous' is not provided, but THESE may have been formed from THIS, in which case the two forms for THESE adduced earlier are indeed ambiguous; this does not apply to KEEP and WE, however (see Section 4.3.4. for a fuller account of Whitehall's observations).

Wyld (1936: 205–7) adduces <i>/<y> for the reflex of OE *ē* from *c.* 1420 onwards, concluding that the 'present sound was fully developed in pronunciation considerably, perhaps fifty years, earlier' than 1420 (1936: 206).[26]

Prins (1942a) refers to an earlier paper (Prins 1940), where he adduced early spellings indicating the shift of ME *ā* > *ǣ* (spellings dated to 1303), and of ME *ō* > [u:] (spellings dated to 1320), but failed to find any for the change eME *ē* > [i:] before *c.* 1420. In the 1942a paper, he quotes early examples for eME *ē* > [i:] as well, taken from the *Interludium de Clerico et Puella* (S Yorkshire or N Lincolnshire, late thirteenth or early fourteenth century), and in *The Poems of William of Shoreham* (Kent, *c.* 1350). Heuser, the editor of the *Interludium*, commented on these spellings, believing they were due to the AN scribe who wrote down the poem (Prins 1942a: 135). In Prins's opinion, however, this does not detract from 'the value of the [...] spellings as evidence for the change *e:* > *i:*. On the contrary, the very ignorance of the scribe in matters of traditional English spelling may have led him to adopt a more or less phonetic rendering' (1942a: 135). The spellings, which have been taken from printed editions, are as follows.

From the *Interludium de Clerico et Puella*
<suythe> SWEET (l. 23)
<suyt> SWEET (l. 50)
<quyne> QUEEN (l. 67)[27]

From *The Poems of William of Shoreham*
<tyde>: <syde> MS <sede> SIDE, OE *sīde* (II: ll. 92 and 94)

As for <tyde>: <syde>, Prins's presentation is somewhat confusing, but it appears that the MS form for SIDE is <sede> (1942a: 136), so that the MS <sede> is a back spelling, indicating the raising of eME *ē* to [i:]. However, the word rhymes with <tyde> 'hour' (OE *tīd*), so Prins seems correct in assuming it implies early vowel shift. The same text has several interesting spellings for eME *ō* also (cf. Section 6.2.4).[28]

On eME *ē* > [i:], Prins (1942b) refers to his earlier article, and to Zachrisson (1913, 1970) and Wyld (1936), who held similar spellings to indicate the 'GVS'. Van der Gaaf, however, rejected many of them on the assumption that <i> here was a simplification of AN <ie> for *ē* (Prins 1942b: 164, and works there cited). Nevertheless, even when questionable spellings are excluded, there are still some 75 <i>/<y> left for eME *ē* from between 1300 and 1400. Prins therefore is convinced that these forms imply eME *ē* > [i:], that the change began in the first half of the fourteenth century simultaneously with eME *ō* > [u:], and that most of them occur 'between dentals, labials and alveolars' (1942b: 165).

Prins also confronts counter-arguments to the early raising hypothesis: the fact that French loans participate in the vowel shift is due to their entering lME (presumably spoken) vocabulary from the written language; besides, the raised reflexes of ME *ē* and *ō* did not merge with ME *ī* and *ū*, because the close vowels had also started to change, that is, diphthongise (1942b: 166). In the later stages of the vowel shift, 'phonematic considerations' are deemed responsible for the 'subsequent development of the vowels' and the 'disappearance of ME *ɛ:*' (1942b: 167).

Black cites <hi> HE, <my> ME, <hire> HERE, <bysyche> BESEECH, <symes> SEEMS (1998: 62), besides irregular spellings for eME *ī*, eME *ō*, eME *ę̄*, and a number of other sounds. These appear in five texts which were originally written by the Lollard preacher William Swinderby in 1390–91, and which were copied into the Bishop's Register in Hereford shortly after. The texts contain 'linguistic forms that seem to reflect the conventions of Welsh orthography' (1998: 62). Among other features, they contain forms that seem to indicate vowel shift, forms which are very similar to those found in the well-known 'Hymn to the Virgin'. Black collates these spellings from the Swinderby papers with forms found in the 'Hymn to the Virgin' and the prayers in MS Llanstephan 117; the similarities are striking (1998: 64). For example, all three texts have <ei> for eME *ī*, <i> for eME *ē*, <ae> for ME *ai*, <uw> for ME *iu*. Black seems convinced that the irregular spellings for eME *ī*, *ē*, *ō*, and *ę̄* are early instances of the 'GVS'. She notes, however, that since the vowel shift affected only the phonetic realisation of the long vowels, and not the phonemic system as such,[29] 'its working is not normally reflected in spelling, and a more specific explanation will thus be needed' for the spellings in question (1998: 62–3):

> In general, spellings that reflect sound changes like the Great Vowel Shift can be expected to occur only where there is contact between different systems. For example, such spellings may [...] appear in texts that involve contact between English and another language, as in the case of English texts written using the orthographical conventions of another language.

A case in point is the retention of NME <o> for [ü:] (< OE *ō*). On the other hand, the possibility of subconscious interference from speech should be permitted: scribes may not have been entirely oblivious of changed phonetic realisations, but they probably were not aware of the distinction phonemic vs. allophonic change. Black goes on (1998: 62):

> However, the spellings of /i:/ with <ey, ei> would here seem difficult to interpret as anything else than an indication of diphthongal pronunciation; also, considering the coexistence of [irregular spellings for other long vowels] in the text, a single, systematic explanation would seem more attractive than a number of separate assumptions of sporadic changes. If it were assumed that the spellings reflect the Great Vowel Shift, a plausible

explanation should then be found for why the shifted forms should be shown in spelling.

If the above spellings are accepted as indicating vowel shift, a number of observations can be made (1998: 63–5): (1) the low front vowel changed 'considerably later than the other front vowels', since there are no spellings indicating the raising of ME [a:]; (2) there is no evidence of the low back [ɔ:] having shifted; (3) the shift affected dialects in different ways, creating different subsystems of long vowels. The last observation can be made from the fact that whereas the long close and long open *e*'s are kept apart in the 'Hymn to the Virgin', the reflexes of the two vowels are both spelt <i>/<y> in the Swinderby papers.[30]

The 'linguistic usage contained in these texts was used as the basis for Linguistic Profile 7400 in *LALME*, and seems to have been used as an "anchor text" for the Hereford area' (1998: 53), which is not unproblematic, as the language is mixed. Black concludes that the linguistic forms of the papers can be 'fitted within two distinct areas, a Southwest Midland one centred on Hereford and a Northeast Midland one, including the Nt-Li area from where Swinderby is assumed to have originated' (1998: 66). Thus, it remains uncertain whether vowel shift should be assumed for Herefordshire or for the NE Midlands.

Wełna (2004) states that the raising of the reflex of OE *ē* to [i:] is part of the 'GVS' and has been dated to the fifteenth century by Luick (1914–40) and Jordan (1968), even though other linguists have questioned this date, given the early occurrence of <i> for earlier <e>. In Laȝamon's *Brut*, which is dated to *c*. 1200, both <spiche> OE *sp(r)ēche* 'speech' and <sichinde> OE *sēcan* SEEK are reported. 'It is even more surprising that the spelling *–hȳdan* for *–hēdan* 'heed' occurs as early as Old English' (2004: 75). In *Sir Ferumbras* (Devon, 1380), frequent forms implying the raising of OE *ē* are found, and even in OE, such forms are not rare; examples are <fyt> FEET, <hir> HERE, <scip> SHEEP (2004: 76). The examples are seen to 'testify to an Old English and Early Middle English tendency to raise long close [e:]' (2004: 76), although Malone (1930) reportedly dismissed them as early evidence of the 'GVS', claiming that they should rather be interpreted as 'survivals of a pronunciation which was more or less current in OE' (2004: 76). Wełna agrees with this view, basing his conclusion on the later development of the words in question.

However, for the paper discussed here, Wełna has collected irregular spellings that testify to early raising of the reflex of OE *ē and* where the vowel was indeed raised early enough for it to participate in the later (vowel-shift) diphthongisation of eME *ī* to PDE /aɪ/. The data is extracted from the *OED* and the *MED*, and consists of the following lexical items, all of which are of French origin (2004: 76; Wełna does not provide etymologies).

> *acquire, choir/quire, entire, friar, inquire/enquire, quire, require, squire, (n) umpire, brier/briar*
> *aisle, contrive, die* (pl. *dice*)[31]

It should be noted that *squire* originates in OFr *esquier*, with [i] as the stressed vowel, which goes unnoticed by Wełna; besides, *entire* seems to go back to OFr *entir* or *entier* (Pope 1934: §411), and *require* to L *requirere.* The early raising of the vowel of some of these words is noted by Luick (1914–40: §481), others by Jordan (1968: §225, Anm. 1).

The first instances of <i>/<y> for *ē* appear *c.* 1290, starting in SQUIRE (but note the earlier *caveat*), then in DICE, REQUIRE, FRIAR, INQUIRE, and CONTRIVE. The irregular spellings are found first in a text from Gloucestershire, then in texts from Shropshire, Lancashire, Oxfordshire, London, Norfolk, and Yorkshire (2004: 78). Wełna then breaks down the spellings into a table where each of the three centuries (1200–1500) is given a column and the number of <i>/<y> versus the number of traditional spellings is given for each word (2004: 79). He concludes that 'the distribution of spellings in time offers a characteristic pattern of lexical diffusion where words affected earlier become the input to the Great Vowel Shift more readily than others' (2004: 79), but since some of the words seem more resistant to the change, this

> makes one wonder how the vowel in that word managed to be captured by the Great Vowel Shift diphthongization rule. It seems that such specific distribution of the change involving affected and unaffected words is yet another proof in support of the validity of the theory of lexical diffusion.

Wełna also groups the early irregular spellings dialectally, and finds that whereas the North and the E Midlands show a moderate tendency to use raised forms, the W Midlands 'can be definitely eliminated as a potential focal area of the change' (2004: 81), despite the fact that the <i>/<y> occur there first. The South-West is also 'slow in introducing the new raised value of the vowel' in these words (2004: 81–2). Rather too much emphasis is placed on early <i>/<y> for the stressed vowel of SQUIRE, given its quality in OFr, but Wełna's other findings seem valid.

According to Wełna, other linguists have also commented on early <i>/<y> for *ē* and interpreted the evidence variously, suggesting, for instance, that the change was combinative and depended on the following /r/. Wełna dismisses this claim, agreeing with Dobson that the raised *ē* 'may have originated in dialects where ME [ɛ:] "tended to be raised to *ē*, and would then be due to an unconscious attempt to preserve the distinction" between ME [ɛ:] and ME [i:] even at the cost of losing the distinction between ME [e:] and ME [i:]' (Wełna 2004: 77, quoting Dobson 1968: §136). However, Wełna does not agree with Dobson's hypothesis regarding the reasons why *ē* was raised in the first place: Dobson suggests that there may have been sociolinguistic reasons, in the sense that educated persons at the time would try to 'render French very tense long close [e:], the result being an *i*-like vowel in that set of words', although 'this explanation does not make it clear why other words with French [e:] failed to become raised to approximate long [i:]' (2004: 77). Against this it may be argued that the raising of *ē* could have been, and probably was, a long process in which certain French words changed first, perhaps depending on the date of their being borrowed into English. Wełna argues in favour of lexical diffusion elsewhere in the same paper, and such diffusion certainly could explain why certain words changed before others (cp. Phillips 2006a; McMahon 1994: 47–55).

Wełna concludes thus (2004: 82):

1. Long close [e:] began to be raised in words like *squire, dice, contrive*, etc. from the end of the thirteenth century onwards;
2. The spellings indicate 'a pattern typical of lexical diffusion';
3. The change started and spread first in the non-Western dialects of England.

Dobson (1968: §§134–6) also thinks the 'raising may have originated in the East and North'.[32] However, it seems far from certain that point 3 would still hold if early <i>/<y> for other words were looked at also: <i>/<y> appear quite early in *LAEME* texts from the W Midlands. However, the instances of early <i>/<y> discussed by Wełna (2004) may indeed have marked the beginning of the 'GVS' for *ē*, given the fact that they overlap with other irregular spellings for other long vowels. Alternatively, they are the 'prelude' alluded to in the title of Wełna's paper, although it is difficult to separate between early <i>/<y> for the French words examined by Wełna, and early <i>/<y> for other words, especially as they are found at the same date. It may also be the case, despite Dobson and Wełna, that the raising of *ē* to [i:], at least in the French words examined, may have been a combinative change at first: in all the words listed by Wełna, except *die/dice* (< OFr *dé/dés*) and *aisle* (< OFr *ele*), the vowel is next to

/r/ (cf. Dobson 1968: §136).[33] Besides, their explanation, i.e., that the raising originated in dialects with a tendency to raise ME [ɛ:] to [e:], and with subsequent raising of [e:] to differentiate it from earlier [ɛ:], appears somewhat *ad hoc*, unless independent evidence from such dialects can be found, testifying to the said 'tendency'.

MS, Northamptonshire Record Office, Finch-Hatton 3047, containing a hitherto unpublished verse charm against thieves, was written in 'the middle to later fourteenth century' (Benskin, forthcoming). It contains several <hiir(e)> HERE. The language probably belongs in either W Lincolnshire or E Leicestershire: Since the document is an extent of lands at Keisby in Lincolnshire, the charm could very well be 'locally rooted', as the language fits there, even though the charm has been written by a different hand than that responsible for the document.

4.3 Summary and conclusions

4.3.1 *Old English* ē

In *LAEME*, forms with <i>/<y> which probably imply vowel shift of eME [e:] to [i:] are found in: Hampshire (1175–99); Worcestershire (from *c.* 1200); Essex and Shropshire (1200–24); Kent (1200–49); Wiltshire (1250–74); Gloucestershire (1275–99); Norfolk (1284–89); Lincolnshire (*c.* 1300); and Oxfordshire (1275–1324). Forms with <ie> (for which it is unlikely that AN spelling practices are to be held responsible) are found in Oxfordshire (from the late twelfth to the early fourteenth centuries); Worcestershire (all through thirteenth century); Wiltshire (1250–74); Cambridgeshire, Gloucestershire, Kent, and Norfolk (1275–99); and Lincolnshire (*c.* 1300). Other such spellings which possibly indicate vowel shift are found in Suffolk (1150–99), Kent and Sussex (1200–49). That is, irregular spellings are most numerous in the SE Midlands and the SW Midlands, which are likely loci of the change. It is also likely that the raising of the reflex of OE *ē*/*ēo* started simultaneously in different and non-adjacent parts of the country.

A few forms with <i>/<y> for OE *ē* reported in *SMED* seem to imply vowel shift. These appear in the North Riding of Yorkshire, Lincolnshire, Huntingdonshire, Warwickshire, and Somerset in the period 1301–33. They are thus scattered across the country, but seem slightly more frequent in the NE Midlands. More uncertain evidence is found in Bedfordshire, Dorset, Norfolk, Nottinghamshire, Oxfordshire, and the West Riding of Yorkshire.

LALME spellings which are likely to indicate vowel shift of the reflex of OE *ē* are found in Kent, Hampshire, Wiltshire, Herefordshire, Oxfordshire, Warwickshire, Norfolk, the West Riding of Yorkshire, possibly also in Essex. Spellings which may indicate vowel shift of *ē* to [iː] are found more frequently before /r/ than before other consonants, which agrees well with the material adduced by Wełna (2004), despite Dobson (1968: §§122, 136).

The additional sources give evidence of vowel shift from S Yorkshire/N Lincolnshire (late thirteenth or early fourteenth century), Kent (*c.* 1350), W Lincolnshire/E Leicestershire (mid-to-late fourteenth century), Devon (*c.* 1380), Herefordshire (1390s), and Nottinghamshire (1435 and 1483). Further, Wełna adduces examples from Gloucestershire, Shropshire, Oxfordshire, Lancashire, Yorkshire, London, and Norfolk, from *c.* 1290 onwards. Thus, the NE Midlands area stands out as an innovative area, which is corroborated by the late forms from Nottinghamshire; the same texts from Nottinghamshire also contain spellings that indicate advanced vowel shift of the reflexes of eME *ī* and *ū*, cf. Chapters 5 and 7. Devon, the West Midlands, and certain parts of the North in all likelihood also underwent raising of eME *ē* at an early date.

Dobson (1968: §136) does not share Wełna's and Wyld's view that the early <i>/<y> spellings for ME *ē* imply vowel shift, but thinks they are instances of 'a comparatively rare process of raising to ME *ī*'; it seems clear that the reason why such a process of raising does not qualify as 'vowel shift' is exactly its early date. Dobson is right, however, in claiming that they are different from the 'Great Vowel Shift', simply because the words that are affected by this early raising process later provide input to the 'GVS'. For example, the stressed vocoid of *briar* and *friar* was first raised to [iː], then diphthongised, in the 'GVS'.

Stockwell's early vowel-shift hypothesis accounts for a seemingly raised long vowel as the output of MEOSL of the half-close vowels, as well as the apparently lowered short vowel as the output of the shortening of close vowels in polysyllabic words. However, Ritt's (1994) account provides an even more convincing explanation.[34]

Since <i>/<y> for eME *ē* are recorded at least from *c.* 1420 in the sources he had consulted, Wyld (1936: 206–7) concludes that

> it is probable that the present sound was fully developed in pronunciation considerably, perhaps fifty years, earlier. A thorough search through the late fourteenth-century texts might reveal examples of *i, y* spellings in these. It

is probable that M.E. *ē* was pronounced very tense, and slightly raised, like the vowel in Danish *se* 'see', which to English ears is almost indistinguishable from [sī]. [...] [ī] was probably fully developed from *ē* before the end of the fourteenth century.

4.3.2 *Old English* ēo

OE *ēo* monophthongised to [ø:] in the eleventh century; this [ø:] was unrounded to [e:] in the North and E Midlands in the twelfth century, but remained and was unrounded to [e:] in the fourteenth or fifteenth centuries in the W Midlands and parts of the South. The following conclusions may be drawn from the ME material extracted.

LAEME sources suggest that vowel-shifting started early in the East/South-East, in the W Midlands, and in the NW Midlands. Material testifying to the monophthongisation and rounding of the reflex of OE *ēo* has not been collected from *LAEME*; this is something that needs to be done in the future.

According to *SMED*, all of the North appears to be an [e:]-area in the first half of the fourteenth century, even the southern part of Lancashire, and so does the E Midlands area. As for the W Midlands, by the early fourteenth century [e:] was found in Derbyshire, Nottinghamshire, Leicestershire, and probably Cheshire. Shropshire, Staffordshire, Herefordshire, Worcestershire, Warwickshire, Gloucestershire, and Oxfordshire probably still had [ø:] or raised [y:], though this [ø:]/[y:] had begun to be unrounded to [e:]. It seems likely that [ø:]/[y:] and [e:] were used side by side for some time. The same is true of at least parts of the South, where the unrounded [e:] appears to be the dominant form in the early fourteenth century, but where rounded reflexes still linger on. In Sussex and Kent, however, spellings indicating rounded variants do not appear, so [e:] seems to have been the current reflex, although the evidence suggests that a raised [i:] may have been used word-finally in Kent.

A few forms with <i>/<y> in *SMED* seem to indicate vowel shifting of eME [e:] > [i:], with subsequent shortening. These are reproduced in Table 4.9.

Apart from the forms found in the North Riding of Yorkshire, Bedfordshire, Somerset, Hampshire, and Worcestershire, forms cluster in the East, from Kent and Surrey via Essex and Suffolk to Norfolk and Cambridgeshire.

Table 4.9 *Potential vowel-shift spellings in* SMED

County	Date	Spellings
North Riding of Yorkshire	1301	<Libreston'> *Lēodbeorht*
Bedfordshire	1309	<Flitt->, <Flytt-> *flēot*
	1332	<Flitwyk>
Kent	1327	<*Try*> TREE
	1332	<*Lyef*> *lēof*
Essex	1327	<*Lief*> *lēof*
Suffolk	1327	<*Lyf*> *lēof*
Somerset	1327	<Lif>, <Lyf> *lēof*
	1333	<Lyf>
Hampshire	1327	<Chil(e)bolton/Chylebolton> *cēola*
Norfolk	1332	<Lyf'> *lēof*
Cambridgeshire	1330	<Gritton> *grēot*
Surrey	1332	<Rydebrok'> *hrēod*
Worcestershire	1327	<Ridmaleye> *hrēod*
	1332	<Rydmerley>

LALME spellings which may indicate vowel shift of OE *ēo* cluster in the North, NW Midlands, NE Midlands, and in Shropshire. The spellings from the NE Midlands thus tie up with the earlier *SMED* spellings from Cambridgeshire and Norfolk; evidence of vowel shift is also early and consistent for parts of the North.

Ek rightly believes the developments of OE *ēo* and OE *ȳ* should be seen as interrelated (Ek 1972: 121). This is especially important for those areas where *ȳ* either lowered to [e:] via [ø:] or was retained at [y:] (cf. Chapter 8), and where *ēo* either remained as [ø:], or was raised to [y:], or unrounded to [e:], since we know with hindsight that the reflexes of the two vowels did not generally merge. Thus, no dialect where the two sounds are kept apart could have had, for example, [e:] for both vowels at the same time (or indeed [ø:] or [y:]). Yet, Kristensson's conclusions seem to suggest that in E Somerset, Wiltshire, E Sussex, E Surrey, Kent, Middlesex, London, most of Hertfordshire, Essex, Suffolk, and the SE part of Cambridgeshire, the reflexes of the two sounds must have merged at [e:], since the reflexes of both OE *ēo* and OE *ȳ* are said to have been [e:] in the early fourteenth century (although [e:] for OE *ȳ* is thought to be only a minor variant in Somerset, Wiltshire, and Berkshire; Kristensson 2001: 119). Clearly, this problem of the chronology of changes and non-merger between the reflexes of OE *ēo* and *ȳ* is a topic for future inquiry.

Table 4.10 LAEME *texts with <i>, <ie>, <y>, <ye>, <ei> etc. for the reflex of eME* ę̄

County	No.	Date	Examples
Essex	4	1150–99	<hie> HE
			<ʒie> YE
			<diere> DEER
			<biede> BĒOD
			<bien> BE inf.
			<lief/lieue> LĒOF
			?<niede> NEED
			<isien(e)> SEE *inf.*
			?<þieue> THIEF
			(<ripen> REAP)
Essex	1200	1150–99	<gie/ʒie> YE
			<lief> LĒOF
			<siene> SEE *inf.*
			<-tien> TĒON *inf.*
Suffolk	1300	1150–99	<wiep> WEEP *pt.*
			<gie/ʒie> YE
			<bien> BE *inf.*
			<diepe> DEEP
			<lief(e)/lieue> LĒOF
			?<nied> NEED
			?<þiefes> THIEF *pl.*
			?<tigeðe> TITHE
			?<tiðinge> TITHE *vn.*
			<wiedes> WEED
			<-tieð> TĒON *imp.*
			<-tigi(n)g> TĒON *vn.*
			(<fieble> FEEBLE)
Oxfordshire	232	1175–1224	<hiere/hier-of> HERE
Hampshire	143	1175–99	<hi> HE
Worcestershire	5	c.1200	<bi-flien> BEFLĒON
Worcestershire	2000	c.1200	<hi> HE
			<icwime> CWĒME
			<greite> GREET *3.sg.pt.*
Worcestershire	2001	c.1200	<g^{i}kisce> GREEK
Lancashire	16	1200–24	<lires> HLĒOR

(*continued*)

Table 4.10 (*cont.*)

County	No.	Date	Examples
Essex	64	1200–24	<biene> BĒN
			<biete*n*> BĒTAN
			<hie> HE
			<hier> HERE
			<diemeð> DEEM
			<fiet> FOOT *pl.*
			<miede> MEED
			<niede> NĒDAN
			<siec(h)> SEEK
			<sliep> SLEEP *pt.*
			<swiete> SWEET
			<ðie> THEE
			<ʒie> YE
			<bie/bieð> BE *imp.*
			<bien> BE *inf.*
			<bie*n*/ibien> BE *pt.ppl.*
			<diepliche> DEEPLY
			<dier> DEER
			<drierj> DREARY
			<life/lieue> LĒOF
			?<nied(e)> NEED
			?<priest> PRIEST
			<ʒesiene/isien> SEE
			<-sien/-sieð> SEE *pl.*
			?<þief/þieues> THIEF (*pl.*)
	65	1200–24	<biene> BĒN
			<hie> HE
			<hier> HERE
			<ʒie> YE
			<beiete> BĒTAN *3.sg.ps.sj.*
			<bieð> BE *imp.*
			<bien> BE *inf.*
			<dier> DEER
			<cnyle> KNEEL
			?<frie> FREE *3.sg.ps.sj.*
			<lieue> LĒOF
			?<nied(e)> NEED
			<isien> SEE *inf.*
			<ʒesiʒen> SEE *pt.ppl.*
			<sien> SEE *pl.ps.sj.*
			<þieue> THIEF
			?<tiʒeþes> TITHE
Shropshire	260	1200–24	<liðerede> LĒPRAN
Shropshire	261	1200–24	<bi-sih> BESEE *imp.*
Shropshire	1000	1200–24	<bisih> BESEE *imp.*

County	No.	Date	Examples
Worcestershire	6	1200–49	?<sciet> SHEET[a]
			<lief> LĒOF
			(<ripen> REAP)
Worcestershire	7	1200–49	(<ripen> REAP)
Kent	8	1200–49	<hi> HE
			<hier> HERE
			<si> SĒ
			<biede> BĒOD
			<bi/bien> BE *inf.*
			<ibie/ibien> BE *pt.ppl.*
			<biflien> BEFLĒON
			<diere> DEER
			<vorsien> FORSEE
			<lief/lieue> LĒOF
			?<niede> NEED
			<(i)sien> SEE *inf.*
			<þieue> THIEF
			(<ripe> REAP)
Sussex	67	1200–49	?<siene> SCĒNE/SCĪENE[b]
Worcestershire	1900	1200–49	<grigcis> GREEK
			<forseiȝen-> FORESEEN-
			?<twinunge> TWĒONIAN
Worcestershire	245	1225–49	?<tiðinge> TITHE *vn.*
			<wrien> WRĒON *inf.*
			<iseien> SEEN
			<iseie> SEE *1.sg.pt.sj.*
Shropshire	275	1200–49	<wrihen> WRĒON *inf.*
Worcestershire	1800	1225–49	<vnwrih> WRĒON *imp.*
Unlocalised	119	1240–50	?<tiheðe> TITHE *inf.*
Unlocalised	121	1240–50	<bisih> BESEE *imp.*
Cheshire	122	1240–50	<wrihe> WRĒON *inf.*
Unlocalised	123	1240–50	<liðerede> LĒÞRAN
West Riding, Yks	231	1225–74	<leise/leyse> LĒSAN (with *ȳ* also)
Worcestershire	277	1250–74	<fiede> FĒGAN *pt.*
			<gric-> GREEK
			<hir> HERE
			<mi> ME
Worcestershire	278	1250–74	<hire> HERE
			<fliȝ> FLEE *imp.*
Wiltshire	280	1250–74	<bieres> BĒRE
			<grickes> GREEK
			<hi/hii> HE
Worcestershire	2	1275–99	<hi> HE
Worcestershire	3	1275–99	?<breist> BREED *2.sg.*
Cambridgeshire	137	1275–99	<hier> HERE

(*continued*)

Table 4.10 (*cont.*)

County	No.	Date	Examples
Kent	142	1275–99	<si> SĒ <bi/bie/bien> BE *inf.* <bieþ> BE *imp.* <i-bye> BEEN <hye/-ie> YE ?<nyede/niedes> NEED
Gloucestershire	161	1275–99	<hir(-), hier*e*> HERE
Unlocalised	179	1275–99	<leys-> LĒSAN (with *ȳ* also)
Gloucestershire	229	1275–99	<hire> HERE
Unlocalised	233	1275–99	<si> SEE *1.sg.ps.* <trie> TREE
Unlocalised	239	1275–99	<bi-sih> BESEE *imp.*
Herefordshire	246	1275–99	<fehid/fehit/feid/feit> FOOT *pl.* <bein> BE *inf.* <beit> BĒTAN *inf.* <heir(e)> HERE <teit> TEETH <seine> SEE *inf.* <þeif> THIEF
Wiltshire	263	1275–99	by-sy BESEE *imp.*
Herefordshire	1100	1275–99	<aweydeþ> AWĒDAN <bi-syh> BESEE *imp.*
Norfolk	1400	1275–99	?<frie> FREE *3.sg.sj.*
Norfolk	1700	1284–89	<hire> HERE
Gloucestershire	2002	1275–99	<drie> DRĒGE <i-seiene> SEEN *pt.ppl.* <i-seien> SEE *pl.ps.sj.*
Lincolnshire	159	c.1300	<suyt/suythe> SWEET <syen> SEEN
Unlocalised	174	c.1300	<vn-seiþe> SEEN
Lincolnshire	182	c.1300	<leyse> LĒSAN (<steide> STEAD)
Gloucestershire	10	1275–1324	(<ripe> REAP)
Ely	282	1275–1324	<seyn> SEEN
Oxfordshire	1600	1275–1324	<i-fielde> FEEL *pt.* <fier> FĒRE <pier> PEER <quiene> QUEEN
Norfolk	155	1300–24	<diep> DEEP <tigðes> TITHE

[a] Regarding SHEET, OE had the weak feminine WS *scīete*, Angl. *scēte*, later *scȳte*[1] (< **skautjōn*, i.e. WS umlaut of OE *ēa*, regularly *īe*, is in contrast with Anglian *ē*), so it is the Anglian form which must be the origin of PDE [ʃiːt], unless the development is different after [ʃ]. The *OED* claims that OE also had the strong masculine *scēat* and weak masculine *scēata*, the former of which is said to be partly the source of PDE SHEET [ʃiːt].

Notes

1 OK *eo* monophthongised to [e] and merged with etymological *e* (Gradon 1979:21).

2 It may be of importance that OE *īo* fell in with *ēo* in all dialects except Kentish, where, as stated earlier, the merger went in the opposite direction.

3 Likewise, when OE *e* had undergone MEOSL, the product was half-open [ɛ:] rather than half-close [e:].

4 The term 'MEOSL' is thus itself a misnomer, according to Ritt's account, since the 'openness' of the syllable is not really what is at issue, but rather the characteristics of the syllable, i.e. moric weight. It seems therefore that MEOSL, homorganic lengthening etc. are instances of compensatory lengthening (1994: 68), which are closely related to the ME loss of final *–e* and of final unstressed syllables in general. Hence, they are similar to other processes of apocope, syncope, and compensatory lengthening witnessed throughout the earlier history of the Gmc languages. Other linguists also prefer the term 'open syllable tensing', e.g. Malsch and Fulcher (1975).

5 If a final syllable was prone to be deleted in ME, and eventually was deleted, it was 'unstable'; if it remains to the present day, it was 'stable'; the apparent circularity of this conclusion seems inevitable, as the prosodic characteristics of earlier stages of the language in most cases can be inferred only from the present-day state of affairs.

6 Lass claims that the lax values [ɪ] and [ʊ] 'cannot be assigned to any period earlier than the 16th-17th centuries' (1988: 404) and that before this date, there were matching sets of phonemically long and short vowels. Lass bases this claim on the statements of the early orthoepists, e.g. Hart. Stockwell and Minkova, on the other hand, state that the tense *vs.* lax opposition goes back to W Gmc or even PrIE (1990: 203–4). Lass's rejoinder (1992) points out that an exclusively quantitative distinction is still found in 'relic' areas, i.e. the

---

Table 4.10 (*cont.*)

LAEME has <sciet> from Worcestershire (no. 6, first half of thirteenth century). The *OED* adduces the form <sheetes> from Chaucer's *The Second Nun's Tale*, dated to c. 1386. The present spelling had thus come into being by (at the latest) the last quarter of the fourteenth century. It may suggest raising of OE *ē*, ME *ę̄*, but, as noted for SHEEN in the note below, <ee> is expected for ME *ē*.

[b] With regard to SHEEN, the OE etymon is *scīene* (as well as *scēne, sceone*), but PDE [ʃi:n] should come from earlier *scēne*. The development may however be different after [ʃ]. There is one <siene> from Sussex (no. 67, first half of thirteenth century). All the other (some 20) tokens in *LAEME* have <e>. The *OED* claims that the sense of the noun was influenced by the root of the verb SHINE, OE *scīnan*, but if that were the case, PDE ought to have [aɪ] for the noun as well. The *OED* has recorded the forms <scienne> from 900 (*Cynewulf*); <scene> from 1000–1300; <schine> from 1300 (*Sir Orfeo*). The present spelling is thus found for SHEEN from the end of the fourteenth century. The *MED* has <sheen> from the beginning of the fifteenth century. It may suggest raising of OE *ē*, ME *ę̄* (cf. SHEET above), but <ee> is expected for ME /e:/, and SHEEN had, seemingly, *ēo* > *ē* as a variant.

northern and southern margins of the Gmc area, and that duration (length) rather than tenseness thus seems to be the original phonemic feature distinguishing certain vowels (short) from certain others (long). Early Gmc spelling supports this statement (since the vowels of both *līf* and *libban*, for instance, are represented by <i>), but to counter Lass's claim that there is no evidence for a tense-lax opposition before the 16th century one could in fact invoke the spellings of the outputs of MEOSL.

7 Schane (1990) suggests that lowered tongue height, laxness, and a retracted tongue root are related: they are instantiations of a phonological feature called 'aperture'; Schane provides both acoustic and articulatory evidence in support of this claim (1990: 11–14).

8 According to Brandl (quoted in Kristensson 1967), the dividing line between areas with and without OE *ǣ* 'passes along the western border of Ca[m] and Hu, the northern border of B[e]d, B[c]k, and O[x], and cuts across southern W[rk] and middlemost Wo[r] to the Severn' (Kristensson 1967: 57). The dialects north and east of this line had OE *ē*.

9 The forms <ihe> and <ihu> for OE *gē* appear in a source text from Norfolk (no. 1400, 1275–99). This source also has <ihu> for OE *ēow*, <ihure> for OE *ēower*, <ihernen> for OE *geornan*, and <ihiuen> for GIVE *ppl.*; <ge–> is the dominant form for the prefix *ge-*, although <gea–> and <i–> both appear also. Thus, <ih> regularly represents initial [j] in this source, and the form <ihe> [je(:)] therefore does not indicate vowel shift. Interestingly, text no. 249 (Herefordshire, 1275–99) has <sige> for the 1.sg.pres.ind. of SAY (< OE *secgan*), but also <saiȝe> and <saþe> for the same part, which might imply some confusion between /i(:)/ and some kind of diphthong. However, it should be noted that <þ> and <ȝ> frequently interchange for [θ, ð], so <saþe> could be a back-spelling for <saȝe> (cf. *LALME* III: xv b). Also, in many southerly dialects, <sigg–> and <sai>/<say> etc. co-occur. There is no reason to suppose that ME <sigge> or <segge> are relevant to diphthongised forms (cf. LIE, which still has [g]-variants in northern dialects).

10 Text no. 246 (Herefordshire, 1275–99) also shows <fehid>, <fehit> (in addition to <feid>, <feit>) for FEET; these seem to indicate that the vowel is perceived as a diphthong with a raised second element, though it is hard to tell whether the first or second vowel received the stress. At least there must have been a perceptible glide or hiatus for the two vowels to be separated by <h>. Similar forms are found for the reflex of ME *ō* also, and are discussed in detail in Section 6.2.1.

11 OE *twēonian* appears with *ȳ* also in OE, so <i> may be entirely conventional.

12 The form <frie> may go back to OE *frīge*.

13 Wallenberg (1931), presenting onomastic material from Kentish charters dated before the Norman Conquest, adduces some <eo> for OE *ēo*, which supports Gradon's claim that OK may have had *ēo*. Examples are <Freondesberiam> with OE *frēond* FRIEND, in Birch's Cartularium Saxonicum (BCS), charter 195 (dated 764); <Fleote> with OE *flēot* 'water, creek, inlet' in BCS 291 (dated 798); possibly <Hafingseota> with OE *sēota* or *seota*, which could

be semantically related to OE *gesetu* 'dwelling', in BCS 289 (dated 798). However, <io> is also recorded for the reflex of OE *ēo*; e.g. <iocled> for *geocled*, in which the first element is OE *geoc* YOKE, in BCS 332 (dated 811).

14 As will be seen in Chapter 5, Kristensson sees all forms with <ei>/<ey> for OE *ī* as back-spellings, based on the development of eME *ēg* into /i:/, e.g. in OE *ēage*, eME *ēge*.

15 However, Serjeantson is quoted as having found some <u> for OE *ēo* in Lancashire in thirteenth-century material (1967: 181), which indicates that Lancashire may have retained the rounded reflex longer than the rest of the northern counties, which lends support to the findings of Moore, Meech and Whitehall (1935).

16 <Hurt(e)>, from OE *heorot* 'hart, stag'.

17 <Louersale>, where the first element is OE *lēofhere*.

18 <Lurebodil>, where the first element is OE *lēofhere*; <Lourbotill>, where the first element is OE *lēofhere*.

19 Internal variation is indeed the conclusion that the non-derivability of attested late WS from attested early WS enforces.

20 A few <ou> and <u> seem to indicate a change OE *eo>ø>y>u* before /r/+consonant (Kristensson 2002: 178). Such a development is restricted to Somerset (1333), Dorset (1327), Wiltshire (1327), and Sussex (1332), and is believed to have taken place in the fourteenth century; Kristensson refers to Sweet (1888: §§657, 682), Wyld (1927: §168 C), and Jordan (1968: §42 *Anm. 1*) for support.

21 Forms with <Priest> for OE *prēost* occur throughout the country, but have not been included, because they are found to be due to the AN spelling practice of writing <ie> for ME *ē* (1967: 177; 1987: 158). Nor have aberrant forms with OE *lēofhere* been included: they are explained as due to shift of stress from the first to the second element of the diphthong, and to subsequent fronting of the stressed *ō* (Kristensson 1967: 176). DEER seems to have had a variant *dīere*, so the two Lincolnshire forms with <i>/<y> probably go back to the latter.

22 Generally however, OE *ēo* is *ẹ̄* or shortened *e* in the North, spelt <e>. Moreover, <ea> and <eo> interchange in the northern part of Northumberland, but the reflex of *ēo* does not seem to fall in with the reflex of OE *ēa*; hence, the first element of the diphthong must have had a closer quality than that of the first element of *ēa* (Kristensson 1967: 176).

23 For EVIL, forms with <e> for the stressed vowel are most numerous, although <i> is not infrequent, and <y> forms are legion; there are also some forms beginning with <u> or <v>, probably corresponding to retained [y]. Pronunciation was probably always with a close front vowel (since the OE etymon is *yfel*), and the fact that the lengthened vowel came to be spelt with <e> testifies either (a) to the raising of etymological *ē* (Stockwell 1985), or (b) to MEOSL, whereby the lengthened [ɪ] (or [ʏ]) was re-interpreted as coming from ME *ē* (Ritt 1994), or (c) to 'the Great Collapse' in Kentish whereby [y(:)] > [e(:)] (Anderson 1988).

24 As for BETWEEN, in so far as the adduced forms really stem from OE *betwēonum*, it rightly belongs in this list. Forms with <ey> for the stressed vowel appear in Derbyshire, Lancashire, Lincolnshire, Norfolk, Nottinghamshire, and the West Riding of Yorkshire; <i> is found in Lancashire, Norfolk, and Yorkshire. Forms with <y> are numerous, and occur in Cheshire, Cumberland, the East Riding of Yorkshire, Ely, Lincolnshire, Norfolk, Northamptonshire, Nottinghamshire, Shropshire, Staffordshire, Suffolk, Warwickshire, and Westmoreland.

25 Stevenson, W.H. (ed.). 1883. *The Records of the Borough of Nottingham. Vol. II.* London.

26 Wyld also remarks that in PDE, in 'vulgar English of big towns [...] there appears to be a tendency to diphthongize [ī] to something like [ə*i*]. This tendency generally goes with a drawling habit of speech which seems incompatible with the preservation of any long vowel as a pure sound' (Wyld 1936: 205).

27 This spelling could be for *quean*, in which case it does not provide early evidence of eME *ē* > *ī*.

28 However, Wełna (2004: 76) comments that 'the early rhymes adduced in Prins's [...] well-known articles cannot be treated as the [*sic*] evidence of early narrowing because of the writer's improper interpretation of the spelling evidence (cf. Ikegami 1997)', although Wełna does not elaborate.

29 By 'phonemic system' is meant the number of distinctive units, i.e. phonemes, before and after the 'GVS'. It is true that the early stages of the shift did not reduce or increase the number of long-vowel phonemes, but the later stages saw the merger of the two previously separate phonemes ME /eː/ and /ɛː/. Also, the reflexes of ME /aː/ and ME /æi/ (and the reflex of ME /ɛː/ in a few words) eventually merged in /eɪ/.

30 Prins quotes <lydy> for LEAD *vb.*, which he dismisses as 'an error', stating that it 'can of course not denote a change *ɛː* > *eː* > (*iː*) at this date' (Prins 1942a: 135, n. 4).

31 *Acquire* is derived from OFr *acquerre*; *choir/quire* from OFr *cuer*; *entire* from OFr *entier*; *friar* from OFr *frere*; *enquire/inquire* from OFr *enquerre*; *quire* from OFr *quaer*, now *cahier*; *require* from L *requirere* < *quaerere*; *squire* from OFr *esquier*; (*n*)*umpire* from OFr *nomper*; *briar* from OE *brǣr, brēr*. Further, *aisle* comes from OFr *ele*; *contrive* from OFr *controver*; *die* (pl. *dice*) from OFr *de*.

32 He refers to the early raising of ME *ē* to [iː] as a 'comparatively rare process [...] whence arises PresE [ai] in *briar, friar, quire, choir*, and *contrive*' (*loc. cit.*). Since it occurs before a limited number of consonants (*r, s, v, k*), it could be a combinative change, but Dobson dismisses this on the grounds that 'raising because of a following *r* is improbable. It must rather be considered an isolative tendency' (*ibid.*). Dobson admits, however, that it 'would be easiest' to interpret some of the cited spellings 'as showing ME raising' of *ē* to [iː] (*op.cit.*: §136, Note 2). Indeed, such raising is deemed 'the likeliest explanation of the fourteenth- and fifteenth-century *spire*' and some other forms, and also of <hirs> HEAR 3. person sg.pres.ind. in an unspecified version of *Cursor Mundi* (*ibid.*).

33 Yet, *V+r* generally involves lowering of the vowel or the development of a non-front glide, whether in OE or in eModE; but that is not to say that <r> implies always the same sound. Dobson (1968: §122) claims that prior to c.1400, *r* may have had a raising influence on the preceding vowel, whereas post-1400, a following *r* lowered the vowel.

34 Still, Stockwell's line of reasoning has interesting consequences also for the general interpretation of <ee> spellings for eME *ẹ̄*: Do they all indicate vowel-raising to [i:]? Do they indicate that the digraph <ee> is associated with the sound value [i:]? Forms with <ee> for eME *ẹ̄* are numerous and appear from *c.* 1265 all over the country in *SMED*. However, <ee> is not the dominant spelling for OE *ē* in the extracted ME material (even if it is a normal spelling in much writing from the C Midlands and London area, *teste* Benskin, pers. comm.). Perhaps it was felt that a new spelling was needed to render the raised reflex of OE *ē*, and that <i> should be reserved for OE *ī*. On the other hand, <ee> for /e:/ often co-occurs with <ij> for /i:/ (and <oo> for /o:/, and the less common <aa> for /ɑ:/), which implies that double vowel-letters are used to indicate vowel length rather than quality. 'Length is in a few cases (and on the whole very rarely) indicated by *ee*, for instance *Preest* ' in the North Riding of Yorkshire in a Roll from 1301, and in the Lincolnshire Roll from 1327 (Kristensson 1967: 177). One might ask how far *SMED* is representative of English as opposed to Latin spelling conventions; it is also relevant that Latin does not use doubled vowel-letters. Thus, doubled vowel-letters are innovations, but their exact phonetic implication remains elusive. In *LALME*, <ee> is found for the singular of WEEK in Essex (LP 6260), Leicestershire (LP 68), Northamptonshire (LP 741), Rutland (LP 554), and Warwickshire (LP 8070), and for the plural in Cheshire (LP 246). The OE etymon here is *wicu* (there was also *wucu*) and pronunciation was always with [i] (and after MEOSL with [i:]), so these spellings may indicate that <ee> had come to be associated with [i:].

CHAPTER 5

The development of ME ī

5.1 Introduction

The core antecedents of ME *ī* were OE *ī*, OE *īg/ig*, and OE *i* lengthened before voiced homorganic consonant clusters. Other sources were:

- OE *ȳ* and lengthened *y* in those dialects where [y] and [y:] unrounded to [i] and [i:].
- OE *i*(*ht*), *eo*(*ht*), *ea*(*ht*) in dialects where these merged at *i*(*ht*), due to palatal mutation (e.g. NIGHT; BRIGHT; MIGHT).
- OE *ēo*(*g/h*) in those dialects where this vowel was raised due to the following palatal(ised) consonant (e.g. FLY v., THIGH).
- OE *ēa*(*g/h*) in those dialects where the vowel was raised due to the following palatal(ised) consonant (e.g. EYE, LYE; HIGH, NIGH).

This ME /i:/ from various sources started to diphthongise to [ɪi] (or [ij]) in the second half of the fifteenth century, and had become [əi] around 1500 (Jespersen 1909: §§8.12–22; Wright 1924: §§73, 77). Dobson (1968: §137) and Luick (1914–40: §483) believe that the first stage of diphthongisation took place earlier and date it to *c.* 1400. So-called 'maximisation' of the diphthong then took place, whereby the articulatory distance between the onset and offset positions became ever larger: [əi] became [ʌi] in the seventeenth century, and finally [ai] in the eighteenth century.[1]

The diphthongisation of ME *ī* is generally not reflected in writing, but the main reason Dobson dated the early stage of it to *c.* 1400, is the evidence afforded by the spelling system of the 'Hymn to the Virgin', in which words with etymological *ī* are spelt <ei>, clearly indicating a diphthong. However, such early irregular <ei>/<ey> for eME *ī* are often dismissed as mere back spellings, modelled on the result of the change of OE *ēah/ēag* > *ī* in ME: the eME reflexes of OE *ēag/ēah* were <ei>/<ey>, and these spellings persisted even after the reflexes of OE *ēag/ēah* presumably raised and monophthongised to [i:]. By analogy, eME *ī* could be spelt <ei>/<ey> without corresponding to a diphthongal pronunciation; that is, they may be back spellings. For this reason, the nature of <ei>/<ey> for eME *ī* will be discussed in detail. By contrast, <ai>/<ay> for eME *ī* are usually accepted as evidence for a diphthong, and hence for vowel shift. Yet, the intermediary stage between eME [iː] and Modern English [aɪ] must have been [əi], and it is at least possible that <ei>/<ey> indicate this.

This chapter provides a substantial collection of irregular spellings for eME *ī*, with a view to assessing whether the conventional dates for ME changes to the front close vowel are correct, and to determining whether any of these spellings indicate early vowel shift.

5.2 The developments of various OE sources to eME *ī*

5.2.1 OE ȳ/y

Even though the reflexes of OE *ȳ* and OE *y* in lengthening contexts eventually merged with the reflexes of OE *ī/i* in most English dialects, their reflexes had different developments in different areas in early ME. The development of eME *ȳ* is therefore treated separately in Chapter 8.

5.2.2 OE ī/i *before* ġ *and voiced consonant clusters*

Late OE *i* lengthened to [iː] before a voiced homorganic consonant cluster. Although the vowel shortened again in eME before certain of these clusters, the long vowel generally remained before *ld, mb, nd, ng* (Jordan 1968 §22; Wright and Wright 1928: §§68–76; Ekwall 1975: §17). Examples are: OE *cild* – later *cīld* CHILD, OE *climban* – later *clīmban* CLIMB.[2] Jordan (1968: §22) dates these changes to the late eighth or early ninth century, whereas Wright and Wright (1928: §68) place them towards the latter part of the ninth century.

In lOE, the *ġ* in OE *īġ/iġ* vocalised to form a minimal diphthong [ɪi] with the preceding vowel, which eventually supposedly became a long monophthong [iː], which fell in with /iː/ (Wright 1924: §73).

5.2.3 The diphthongs io, eo, ea

Breaking

The OE diphthongs *io, eo, ea* (long and short) were mostly the result of breaking of earlier *i, e, æ* (but also of palatal diphthongisation and back mutation). Breaking of PrOE *i/ī, e/ē, æ/ǣ* affected OE dialects in different ways, as indicated in the following text.

Breaking of PrOE *æ+lC* gave <ea> in Saxon and Kentish, <a> in Anglian by retraction (Campbell 1959: §143–4). Breaking of *æ+rC* gave <ea> in Saxon, Kentish, Mercian, and <a> after a labial consonant in Northumbrian. Breaking of *æ*+[x] gave *ea* with great regularity; retraction to *a* was rare (1959: §145). Broken PrOE *æ* was often written <a> in later Anglian texts, whereas <ea> is most common in WS and Kentish (1959: §143).

PrGmc *ǣ* gave WS *ǣ* and non-WS *ē* (Campbell 1959: §§151–2). WS *ǣ* was broken to *ēa* before [x] and retracted to *ā* before *w*. Anglian *ē* was broken before [x], but due to Anglian smoothing (see the following text), broken forms are only found in forms where the [x] was lost. In Anglian and Kentish, breaking of *ē* from PrGmc *ǣ* was prevented before [x] when *i* appeared in the next syllable; hence, **nēhist* is *nēst* in Anglian. WS *ǣ*, from PrGmc *ǣ*, was broken to *ēa*, which became *īe* by *i*-mutation, giving *nīehst* (1959: §154). The reflex of OE *ēa* began to be spelt <æ> *c.* 1000, and eventually <a> (just like OE *æ*) *c.* 1100 in Southern, Eastern, and Northern texts, in the thirteenth century in the W Midlands, and in the fourteenth century in Kent (1959: §329).

Breaking of PrOE *e* gave *eo* in all dialects (Campbell 1959: §146). In the North, the product was spelt <o> when *e* came before *wC/rC* when the following *C* was not *c/g/h* (1959: §147). Breaking of *ē* before [x] gave *ēo*.

Breaking of PrOE *i+wC/hC* gave *io* in all dialects, but the spelling <io> gave way to <eo> in OE (Campbell 1959: §148). Breaking of *ī* gave *īo* before [x] and before [x]+consonant, but it is reflected as *ēo* (1959: §153). In non-WS, the product is spelt <u> when the *i* appears before *wC/rC* and the *C* is not *c, g, h* (1959: §§149–50).

Anglian smoothing

The process called 'Anglian smoothing' monophthongised PrOE long and short *ea, eo, io* before *c/g/h* and before *r/l+c/g/h* to long and short *e, e,* and *i*, respectively, thus counter-acting the effect of breaking (Campbell 1959: §§222–33). Hence, <mæht> 'marrow', <feh> 'money', <cneht> KNIGHT, <werc> WORK, <flege> FLY n., <gesihð> SIGHT, <birhtu> BRIGHTNESS. For *æ* before *r/l*+back consonant, the vowel was sometimes spelt <æ>, sometimes <e>. In Old Northumbrian, *ea* before final [xs] gave *e* due to the final consonant cluster, which was palatalised (1959: §224).

Sometimes there was variation between <æ> (from smoothing) and <e> (due to *i*-mutation), for example, <æhher> or <eher> 'ear of corn'. When *ēa* came before a back consonant, it was first smoothed to *ǣ*, then raised to *ē*, for example, <hēh> HIGH, <nēh> NIGH. In some words, a [x] 'before a consonant disappeared early, and a preceding diphthong was not affected [by smoothing]: Cp. *hēalēcas*' (1959: §230), thus producing variation in Anglian between, for example, smoothed *hǣh, hēh* and unsmoothed *hēalēcas*. The *ǣ* from PrOE *ā+i/j* did not raise to *ē*; hence, *ǣht* 'property', *cǣg* KEY, *rǣcan* REACH V.

Traces of smoothing are seen in WS and Kentish texts too, but this must not be confused with a later WS process of smoothing of long and short *ea* (1959: §§226, 312–14). The later WS smoothing affected *ea* as a falling diphthong only: *ea* monophthongised to *e* before *c/g/h*, and after *ċ/sc/g*; for example, *seah* > *seh* SEE pt., *ēage* > *ēge* EYE. By a similar process in ninth-century Kentish, *ēa* was monophthongised to *ǣ*.

The later history

The later history of the diphthongs is as follows (Campbell 1959: §§293–301). In Northumbrian, *io/īo* remained unchanged; in early Mercian, *io/īo* and *eo/ēo* remained distinct, but later, they had fallen together under *eo/ēo*; in WS, the reflexes of *eo/ēo* and *io/īo* seem to have merged, but there are remnants of a previous distinction; in late WS, the use of *io/īo* was discontinued. In Kentish of the ninth century, *ēo* became *īo*, spelt <io> or <ia>, whereas *eo* and *io* merged at *eo*, spelt <eo>, as in WS and Mercian. In early WS, *īe* was often reflected as *ī*; in late WS, *īe* > *ī* before palatal consonants, and *īe* > *ȳ* elsewhere. Soon after 1000 AD, the OE diphthongs, long and short, were monophthongised (1959: §329). Generally, *ea/ēa* became *æ/ǣ*, and *eo/ēo* became *ø/ø̄*; *io/īo* had become *eo/ēo* in Northumbrian, whereas it still existed in Kentish. In Kentish *ea/ēa* became level or rising diphthongs, not monophthongs; and PrOE *eo/ēo* and *io/īo* had merged at *io/īo*, which also became level or rising diphthongs, not monophthongs.

5.2.4 *Palatal mutation*

By palatal mutation (Campbell 1959: §§304–11), *e/eo/i/io* + *ht/hs/hþ* (+ *e*) became *i*. In this phonetic context, *io* and *eo* would have been found only in WS and Kentish, since Anglian would have had smoothed *i* and *e*; contrariwise, *e* would not be found before [x]-clusters in WS or Kentish, due to breaking. Since palatal mutation affected the vowels before the consonant groups *ht/hs/hþ* when these groups were in final position or came before *e*, it is reasonable to assume that the [x] was palatalised to [ç] first, and that the vowels were palatalised only after the consonant had palatalised (1959: §311). In Kentish, there were two stages of palatal mutation: (1) *eo* > *e* and *io* > *i*; (2) *e* > *i*.

The evidence is much earlier for Kentish and WS than for Mercian and Northumbrian; the earliest Northumbrian texts are from the late tenth century, and with the exception of WS, evidence is generally patchy. In Campbell's opinion, palatal mutation must have started in the South, with Kentish being affected first, in the ninth century, whereas in WS, palatal mutation had 'affected all possible short sounds by 900' (1959: §311); Mercian was affected in the tenth century, and Northumbrian even later. There is apparently no OE evidence of palatal mutation in Northumbrian, for the reason stated earlier, but ME spellings suggest that palatal mutation reached the North as well.

Long OE *īo* and *ēo* were generally not subject to palatal umlaut, but there are indications in lOE and eME that some of the eligible lexis was affected, for example, OE *lēoht*, ME *līht* LIGHT, and OE *nīhste* (< *nēhste*) 'nearest'.

Wright and Wright (1928: §46) state that late OE *i+ht* 'remained throughout the ME period in the northern and north Midland dialects, but in the south Midland and southern dialects it became lengthened to **ī** with gradual loss of the spirantal element from about the end of the fourteenth century'. Dobson (1968: §§140–3) believes variants with a retained fricative survived to the mid-seventeenth century in educated speech in parts of the country. In Kentish, PrOE *ēo* is supposed to have merged with *īo*, although Gradon (1979: 30–4) states that this is not a necessary assumption. OK *eo* (1) generally monophthongised to [e] and merged with /e/; or (2) raised to [i] and merged with /i/ before [ç] + non-velar consonant, 'as in *kniȝt, riȝt, uiȝt*' (1979: 21). OE *ea* (1) generally lowered and joined /a/; or (2) merged with /e/ before /x/, and before [ç k] + consonant, 'as in *eȝte, eȝtende, ulexe, wex, izeȝ*' (1979: 21). Thus, 'Glide vowels do not appear between a vowel and [x]', and the spelling evidence suggests that [ɣ] had not vocalised in the language of the *Ayenbite of Inwyt c.* 1340 (1979: 38). This source uses <iȝt> for the reflex of OE *iht* and *eoht*, and <eȝt> for OE *eaht*, where <ȝ> presumably corresponds to to [ç] and [J][3] (1979: 44–5). However, the <t> is often lost before another consonant, for example, <briȝnesse> BRIGHTNESS, which 'may be a sandhi phenomenon [...] or it may be due to lack of stress' (1979: 49); sometimes the <ȝ> is lost, for example <ryȝuollyche>, where the velar fricative may have 'become palatalized and then been absorbed by the root vowel' (1979: 50).

5.2.5 *Other considerations*

The diverging developments of *ē+*g^1 (as in *tweyn* < OE *twēgen*) and *ē+*g^2 (as in *eye* < OE *ēage*) are due to a qualitative difference in the sounds corresponding to *g*: the former *g* comes from an OE originally voiced *palatal* fricative (or semi-vowel) and, in combination with pre-consonantal *ē*, gives PDE /eɪ/; the latter comes from *g* from a voiced *velar* fricative before an originally back vowel which was fronted in unstressed syllables, whence it became a *palatal* fricative, and gives PDE /aɪ/ in combination with pre-consonantal *ē*; cf. Campbell (1959: §§427–39) and Kristensson's 'secondary palatal fricative' (e.g. 1987: 182).[4]

At any rate, the reflexes of OE *eoh+t, eah+t,* and of OE *ēog, ēoh, ēag, ēah* are believed to have generally become [i(:)çt] and [i:j] at different stages in various dialects during the ME period, and fell in with /i:/. Part of the purpose of this chapter is to determine whether this was indeed the path of change.

5.3 On <ei>/<ey> as evidence of diphthongisation of ME *ī*

5.3.1 *Arguments against interpreting <ei>/<ey> as evidence of diphthongisation*

ME texts provide a number of interesting forms for the reflex of ME *ī*. There are, for example, such forms as <a-beydin> ABIDE, <breyt> BRIGHT, <leif> LIFE, <mayȝth> MIGHT, <weyte> WHITE. Although such spellings become increasingly frequent in lME and eModE, they are not rare in eME. It would seem that the cited spellings offer early evidence of vowel shift of ME *ī*. However, problems arise when they are to be interpreted in terms of sound-values: some of the spellings suggesting early phonetic change have not gone unnoticed by earlier philologists, but have merely been discarded as evidence of early diphthongisation for various reasons. This is particularly the case for the close front vowel, which poses a greater challenge than the other long vowels, due to other sound changes that involved the close or half-close front vowels during lOE and ME, with concomitant orthographical changes. These changes have been dealt with briefly in the preceding sections. Chiefly, when the reflexes of OE *ēog*/*ēoh* and *ēag*/*ēah* were smoothed and consecutively raised to [i:], they were still in many cases spelt <ei>/<ey>; therefore, it may be claimed, when the reflex of ME *ī* is spelt <ei>/<ey>, these are just back spellings. The logic is as follows: if *ēog*/*ēoh* and *ēag*/*ēah* = [i:] and are spelt <ei>/<ey>, then ME ī = [iː] may also be spelt <ei>/<ey>. The digraphs therefore may not indicate a diphthong. Reservations of this kind will be examined carefully in what follows.

In his extensive discussion of the issue, Dobson investigates 'Evidence apparently showing [ei] or [ɛi] for ME ī' (1968: 662). The sources of this evidence are the following: 1. foreign orthoepists, 2. occasional spellings, and 3. 'alleged rhymes' between *ei*-words and *ī*-words. Each of these will be treated in turn.

1. Orthoepists

Despite Dobson's explicit reference to *foreign* orthoepists as offering evidence of the diphthongisation of historical ī, he merely refers the reader to Zachrisson (1913), and turns his attention to the statements of *native* orthoepists. Nearly all the early orthoepists[5] (a) describe a diphthongised reflex of ME ī, (b) describe a diphthong where the second element is a tense, close [i], and (c) have problems describing the first element, which is variously described as a 'thinner (more obscure) sound' or as a 'feminine *e*', or the diphthong is described as a 'foreign' [ei] or [ɛi]. Dobson concludes that they are trying to describe a diphthong where the first element is centralised, and where the second element is the more prominent, hence [əi] or [ᵊi]. Clearly, the orthoepists tried to describe a relatively 'obscure' sound by means of the Roman alphabet. The Roman alphabet has no letter specifically representing the schwa (nor central and front rounded vowels in general), so the letter with the nearest sound-value was <e>. Dobson appreciates this, observing that (1968: 660; my italics)

> In these cases the identification does not mean merely that Latin *ei* or Greek ει were identified with ME ī in the English pronunciation of these languages [...], but that an attempt is being made to find means of expressing the degree of diphthongization; *such statements are a pseudo-learned variation* on the ordinary transcription *ei*.

Further down on the page he admits that there 'are indications in various orthoepists that the transcription *ei* was only approximate'.

2. Occasional spellings

Some of the occasional spellings are dismissed on the grounds that (1968: 662)

> they may be due to the variation between *ei* and ī in a number of common words such as *eye* and *height* – an explanation which is inherently more

likely for such spellings when they occur in conventional orthography than the hypothesis of phonetic intention.

That is, simultaneous *variation* in the pronunciation is seen as the mechanism behind the scribes writing <ei>/<ey> for ME *ī*. The logic is that some words were sometimes pronounced with [ei] or [e:], and sometimes with [i:]. These were traditionally spelt with a digraph <ei>/<ey>. The digraphs thus corresponded to the phonetic reality [i:] *as well as* [ei]. By analogy, words whose pronunciation was only with [i:] may also be spelt with <ei>/<ey>. Dobson does not explain exactly what constitutes a 'conventional orthography', nor does he produce an explanation for the <ei>/<ey> spellings when they occur in an *unconventional* orthography – this is more than a mere quibble, as most ME orthographical systems are individual.

In conclusion, Dobson does *not* claim that <ei>/<ey> never indicate diphthongisation, but that they do not represent the diphthong [ei], with which one must concur, as (a) [əi] is a regular reflex for ME *ī* in many PDE non-standard accents, especially before /t/, and (b) it has been established from modern evidence that when /i:/ has diphthongised in more recent years, for example, in Cockney and Australian English, the first element has taken a *centralised*, not front, path. A front path still remains a theoretical if improbable possibility.

3. Rhymes

Regarding the rhymes adduced, Dobson maintains that all but one of the examples are cases of ME *ī* rhyming with the reflexes of OE *eġ*. The only examples cited are *side: leyde*, and *by: wey*. Dobson's argument is as follows: since OE *eġ* is commonly [aɪ] in the modern dialects, the development must have been OE *eġ* > *iġ* > *ī*.[6] That is, these are rhymes between ME [i:] from ME *ī* and ME [i:] from OE *eġ*, ME *iġ/ī*. However, OE *eġ*-words regularly have PDE /eɪ/, not /aɪ/ – certainly, the words adduced by Dobson do. Therefore, the rhymes cited are between words with ME *ī* and PDE [aɪ] on the one hand, and words with ME *and* PDE [eɪ] on the other, that is, *laid, way*. The exception is the rhyme *enmie: obeye*.[7]

Stockwell (2006), in a paper written in response to Stenbrenden (2003a), seemingly calls into doubt his earlier position that the vowel shift was very much earlier than has been assumed, discussing the status of <ei>/<ey> as evidence for early vowel shift. However, Stockwell here discusses <ei>/<ey> for etymological *ai* and *ei*, which only merged with the reflex of OE *ī* in the W Midlands, evidence of which is found in *SED* (Orton and Dieth 1962). Against this it must be said that in my paper, I discussed mainly <ei>/<ey> for etymological *ēag/ēah*, the reflexes of which *did* merge with the reflex of OE *ī* in StE. Insofar as spellings for etymological *ai, ei* were examined in some detail, they were so because Dobson discusses rhymes between *ai, ei* and ME *ī*. But Dobson clearly draws the conclusion that no rhymes between the reflexes of ME *ī* and ME *ei* can be exact, since the two sounds never merged; that is, they are rhymes between [əi] for ME *ī* and [ei] for ME *ai, ei*, with which Stockwell and the present writer both agree. Clearly, identity of spelling need not entail identity of pronunciation.

It is curious, however, that Dobson does not apply the same counter-arguments against using <ai>/<ay> for ME *ī* as evidence of diphthongisation. In note 4, he accepts rapid diphthongisation of ME *ī* to [aɪ] in the East, and the consequent 'confusion between dialectal [ai] < ME *ī* and StE [ai] < ME *ai* ' (1968: 663). Hence, he does not discard <whrayt> WRITE in the *Cely Papers* (Essex), and simply says it 'seems to depend on the identification of an advanced pronunciation of ME *ī* with a conservative one of ME *ai* ' (1968: 663).[8] No mention is made of the fact that the reflexes of ME *ī* and ME *ai* never became identical, which is the crucial point of his argument concerning <ei> for ME *ī*. The only difference may be that <whrayt> does not appear in rhyming position. Also, given the later date for these spellings, Dobson may simply have tacitly accepted that the maximal diphthong would have been reached. There are earlier <ay> for *ī*, however, even in ME.

Quite apart from these considerations, the various versifiers themselves found ME *ei* and the reflex of eME *ī* sufficiently similar to use them in rhymes, which raises the following question: Why would any writer (a) use <ei>/<ey> to represent the reflex of eME *ī*, (b) *and* let the words rhyme with ME *ei*-words, unless ME *ī* really had diphthongised? The bottom line is that rhymes between ME *ei* and ME *ī*, however inexact, go to show that the reflex of ME *ī* actually *had* diphthongised.

Kristensson's reasons for discarding <ei>/<ey> as evidence of diphthongisation of eME *ī* partly overlap with Dobson's arguments regarding point 2. Kristensson's view is that <ei>/<ey> for eME *ī* are analogical spellings, for the reasons pointed out in the preceding (Kristensson 1987: 65).

The conclusions are thus a little different for Dobson and Kristensson: Kristensson claims that <ei>/<ey> for ME *ī* cannot be used as early evidence of diphthongisation of *ī at all*; Dobson's view is that <ei>/<ey> cannot be used as evidence for a stage [ei] with a front first element. It is easy to agree with Dobson's conclusion; Kristensson's stance, however, seems overly restricted. Stockwell notes (2006: 178), with respect to Kristensson's claim that

> There is no way to defeat this argument directly. To accept it, we have to assume that the force of spelling analogy may be sufficiently strong to blot out the force of phonetic similarity. One may add a plausibility argument to the effect that this is especially likely to be true of scribes to whom carry-over of graphological analogies might seem more natural than phonetic similarities. On the other hand, his view is rendered somewhat suspect, because there should be replacements in the opposite direction; *<i>* spelled for etymological *<eg>*, and there seem to be none such.

5.3.2 Arguments for using <ei>/<ey> as evidence of diphthongisation

In this regard, arguments set forth by Kuhn and Quirk (1953) with respect to breaking diphthongs may be of interest. Kuhn and Quirk respond to claims made by Daunt (1939) and Mossé (1945) that the digraph spellings for the products of breaking, palatal diphthongisation and back mutation did not correspond to phonetic or phonemic diphthongs – Mossé and Daunt think the last element of the digraph was simply a diacritic indicating the quality of the following consonant. Kuhn and Quirk show that the digraph spellings corresponded to phonetic diphthongs. For example, in late WS, broken and unbroken reflexes of WGmc *a* (> OE *æ*) are kept clearly apart, as are broken and unbroken reflexes of WGmc *e* (> OE *e*). Normally, broken *e* is <eo>, but sometimes the reflex is spelt <u> or <o>, indicating a rounded sound. More interestingly, back spellings with <eo> for the reflex of OE *o* are found, for example, <geweorhte> for *geworhte*, <weorde> for *worde* (1953: 51). Kuhn and Quirk draw three conclusions from this fact: (1) broken and unbroken reflexes of WGmc *e* 'had diverged so far as to be recognized by the scribe as being "differents"'; (2) broken *eo* corresponded to a vowel very different from [e] or [ɛ], so much so that <eo> could be used for a rounded vowel; (3) the second element of <eo>, that is, <o>, was not a diacritic, 'but an integral part of the vocalic symbol *eo*, which could be transferred as a whole from its original predictable context' (1953: 52). It is the last observation that convinces Kuhn and Quirk of the phonemic status of the breaking diphthongs. 'Those forms cited immediately above, in which *eo* has been transferred from its original limited context to represent other sounds phonemically distinct from /e/, point to a phonemic distinction in the uses of *eo* and *e*' (1953: 52).

Moreover, *æ* and *ea*, and *e* and *eo*, 'were no longer in strict complementary distribution as early as the first part of the ninth century' (1953: 52). Kuhn and Quirk even adduce minimal pairs and analogous pairs, although the number of such pairs is necessarily limited, as for example *ea* was regularly a conditioned allophone of *æ*, and <æ> and <ea> hence would not appear in the same environments. Kuhn and Quirk thus essentially redefine the concept of a phoneme: the existence of minimal pairs is not the only sensible criterion for recognising a distinctive unit.

Against Kuhn and Quirk's assumption that <eo> in *weorde* and *geweorhte* are back spellings, it may be said that strong verbs are often subject to paradigmatic levelling, and that <eo> in the preterit could be an analogical re-formation, a simple extension of the root vowel of the present stem (*weorðan* 'be, become' and *wyrcan/weorcan* WORK) to the preterit.[9] In that case, <eo> is not indicative of sound change and need not imply phonemic contrast. Their account would therefore be more convincing if such spellings were found in forms which are not paradigmatically related.

At any rate, the very existence of back spellings with <eo> for an etymologically rounded vowel seems sufficient proof to Kuhn and Quirk that the sound normally reflected as <eo>, that is, broken *e*, had phonemic status. There is, however, an important underlying assumption which Kuhn and Quirk fail to consider explicitly, which is *similarity of sound*: back spellings by definition presuppose a similarity of sound between some of the allophones of the two phonemes affected. However, this need not always be so. In this case, the development of front rounded vowels from *eo/ēo* (most likely [ø] and [ø:]) triggered new spellings <u> or <o> instead of traditional <eo>. Therefore, since traditional <eo> could sometimes be spelt <u> or <o>, traditional <o> could also sometimes be spelt <eo>. The two sounds [o] and [ø] would probably have had the same height, and they would both have been rounded, but it seems doubtful whether any of the allophones of etymological *eo/ēo* and *o/ō* would ever have been identical. The back spellings adduced by Kuhn and Quirk are therefore different from the back spellings used for illustration in Chapter 1: the mergers in twelfth-century High German dialects between [ø] and [e] at /e/ and between [y] and [i] at /i/ resulted in occasional spellings <e> for etymological <ö>, and <i> for etymological <ü>, but they also resulted in back spellings <ö> for /e/ and <ü> for /i/. Here, the rationale behind the back spellings is true merger, that is, identity of sound. Kuhn and Quirk's back spellings, on the other hand, do not presuppose merger at all, which seems to go against Penzl's claim that 'Reverse or inverse spellings [...] always indicate a phonemic coalescence' (1957: 16). Instead, the rationale behind <eo> for etymological *o* is as follows: the sound [ø(:)], developed from *eo/ēo* had different orthographic representations, including <eo>, <eu>, <u>, and <o>; by analogy, [o(:)], usually spelt <o>, could also be spelt <eo>. The common ground is the spelling <o>. The digraph <eo> was thus analogically transferred to words where it did not belong, due to simple graphemic extension, not merger.

Kuhn and Quirk's argument for regarding breaking diphthongs as phonemically distinct could apply also to <ei>/<ey> for eME *ī*. The digraphs <ei>/<ey> (whatever their phonetic correspondence) in words of the HIGH and EYE sets were originally found in predictable contexts, that is, before [ç] or [J] (and possibly as allophones co-varying with [i:]), and the fact that they were lifted in their entirety from the original, limited context to represent the sound corresponding to *ī* not followed by [ç] or [J], would indicate phonetic similarity, at the very least, between the sounds regularly represented by <ei>+C and <i> respectively.

5.3.3 The chronology of changes in the front vowel area

If Kristensson's and Dobson's claims presented in the previous section are taken literally, almost none of the ME irregular forms for the reflex of ME *ī* may be used as evidence of early diphthongisation. Clearly, the chronology of changes to the reflexes of OE *ig, iht, eoht, eaht, ēog/ēoh, ēag/ēah* must be established. The discussion which follows is for the most part relevant also to systemic considerations regarding the development of OE *ū* and OE *ūg/ug/ōg/og*; therefore, the arguments put forward will not be repeated in Chapter 7, though the spelling evidence for eME *ū* will be discussed in detail there.

The interplay between vocalic and consonantal changes

The traditional view is that the vowels of OE *īg/ig* merged with the reflexes of OE *ī* and lengthened OE *i* at /i:/ in lOE, that this process was repeated (1) in eME with the reflexes of OE *iht, eoht, eaht* (Anglian *iht, eht, æht* by smoothing, and *iht, iht, æht* by palatal mutation) and (2) in lME with the reflexes of OE *ēag, ēog, ēah, ēoh*. Thus, the /i:/ phoneme may have been 'destabilised' three times in ME, that is, received diphthongal allophones. In the case of *iht*, the post-vocalic fricative or semi-vowel eventually vocalised completely and was lost; some handbooks claim that the [çt] survived into eModE; it certainly did in Scots. For instance, Dobson (1968: §§140–3) thinks there was variation in words of the NIGHT set between [ɪç], [i:] and [əiç] in lME and eModE, and that words of the

HIGH set (with lME [i:ç]) had similar variants, due to analogy with the NIGHT set.[10] Dobson insists that the first variant [ɪç] survived until the mid-seventeenth century (1968: §143), and that this variant was simply 'displaced by the alternative [əi] pronunciation developed from late ME *ī* ' (1968: §143). The first claim is possible, at least for educated Southern speech, and the second claim is highly likely, regardless whether the 'displacement' took place in lME or in the seventeenth century – it was probably a long-term process which affected various regional variants at different times.

As stated before, ME /i:/ from various sources later diphthongised in the 'GVS', first to [ɪi], later to [əi] and [ʌi]. As to why OE *ēag/ēah, ēog/ēoh* eventually merged with the reflex of OE *ī* (when OE *ēa regularly* merged with eME *ę̄*, and OE *ēo regularly* merged with OE *ē*), most handbooks state that when OE *ēa* and *ēo* were followed by *g/h*, these palatal consonants caused (1) the off-glide [ə] to rise to [ɪ] in ME, and (2) early raising of the preceding vowel *ē* to [ɪ:] or [i:], such that it was absorbed by etymological *ī*; finally, the postvocalic palatal consonant was completely vocalised and lost. In other words, there was a long process of regressive assimilation. The chronology of changes could have been as follows.

1. *īġ/īw > ī*
2. *iġ > ī*
3. *iht/eoht/(eaht) > īht > īt*
4. *ēog/ēoh > ē(i)ġ > ēj/īj > ī*
5. *ēag/ēah > ē(i)ç > ēj/īj > ī*

This linear chronology is not supposed to suggest that the development of each lexical set was brought to completion before the next set started to change; there might have been temporal overlap between the late stages of change for one set and the early stages of change for the next. Additionally, there is no evidence for any absolute dating, and there is no clustering of evidence for points 1–5 at separate times. Since the reflexes of OE *īġ/iġ, īw, iht*, and *ēag/ēah, ēog/ēoh* all end up as PDE /aɪ/, it seems logical that they must first have been subsumed under ME *ī* (either as long monophthongs or as minimal diphthongs) and then diphthongised (further). Alternatively, the reflexes of OE *ēog/ēoh* and *ēag/ēah* had variant pronunciations, and the relevant sets of words merged with the reflex of ME *ī after* the latter had started to diphthongise, and had reached [əi].

As previously mentioned, it is the assumed development of OE *ēag/ēah* and *ēog/ēoh* to [i:] which lies behind the claim that <ei>/<ey> for ME *ī* are merely back spellings, and hence not admissible as evidence for early vowel-shifting. A few points are worth making here. First, <ig(h)> and similar spellings would not be expected for older <ēg>/<ēh> (<OE *ēag*/*ēah*), unless the postvocalic fricative was still pronounced. If it had already vocalised or been 'absorbed' by the preceding vowel, the spelling <i> is what one would naturally expect; that is, unless the postvocalic fricative in words with short *iht* had already been vocalised, so that the <ȝ>/<g> etc. could be used merely as a marker of length. Second, ME <eih>/<eyh> for the reflexes of OE *ēag/ēah* (and *ēog/ēoh*) make sense only if they represent the [e:ɪj] and [e:ɪç] stage in their development.

Stockwell (1960, 1964, 1972, 1978), and Stockwell and Minkova (1988a, 1988b) have been arguing for a long time that the course of change could be the other way round: their argument is that English saw an early stage of vowel shift in the merger of OE *ī* with the reflexes of OE *ig/īg* (and of OE *ū* with the reflexes of OE *ug/ūg* > lOE *uw/ūw*); they also hold that this pattern was repeated in ME with the merger of eME *ī* and *ih(t)*. This large-scale merger between the reflexes of OE *ī/ȳ, īh/g, ȳh/g, ig, iht/yht* in the front series would necessarily have resulted in co-varying monophthongal and diphthongal allophones of the high front vowel phoneme for some period, unless sound change works overnight and for all coaeval generations at the same time. The existence of diphthongal allophones could actually have triggered the further diphthongisation of ME *ī* in the 'GVS': it has been observed that when a diphthong *has been* produced, the articulatory distance between the first and the second element tends to become larger, probably for perceptual reasons. This is referred to as 'glide maximisation' by Stockwell (1978) and 'diphthong maximisation' by Labov (1994: 249).[11] It is very possible that this is what happened to the diphthongised result of the mergers in the close(-mid) front area. The first element of the diphthong may have been on its way down in phonological space when the reflexes of OE *ēag/ēah* saw vocalisation of the consonant and raising of the vowel. If so, this is where the merger may have taken place between eME *ēg/ēh* and eME /i:/: at a point where [i:] was still a phonetic reality, but where the majority of allophones had a lowered first element.[12]

Traditionally, the output of the merger between the reflexes of OE *ī* and OE *īg/ig* is represented as [i:], that is, a long monophthong, but the possibility remains that it was realised as a minimal diphthong [ij] (> [ɪi]). *Post facto* it can only be stated that any difference between [i:] in, for example, WHITE and [i:j]/[ij] in, for example, *stīg* STY was not great enough for the sounds to develop into two contrastive phonemes; that is, there seems to have been a lack of minimal pairs distinguished by [i:] and [ij]/[ɪi]. Hence, the vowels of the words in question collapsed into one phoneme, which still may have had simultaneous monophthongal and diphthongal allophones. One would consequently expect some fluctuation between the different realisations, and not always on a historically correct basis. When the OE *ēog/ēoh, ēah/ēag* words later underwent vocalisation of the fricative, and raising of the vowel, the implication is that ME /i:/ received further diphthongal variants.

Other considerations need to be addressed as well. If OE *ēog/ēag* > *ēg* [e:j] > [e:ɪ] > [i:], and if OE *ēah/ēoh* > *ēh* [e:ç] > [e:ɪç] > [ɪ:j] > [i:], there should be early occasional spellings with <i>/<y>, <ie>/<ye>. Such spellings are quite frequent in *LAEME* sources for OE *ēog/ēoh*, even from the early period, but very rare indeed for OE *ēag/ēah*. Instead, such spellings feature in great numbers in *late* ME, that is, at a point in time where [e:j] by all accounts should have been raised to [i:(j)], and the glide should have been 'absorbed' by the long vowel. The absence of such spellings in eME could imply (a) that the raising and vocalisation took longer than assumed, and/or (b) that <eʒ>, <eh>, <ei>/<ey> were after all the best written representations of the phonetic realisation of the reflex of OE *ēag/ēah*. It is a fact that OE *ēag/ēah* 'joined' the eME /i:/ phoneme, but whether this happened at [i:] or [ij]/[ɪi] (or [əi]) is an open question. Stockwell entertains similar views, saying that to account for <i>/<y> for etymological *ēag/ēah* in the traditional view, 'without the EVS [= Early Vowel Shift] hypothesis, one has to assume total de-diphthongization (becoming [i:]), a retrograde development which seems unlikely in a set of phonological entities that were, on all testimony, shortly to undergo diphthongization anyway' (2006: 177).

To be sure, both diatopic and diachronic variation may have been found even in eModE. Support for this hypothesis is found in dialects of Scots, where the modern realisation of, for example, HIGH is [hi:] (alongside /həi/), which presupposes older [e:]. Besides, rhyming evidence strongly suggests that monophthongal and diphthongal allophones of eME *ī* survived into lME and eModE in certain dialects. However, in order to draw any certain conclusions regarding this, one would have to establish (a) that the rhymes are exact, and (b) what sounds likely correspond to the <ei>/<ey> spellings. This brings to centre-stage an important issue: namely, what systems do these spellings inhabit? Is, for instance, <ey> to be interpreted as corresponding to the same sound(s) no matter what spellings are used for other vowels in the systems in which <ey> is found? It would hardly be surprising if various scribes were to use the same orthographical means to indicate different phonetic realities. Wyld expresses the same view regarding <ei>/<ey> for the reflex of ME *ī*: 'it seems clear from other evidence that they do not always express the same diphthong' (1936: 223).

If variant pronunciations existed, the inference is that the collapse in the (half-)close front vowel area could be due to allophonic variation rather than true phonetic change: co-variants developed side by side, and merger eventually took place when one type of variant (i.e. [i:]) was analogically *replaced* by another (i.e. [ɪi]/[əi]). Variationist linguistics recognises (a) the synchronic existence of variants, and (b) the power of frequency of occurrence, and assumes that many types of change are due to a change in the frequencies with which the different variants occur. Thus, if a particular variant becomes more frequent (for whatever reason), the result may be a change in prototype, which in essence is an analogical process; thus, the possibility for analogical replacement has been opened. More specifically, the diphthongal variants, front and back, may have become more and more frequent in ME, to the point where they replaced any monophthongal variants that may have remained. On the other hand, the issue may rather be salience than simple frequency of occurrence. And what variationist linguistics happens to recognise is of course not in itself evidence that it happened thus.

The difference between this hypothesised course of events and the traditional scenario is the following. If the relevant changes were truly and only phonetic in nature (the traditional account), this implies that [i:ç(t)] from all sources first became [i:j(t)], then [i:(t)], at which point it merged with /i:/, then diphthongised again to [ɪi(t)] ('GVS') and finally to [əi(t)]. The variationist approach, on the other hand, assumes that /i:/ had co-varying allophones [i:], [ij], [ɪi] (and perhaps even [əi]) for a lengthy period of time, and that when the diphthongal allophones analogically replaced the monophthongal ones, this may have been the first stage of the 'GVS'. The arguments apply equally to /u:/. Clearly, the conception of the mechanics of the variationist approach does not differ from that of Stockwell.

The later development of the reflex of eME *ī* shows that it *did* diphthongise at some stage. How would a scribe represent such a diphthong, and what options were at his disposal? If he was trying to record a minimal diphthong, he could write <i>, <ii>, <ij>, <iy>, <yi>, <ie>, <iȝ> (the latter spelling was only possible after the sound represented by <g>/<ȝ> had been vocalised); if the phonetic space between the elements of the diphthong had become greater, and the first element had not been rounded or backed, he could write <ei>/<ey>, or even <ai>/<ay> if the first element had become an open vowel. If the first element had been rounded and backed, he could write <oy>. *All* of these spellings appear in the

ME material considered here. On the other hand, the question remains how many scribes were indeed trying to record *segments* as opposed to *words*. Whereas some certainly did, it is not obviously the norm of scribal behaviour.

Stockwell and Minkova's stance that the initial stages of the 'GVS' included the vocalisation of *g* and *w* has received attention and support in more recent years, from Wełna (1988), Pilch (1997), and Steponavičius (1997 and 2005). Their claims are relevant to the 'GVS' as a large-scale and long-term shift of a systemic kind, but they are especially relevant to the development of ME *ī* and *ū*, in that they bear directly on the chronology of lOE and ME changes in the close front and back areas. Their claims will therefore be summarised later. It may be of interest, however, to note first certain statements made in a much earlier works by Sundby (1963) and Wyld (1927).

Sundby (1963) provides tables of spellings for OE *dēagian* DYE v., OE *hēah* HIGH, OE *lēah* 'clearing, open land' in onomastic material from Worcestershire from the twelfth century to *c.* 1500. Sundby finds that forms without a post-vocalic consonant appear before 1250, but in greater numbers after 1250. He concludes that raising of /e:/ to [i:] took place in the thirteenth century when the vowel came before [j], and a century later when it came before [ç]; the vowels went through a diphthongal stage 'as indicated by the spelling *ei*' (1963: 176). He admits that 'the two types cannot be sharply distinguished, however, because we must reckon with analogies and overlapping' (1963: 176). In other words, the reflexes of OE *ēag* and *ēah* developed at different rates towards ME /i:/.

Wyld (1927) takes a different view, and notes on the vowels of the EYE and HIGH sets that they are usually spelt *ēi* or *ē* in both ME texts and place-name material, and that <i>/<y> start appearing from the mid-thirteenth century onwards for both reflexes, although the 'scribes appear to have avoided these latter spellings'. Indeed, 'So infrequent are the *y, i*, spellings that even the slightest trace of them in a document may be significant of the new pronunciation in the dialect of the area whence it comes, or at least in that of the scribe' (1927: 1267). Wyld observes that (a) sources from Wiltshire show more <i>/<y> spellings than those from any other county, (b) texts from London,[13] Cambridgeshire, Norfolk, Suffolk, Essex, and Kent show no such spellings up until the fourteenth century, and (c) neither do texts from Lancashire or Cheshire, (d) nor place-name material from Gloucestershire, Somerset, Devon, and Dorset. The W Midlands, Central Midlands, and the Central Southern areas are therefore believed to be the loci of change, and to have had [i:] for the reflexes of both OE *ēag* and *ēah* from the first half of the thirteenth century.

Wełna's (1988) observations are relevant for the development of OE *ī(g)* and OE *ū(g)* in ME, and the vowel mergers in the (half-)close front area. His paper investigates diphthongs formed from combinations of vowel plus vocalised fricatives in ME, and establishes stages in the development of OE monophthongs and diphthongs, especially in the period *c.* 1200–1300. These stages are based on those suggested by Luick (1914–40). Wełna's account of these changes involves a postulation of different phonemic vowel heights in the history of English. He also treats the chronological stages of the *system* of diphthongs and the consequences of change in detail. Wełna (1988: 421–5) first explores the different stages of vocalisation, which may be summarised as follows: *g/w* were vocalised after front and back vowels respectively in the ninth century, but the fricative was restored. New vocalisation took place after short vowels in the late twelfth century, and after long vowels soon after 1200. Post-1225, diphthongisation affected the long front vowels before original *w*; around 1250, diphthongisation affected (a) front vowels before the secondary palatal fricative, and (b) back vowels before a voiced velar fricative, which restored [ei ou]. After 1250, [i] and [u] were inserted between (a) front vowels before a voiceless palatal fricative, and (b) back vowels before a voiceless velar fricative. Between 1275 and 1300, [ei ou] had their first element raised, producing [ii uu], which – it is assumed – fell in with /i:/ and /u:/. However, the possible diphthongs [ii uu] are 'disregarded since from the very beginning they must have corresponded to long monophthongs', namely, [i:] and [u:] (1988: 421). This claim seems to apply to OE *ig* and *ug/uw*, but it goes against what Wełna says about Stage 1, where OE *g/w* were vocalised, but were 'restored due to the impact of the inflectional paradigm' (1988: 421), suggesting paradigmatic variation between minimal diphthongs and combinations of close vowel plus fricative. Wełna's chronology regarding the crucial early stages of vocalisation of fricatives after close vowels therefore remains unclear.

Wełna also gives an outline of the chronology of the various changes that produced the vowels of the sets HIGH, EYE, EIGHT, BOUGH, and BOUGHT (1988: 426).[14] Stage 1 involved pre-vocalic shortening, for example, [e:iə] > [eiə] EYE, whereas Stage 2 involved the lengthening of vowels before *h*, for example, [bɔhtə] > [bɔ:htə] BOUGHT. The final Stage 3 saw the insertion of a glide before *h*, for example, [he:h] > [he:ih] HIGH. Stage 1 thus (a) effectively eliminated 'over-long' or trimoric vowels, and (b) presupposes the complete vocalisation of post-vocalic [j] and [w].

According to Wełna's chronology, the stages included in the table must have taken place before 1275 (1988: 426–7). Wełna's dating thus agrees with Sundby's in claiming that the vowel in the EYE set was raised to [iː] in the late thirteenth century, whereas that of the HIGH set was raised in the late fourteenth.

Pilch (1997) also provides new analyses regarding the system of ME sounds, invoking evidence from spellings (which however are deemed haphazard), from PDE phonetics and morphophonemics, from ME structural evidence, from English loans in Irish and Welsh, and from syllabic types ('shape types'; 446 ff.).

Regarding the 'GVS', Pilch draws attention to the fact that in ME, change had spread from the North to the South/London, until the upper classes exchanged English for French in the late fourteenth century. Subsequently, English became prestigious and change started to spread from London to other areas; that is, London went from being a 'relic area' to becoming a 'focal area' in Pilch's terminology (1997: 450–1). But London English apparently had 'a skew system', where 'the low row of "long" vowels was overcrowded with the three different phonemes /æ. a. ɑ./' (1997: 451). Such asymmetric vowel systems can live on, Pilch claims, for a long time in 'relic areas', but not in 'focal areas' (1997: 451). The vowel shift is supposed to have started when London English reinforced (1997: 451–2)

> the difference between the shape types [i.e. the mismatched quantity correlation between short and long vowels after MEOSL] not by 'lengthening' of vowels, but by removing whatever vague phonetic similarity was left between the 'long' vowels and their 'short' correspondents. [...] It achieved this by diphthongizing /i· u·/ in shape type (ii). This is what started the Tudor Vowel Shift. [...] Additional pressure on /i· u·/ to diphthongize came from the 'vocalization' of /ç j/ > /i/, /ɣ χ/ > /u/ [...] As we know from typological experience, the diphthong becomes better audible as such when the two elements become differentiated. We thus view the Tudor Vowel Shift as two parallel circular drag chains (in terms of features):
>
> /e/ → /i/ /o/ → /u/
> ↑ ↓ ↑ ↓
> /æ/ ← /ai/ /ɑ/ ← /au/

However, Pilch's postulated phonemes /æ· a· ɑ·/ for late-fourteenth-century London English correspond to /æː aː ɔː/ in the traditional view, where the last is not a front phoneme, which vitiates the 'skewed' argument. Pilch's argument may still be linked with Stockwell and Minkova's analysis that the vocalisation of *g/w* in lOE triggered the vowel shift, although Pilch does not refer to this stage of vocalisation, but rather to the vocalisation of *h* in *ht* after a front vowel in ME. Pilch's account is valuable for suggesting that vowel-change is not independent of vocalisation of consonants or of changes to syllable structure; still, he has too much faith in *systems* and that systems must be symmetrical. Further, some of Pilch's explanations are overly teleological, and his article deals with phonemics and structurally distinctive units rather than phonetic realisations, despite the paper's title.

Steponavičius (1997) states that *c.* 1200, the correlation between long and short vowels was replaced by a correlation between free and checked vowels. Therefore, he claims, the 'GVS' was a necessary structural reshuffling, apparently triggered by this systemic change, from long monophthongs to vocalic nucleus plus off-glide. However, it is not entirely clear why a structural change was *needed*, that is, why the long monophthongs *needed* to be restructured into vocalic nucleus plus off-glide (despite the vocalisation of *g/w*). The long monophthongs could have simply remained. To be sure, what happened to the close vowels in the 'GVS' was most likely the development of a minimal diphthong, but these diphthongs consisted of on-glide plus vocalic nucleus, not a vocalic nucleus plus off-glide. In other words, it seems that the vocalisation of *g/w* could cause a shift in the correlation short/long to checked/free only if the outputs of the vocalisation were sounds which were not part of the OE system already. Rather, the identification of the vocalised output (minimal diphthongs) with already existing (phonemic) long *monophthongs* implied allophonic variation within the phoneme, between monophthongal and diphthongal variants. Also, even if the vocalisation of *g/w* triggered the 'GVS', making the shift a 'pull-chain' process in conventional terminology, Steponavičius does not give any reasons why the 'GVS' also involved raising of the non-high vowels.

In his later article, Steponavičius (2005) states again that the change from OE long vs. short vowels, to free vs. checked vowels was due to the vocalisation of postvocalic fricatives, the development of glides before fricatives, and the loss of the length contrast in the vocalic segment; all of this created a new system of free ('long') vowels. The 'GVS' is seen as a continuation of this, which involved the elimination of level-glide free vowels (= long monophthongs), which were supplanted by out-gliding diphthongs in [-i] or [-u]. Against this it may be argued that level-glide free vowels were never eliminated, as witnessed by the presence in present-day RP of /iː/, /uː/, /ɜː/, /ɔː/, /ɑː/ – all it comes down to is the *linguist's* analysis of phonemic systems and the transcription, which is a consequence of this analysis.

The strength of Steponavičius's approach is that he, like Wełna and Pilch, connects vowel-change to consonantal change, and sees the vowel shift in a much larger perspective. The weak points are, first, that typology is used as an explanation for change; second, that Steponavičius believes in 'stable' systems, whose definitions are tautological; and third, that he makes no room for allophonic variation within each phoneme.

The preceding discussion leaves little doubt that the development of ME *ī* and *ū* did to some extent depend on the vocalisation of post-vocalic fricatives, first in lOE, later in ME. The dating of these processes is therefore investigated in what follows.

Conclusions regarding the chronology of changes

The chronology of changes in the front vowel area is obviously important, perhaps especially the development of the reflexes of OE *ēag* and *ēah*. Spellings have been extracted from all three ME corpora in the hope that they may shed light on (1) when the reflexes of OE *yht, eoht, eaht* merged with that of *iht*, (2) when the post-vocalic semi-vowels and fricatives vocalised, and (3) whether the development of OE *ēag*/*ēah* and of OE *ēog*/*ēoh* in terms of spelling was either (a) <eah>/<eag> → <ey> → <igh>, or (b) <eah>/<eag> → <igh> → <ey>, and to ascertain whether the same order of events took place everywhere. For tables of all the spellings extracted and analysed, see Stenbrenden (2010: Chapter 4).

With regard to (1), *LAEME* material reveals that the reflexes of OE *iht* and *yht* merged first, at *iht*, in those dialects where OE *ȳ*/*y* were unrounded, that is, in the eastern part of the country; this was certainly taking place in the latter half of the twelfth century. Western texts are generally more consistent in having <u>-type spellings for OE *yht*, although <i> is certainly not infrequent either, especially for OE DRYHTEN and cognates; <u>-type spellings become increasingly rare from the mid-thirteenth century, but there are odd occurrences as late as *c.* 1300 in southern and western texts. Next, the reflex of OE *eoht* merged with *iht*;[15] <e>-type forms are only occasional after the mid-thirteenth century. The reflex of OE *eaht*/*æht* merged with the others later. Given the high number of digraphs for this vowel, for example, <ea>, <eæ>, <ei>, <au>, words with OE *eaht* may have retained a diphthongal pronunciation for a long time, and may in fact have acted as a bridge in the development of a diphthong for the reflex of eME *ī*.

Regarding (2), *LAEME* sources indicate complete vocalisation of [j] after [i] (< OE *ig*) in sources from Essex in the late twelfth century, and in the (S)W Midlands (Worcestershire, Herefordshire, Gloucestershire, and Oxfordshire) from *c.* 1200 onwards. Complete vocalisation of [ç] from OE *h*+*t*+front vowel is in evidence in the E Midlands (Suffolk, Northamptonshire, Essex, Norfolk, Ely, and Huntingdonshire) and the (S-)W Midlands (Gloucestershire, Worcestershire, Wiltshire, Herefordshire, and Oxfordshire) in the late twelfth and early thirteenth centuries, and in Cheshire in the late thirteenth century. Hence, the handbooks may not be correct in assuming that the fricative part of OE *–ht* was preserved far into the ME period or even into the eModE period in all dialects.

Vocalisation of [x] or [ɣ] after a back vowel is suggested in a number of *LAEME* sources: it seems to have taken place first in Essex and Berkshire in the latter half of the twelfth century; in the W Midlands (Worcestershire, Gloucestershire, Shropshire, and Herefordshire) from *c.* 1200; in the NE Midlands (Cambridgeshire, Lincolnshire, Ely, and Norfolk) from the late thirteenth century; and in the North (Cheshire, Durham, and Yorkshire) in the late thirteenth and early fourteenth centuries. The [ɣ] appears to have vocalised before preconsonantal [x], but there are very early spellings indicating vocalisation of [x] also.

Thus, *LAEME* sources reporting spellings which indicate complete vocalisation of both the palatal and the velar fricatives have been entered in the E Midlands (Essex, Ely, Norfolk, Lincolnshire, and Berkshire) from the latter half of the twelfth century; the W Midlands (Gloucestershire, Worcestershire, Herefordshire, and Wiltshire) from the early thirteenth century; Cheshire (1275–99) and Yorkshire (1300–50). The Worcestershire-Gloucestershire area and Essex therefore stand out as loci of vocalisation. It is difficult to date the vocalisation of post-vocalic [j], [ç], [x], and [ɣ] in the North, due to the paucity of northern texts from the early period, but all the northern texts from the early fourteenth century give evidence of vocalisation.

However, it should be pointed out that the majority of relevant spellings extracted from *LAEME* show some kind of post-vocalic consonant, for example, <h(t)>, <kt>, <st>, <th>, <þt>. As the words in question are still spelt with a post-vocalic consonant cluster in PDE, this is hardly surprising, and need not imply retention of the fricative before /t/. Once standardisation and printing conventions were established, the game had changed: <ght> in pre-1470 English is not the same as <ght> post-1550, and <ght> in fourteenth-century English need not be supposed conservative in respect of spelling. Still, forms such as <nicht> NIGHT, <richt> RIGHT and <michti> MIGHTY (text no. 232), and <nikt> NIGHT and <rikt>

RIGHT (no. 228), suggest that a palatal fricative (or even plosive) remained before the /t/ in such dialects. When the proportion of tokens showing non-retention of the fricative is calculated for the items BRIGHT, FIGHT (verb and noun), FLIGHT, FRIGHT, KNIGHT, LIGHT, NIGHT, RIGHT, SIGHT and WRIGHT, the number comes out between 0% (for WRIGHT) and 8.82% (for FLIGHT); on average, 3.34% of the tokens imply complete vocalisation of the [ç] before /t/. These examples are thus more than just sporadic, but they certainly do not constitute the bulk of the evidence either, so the handbooks are not wholly misleading. Quite a few spellings are hard to interpret: <w> for OE *g* may or may not imply complete vocalisation, but certainly does indicate weakening of the fricative to a semi-vowel.[16] Numerous source texts also show variant forms which seem to contradict each other in terms of implied sound value. A case in point is the source text for no. 273 (Herefordshire, 1225–49), which has <vchtsong> for OE *ūhtsang* 'matins, morning song', which indicates a retained fricative, as well as <vtsong>, indicating complete vocalisation. The only logical inference is that variant forms with or without a post-vocalic consonant must have existed side by side for centuries; this is demonstrably so in some texts, which have 'bare' <ei>/<ey> or <ut> forms co-varying with <eih> or <uht>.

The relevant spellings in *SMED* suggest strongly that post-vocalic *ġ* [j] after a front vowel was certainly in the process of fusing, or had fused, with the preceding vowel from the early fourteenth century onwards, whereas the secondary palatal fricative was retained a little longer. Post-vocalic [ɣ] after a back vowel lingered on a little longer in Lancashire, Gloucestershire, Norfolk, Suffolk and the South, but was vocalising elsewhere in the early fourteenth century (cf. Prins 1942a: 137). In the reflex of OE *–ht*, the fricative was generally retained longer all over the country, except in Lincolnshire, where vocalisation seems to have been completed. However, spellings indicating vocalisation are also found in most of the country, albeit more infrequently in the South than in the rest of the country.

As for (3) mentioned earlier, it seems that *ēog/ēoh* and *ēag/ēah* must be kept apart, as their developments were clearly not identical (cf. Sundby 1963), and that the chronology may have been that of (a) mentioned earlier for *ēag/ēah*, but (b) for *ēog/ēoh*. In the earliest *LAEME* texts, the reflexes of OE *ēog/ēoh* are spelt <i> (+consonant), at least in the East and South-East (Essex, Suffolk, and Kent); thus, <i>-type spellings are in fact slightly earlier than <ei>-type spellings in these areas. In other dialects, especially in the W Midlands, the development of OE *ēog* seems to have been the same as that of OE *ēo* in general, that is, to [ø:], at least in given words.

For OE *ēah/ēag*, however, <ei>-type spellings predominate from the earliest ME texts; <eh>- and <eȝ>-type spellings are also found from the latter half of the twelfth century onwards, but these are not nearly as frequent as <ei>/<ey>. Again, although forms with a post-vocalic consonant seem more numerous than 'bare' forms, such bare forms are found already in the second half of the twelfth century, and appear in some quantity from the early thirteenth century onwards. Thus, it seems more and more difficult to maintain that the post-vocalic consonant was retained even into the eModE period. At least in certain parts of the country, the post-vocalic palatal semi-vowel and fricative appear to have been in the process of being vocalised as early as the late twelfth century. The same seems to be the case with the post-vocalic velar semi-vowel and fricative; cp. Chapter 7. However, with respect to the inflected forms with contraction, or medial <w>, it is difficult to ascertain whether the corresponding simplex in ME, if lacking <(g)h>, <ȝ> etc., shows vocalisation rather than re-formation.

In the *LAEME* corpus, there is only a handful of <i> for OE *ēah*. These forms suggest that the raising of the reflex of OE *ēah* to [i:] was taking place possibly in the early thirteenth century in Essex, and probably from the mid-thirteenth century onwards in Worcestershire, Oxfordshire, Ely, and Norfolk. Furthermore, this process seems to have only just begun by the end of the period covered by *LAEME*. In part, this goes against the claims made by Wyld (1927: 126–7) that <i>/<y> for OE *ēag/ēah* are not found at all in the E Midlands up until the fourteenth century.

In *SMED*, forms with <i>/<y> for OE *ēah/ ēag* are indeed more numerous than in *LAEME*, though <ei>/<ey> remain dominant; <i>/<y> are found in all of England south of the Humber for the reflex of OE *ēag*, and in the South as well as in Leicestershire and Northumberland for OE *ēah*. Kristensson concludes that the [i:]-stage had been reached in most counties by the early fourteenth century, except in Kent, Devon, and Dorset, which had [ei:], and in Westmorland, Lancashire, the North, East, and West Ridings of Yorkshire, which had retained [e:].[17] In *LALME*, spellings with <i>/<y> for the reflexes of OE *ēag/ēah* are extremely frequent, but so are <ei>/<ey> also.

Another interesting fact emerges from the extracted material: even in the late period covered by *LAEME*, there are texts which show occasional <i> for the reflex of OE *ēah*, but which also show very frequent <a>, <ai>, <æ>, etc. spellings for the same (e.g. text nos. 277 and 278, Worcestershire, 1250–74). The dominant spellings appear to indicate an open vowel, or at least a half-open one. These spellings could imply variant pronunciations, as has been proposed in the discussion earlier, which corroborates Stockwell and Minkova's suggested development. However, the eME material does not give much evidence for an [i:] stage for the reflex of OE *ēag*: the few <i>/<y> that appear, are for the reflex of OE *ēah*.[18] Therefore, it must be concluded that the raising of the vocalic nucleus of the reflexes of OE *ēag/ēah* was in its early stages *c.* 1300. However, from the *LAEME* material it cannot be concluded that OE *ēag* was raised a whole century before OE *ēah*, as claimed by Sundby (1963) and Wełna (1988) – rather, the distinction is between *ēog/ēoh* and *ēag/ēah*. The *SMED* material is similarly inconclusive, although <i>/<y> are slightly more numerous for OE *ēag* than for *ēah*.[19]

As pointed out earlier, the development of the reflexes of OE *ēog/ēoh* was different from that of OE *ēag/ēah*, which etymologically should be expected: OE *ēa* < *ǣa*, *au*, and is ME /ɛ:/, whereas OE *ēo* < *eu/iu* and broken *ē*, and is ME /e:/. Judging by the eME spellings, the vocalic nucleus of these etymological diphthongs was either raised to [i:] early on, or monophthongised to [e:]. The <ie> forms in no. 4 from Essex (1150–99) could be AN spellings for [e:], but there are equally early <i> spellings from for example, Worcestershire, in texts which do not generally show AN <ie> for [e:]. Forms with <e> and <i> are about equally frequent in the *LAEME* material. Hence, the raising of the nucleus of OE *ēog/ēoh* must have started at least in the latter half of the twelfth century, and it may have started in the SE Midlands (Essex and Suffolk) as well as in the W Midlands (Worcestershire and Shropshire). Spellings with <ei>/<ey> do not appear until *c.* 1250; these could imply insertion of a glide-vowel after [e:] before the palatal semi-vowel, or the vocalisation of the semi-vowel, or both. They are recorded in Wiltshire, Cambridgeshire, Essex, Herefordshire, and Gloucestershire. Again, it appears that variants with raised [i:] and variants with monophthongised [e:] existed side by side in the same idiolects or dialects, as many source texts report co-variants with <i> and <e(o)> (e.g. no. 1900, Worcestershire).

Spelling evidence for all the changes enumerated earlier is recorded in numerous *LAEME* source texts; *all* of them seem to have taken place or to be taking place in Worcestershire, Oxfordshire, and Ely, which therefore could be loci of change. The E Midlands, W Midlands, and Kent clearly stand out as showing an advanced pronunciation from an early stage, but the paucity of eME material from the Central Midlands and (parts of) the North suggests that caution is needed when conclusions are drawn. However, all counties are represented in the *LALME* material, which indicates complete vocalisation of post-vocalic [j] across the country, although the Midlands are better represented than the North and the South; the same applies to [x]. Vocalisation of [ç] seems to have started later, and/or been effected more slowly, in the North. The opposite seems to have been the case for post-vocalic [ɣ]: there are fewer spellings indicating vocalisation in the South than in the North and the Midlands. That is, the locus of change for the ME vocalisation of post-vocalic fricatives must probably be sought in the Midlands, whence it must have spread southwards and northwards, following patterns typical of lexical diffusion: some words seem to be affected by linguistic change first, and are 'leaders'; other words gradually follow suit.[20] The reason why some words are affected first may be that they are very frequent, or – in combinative change – that the phonetic conditions that trigger or favour the change are present in these words. The words which are affected later, are affected due to simple analogy. The following chronology of change is thus suggested by the ME material.

1. *īġ/īw* > *ī* (lOE); *ȳ* > *ī* and *yht* > *iht* in certain parts of the country
2. *iġ* > *ī* (lOE)
3. *iht* > *īht* > *īt* (eME)

4a. *eoht* > *eht* > *iht* > *īt* (lOE or eME)
4b. *ēog/ēoh* > *īġ/īh* (lOE or eME)
    > *ēiġ/ēih* > *īġ/īh* (eME and throughout ME)

5. *eaht* > *æht/eht* > *iht* > *īt* (lOE/eME and throughout ME)
6. *ēag/ēah* > *ēg/ēh* > *ēiġ/ēih* > *īġ/īh* > *ī* (eME and throughout ME)
    > *ei*

Moreover, irregular <ei>/<ey> for ME *ī* start to appear at about the same time as <i>/<y> start to appear for the reflexes of OE *ēag/ēah*, which may suggest confusion between the two sets. It seems also that the reflexes of OE *ēog/ēoh* could have provided a 'bridge' between the two classes: the eME spellings indicate that OE *ēog/ēoh* were raised to [ɪː], [iː], or [ij] early on, at least in some dialects, but forms with [e] or [ei] for the same reflexes existed side by side with the raised variants. Hence, variant pronunciations with a close vowel, a half-close vowel, or a diphthong, appear to have arisen quite a bit earlier for OE *ēog/ēoh* than for OE *ēag/ēah*; this is not surprising, given the etymologies and later developments of OE *ēo* and *ēa* in ME.

Interestingly, virtually all the *LAEME* texts which show (potential) vowel-shift spellings for eME *ī* also show complete vocalisation of the post-vocalic semi-vowel and fricatives. In other words, these are texts by scribes whose orthographical systems imply an advanced pronunciation.[21]

Thus, analysis of *LAEME* spellings for the reflexes of OE *ī*, lengthened *i, iht/eoht/eaht, ēog/ēoh, ēag/ēah* strengthens the assumption that <ei>/<ey> for at least *ī* and lengthened *i/iht/eoht* could show early vowel shift, especially in sources which do not show general <ei>/<ey> for these reflexes. A case in point is no. 282 from Ely (1275–1324), which shows <it>, <itt>,[22] <ith>, <iȝth>, <yt>, and <yȝt> for the reflexes of OE *iht* and *eoht*, but which shows one <pleyt> PLIGHT.[23] However, *LAEME* source texts with <ei>/<ey> for these reflexes also generally show <ei>/<ey> for the reflexes of OE *ēag/ēah*, so the possibility remains that <ei>/<ey> for ME *ī* might be back spellings.

5.4 Discussion of ME potential vowel-shift spellings for *ī*

Irregular spellings for OE *ȳ/y* are treated in Chapter 8, although in areas where the reflexes of these were unrounded to [i(:)], the output merged with that of eME *ī*.[24]

5.4.1 Discussion of LAEME *material*

OE ī

For eME *ī* the material shows some <e>, <u>, and <o>, and quite a few <ei>/ey>. The irregular spellings start appearing in the latter half of the twelfth century, and they appear regularly throughout the thirteenth century. The digraph <ai> occurs once for the vowel of WISE, in text no. 262 from Shropshire (1200–24). The form in question is <waisdom> and is difficult to assess, as the stressed vowel is short in PDE.

Some of the items recorded (Table 5.1) seem to have had variant pronunciations in OE, and <e> in these cases may therefore reflect the regular development of OE *ē*; examples are OE *drīge* DRY, which had variant forms with *ē* (and *ȳ*), and OE *sīclian* SICKEN, for which variants with *ǣ, ē, ēo*, and *ȳ* are attested. Forms which may attest regular developments of vowels other than *ī* are therefore preceded by a question mark in the table.[25] The remaining forms appear in the SE Midlands, the SW Midlands, and the NE Midlands, starting in the early thirteenth century.

Forms[26] with <ei>/<ey> (Table 5.2) are particularly frequent in no. 161 from Gloucestershire, where they are dominant. The earliest <ei>/<ey> cluster in Essex and Suffolk in the late twelfth and early thirteenth centuries, and in the W Midlands (Shropshire, Worcestershire, Herefordshire, and Gloucestershire) from the early thirteenth century onwards.

Table 5.1 LAEME *incidence of* <e>, <eo> *for OE* ī *(and* ēog*)*

County	No.	Date	Spellings
Essex	64	1200–24	<bleðeliche(r)> BLITHELY
	160	1275–99	<stref> STRIFE
Sussex	67	1200–49	<ste> STĪGAN *inf.*
Kent	8	1200–49	<bleðeliche(r)> BLITHELY
			<ʒetseres> GĪTSERE *pl.*
	142	1275–99	<bleþeliche> BLITHELY
Worcestershire	1900	1200–49	<teʒeþ> TIE *3.sg.ps.*
	245	1225–49	?<seclie> SĪCLIAN *3.sg.ps.sj.*
	278	1250–74	<ʒets-> GĪTSIAN *vn.*
	3	1275–99	<leþ> LIE *3.sg.ps.*
Cheshire	118	1240–50	?<seclie> SĪCLIAN *3.sg.ps.sj.*
Gloucestershire	161	1275–99	<ste(n)> STĪGAN *inf.*
	229	1275–99	<steheþ> STĪGAN *3.sg.ps.*
	2002	1275–99	<lekþ> LIKE *v. 3.sg.ps.*
			<seʒin> SĪGAN *inf.*
	10	1275–1324	?<dreʒ> DRY
			<bleþeli(che)> BLITHELY
			<ʒevernesse> GĪVERNESS
			<bleþeliche> BLITHELY
			<ʒeseres> GĪTSERE *pl.*
Herefordshire	246	1275–99	<sten> STĪGAN *inf.*
	247	1275–99	<sten> STĪGAN *inf.*
	1100	1275–99	<steo> STĪGAN *inf.*
Norfolk	1700	1284–89	<bleþeliche> BLITHELY
Unlocalised	265	13th c.	<steheþ> STĪGAN *3.sg.ps.*
Unlocalised	238	1275–99	<steo> STĪGAN *inf.*
Lincolnshire	169	1325–49	<be-sweke> BESWĪCAN

Three texts from the W Midlands report <ij>, <iiʒ>, <iʒ> for eME *ī*. No. 1600 (Oxfordshire, 1275–1324) has several <ij> for OE *ī*, *iht, yht*; this spelling probably simply indicates a long monophthong. However, the source in question shows potential vowel-shift spellings for eME *ē* and *ō*, and possibly for eME *ū*, as well, so <ij> may correspond to a minimal diphthong. Forms with <iʒ> are found in 3 tokens in Worcestershire (no. 277, 1250–74) for WILE and cognates. These imply vocalisation of etymological *g/ʒ* after *i*, such that <iʒ> may represent /iː/; it is an open question whether the digraph indicates a phonetic monophthong or a minimal diphthong. The forms <miiʒt> MIGHT *n.* and <siʒtte/siiþe> SIGHT are found in no. 2002 (Gloucestershire, 1275–99), which also has a number of other irregular spellings.

Table 5.2 LAEME *incidence of <ei>/<ey> etc. for OE* ī, *(ȳ),* ēog

County	No.	Date	Spellings
Essex	1200	1150–99	<itei(e)d> TIE *ppl.*
	64	1200–24	<leðebei(h)/leðebeiȝe> LIÞEBĪGE
Suffolk	1300	1150–99	<teid> TIE *ppl.*
Worcestershire	2000	c. 1200	<leit> LIGHTNING
	1900	1200–49	<unteiȝe> TIE *ppl.*
			<teȝeþ> TIE *3.sg.ps.*
	245	1225–49	<iteied> TIE *ppl.*
	1800	1225–49	<creie> CRY
			<iteied> TIE *ppl.*
	276	1250–74	<teiet> TĪEGAN *3.sg.ps.*
	2	1275–99	<iteid> TIE *ppl.*
Shropshire	260	1200–24	<iteiet> TIE *ppl.*
	262	1200–24	<leoðe-bei> LIÞEBĪGE
			<iteiet> TIE *ppl.*
	1000	1200–24	<iteiet> TIE *ppl.*
	272	1225–49	<iteiet> TIE *ppl.*
Herefordshire	273	1225–49	<iteiȝet> TIE *ppl.*
	246	1275–99	<þestrei> ÞȲSTRIG
	249	1275–99	<leþe-bei> LIÞEBĪGE
	1100	1275–99	<i-teyed> TIE *ppl.*
Gloucestershire	161	1275–99	<a-beydin> ABIDE
			<be-teyden> BETIDE
			<bleyþit> BLĪÞIAN
			<to-dreyuen> DRIVE
			<leif/leyf> LIFE
			<seyde(n)> SIDE
			<seyþe> SWĪÞE
			<weyue> WIFE
			<e-leyt> LIGHT *ppl.*
			<leyt> LIGHT n.
			<þondir-leyt> THUNDERLIGHT n.
	229	1275–99	?<dreiȝ> DRY
	2002	1275–99	?<-drei> DRY
			<flei> FLY *n.*
			<fleye> FLY *v. inf.*
			<þei> THIGH
Unlocalised	121	1240–50	<iteiet> TIE *ppl.*
	123	1240–50	<iteied/iteiet> TIE *ppl.*
	19	1300–24	?<dreie> DRY

Table 5.3 LAEME *incidence of* <u>, <o>, *etc. for the reflexes of eME* ī

County	No.	Date	Spellings
Oxfordshire	232	1175–1224	<suhðe> SIGHT
Shropshire	262	1200–24	<bluðeluker> BLITHELY
Unlocalised	120	1240–50	<huine*n*> HĪGAN
Wiltshire	280	1250–74	<bloþeliche> BLITHELY
Worcestershire	278	1250–74	<bluðeliche> BLITHELY
Devon	147	1275–99	?<buswide> BESĪÞIAN
Herefordshire	246	1275–99	?<wuile> WHILE
Durham	188	1300–49	<scoyer> SQUIRE

Most <u>, <o>, etc. (Table 5.3)[27] are recorded in texts localised to the W Midlands and appear throughout the thirteenth century. In <scoyer> SQUIRE in no. 188 from Durham, there is a remote possibility that <o> is supposed to indicate [w] and the <y> [iː], in which case the spelling is unremarkable, but such an interpretation of <o> is not very likely in a non-minim cluster. That is, this is more probably a vowel-shift spelling.

If the diphthongal spellings <ei> and <ey> indicate early diphthongisation of etymological *ī*, the change seems to have started in the South-East and East Anglia, and independently in the W Midlands (Shropshire, Herefordshire, Worcestershire, and Gloucestershire).

OE i *in lengthening context*

The material is extracted for OE *i* before (a) voiced homorganic consonant clusters (e.g. BLIND, WIND), or (b) OE or eME *ġ* (e.g. NINE, SIGN), or (c) OE *ht* (e.g. MIGHT n., NIGHT, RIGHT).

The two forms in Table 5.4 are interesting: <suhðe> may demonstrate the development of OE *y*, but <bland> is remarkable, especially in such an early text.[28]

In Table 5.5, forms with the reflex of OE *y* in lengthening contexts have been asterisked, and are treated in Chapter 8. Lexical items that are recorded with OE *iht* as well as with *eoht, eaht*, etc. are preceded by a question mark.

For OE *i+ġ*, <e> appears in Kent, Wiltshire, and Essex; two are for NINE, but as this numeral is recorded with *e* for the stressed vowel in OE, the *LAEME* forms may reflect the regular development of OE *e*. The same may be true of the three tokens with <ei>/<ey> in NINE and NINTH from Yorkshire. The two forms for LIE (text no. 160, Essex) may have <e> by analogy with the preterit. One form with <ei> for unstressed OE *ig*

Table 5.4 LAEME *incidence of <a>, <u> for the reflexes of OE* i/y *in lengthening contexts, and OE* eoht, eorht, eaht

County	No.	Date	Spellings
Oxfordshire	232	1175–1224	<suhðe> SIGHT
Essex	65	1200–24	<bland> BLIND *imp.*

is recorded in a source from Herefordshire; the word in question is OE *þȳstrig, þēostrig* 'dark, obscure', and the form is <þestrei>. The same source has one <ui> spelling and one <e> spelling for words with OE *ī*, as well as <seisþe> for SIGHT; a diphthongised reflex of ME *ī* may be implied. For BUY and LIE 'untruth', both with OE *y*, <ei>/<ey> are found in Essex, Shropshire, Kent, Cambridgeshire, Gloucestershire, Norfolk, and Lincolnshire, starting in the early thirteenth century; these seem to indicate vowel shift.

The form <bleint> may correspond to a diphthong. For OE *y* before a voiced homorganic consonant cluster, no. 161 (Gloucestershire) has <man-keyne> MANKIND; this text has a truly idiosyncratic orthography, with <ey> very frequent and dominant for the reflex of all eME *ī*; this form may therefore testify to early vowel-shifting.

For OE *i* before *ht*, <e> is recorded in Worcestershire; <ee> appears in Durham. Some of the items in question (i.e. NIGHT and RIGHT) are recorded with *æ/e/eo/ea* in OE, which implies that the forms with <e> may go back to OE variants with a non-close vowel. However, palatal mutation (Campbell 1959: §§304–11) would have raised *e/eo* + [x]-clusters + *e* to *i*, starting in Kentish in the ninth century, and spreading northwards in the tenth and eleventh centuries. This suggests in turn that the forms with <e>/<ee> for NIGHT and RIGHT do reflect eME *iht*. Since palatal mutation only affected forms where *io/e/eo*+[x]+C were followed by *e*, it resulted in paradigmatic variation between [içt] and [e(ə)çt], for example, *cniht – cneohtas* KNIGHT, but also in analogical forms such as *cneoht, cnihtas*. Forms with <ei>/<ey> occur in Essex, Herefordshire, Gloucestershire, Norfolk, Ely, Durham, and in an unlocalised text. For OE *yht*, <ey> for *y* is found in Gloucestershire and Lincolnshire from the late thirteenth century. The form <freyð> OE *friþ* 'peace' in no. 132 from Cumberland is remarkable, in that it is the reflex of OE *i*, but not before a homorganic voiced consonant cluster. The later history of English shows lengthening of vowels before voiceless fricatives (the so-called 'TRAP-BATH split'); this may be an early similar case, but it is difficult to tell.

Table 5.5 LAEME *incidence of <e>, <ei>/<ey>, etc. for OE* i/y *in lengthening contexts*

County	No.	Date	Spellings
Worcestershire	2000	c. 1200	?<mehtiȝan> MIGHTY *n.*
	3	1275–99	<rehte> RIGHT
Essex	64	1200–24	<seihtþe> SIGHT
	65	1200–24	*<beið> BUY *3.sg.ps.*
	160	1275–99	<leȝe> LIE *imp.*
			<leȝen> LIE *3.pl.ps.*
			*<for-beyen> FORBUY *inf.*
Shropshire	260	1200–24	*<ley> FALSEHOOD
			<blent> BLIND *3.sg.ps.*
	261	1200–24	<iblend> BLIND *ppl.*
	262	1200–24	<iblend> BLIND *ppl.*
	1000	1200–24	<blent> BLIND *3.sg.ps.*
	272	1225–49	<blent> BLIND *3.sg.ps.*
Kent	8	1200–49	<neȝende> NINE
			*<beið> BUY *3.sg.ps.*
Herefordshire	273	1225–49	<blent> BLIND *3.sg.ps.*
	246	1275–99	<seisþe> SIGHT
			<þestrei> ÞȲSTRIG
	1100	1275–99	<blende> BLIND *3.sg.pt.*
Unlocalised	120	1240–50	<blend> BLIND *3.sg.ps.*
Cumberland	132	13th c.	<freyð> FRIÞ
Unlocalised	139	13th c.	<bleint> BLIND *aj.*
Wiltshire	280	1250–74	<neȝentene> NINETEEN
Cambridgeshire	137	1275–99	*<bein> BUY *inf.*
Gloucestershire	161	1275–99	<areyt> ARIGHT
			?<god-al-meyte> ALMIGHTY
			?<meytin> MAY *1.pl.pt.sj.*
			?<meyte> *3.sg.pt./3.pl.pt.(sj.)*
			?<meyte> MIGHT *n.*
			<reyt(e)> RIGHT
			<reyt-weysnesse> RIGHTEOUSNESS
			<reyt-folnesse> RIGHT-FULNESS
			<seyte> SIGHT
			*<dreyte> DRYHTEN
			*<fleyt> FLIGHT
			*<vreyte> FRIGHT
	2002	1275–99	*<man-keyne> MANKIND
	10	1275–1324	<wende/wendis> WIND *n.*
			*<beye> BUY *inf.*
			*<forbeyen> FORBUY *inf.*
			*<beiþ> BUY *3.sg.ps.*
Norfolk	269	1275–1324	*<beyn> BUY *inf.*

(*continued*)

Table 5.5 (*cont.*)

County	No.	Date	Spellings
Unlocalised	241	1275–99	<blende> BLIND *3.sg.pt.*
Lincolnshire	159	c.1300	*<ley> FALSEHOOD
	169	1325–49	*<fleyt> FLIGHT
Ely	282	1275–1324	<pleyt> PLIGHT
Durham	188	1300–49	<reeth/reith> RIGHT
East Riding Yks	297	1300–49	<nein> NINE <neynd> NINTH
North Riding Yks	298	1300–49	<neynd> NINTH

The spellings <ei>/ey> for OE *i* certainly indicate that the vowel had been lengthened and may suggest diphthongisation. If so, the change seems to have started in Essex, Kent, and Herefordshire, and to have been effected a little later in Cambridgeshire, Gloucestershire, Norfolk, Lincolnshire, and Ely; diphthongisation may have started independently in Cumberland and Durham. However, it is difficult to determine the difference between sporadic and fortuitous coherences in patchy and partial data: the North in particular is poorly attested in the *LAEME* material. Hence, any conclusions must be tentative.

OE eah(t) *and* eo(r)ht

LAEME sources record potentially interesting spellings for OE *eaht* and *eo(r)ht*, as appears in Table 5.6.[29]

Digraph spellings for OE *eaht* are recorded in Essex and Worcestershire, then in Gloucestershire. However, in Anglian, smoothing of broken *ea* would have given *æ* (sometimes *e*, cf. Campbell 1959: §§222–33), which suggests that <ei>/<ey> could indicate [e] or [æ] plus a glide developed before the palatal fricative. If the product of smoothing had been raised to *e*, however, palatal mutation would have raised the vowel to *i* before [x]-clusters+*e*, suggesting that the <ei>/<ey> spellings adduced earlier do indeed reflect eME *iht* (Campbell 1959: §§304–11).

There are some <ei>/<ey> for the reflex of OE *eoht*, in Gloucestershire, Worcestershire, and Norfolk, from the late thirteenth century onwards. In addition, the form <fexit> for FIGHT n. appears in Durham (no. 188) and may indicate diphthongisation of the vowel; at least, the <i> may correspond to a glide between etymological *h* and *t*. Variants with *e* for the vowel are recorded in OE for both BRIGHT and FIGHT, so <ei>/<ey> could correspond to [e] plus a glide developed before the palatal fricative. However,

Table 5.6 LAEME *incidence of <e>, <ei>, <ey>, etc. for the reflexes of OE* eoht, eaht

County	No.	Date	Spellings
Worcestershire	2000	c. 1200	<mehtiȝan> MIGHTY *n.*
	277	1250–74	<feiht> FIGHT *3.sg.pt.*
			<feihten> FIGHT *inf.*
Essex	64	1200–24	<hleit> LAUGHTER
Gloucestershire	161	1275–99	<god-al-meyte> ALMIGHTY
			<meytin> MAY *1.pl.pt.sj.*
			<meyte> *3.sg.pt./3.pl.pt.(sj.)*
			<meyte> MIGHT *n.*
			<breyt(e)> BRIGHT
			<feyte/feytin> FIGHT *inf.*
			<feytinge> FIGHT *vn.*
	2002	1275–99	<feite> FIGHT *inf.*
			<ounmaute> MIGHT *n.*
Norfolk	1700	1284–89	<feiteinge> FIGHT *vn.*
			<feite> FIGHT *3.sg.ps.sj.*
Durham	188	1300–49	<fexit> FIGHT *n.*

as noted earlier with respect to the reflex of OE *eaht*, palatal mutation would have raised *e/eo*+[x]-clusters+e to *i* in late OE or early ME. Thus, <breyt> and <feit>, etc. for BRIGHT and FIGHT most likely reflect eME *iht*.

OE ēag/ēah, ēog/ēoh

From the spelling evidence collected, one may conclude that for the reflexes of OE *ēag/ēah*, <ei>, <eȝ>, <e>, and similar spellings are dominant in the period covered by *LAEME*. The only six tokens with <i>/<y> are found for NIGH and HIGH (Table 5.7).

Although <ei>-type spellings are dominant, <e>-type forms with a post-vocalic consonant (clearly indicating [e(:)] + a fricative, rather than a glide or semi-vowel) are very numerous also. This must be taken as relatively solid evidence that around *c.* 1300, the reflexes of OE *ēag/ēah* had not been raised to [i:], nor were in the process of merging with the reflexes of OE *ī* or *iht/yht/eoht/eaht*. The situation was clearly different for the reflexes of OE *ēog/ēoh*: even the earliest source texts for *LAEME* have <i>-type spellings for these, for example, text nos. 4 (Essex, 1150–99) and 1300 (Suffolk, same date). Forms with <e> are also numerous, especially in the W Midlands, but even in these sources, <e> frequently co-varies with <i>-type spellings. Whether this suggests that the alleged raising of the reflexes

Table 5.7 LAEME *incidence of <i> and <y> for OE* ēah

County	No.	Date	Spellings
Essex	65	1200–24	<nieh> NIGH
Worcestershire	277	1250–74	<nih> NIGH
	278	1250–74	<nig> NIGH
Norfolk	269	1275–1324	<hithe> HIGH
Ely	282	1275–1324	<ny> NIGH
Oxfordshire	1600	1275–1324	<hiȝe> HIGH

of OE *ēag/ēah* happened by analogy with those of OE *ēog/ēoh* is uncertain. It also leaves open the possibility that the reflexes of OE *ēag/ēah* merged with that of eME *ī* only when the latter had started to diphthongise.

Text no. 246 reports some <ii> for eME *ī*; OE *iht* is here almost always <ist>, or <it>. OE *hw* is generally <w> in this text, but WHILE is <wuile> once, which again could imply diphthongisation, although <ui> would be an odd diphthong development; it could also correspond to [y:], with rounding after [w].[30] Diphthongisation may be implied by <seisþe> SIGHT in the same source. This text has a high number of <ei> spellings for eME *ē*, and quite a few <oi> for eME *ō*; these could indicate length or raising (they occur also for BED and RED); <–ist> is also used in words where OE did not have an [s], for example, <fiste> FIFTH, <aiste> OE *ǣht*, <bitaiste> OE *betǣcan*, so <–ist> in this context may denote [çt] or [θt]. OE *iht* and *eoht* seem to be <ist>, but OE *meaht(e)* is <maist>, <mast>.[31]

Analogical <i> for ME ei

One <awi> AWAY appears in no. 278 from Worcestershire (1250–74). This source otherwise has <ei>, <æi>, <ai> for the reflexes of OE *ėg/æġ* and <i> for the reflex of OE *ī*, though there is <bluðeliche> BLITHELY and <ȝets-[in]ge> OE *gītsian* 'to long for, covet'. It is possible that this is a back spelling, indicating diphthongisation of OE *ī*. Curiously, Zachrisson does not draw the same conclusion with respect to <wye> WAY in the Paston Letters, but merely states that it may be an error (Zachrisson 1913: 74). He concludes that <ey> for eME *ī*, <au>/<aw> for eME *ū*, <u> and <ou>/<ow> for eME *ō*, and <i>/<y> for eME *ē* in the same sources clearly indicate vowel-shifted sounds, and he defines 'analogical spellings', so it is surprising that he does not make the obvious inference. There remains the possibility that <–wi(e)>/<–wy(e)> indicate reduction of the second

Table 5.8 SMED *incidence of <ey> for eME* ī, ī+w

County	Date	Spellings
Cambridgeshire	1330	<Weytefot'> WHITE
Hertfordshire	1307	<le Leymbrenne'> LIME
Kent	1327	<Weys> WISE
Northumberland	1316	<Weydon> WIDE
Staffordshire	1327	<Heyne> ME *hīne*
Warwickshire	1332	<Sweyn> SWINE
Wiltshire	1332	<Hardeneheiwich> OE *hīwisc*
Worcestershire	1332	<Steyward> STEWARD

element of the compound, but since the second syllable carries the stress, it seems unlikely.

5.4.2 *Discussion of* SMED *material*

OE ī

There are a few <iy> for the reflex of OE *ī*, found in the North Riding of Yorkshire (LSR for 1301). In Kristensson's view (1967: 73), <iy> merely indicates vowel-length, by which he probably means a long monophthong, much like <ij> in *LAEME*; the digraph could also imply a minimal diphthong. <Swenhurde> with SWINE (Somerset, 1327) is likewise difficult to assess. Occasional <ey> is recorded in Table 5.8.

In Kristensson's view, <ei>/<ey> forms for both OE *ī* and OE *ig* are back spellings, 'reflecting the change of OE *ēȝe* into ME /i:/' (1995: 45, 141; cf. 1967: 74; and 1987: 65, 147; and 2001: 65). In *SMED4*, however Kristensson admits the possibility that OE *ī* was being diphthongised in the early fourteenth century, not because of the <ey> spellings, but for more systemic reasons: 'The reflex of OE *ī* is spelt <i/y> denoting /i:/ or […] [ɪi] in at least parts of the area under examination' (Kristensson 2001: 65). In the chapters on eME *ē* and *ō* it will be seen that there are numerous irregular spellings for the reflexes of these two sounds in the central Southern counties. Therefore, Kristensson draws the conclusion that eME *ē* and *ō* had been, or were being, raised to [i:] and [u:] respectively at the beginning of the fourteenth century (Kristensson 2001: 78–9). Yet, the reflexes of these two sounds never merged with the reflexes of etymological *ī* and *ū*, as witnessed by the PDE reflexes. To account for this (2001: 79–80),

> we must assume that ME /i:/ and /u:/ had developed, or were developing, into diphthongs at the time when ME /e:/ and /o:/ were raised. I think that ME /i:/ had become [ɪi], but – as was generally the case in the Great Vowel Shift – the old spelling was retained. So by this time the letter value of <i> was [ɪi], and therefore the scribes avoided <i> to denote the 'new' /i:/. [...] All this amounts to suggesting that the tendencies which eventuated in the Great Vowel Shift were beginning to assert themselves in the Central Southern dialects in the early 14th century.

This applies to <Steyward> also. One cannot help wondering whether irregular forms from the North and the Midlands could be accounted for in similar manner. The view that OE *ī* had diphthongised is actually corroborated by other Southern material, in a few <y(e)> spellings for OE etymological *eġ*: <Whybulle> with OE *hweġ* WHEY (Hampshire, 1333), and <Holewye> with OE *weġ* WAY (Somerset, 1333), cf. the section on 'Analogical <i> for ME *ei* ', and later under OE *ēġ*. The <–wye> may also indicate vowel-reduction in a compound.

If the <ei>/<ey> spellings are indicative of diphthongisation of the reflex of OE *ī*, this change seems to have taken place simultaneously in different locations: Northumberland, the Cambridgeshire-Hertfordshire area, the Staffordshire-Warwickshire area, and perhaps Kent. The back spellings from Hampshire and Somerset may indicate vowel shift in the South as well.

OE i *in lengthening contexts*

Two <ye> for OE *i* in lengthening contexts appear in Essex (1327) and Somerset (1333); it may indicate a minimal diphthong, but it seems unlikely and it is difficult to know for certain without having analysed the scribe's orthography in detail. For Kristensson's explanation of these forms, see the preceding section, under OE *ī*.[32] *SMED* reports <ey>, <egh>, etc. as in Table 5.9.

Some <eg(h)> for OE *ig* are reported in the South (Kent and Somerset). The Kentish forms 'go back to OE *u*-mutated forms [...] and [...] presuppose OKent *eo* from earlier *io*' (Kristensson 2001: 61). As for <Neghenhude> with NINE and <Steghel> with STILE from Somerset, it is claimed that they are examples of the lengthening of /i/ to /e:/, that they thus 'contain /e:/ and that the tendency to lengthening of /i/ in an open syllable obtained in the whole of England' (2001: 61; see also Kristensson 1987: 65). However, in the early vowel shift model, innovative <e> for the MEOSL product of /i/ indicates vowel shift of /e:/ to [i:]. Both of these accounts go against the traditional view that *i* lengthened only in the North and in East Anglia.[33]

Table 5.9 SMED *incidence of <ey> etc. for OE* i+g

County	Date	Spellings
Essex	1332	<Steyle> STILE
		<Teilere> TILE
Kent	1327	<Steghel> STILE
		<Teghelere>, <Theghelere> TILE
	1332	<Steghel>, <Stegule> STILE
		<Teghelere> TILE
Lincolnshire	1327	<Steygle> STILE
Norfolk	1332	<Steyle> STILE
Somerset	1327	<Neghenhude> NINE
		<Steghel> STILE
	1333	<Neghenhude> NINE

On the two <ey> in reflexes of OE **Peohtla* in Leicestershire (1327, 1333), Kristensson (1987: 122) comments that 'OE *eht* (< *eoht*) followed by a velar vowel has become *eyght* (with a glide before /χ/)'.

The three <ey>-forms in Table 5.10 are explained as 'due to influence from the plur. *cneohtas*' (Kristensson 1995: 93). The processes in question, 'Anglian smoothing' and 'palatal umlaut' (Campbell 1959: §§304–11), took place in (late) OE. East Anglian would therefore have had *cniht-* in both the singular and the plural by this date; thus, the forms may indicate vowel shift.

Analogical <y> for ME ei

Two interesting spellings for OE *eġ* appear in the South. <Whybulle> with OE *hweg* WHEY appears alongside <Weybole>, <Wheybole> in Hampshire (1333). <Holewye>, with OE *weġ* WAY, occurs in Somerset; <–weye> is dominant, but there are also forms with <–wey>, <–wai>. Kristensson merely comments that <Whybulle> in Hampshire 'is probably a scribal mistake for *Wheybulle*' (Kristensson 2002: 256), whereas <Holewye> is overlooked. Although it must be allowed that the second element of compounds are sometimes a special case, these two forms with <y(e)> for [ei] or [æi] may also be back spellings, indicating that etymological *ī* had diphthongised, in that etymological *eġ* [ei] was never raised to [i:]. If, however, etymological *ī* had diphthongised, but was still spelt <i>/<y>, this spelling might represent a phonetic diphthong as well as a monophthong; in other words, forms with <i(e)> or <y(e)> for etymological *eġ* are back spellings.

Table 5.10 SMED *incidence of <ey> for OE* iht, eoht

County	Date	Spellings
Bedfordshire	1309	<Kneygh/Kneyt> KNIGHT
Cambridgeshire	1330	<Kneyth> KNIGHT

5.4.3 Discussion of LALME *material*

OE ī

For OE *ī*, *LALME* reports some <ei>/<ey>, as indicated in Table 5.11.

Thus, vowel shift is indicated in Cumberland, Ely, Leicestershire, Lincolnshire, Norfolk, and Wiltshire. As the table shows, LP 5371 (Wiltshire) has a high frequency of <ey> spellings for etymological *ī*; these often co-occur with <y>. A new, full analysis for LP 5371[34] has been made available by Benskin, which reveals that the irregular spellings are more numerous than the limited range of the LP suggests. It is an open question how many other irregular spellings would be uncovered if more source texts were given the same degree of scrutiny.

There are also a very few <ye> (Leicestershire and Lincolnshire), and <yi> (Derbyshire, Ely, Leicestershire, Lincolnshire, Norfolk, and Suffolk) for FIVE, FIFTH, and LIFE; these are hard to interpret, but they might indicate a (minimal) diphthong. If so, the NE Midlands, Cumberland, and Wiltshire stand out. LPs 4662 (Norfolk) and 5371 (Wiltshire) are of particular interest in that they have more than one <ei>/<ey> for the reflex of ME *ī*. For LIFE, <liȝf> is recorded in Huntingdonshire, and <lyȝf> in Ely. These forms suggest that the sound originally corresponding to <ȝ> had been vocalised, and the preceding vowel lengthened, such that <i>/<y>+<ȝ> could be used as a digraph corresponding to [iː].

The lists in the *Appendix of Southern Forms* show that <ei>/<ey> for ME *ī* are not really rare in lME. Forms with <ie>/<ye>, <ij>, <iȝ>/<yȝ> are also recorded in some quantity, but since individual words are not specified in the LPs, the original MSS or documents, or the *LALME* archives, should be examined again in order for these spellings to be properly assessed. However, there is no good reason for thinking <ij> is for a diphthong: in the Central Midlands, it is widespread for all /iː/, and is found in the same systems as <ee>, <oo>, and (less commonly) <aa> are found. One would not want to claim that <ee>, <oo>, and <aa> correspond to diphthongs; hence, <ij> is simply <i>+<i> with the second <i> written long. Forms with <iy> may be similarly interpreted.

Table 5.11 LALME *incidence of <ei>/<ey> for OE* ī

County	LP	Spellings
Cumberland	354	<feyfte> FIVE *ord.*
Ely	4565	<leyf> LIFE
Leicestershire	1	<feyfte> FIVE *ord.*
Lincolnshire	492	<thei> THY
Norfolk	634	<þein> THY
	4662	<wheyl>, <wheyl-þat> WHILE
		<þeyn> THY
Wiltshire	5371	<a-ueyse> ADVISE
		<aleyue> ALIVE
		<bleyde> BLIND
		<leyue/leyf> LIFE
		<seyde> SIDE
		<streyf> STRIFE
		<þeyn> THY
		<weyle> WHILE
		<weyte> WHITE

In the *Appendix of Southern Forms*, the following have been recorded (though often not included in the LPs):

Occurrence of <ei>/<ey> for ME *ī*

Bed 8190, Bck 6690, Cnw 5010, Dvn 5040, Ely 4565, Ex 6321, Gl 7040 7120, Ha 5511 5570, Hrf 7400 7520, Htf 6561, Nfk 4656, Sal 4239, Som 5180 5210 9390, Sfk 4266 6140, Sur 5630 5651 5730, Sx 5680 5720 5860, Wrk 4285, Wlt 5411 5420 5440, Wor 7710 7841, Mon 7250.

Occurrence of <ye> for ME *ī* (e.g. <lyef> LIFE)

Brk 6751, Bck 6720, Nfk 4668, Sal 4239, Sfk 8380.

OE i *in lengthening contexts*

From the foregoing discussion, it may be inferred that *LALME* <ei>/<ey>, etc. for OE *i* in lengthening contexts indicate vowel shift; these are recorded in Table 5.12.

Again, a full analysis of Wiltshire 5371 reveals an unusually high number of <ey> for the reflexes of OE *–ig* and *–iht*.

KNIGHT <kneytt->
LIGHT <ley3th>, <ley3t>, <leyt>
MIGHTY <meyty>, <mey3ty>

Table 5.12 LALME *incidence of <ey>/<ei>, etc. for OE* i *in lengthening contexts*

Lexeme	County	LP
BRIGHT	Essex	6321
FIGHT	Berkshire	6751
	Cambridgeshire	672
	Derbyshire	54, 61, 188, 201
	Essex	6321, 6330
	Herefordshire	7370, 7391
	Hertfordshire	6600
	Lincolnshire	16, 75, 194, 226, 492, 587, 913
	London	6380
	NME	471
	Norfolk	666
	Northamptonshire	736
	North Riding of Yks	457
	Somerset	5280
	Staffordshire	177, 215, 702
	Suffolk	8380, 8420
	Surrey	5740
	Warwickshire	699, 8010
	West Riding of Yks	262
	Wiltshire	5411
	Yorkshire	375
LIGHT	Hampshire	5530
	Oxfordshire	6820
MIGHT *v.*	Devon	5050
	Essex	6321
	Norfolk	4290
NIGHT	Devon	5110
	Essex	6100
NINE	Lancashire	154
	Lincolnshire	45, 69, 212, 587
	Norfolk	637
	Northamtonshire	225
	NME	22, 478, 525, 599
	North Riding of Yks	190, 197, 487, 1212
	Shropshire	4239
	Staffordshire	238
	Warwickshire	534
	Westmoreland	389
	West Riding of Yks	5, 116, 348, 358, 410, 460, 488
	Yorkshire	375
RIGHT	Essex	6321
	Wiltshire	5420

NIGHT <neyȝte>, <neyȝt>, <neyȝth>
NINE <neyne>
RIGHT <reyȝt>, <reyȝt->, <reyt->
SIGHT <seyȝt>
SIGN <seyne>

The frequency and regularity with which the digraph occurs in this source seem to support the view that it indicates diphthongisation of ME *ī*; this interpretation would, however, be even more convincing if there were <ey> for OE *ī* not before *g/h* in this text.

For ME final unstressed *–y*, some forms with <ei>/<ey> are recorded in Derbyshire, Essex, Gloucestershire, Hampshire, Herefordshire, Lincolnshire, Norfolk, Nottinghamshire, Somerset, Staffordshire, Surrey, Sussex, and Wiltshire. For *–ly*, <ley> is found in Cheshire, Durham, Hampshire, Herefordshire, Norfolk, Suffolk, Staffordshire, Surrey, Sussex, and the Isle of Man. These could either be (1) back spellings based on the change ME *ēg/ēh* > *ī*, or (2) indicative of vowel shift, in which case they imply vowel length retained in an unstressed or half-stressed syllable. The latter is possible – consider HAPPY-tensing in London [sɪtəi] CITY, with [əi] as a co-variant of /i:/ from OFr *–ée* [e:].

OE ēah

For OE *ēah*, there is one <ay> in HIGH in a source from Norfolk; for a discussion of its implications, see the section on 'Discussion of <ay>/<aȝ> for eME *ī*'. For HIGH, both <hi>/<hy> and <hei>/<hey> are numerous indeed, but <ei>/<ey> appear to be more common in the South, although they do appear in the North as well, particularly in the West Riding of Yorkshire. It may of course be the case that there are fewer attestations of HIGH in the North, generally speaking, but the *County Dictionary* does not suggest that such is the case. For the comparative and superlative forms, <ei>/<ey> are still more frequent in the South, though the frequency of such forms in the North is higher, relatively speaking, than for the positive form. In the comparative and superlative forms of HIGH, OE had *ī*, which may or may not have been a contributing factor when HIGH joined ranks with OE *ī*-words. For the vowel of NIGH, <ei>/<ey> occur throughout the country, although they seem to be slightly more frequent in the Midlands.[35]

Discussion of <ay>/<aȝ> for eME ī

With respect to <ay>/<aȝ> for the vowel of the reflexes of HIGH and lengthened OE *i* (Table 5.13), it is difficult to see how these could *not*

Table 5.13 LALME *incidence of <ay> for OE* ēah *and* i *in lengthening contexts*

County	LP	Spellings
Cornwall	5010	<mayȝth> MIGHT *v.*
Norfolk	626	<fayt-> FIGHT
	4567	<hay> HIGH
Staffordshire	189	<maȝt> MIGHT *v.*

indicate a diphthong. An examination of the entire orthographical systems of the source texts in which they occur might settle the case. The spelling <ay> in FIGHT and MIGHT could represent [əi] or [ʌi], and since the etymological diphthongs OE *eġ* and OE *æġ*, which appear to have merged in eME, were spelt either <ai>/<ay> or <ei>/<ey>, a newly developed diphthong with a similar phonetic make-up (in terms of the distance between nucleus and glide) could be spelt similarly. At any rate, <ay> for earlier *i, eoht, eaht* must indicate a diphthong, not a monophthong. The digraph <ay> could also indicate a diphthong whose first element had gone all the way down to [ʌ] or [a].

The orthographic systems of the sources showing <ay>/<aȝ> for ME *ī* need to be examined (Table 5.13).[36] LP 5010 (Cornwall) features the form <mayȝth> MIGHT v. and also <myȝth>. It has <ay> for the vowel of DAY, as well as for the present and preterit of DIE (<day> and <dayd> respectively). Other <ei>/<ey> spellings for ME *ī* are also attested, according to the *Appendix of Southern Forms*. There is a (possibly analogical) form <þy> THEY; but THEY has not always had a diphthongal pronunciation – personal pronouns are notoriously subject to diverse developments when unstressed, cf. Wright (1905: §419 and Index), who cites *ði* as the unstressed form in S Lancashire, Cheshire, Staffordshire, Derbyshire, W Shropshire, S Somerset, and N Devon. HIGH appears as <hye>.

LP 626 (Norfolk) has <fayt–> FIGHT and <heyght> HIGH; it reports <dye> DIE, <myght>, <myth> MIGHT *v.*, <myty> MIGHTY, and <nye> NIGH. The singular of DAY appears as <day>; and EYE is both <ye> and <eye>. LP 4567 (Norfolk) has <hay> HIGH; <eye> EYE; <fyte> FIGHT; and <deye> DIE. The same source has <ay> for the vowel of DAY and SAID.

LP 189 (Staffordshire) has <maȝt> MIGHT v. and <myȝt> (the latter is dominant). This source has a number of more or less irregular spellings: EYE appears as <ye>, <hee> in the singular, as <eyne>, <ene>, <ȝene> in the plural; FIGHT is <feȝt>; FIRE is <fouyre> and <fuyre>; LADY

Table 5.14 LALME *incidence of back spellings <i>/<y> for ME* ai/ei

County	LP	Spellings
Buckinghamshire	6690	<wyes> WAY
Cambridgeshire	4271	<side/syde> SAY *pt.sg.*
	6180	<dyis> DAY
Cumberland	355	<die> DAY
Ely	60	<þir> THEIR
	4565	<syn> SAY *pl.*
Kent	9470	<thier> THEIR
Lincolnshire	198	<my> MAY
	551	<þir> THEIR
Norfolk	4668	<alwy> ALWAYS
		<wy> WAY
	4670	<wye> WAY
NME	484	<my> MAY
Shropshire	4239	<awy> AWAY
Sussex	5840	<wi> WAY

is <laday>, <lade>, <ladi>, <lady>, <ladye>; HIGH is <hi>, <hy>, <hye>, <hyȝ>; NIGH is <ne> and <nyȝ>. For DIE, <dy>, <dye> appear, and <day> occurs for DAY. In this source, SAY is usually <say->, although <sad> for the preterit singular appears also; the preterit singular of SEE is <syȝ> as well as <sau>, <saw>, <se>, <sey>; THEY appears as <þai>/<þay>, <þei>/<þey> and as <þi>, which may be an analogical spelling, although a reduced unstressed form may be indicated.

Thus, the source texts for all four LPs reporting <ay>/<aȝ> for ME *ī* have <ay> for etymological *ai*. Additionally, some of the texts have analogical <i>/<y> for etymological *ai*, which suggests that <i> and <y> were associated with a diphthong. This is corroborated by the fact that some words appear with both <ei>/<ey> and <i(e)>/<y(e)>, though the traditional explanation for this is that some words had both [i:] and [e:i] variants in ME. This traditional explanation almost certainly is true for some words, and in fact it seems to strengthen the case for interpreting the <ei>/<ey> as actually corresponding to diphthongs in words which did *not* have etymological [ei] variants in ME, such as WIFE, WHITE, FIVE, and the like.

Analogical <i>/<y> for ME ai, ei

Forms with <i>/<y> for ME *ai* (Table 5.14) are of special interest,[37] as these spellings appear to be analogical: compare <wyes> WAYS with <dayes>

DAYS, <hye>/<hyi> HIGH in the same source text (LP 6690). If so, they imply that the nucleus of diphthongised ME *ī* was well on its way down in articulatory space.[38]

There are also the following analogical spellings with <i>/<y>, etc. for THEY, but they could (1) be unstressed variants (cf. the discussion earlier), or (2) be due to confusion with THY.[39]

<thi> Cam 4271, Hrf 7400,
<thy> Cam 4271, Ex 6360, Sur 5730, NRY 1034,
<thye> Dvn 5040, Nfk 4670, Wlt 5293,
<þi> Nfk 4670, Stf 189, Sx 9310, Wor 7761,
<þ^{i}> Nfk 4656, Nht 562, Sfk 4266,
<þ^{i}> Nfk 4103,
<þy> Cnw 5010, Hrf 7300, Som 5280, Sur 5810, Sx 5680,
<þ^{y}> Stf 702,
<þye> Dvn 5040, Wlt 5420,
<þyi> Wlt 5420.

There are very similar spellings found in *LAEME* and *SMED*, which have been discussed in the relevant sections.

Finally, there are miscellaneous spellings in the *Appendix of Southern Forms* (*LALME IV*: 318 b) that deserve mention. Unetymological <iȝ> and <yȝ> for OE *ī, ȳ, y+nd* suggest that (a) post-vocalic etymological ȝ had vocalised completely, and (b) the preceding vowel had been lengthened, and (c) the etymological <ȝ> often remained in the spelling; <ȝ> could therefore be used as a marker of length. The form <doy–> DIE in Dvn 5090 (*County Dictionary*: 151 a) is interesting in that it implies a maximal diphthong with an open and *back* first element. This lends further support to the claim that DIE has always had a diphthongal pronunciation, that it never raised and monophthongised to [i:], and that the spelling <die> is an analogical spelling which came to be used after the reflex of ME *ī* had diphthongised. Early <die>/<dye> for DIE may thus imply early vowel shift.

5.4.4 Discussion of material from additional sources

Zachrisson (1913: 71–3) quotes <ei>/<ey>, <ay>, and <oi> for eME *ī* in fifteenth-century documents from London, and private letters from Norfolk (*Paston Letters*) and Essex (*Cely Papers*). The following list is not exhaustive.[40]

<abeyd> ABIDE (Paston Letters)

<deseyre> DESIRE (Paston Letters)
<feynde> FIND (Paston Letters)
<leyke> LIKE (Cely Papers)
<meyll> MILES (Cely Papers)
<otherweys> OTHERWISE (Paston Letters)
<reyde> RIDE (Cely Papers)
<reight> RIGHT (State Papers, London)
<whrayt> WRITE (Cely Papers)

In Zachrisson's opinion, '*ei* is a phonetic spelling, used to symbolize the diphthong into which ME *ī* had developed' (1913: 73). He concludes that this diphthong must have been [əi], whereas <ay> could correspond to [əi] or [ai]; the occasional <oi> for *ī* suggests [ʌi]. Zachrisson maintains that the [əi] stage was probably reached in the fifteenth century (1913: 76). Interestingly, he holds that a number of <e> for *ī* also 'denote the diphthong [the writers] used in their pronunciation of ME *ī*, although only the first element of the diphthong was thus graphically represented' (1913: 75). Some <e> for *ī* are recorded in *LAEME*, which could be similarly explained, but they could also indicate shortening to [ɪ], spelt <e>.

Whitehall draws attention to irregular spellings in *The Records of the Borough of Nottingham*,[41] noting that two major points regarding the 'GVS' 'remain largely unexplored' (Whitehall 1935: 61), namely, the diphthongisation of eME *ī* and that of eME *ū*. He states that the spellings are numerous enough (1935: 61–2)

> to obviate charges of accidental and meaningless misspelling, they occur in documents bearing every outward sign of strong dialectal influence, and they are at least as unambiguous as anything previously cited. On one count they may be reckoned more trustworthy than the general run of 'occasional' spellings. Whereas orthographic evidence for the 'great vowel shift' is usually painstakingly culled from widely separated contexts in works of considerable length, the forms to be given here occur within a few lines of one another in three short documents. The probability of subconscious phonetic intention behind the spelling trends of the writers is thus greatly strengthened.

In 'Bills for Debts Due to John Lawson, Weaver'[42] (dated 1496) are found <maynde> MIND (twice), <prays> PRICE, <wayt> WHITE. Whitehall also notes that earlier occasional spellings taken to imply the diphthongisation of eME *ī* have usually had <ei>/<ey>, though <ui> is found twice in <ruight> RIGHT in the Cely Papers. These have all been interpreted as indicating [ei] or [əi]. A hitherto unnoticed <quoyt> WHITE is found once, in a Lancashire Indenture (dated 1431). In Whitehall's opinion, the consistent <ay> in the *Nottinghamshire Records* indicates an advanced stage of diphthongisation. Other occasional spellings with <ai>/<ay> appear later. Whitehall observes (1935: 63):

> An isolated *kainde* ('kind') occurs in the *Verney Papers* (1639), the Scots dialect-speaking parson of Wood's *Conflict of Conscience* (1581) is given the forms *ay, bay, Chrayst, assaygned, Frayday*, and *maynd*, and Shadwell writes *ay* fairly consistently for the Lancashire dialectal pronunciation in his *Lancashire Witches* (1682).

Whitehall offers three possibilities regarding the phonetic implications of these spellings, based on the later development of eME *ī*: <ay> indicates (a) [ɑi], or (b) [əi] or [ʌi], or (c) [ei]; the last alternative must be considered carefully, given the consistency of <ei>/<ey> and <ai>/<ay> for ME *ai* (as in *day, way*), which gives PDE /eɪ/. Thus, it seems certain to Whitehall that <ay> for ME *ī* indicates a diphthong of some kind. He finds that the first interpretation ([ɑi]) is inconceivable, since the etymological diphthong *ai* seems *not* to have 'retained something approaching its original pronunciation' at this date, but that raising had started (1935: 64). This argument fails to acknowledge the fact that if the scribe was writing as he spoke, he might very well use <ay> as 'an unconscious semiphonetic spelling' for a maximal diphthong, something Whitehall uses as an argument in favour of using <au>/<aw> as evidence of a maximally diphthongal reflex of OE *ū* (1935: 67; cf. Section 7.2.3). The difference is that for *ū*, the ME merger of related diphthongs does not cloud the issue, as it does for *ei/ai*. Whitehall believes the same arguments apply against the second alternative ([əi] or [ʌi]): '*ay* is equated with front sounds rather than back sounds in the spellings of the various documents examined, and would therefore be little likely to symbolize any diphthong containing a back or mixed front element' (1935: 65). For a diphthong with a central first element, Whitehall would expect <ui> or <oi>, neither of which occurs except in the instances cited earlier. However, both <ui> and <oi> are believed, at that date, to have corresponded to a diphthong with a rounded first element, though Zachrisson (1913: 76) maintains that the occasional <oi> for ME *ī* in his sources suggests [ʌi]. The inability to represent central vowels is a weakness of the Roman alphabet, but the modern language has shown that a centralised path for the first element of diphthongised *ī* is indeed the most likely scenario (Dobson 1968: §137). Besides, the same arguments could be marshalled against using <ui>/<oi> as evidence for the diphthongised reflex of eME *ī*, namely that both <ui> and <oi> were used for etymological diphthongs of French origin, with which the reflex of eME *ī* did not generally merge. Whitehall concludes, therefore, that <ay> must imply the pronunciation [ei] (1935: 65). Although Whitehall is likely wrong in concluding that <ay> corresponds to [ei], he is right in viewing the digraph as representing a diphthong.

Wyld (1936: 223–6) quotes <ei>/<ey> for ME *ī* from various sources: *St. Editha* (Wiltshire, *c.* 1420), the *Paston Letters* (Norfolk, 1440–70), and the *Cely Papers* (Essex, 1475–88). Wyld makes the same mistake as Whitehall in assuming that the second stage was [ei], which forces him into a lengthy discussion (1936: 223–5), postulating two lines of development for this [ei]. The problem is that the later evidence, such as the statements of orthoepists, suggests a central first element, and that in some dialects, the reflexes of ME *ī* and ME *oi* seem to have merged at some stage. Wyld transcribes this stage as [ai], but he uses the symbol [a] for IPA [ʌ], so it is very clear from the context that [ʌi] is what he has in mind. Evidence for [ʌi] is also seen in the spelling <ruight> RIGHT in the *Cely Papers* (1936: 224). Wyld does seem to recognise the fact that [əi] may be what the orthoepists are trying to describe, and he correctly observes that RP /iː/ tends to be diphthongised in 'vulgar English of big towns' to [əi] (1936: 205), so it is surprising that he does not see the relevance of this to the development of ME *ī*. The available ME and eModE evidence makes Wyld conclude that there may have been two different types of pronunciation for the reflex of eME *ī* existing side by side from the fifteenth century to the seventeenth, and that a diphthong had developed at least from the early fifteenth century (1936: 223–5).

Black (1998) adduces <dreyfe> DRIVE and <feife> FIVE from the Swinderby papers (*c.* 1390–1). The language of these documents shows at least two distinct usages (cf. Section 4.2.4), and Black fits these forms 'within two distinct areas, a Southwest Midland one centred on Hereford and a Northeast Midland one, including the Nottinghamshire-Lincolnshire area from where Swinderby is assumed to have originated' (1998: 66). The documents also contain several (other) forms that show Welsh orthographic conventions, and since <ey> corresponded to a diphthong in Welsh at the time, <dreyfe> and <feife> almost certainly testify to vowel-shifting in whatever English informed the scribe.

Some other irregular spellings which may indicate vowel shift are given in Table 5.15. They suggest that the vowel shift was under way in the NW Midlands around 1320–30,[43] in the W Midlands in the mid-fourteenth century, and in whatever language informed the *Piers Plowman* writer in the 1370s.[44]

Table 5.15 *Incidence of <ei> and <ey> for eME* ī *in additional sources*

County	Text	Date	Spellings
Ely/W Norfolk	HB2	1320–30	<greind/greynd> GRIND *imp.* <neyt> NIGH
Ely/W Norfolk	HB3	1320–30	<greind> GRIND *imp.* <greinden> GRIND *inf.* <þein> THY
London or Oxfordshire	Bu 11.2	1377–79	<ableinte> BLIND *v. pt.*
?W Midlands	Br 14.34	before 1350	<meynde> MIND

A few analogical <i>/<y> for etymological *ei* seem to furnish indirect evidence for the diphthongisation of ME *ī*. These are (a) <lyne> LIE past ppl. in a Northern/Scottish texts dated to 1568;[45] (b) <pris> PRAISE in a late fourteenth century London text,[46] although this may depend on a variant *prise* (< OFr *prisier*) besides *praise* (< OFr *preisier*), cf. Dobson (1968: §137); (c) <hye> for EGG in Ely/W Norfolk c. 1320–30 (Hunt and Benskin 2001: 224, T1); possibly also (d) <leyen> (as well as <lye>) for LIE inf. (Hunt and Benskin 2001: 226, T2).

5.5 Summary and conclusions

The ME material extracted indicates that post-vocalic [j], [ç], [ɣ], and [x] started to be vocalised at an early date, and that this process is relevant to the diphthongisation of ME *ī* and *ū*.

Evidence for the diphthongisation of the reflex of ME *ī* may be grouped into two categories: (1) digraphs like <ei>/ <ey> and <ai>/ay>, which in some cases almost certainly are semi-phonetic spellings implying a diphthong, and (2) analogical spellings with <i>/<y> for etymological *ei, ai* (in words which have always had [eɪ], [æɪ] or [aɪ]), which indicate that <i>/<y> have come to be associated with a diphthongal pronunciation. Dobson's and Kristensson's arguments for seeing <ei>/<ey> as mere back spellings reflecting the change ME *ē̆g/ēh* > *ī* cannot, and have not, been ignored, but the sheer number of such digraphs for the reflex of ME *ī* from a very early date makes it difficult to dismiss all of them as evidence of the diphthongisation of ME *ī*. It also seems that two variant pronunciations continued to exist in the HIGH and EYE sets far into the eModE period (cf. Dobson 1968). If so, the diphthongisation of ME *ī* could be at least partly analogical: if some words with [iː] could also be pronounced with [ei]/[əi] or a similar diphthong (i.e. the HIGH and EYE words), then other [iː] words (the WHITE set) could be pronounced with a diphthong also. The preceding examination of ME changes affecting the front close and half-close vowels has revealed that at least some of the irregular spellings in all likelihood indicate vowel shift. Analogical spellings with <i>/<y> for ME *ei, ai* are rarer, but provide even more reliable evidence for the diphthongisation of ME *ī*. In the following brief summary, spellings whose evidentiary status is uncertain have been left out.

In the *LAEME* material, vowel shift of eME *ī* is implied by forms found in Essex, Shropshire, Worcestershire, and Gloucestershire. The source text for no. 161 from Gloucestershire (1275–99) shows a very idiosyncratic orthography, with <ey> dominant and almost exclusive for the reflexes of ME *ī*. For OE *i* in lengthening contexts, diphthongisation is implied in Essex, Ely, Cumberland, Durham, Herefordshire, besides Gloucestershire. For OE *eoht*, <ei>/<ey> are found in Worcestershire, Gloucestershire, and Norfolk. For the OE suffix *–ig*, <ei> appears in Herefordshire. The status of <ei>/<ey> for the reflexes of OE *eaht* remains uncertain, but they are reported in Essex, Worcestershire, and Gloucestershire. The digraphs in *LAEME* appear from the first half of the thirteenth century onwards. The analogical form <awi> AWAY is found in Worcestershire (mid-thirteenth century), and strongly suggests an [əi]-like diphthong for eME *ī* in the W Midlands.

In material from *SMED*, diphthongisation of eME *ī* is indicated as follows. For OE *ī*, <ey> is found in Northumberland, Staffordshire, Warwickshire, Cambridgeshire, Hertfordshire, and Kent, in the period 1307 to 1330. The earliest such spellings are found in Hertfordshire and Northumberland. There are a few <ei>/<ey> in Essex, Lincolnshire, and Norfolk for OE *ig*. For late OE *–iht*, there are some <ey> in Leicestershire, Bedfordshire, and Cambridgeshire. Analogical <y> for etymological *ei* is attested in Hampshire and Somerset. Diphthongisation of eME *ī* is therefore indicated in the E Midlands and the South in the early fourteenth century.

In *LALME*, forms with <ay> etc. for ME *ī* are found in Cornwall, Norfolk, and Staffordshire. For the reflex of OE *ī*, numerous <ey> are found in the Wiltshire LP 5371; other forms with <ei>/<ey> are found in Cumberland, Ely, Leicestershire, Lincolnshire, and Norfolk, pointing to the NE Midlands as a locus of change. For OE *i* in lengthening environments, <ei>/<ey> appear all over the country; for OE *ēah*, one <ay> is recorded in Norfolk, and there are countless <ei>/<ey> all over the country. Analogical <i> and <y> for etymological *ei, ai* are found all over the country by this date.

Material from additional sources indicates vowel shift in Ely or W Norfolk around 1320–30 (Hunt and Benskin 2001), and in Nottinghamshire or Herefordshire *c.* 1390 (the Swinderby papers, Black 1998). The <ay> forms from the *Records of the Borough of Nottingham* (*c.* 1496) adduced by Whitehall (1935) are certainly indicative of advanced diphthongisation of the reflex of ME *ī* in the NE Midlands in the late fifteenth century.

Clearly, the Midlands, both East and West, stand out as a locus of change, and more work needs to be done on documentary material from this area, as it may uncover many more irregular spellings, not just for the reflex of ME *ī*, but for all the long vowels. Stockwell concludes from ME as well as modern dialectal evidence that 'the vowel shift *must* have gotten a head start in this part of the country' (2006: 179; his emphasis), referring especially to Gloucestershire, but also to Wiltshire, Devon, Somerset, and Dorset, that is, the SW Midlands. However, vowel-shift spellings are found all over the country, although in smaller numbers in the North and the South. Ogura (1985, 1990) has found that the most advanced PDE pronunciations of the reflexes of ME *ī* are found in Essex and Oxfordshire, and that these hence were likely loci of change in ME, at least with respect to the 'GVS'.

Maci (2006) examines <ei>/<ey> in four fifteenth-century Norfolk plays, and compares them to similar spellings in the *Paston Letters*. Although the frequency of <ei>/<ey> is negligible in comparison with traditional <i>/<y>, they are still recorded in some quantity in the texts investigated.[47] For 37.5% of the words with <ei>/<ey> for ME *ī*, she is unable to find any 'etymological reason' (2006: 159). Maci finds that the use of <ei>/<ey> is not socio-linguistically motivated, since it is not confined to the speech of lower-class or 'negative' characters (2006: 153–5); nor is it confined to (Paston) letters written by women (2006: 160). What is more, words with etymological ME *ī* are never made to rhyme with ME *ei, ai*, even when they are spelt with <ei> or <ey> (except once, where a rhyme is made between <pray> PRAY and <dey> DIE; (2006: 157).

Maci clearly thinks <ei>/<ey> for ME *ī* are 'a diacritic mark indicating the initial process of diphthongization' of the reflex of ME *ī* (2006: 159). To explain the relative rarity of such spellings, Maci quotes Lass, who says it is to be expected in the initial stages of sound change, as there are usually 'long periods of variable change. It is never the case that a change hits every item in the lexicon at once'; rather, 'there are particular words which are "leaders": the change hits them first and gradually diffuses through the lexcion' (2006: 159).

Additionally, Maci finds that the digraph spellings pattern in an interesting way: they occur (a) when ME *ī* is word-final, (b) when ME *ī* is in monosyllables, and (c) when ME *ī* is in disyllabic words at a syllable boundary, where it is followed (i) either by a vowel, or (ii) a dental, dentalveolar or alveolar consonant; the digraphs are also more frequent before the voiced consonants than before the voiceless consonants in the categories specified in (c) (2006: 161). As English long vowels tend to be diphthongal, Maci thinks point (a) above is natural and predictable (although the reasoning here is more like a *post facto* observation); the development of an off-glide in (c i) is also deemed natural before a vowel, 'to avoid hiatus' (2006: 161). As for (c ii), that is, the development of a diphthong before certain consonants, this is considered a result of *co-articulation*: in connected speech, each phoneme is not pronounced distinctly; instead, 'some of the characteristics of the previous sound are carried on to the following one' (2006: 161), and adjacent sounds influence each other. Since high front vowels are pronounced with the blade or back of the tongue raised, they may be slightly changed when they are followed by dental or alveolar sounds, which are produced with the tip of the tongue raised, for ease of articulation.

> Therefore, under the coarticulation phenomenon, the presence of dental or alveolar consonants may have influenced the tongue position while pronouncing the long vowel and brought it to a slightly flatter level, with the result that the long vowel is lowered toward /ɛ/ or centralized toward /ə/. (2006: 164)

Additionally, there is an 'intrinsic tendency for long vowels to be perceived as lower' (2006: 164; cf. Jones 1989: 202), which may have helped to lower the on-glide further. Hence, words in which ME *ī* was followed by a dental or alveolar consonant were 'leaders' in the diphthongisation of the reflex of ME *ī*, and the diphthongal allophones may subsequently have been analogically extended to all phonetic environments. Finally, it is a well-known fact that vowels are temporally longer before voiced consonants than before voiceless ones. It is therefore not surprising that phonetically conditioned lengthening and diphthongisation should happen earlier and more frequently before voiced consonants. Phillips (2006b) and Ogura (1995) have found similar patterns.

Quite apart from the preceding, the most convincing albeit circumstantial 'evidence' implying that ME *ī* must have diphthongised earlier than 1400 is in fact the material adduced for the raising of ME *ē*: <i>/<y> for the reflex of ME *ē* are recorded from the thirteenth century onwards, and Wyld (1936: 205–7) concludes that the [iː] stage was fully developed perhaps as early as 1370. Since the reflexes of ME *ē* and ME *ī* did not merge, the reflex of ME *ī* must have started to diphthongise around the same date.

Notes

1 In the North, the maximal diphthong is in evidence from the sixteenth century (Zachrisson 1913: 76).

2 However, if a third consonant followed the consonant groups in question, the vowel remained short, e.g. in *cildru* CHILDREN *pl.*

3 [j˔] is the most commonly used IPA symbol for a voiced/lenis palatal fricative, i.e. the voiced/lenis equivalent to [ç]; however, to avoid confusion between the semi-vowel and the fricative, [J] may also be used for the latter (Endresen 1988: 56).

4 In this context, the assumed development of the originally velar sounds corresponding to <c> and <g> may be worth considering. Campbell suggests the following course of events (1959: §§426–34). First, <c> [k] became [c] before a front vowel in PrOE, whereas <g> [ɣ] became [J] in the same context at the same time. In final position, [k] became [c] and [ɣ] became [J] after front vowels in OE. The geminate <cc> [kk] became [cc], and the geminate <gg> [ɣɣ] is reflected as <ċġ>. The later history of <ġ> [J]/[j] is that it remained initially, but combined with a preceding vowel to form long monophthongs or diphthongs; velar <g> [ɣ] became [ɡ] initially in late OE, but remained medially and finally until after *c.* 1200, when it became [J]/[j] or [w] and formed diphthongs with the preceding vowel. The palatal stops <ċ> [c] and <ċċ> [cc] underwent affrication and assibilation to [tʃ]; likewise, <ġ> and <ċġ> became [dʒ]; in some cases the palatal stops retracted and became velar stops. The processes of affrication and assibilation are believed to have taken place in eWS, and the processes may have involved the stages [J] > [tJ] > [tj] > [tʃ], and [JJ] > [dJ] > [dj] > [dʒ]. Even in early OE, *ġ* vocalised after a front vowel and formed either a long monophthong [i:] (e.g. *wīġ* > *wī*) or a diphthong (*weġ* > *wei*), but the semi-vowel was often analogically restored (1959: §266). It is this process which in Stockwell and Minkova's view (1988a, 1988b) destabilised the /i:/ phoneme because the phoneme now had monophthongal as well as diphthongal allophones, assuming that the vocalisation of *ġ* produced [ij] or [ɪi], not [i:]. In post-Alfredian English (i.e. in late WS for most words), final *ȝ* unvoiced to [h], which is evidenced in the increasingly common use of *h* for previous *ȝ*; examples are *burh* 'city', *genōh* ENOUGH, *plōh* PLOUGH, *bēah* 'ring', *fuhlas* 'birds' (Campbell 1959: §446).

5 The notable exception is John Hart (whose orthoepistical works were published in 1551, 1569, and 1570); Alexander Gil (whose *Logonomia Anglica* was published in 1619) later dismisses Hart's description as being that of the 'Mopsae' pronunciation, named after Sidney's character Mopsa (in *Arcadia*, 1580), an ugly, ill-mannered, unintelligent and affected woman, who is also funny, lively and harmless (Dobranski 2005). The term 'Mopsae' refers to London society ladies. Their (long) vowels are described as being far ahead of the standard speech of their time.

6 However, if this is the case, it seems strange that there are no spellings with <ig>, <iȝ>, <i> for OE *eġ* in lOE or eME. There are indeed a few such spellings in late ME, but these are probably too late to support Dobson's hypothesis. *Sir Orfeo* has <on wy>/<owy> for *on wege*, e.g. in line 96 of Sisam's edition in *Fourteenth Century Verse and Prose* (1962: 13–31). Sisam's 'text follows the Auchinleck MS' (MS, Edinburgh, National Library of Scotland, Advocates 19.2.1), which is entered in Middlesex as LP 6510 in *LALME* (*Vol. I*: 88), and is dated to *c.* 1330–40. In line 96, <owy> is in rhyming position, so an unstressed variant seems out of the question; interestingly, it rhymes with <cri> CRY, which suggests either that WAY had a variant with [i:] for the vowel, or that the vowel of CRY had diphthongised to [əi], so that the <y> in both cases corresponds to a diphthong.

7 But ENEMY has fourteenth-century forms <ennymei>/<en(e)me>, and a fifteenth-century form <enmei>, in which the final vowel is altered, in Dobson's opinion, due to analogy with French words with English final *–ey* (e.g. *valley, alley*). Another case is found in *Kyng Alisaunder* (Bennett and Smithers 1966: text extract no. 2), which shows a rhyme pair between <exyl> EXILE and <Abigayl>. The MS (Oxford, Bodleian Library, Laud Misc. 622) is dated to *c.* 1400 or the late fourteenth century (cf. Smithers 1957: 3), and the language has been localised to Essex and is part of *LALME* LP 6260.

8 Although the use of <whr> for etymological *wr* in the same word may suggest that the writer was in fact more conservative than the <ay> for ME *ī* indicates.

9 Additionally, *weorðan* is also recorded with <u> and <y> for the stem vowel, and <y> is most common in *wyrcan*.

10 In Dobson's view, the OE pronunciation [ɪç] survived into the Modern period, principally in Northern dialects, and has given PDE forms such as [nɪt] for NIGHT, by deletion of the fricative, and [ni:t], by 'vocalization and absorption of the consonant' (1968: §140). The second variant, [i:] was due to a process [ɪç] > [ɪj] > [i:] which was complete by 1400 and was chiefly Eastern; the later development was to [əi], and this variant came into London English from the East (*ibid.*). The third variant, [əiç], is explained either as a blend of the first two variants, or as due to analogy with the HIGH set, or as in effect being the same as the second variant, but with retention of the fricative (*ibid.*).

11 But see Lass (1988) on the vacuity of the diphthong optimisation principle. A diphthong may essentially develop in three ways: (1) it remains the same, or (2) the two elements of the diphthong become increasingly similar, or (3) the two elements of the diphthong become increasingly differentiated (diphthong optimisation). 'That one kind of VV cluster tends to turn into another, and which way the movement goes, merely reflect the limits of what's available' (Lass 1988: 401). Put differently, there is a 33.33% chance of either development taking place, so the 'diphthong optimisation' principle loses any explanatory or predictive force. However, 'diphthong maximisation' is here used merely as an empirically based description.

12 Wolfe (1972: *passim*, e.g. pp. 148–56) presents counter-arguments against Stockwell's hypothesis that the close vowels diphthongised early because of the vocalisation of (*i*)*ġ* and (*u*)*g* to /iy/ and /uw/. Although Wolfe leaves open the possibility that (*i*)*ġ* and (*u*)*g* became /iy/ and /uw/, the development could also have been that assumed in traditional handbooks, and she concludes that 'There is no proof either way' (1972: 148).

13 Wyld remarks that the lack of <i>/<y> in London sources 'before the fifteenth century is puzzling in view of Chaucer's rhymes' (1927: 127), which indicate the sound [i:] for e.g. *eye* 'in all cases where the word occurs in rhyme' (1927: 126).

14 It is unclear what sounds are believed to correspond to *h* in the following – [ç], [x], or [ɣ].

15 OE *feoht(an)* and cognates seem to have kept the original vowel longer than the rest of the OE *eoht* words.

16 One should also consider how <w> postvocalically is used in other contexts; what sense does it make to suppose the vowel in <owt> OUT different from that in <own> or <own> OWN, for example? In the former case, <w> is considered part of a digraph corresponding to [u:] (i.e. <ow>+<t> for OUT), whereas in the latter case, <w> corresponds to the weakened reflex of OE [ɣ] (i.e. <o>+<w>+<n> for OWN).

17 No conclusions are drawn for Herefordshire and Cheshire, due to the paucity of material.

18 There is one <yhe> for EYE in Lancashire 151 (1275–99), but analysis of this scribe's orthographic system reveals that initial <yh> may correspond to [j].

19 Kristensson concludes, however, that the [i:] stage had been reached (for the reflexes of both OE *ēag* and *ēah*) in most of the country by the early fourteenth century, except in some southern counties, which had [ei:], and in some northern counties, where [e:] remained.

20 In *LAEME*, a leader in the vocalisation of [ç] may have been FLIGHT; leaders in the vocalisation of *g* in OE *ug* may have been FOWL and BOUGH. In *LALME*, leaders in the vocalisation of [j] seem to have been EYE and HOLY; in the vocalisation of [ɣ] OWN stands out; in the vocalisation of [x], THROUGH, THOUGH and (possibly) SAW may have led the way.

21 The only sources which have <ei>/<ey> for eME *ī*, and which do *not* contain spellings indicating complete vocalisation of [j] or [ç], are the following: no. 2000 (Worcestershire, *c.* 1200); no. 64 (Essex, 1200–24); and no. 188 (Durham, 1300–49). Of these, however, no. 2000 has a spelling indicating the complete vocalisation of OE *o*+(*r*)*ht*, and no. 188 has a spelling indicating the complete vocalisation of OE *ug*.

22 This spelling suggests the possibility of early shortening, but the *English Dialect Grammar* (Wright 1905: Index) goes against it: [i] is recorded in N Cumberland, mid-Yorkshire, NW, and mid-Lancashire, N Derbyshire, and N Shropshire for a few such words (e.g. LIGHT, NIGHT, RIGHT, SIGHT), but the reflexes are generally a long monophthong or a diphthong.

23 Likewise, no. 169 from Lincolnshire (1325–49) shows <ith>, <itht>, <ydh>, <yt>, <yth> for the reflexes of OE *iht/eoht* and even for *eaht* (once), but has one <fleyt> FLIGHT. Similar cases are found in no. 64 from Essex (1200–24), no. 246 from Herefordshire (1275–99), no. 2002 from Gloucestershire (1275–99), no. 1700 from Norfolk (1284–89), and no. 188 from Durham (1300–49). No. 161 from Gloucestershire (1275–99) has a very idiosyncratic orthography showing dominant (and virtually exclusive) <ey> for all reflexes of OE *iht/yht/eoht/eaht*, in addition to some for OE *ī* and for *i* in lengthening contexts.

24 Spellings that indicate unrounding of the reflex of OE *y* in the SW Midlands are quoted by Gradon (1962). She also cites spellings that seem to indicate *conditioned* rounding of the reflexes of OE *i* and *ī*, and a number of these cannot be simply dismissed as back spellings (1962: 67), although occurrences of <y> for OE *i* in a set of Exeter documents likely are analogical spellings due to the change *y/ȳ* > *i/ī* (1962: 66). More specifically, OE *ī* after *w* seems to have undergone rounding, given such ME forms as <hwule> WHILE and <s(w)uþe> OE *swīþe* 'very' (1962: 71).

25 For OE *blīþian* 'to make glad', <e> is recorded for the stressed vowel in Essex, Kent, Norfolk, and Gloucestershire, i.e. in the South-East from the early thirteenth century, then in the North-East and South-West towards the end of the same century. Gradon (1979: 16–17) observes that <bleþeliche> in the Kentish *Ayenbite of Inwyt* 'constitutes a special problem'. She dismisses influence from *bleaþ* 'gentle, shy, timid' or *blessen, bletsian* 'to consecrate, ordain' on both phonological and semantic grounds, and agrees with Wallenberg that <e> here is due to shortening in a polysyllabic word followed by laxing and lowering. She also notes that such a development would not have been specifically Kentish, as similar forms are recorded elsewhere, which agrees with my findings.

26 Forms with <ei>/<ey> appear also for OE *drīge/drȳge* DRY and OE *sīon* 'strain, filter', but as these words are recorded with vowels other than *ī* in OE (i.e. *ē, ēo, ȳ*), <ei>/<ey> need not imply vowel shift; such forms have not been included. OE *tīþian* 'to give, grant, bestow, permit; tithe' may have had forms with *ēo*, by analogy with OE *tēoþa* TENTH and cognates, so these forms must also be treated with caution.

27 The form with <wi> for the stressed vowel of OE *besīþian* 'to go, depart, travel' is questionable: the cognate *sīþ* 'going, motion, journey' is recorded with *ȳ* also, so the digraph may correspond to [y:].

28 Some forms with <a> and <ai> in NIGHT (in Worcestershire, Shropshire, Herefordshire, and Norfolk) probably go back to OE *nahtes* or *neahtes*, and have not been included; <ounmaute> MIGHT n. (Gloucestershire) likely goes back to OE *meaht* or Anglian *mæht* after smoothing (cf. Campbell 1959: §145), and has also been excluded.

29 Forms for OE *sēon* SEE have not been included in the table, since levelling and analogical processes make it difficult to determine the source vowel of given ME forms.

30 However, the <wuile> form may be due to a litteral substitution set, whereby <w> = <uu>/<vv>, therefore 2 = 1; thus, <w+u> = <v+v> = <w>. In that case, the form is unremarkable.

31 In this context, the following may be noted. The extracted ME material suggests that the consonant corresponding to *h* in the cluster *ht* started to vocalise very early, in lOE or eME. Similar tendencies existed in Gallo-Roman and Old and Middle French. In Gallo-Roman, the Latin cluster [kt] > [xt] > [çt] > [jt] > [it] (Pope 1934: §324), but the change is reflected in spelling, e.g. *factum* > *fait*. In Frankish, [x], spelt <h>, 'was in use […] in the intervocalic group **χt** as in Gallo-Roman', which was palatalised like the identical Gallo-Roman cluster (1934: §635). The group *kt* was palatalised (as were many other consonant clusters consisting of a velar plus a dental consonant) in OFr, but due to Carolingian spelling and pronunciation reforms, this tendency was checked (1934: §§646–7). However, in Old and Middle French, the reduction of certain intervocalic consonant clusters, including *kt*, continued; in *kt*, the [k] was lost; Middle French spellings sometimes reflect this sound change, e.g. *suspectum* > *sospet* (1934: §650). In the Renaissance, reformers attempted 'to restore the pronunciation of **h**', and 'Full value was attributed to the consonantal groups […] **kt, ks**', at least in loan-words (1934: §655). As the sound corresponding to *h* had been reduced and later lost before [t] in French, it is possible that ME <–it> etc. for OE *–iht, –eoht, –eaht* is an AN back spelling, but it can be a back spelling only if the <h> was retained in French spelling after it ceased to be pronounced. If so, it cannot be concluded from (early) ME <–it> that the postvocalic [ç] had vocalised completely in early ME, even if numerous spellings seem to indicate it. In addition, [s] before dental fricatives was changed in OFr to a palatal or velar fricative, [ç] or [x], which was spelt <h>, beginning in South-Western French in the late twelfth century and spreading northwards (1934: §378). This change is reflected in the spelling of French loans in contemporaneous German poetry, e.g. <tschahtel> *chastel* CASTLE, and <foreht> *forest*, later *forêt* FOREST. This development may explain the <–st> forms for etymological *–ht* in ME, i.e. they are AN back spellings, and correspond to [çt], not to [st]. However, a ME weakening [çt] > [st] (spelt <st>) or [çt] > [θt] (spelt <tht>, <þt>, etc.) does not seem entirely implausible. Pope refers to the *Orthographia Gallica* (cf. Stürzinger 1884: 49ff.; Johnston 1987: 35), which says that any syllable which is pronounced with aspiration, may be spelt <st>; MS H adds that 'Quant *s* est joynt [a la *t*], ele avera le soun de *h*, come *est, plest* seront sonez *eght, pleght*' ('When *s* is joined [to the *t*], it will have the sound of *h*, so *est, plest* will be sounded like *eght, pleght*' (Pope 1934: §378; my translation). This explicitly equates <st> with <ght>, and clearly implies weakening of [s] to the point that the only trace left of it is pre-aspiration of the following [t].

32 Spellings like <beye> BUY also seem like solid indications that eME *ī* had diphthongised, except in Kentish, which had *e*/*ē* from OE *y*/*ȳ*. In *LAEME*, such digraphs for OE *licgan, bycgan* start appearing from the early thirteenth century onwards (see Chapter 8): in Cambridgeshire (no. 137), Gloucestershire

(nos. 2002 and 10), Norfolk (no. 269), and Essex (nos. 65 and 160). London influence could be held to disseminate Kentish elements, as Kent was close and many Londoners were of Kentish origin. OK had *e/ē* for OE *y/ȳ*, and so did some other counties, at least in some *y/ȳ* words. *LALME* has frequent <dede> (< *dyde*) for DID in East Anglia.

33 The traditional tale may seem to be tacitly endorsed by Ritt's treatment of OSL (Ritt 1994), but in fact he assumes lengthening of lax [ɪ] to [ɪ:], which was re-analysed as an allophone of tense /e:/, as there were no lax long monophthongs.

34 The language of this source is mixed, so the hands have been assigned to different LPs, 5371 (Hands A and C) and 5372 (Hand B, a mixture of Salisbury and NE Midland language). See Sections 1.4.3 and 7.2.3 for details.

35 The heading for NIGH suggests that forms were recorded in the northern area of survey only, but there are numerous attestations in e.g. Cambridgeshire, Ely, Leicestershire, Derbyshire, and even in Bedfordshire.

36 LP 5920 (Sussex) has <hauy> (as well as <y>, <I>, <I.>) for the 1. p. sing. pers. pronoun. However, closer inspection reveals that it is a fused form of HAVE+I, which Samuels noted once in the analysis, without comment (Benskin, pers. comm.); cf. <haddy> for 'had I' in LP 5690 (Sussex).

37 Forms with <i>/<y> etc. for DIE, EYE and SEE are numerous and have not been included.

38 These are from the *Appendix of Southern Forms* (*LALME IV*: 316 b): <alwy> is recorded in the source text for Nfk 4668 (which also has <wy> for WAY); <awy> in Sal 4239; <wi> in Sx 5840; <wyes> in Bck 6690. The form <wye> in Nfk 4670 is recorded both in the *County Dictionary* and in the *Appendix*, but it is preceded by a question mark in the Linguistic Profile (*LALME III*: 364 c). The other forms from the *Appendix* are not recorded in the Linguistic Profiles (*LALME III*).

39 Additionally, for the stressed vowel of TWO, <i>/<y> appear in Berkshire, Devon, Essex, Gloucestershire, Somerset, Staffordshire, and Sussex. Forms like <twyn(e)> or <twynne> could have [ɪ], not [i:], so <twy(e)> etc. are the relevant forms. The etymology could be either the OE prefix *twi-*, in which case these forms are unremarkable, or OE *twēgen masc.*, in which case they may be analogical.

40 To the forms cited by Zachrisson may be added (all from the *Cely Papers*; the numbers refer to letter and line numbers in Hanham 1975): <bey> BUY (5/20, 39/35); <bey> BY (58/14); <Freyday> FRIDAY (39/4); <reydyng> RIDING (40/10); <ryught> RIGHT (84/22, 86/26, 95/1, 96/1, 108/1).

41 Stevenson, W.H. (ed.). 1883 and 1885. *The Records of the Borough of Nottingham. Vols. II & III*. London.

42 In Stevenson (1885, Vol. III, No. 17).

43 HB2 and HB3 are two of the medical texts edited in Hunt and Benskin (2001).

44 The text labelled *Bu* is found in Burrow (1992); the number refers to the text number as given in this edition. No. 11 is MS, Oxford, Bodleian Library, Laud Misc. 581: *Piers Plowman* (extracts). The text labelled *Br* is found in

Brown's edition of lyrics of the 14th century (Brown 1952); the poem starts 'Wele heriȝyng and worshype boe to crist'. The form <boe> BE suggests W Midlands or SW origins.

45 MS, Edinburgh, National Library of Scotland, Advocates' 1.1.6 ('Bannatyne MS'): *Of the Resurrection of Christ* (W. Dunbar).

46 MS, Cambridge, St John's College, L.1: *Troilus* (extract) (G. Chaucer).

47 Maci includes <ei>/<ey> for EITHER and NEITHER also, which is unfortunate, and she wrongly dismisses some <ei>/<ey> spellings on etymological grounds (e.g. for ITEM); this does not seem to invalidate her findings, however.

CHAPTER 6

The development of OE ō

6.1 Introduction

OE *ō* is believed to have developed along the following lines in ME and ModE. North of the Humber, OE *ō* was fronted to a sound similar to [ø:] around 1300, and was then raised to [ü:] in the fifteenth century (Jordan 1968: §54). In many northern dialects, the [ø:] or [ü:] has remained to the present day (Wright and Wright 1928: §55; Luick 1914–40: §406). This process is usually referred to as Northern Fronting (NF). It should be noted here that the reflex of OE *ēo* also monophthongised to [ø:] in all dialects (Chapter 4), but this sound did not merge with the reflex of OE *ō* in the North. The change of OE *ēo* > [ø:] is supposed to have taken place in lOE, and the output to have unrounded to [e:] in the twelfth century, at least in the North and East. This indeed seems to be the only path of development possible, if only in those northern dialects where the reflexes of OE *ēo* and OE *ō* did not merge.

In southern dialects, eME *ō* raised to [u:] around 1500 (Wright and Wright 1924: §§74–5; Ekwall 1975: §§83–7). Jordan (1968: §53), however, dates this change to *c.* 1400 (cf. Luick 1914–40: §581-2.; Dobson 1968: §157); Jespersen (1909: §8.31), assuming the raising to have begun in unstressed syllables, dates the early stages of it to the fourteenth century. Dobson seems to think that ME *ō* raised to [u:] in some words in the early fourteenth century in a process unrelated to the 'GVS' (Dobson 1968: §158). The 'Hymn to the Virgin' uses the spelling <w> for etymological *ō*, which unambiguously corresponds to [u(:)], so there is no doubt that the raising must have started before 1500 in whatever English informed the writer of the Hymn. The /u:/ < ME *ō* remains unchanged in the standard language, though in some dialects, it started to diphthongise to [ʊu] in the nineteenth century, and in Cockney is reflected as [ə̆ü] (Sivertsen 1960) or [ʌʉ] (Wells 1982).

MEOSL lengthened eME *u*, the product of which appears as <o>, which seems to indicate lowering; this new *ō* merged with etymological *ō* and shared its subsequent development.[1] However, Stockwell's early vowel-shift hypothesis implies that eME *ō* had already been raised to [u:] before MEOSL, so <o(o)> corresponded to [u:]; thus, when short *u* lengthened to [u:] in MEOSL, the output was naturally spelt <o(o)> (Stockwell 1985). Ritt (1994) maintains that there arose a tense-lax distinction in ME, whereby the etymological long vowels became tense, and the etymological short vowels became lax. After MEOSL, which lengthened lax/short vowels, the new *lax and long* vowels were re-interpreted as belonging to the (etymologically speaking) lower long tense vowels; hence the perceived lowering of the MEOSL output; cf. Section 4.1. Yet another view of the output of MEOSL is put forward by Britton and Williamson (2002), and is discussed in Section 6.2.5.[2]

Another change, namely the unrounding of ME *u* [ʊ] to [ʌ], also took place south of the Humber in eModE (but with numerous exceptions), causing what is termed 'the FOOT-STRUT split'. Sweet (1888: §§791–800) seems to date the beginning of this split to the sixteenth century; Zachrisson (1913: 81) adduces spellings dating the beginnings of the split to the fifteenth century; Dobson (1968: §93) gives a later date for StE. It is relevant here because the change affected not only (a) words with etymological [u], and (b) words with a shortened [u:], but also some words which had OE *ō* (not OE *ū*, as expected), for example, OE *blōd* BLOOD and OE *brōþor* BROTHER, and other OE *ō* words appear with PDE (RP) [ʊ] instead of the expected /u:/ (post-GVS) or RP /ɒ/ (the normal shortened product of *ō*). It has been suggested, therefore, that when eME *ō* shortened, the output was a *close* short vowel [ʊ], which provided input to the FOOT-STRUT split. However, if the early vowel-shift hypothesis is correct, these forms all make sense: the reflex of OE *ō* had become [u:] already, then was shortened to [ʊ] in words such as BLOOD and GOOD, which later took part in the FOOT-STRUT split or not, producing [ʌ] and [ʊ] respectively.[3]

This chapter is not primarily concerned with the eModE FOOT-STRUT split, since it affected short vowels, nor with MEOSL as such, although the latter may seem to involve long-vowel shifting. This chapter examines ME spellings which could indicate early vowel shift of the reflex of OE *ō*, whether of the presumably earlier NME type to [ü:] (NF) or the supposedly later SME kind to [u:] ('GVS'). However, the outputs of MEOSL and of the FOOT-STRUT split, and the later development of these outputs, may throw light on (a) the early stages of vowel shift for OE *ō* and *ū*, and on (b) which dialects underwent NF. Therefore, these processes will be dealt with also, particularly in Section 6.2.5, in so far as they are deemed relevant. The NME system of long vowels is investigated in more detail in Section 6.3.2.

6.2 Discussion of ME spellings

6.2.1 Discussion of LAEME material

LAEME reports <e> as well as <oe>, <oi>/<oy>, and <ou>/<ow>, <ov>, <u>, <uo> for eME *ō*. Potential vowel-shift spellings are recorded in Table 6.1.

Thus, forms with <e(o)> and <oe> for OE *ō* are virtually confined to the W Midlands. They are difficult to interpret: (1) <e> may be used as a marker of length, much like <i> is used further north at a later date; (2) they could be errors, but as they appear several times, this seems unlikely; (3) they could indicate laxing of the second mora, much like PDN /eː/ is sometimes realised as [eɛ] or [eə]. The form <oe> for OE *ō* could also be a back-spelling: if <oe> is used for OE *ēo*, thence for OE *ȳ*, it could be used for raised and fronted *ō* as well. Had the <oe> forms occurred further north, they could have been interpreted as indicating fronting; this is hardly the case here, as OE *ō* is not generally believed to have fronted in the SW Midlands. However, Wright (1905: §§161ff.) states that [iu] is the normal development of OE *ō* in Staffordshire, Warwickshire, Worcestershire, Shropshire (and in northern dialects); [œu] is found in S Cheshire. Besides, shortening has produced [iu] in Staffordshire, Shropshire, W Warwickshire, and [œu] in S Cheshire, E Staffordshire. Fronted reflexes are also common in Somerset and Devon. In other words, fronting of ME *ō* must have taken place in certain areas of the W Midlands also. However, in text no. 2002, <goed> rhymes with <hounderstod> UNDERSTAND pt., <ouermod> *ofermōd* 'pride, insolence', <wod> *wōd* 'mad, insane', all of which have conventional <o> for the reflex of ME *ō*.[4] Interestingly, there are a few occurrences of <goed(e)> in *LALME* sources from Gloucestershire and Worcestershire. The one simple <e> for OE *ō* in *LAEME* appears in a compound (<geddede> 'good deed'), so it could indicate lack of stress and subsequent shortening and/or reduction to schwa.[5] The <eo> and <eou> appearing in Worcestershire seem to indicate diphthongisation and perhaps fronting; at any rate, they are almost certainly indicative of change of some kind, for the source text in question (no. 278) shows <ou> spellings for eME *ō* also, and has frequent <eou> as well as one <uo> for the reflex of OE *ū* (cf. Chapter 7).

Table 6.1 *Incidence of <u>, <ou>, etc. for eME* ō (LAEME)

County	No.	Date	Spellings
Essex	1200	1150–99	<cumen> COME *1.pl.pt.*
Suffolk	1300	1150–99	?<blouwen> BLOW *3.pl.ps.*
Worcestershire	5	c. 1200	<frure> OE *frōfor n.*
	2000	c. 1200	<bleode> BLOOD
			<muste> MUST *3.sg.pt.*
	2001	c. 1200	<touward> TOWARD
			<in-tou-> INTO
Herefordshire	189	1200–24	<bune> BOON
Worcestershire	6	1200–49	<tu> TOO
	1900	1200–49	?<touwar(de)/towwerde/touwerdu*m*> TOWARD
			?<unifouh> OE *ungefōg n.*
	245	1225–49	?<(-)touward> TOWARD
			<untouwe> OE *untōhen*
			?<wowunge> WOO *vn.*
			?<wouh> OE *wōh*
	1800	1225–49	?<auouh> OE *fōn imp.*
			?<touward> TOWARD
			?<wowen> WOO *inf.*
Unlocalised	119	1240–50	<lowse> LOOSE
Gloucestershire	158	1250–74	<pulle> POOL
			?<wouȝ> *OE wōh*
Worcestershire	277	1250–74	<cum> COME *1/3.sg.pt.*
	278	1250–74	<breoðer/breoþor> BROTHER
			?<ifrouuerð> OE *frōfrian pt.pl.*
			<goud(ne)> GOOD
			<leo(u)/lou> LO!
			<seone> SOON
			<seoð/seoh> SOOTH *n.*
			?<tou(-)ward(e)> TOWARD
Wiltshire	280	1250–74	?<bloude> BLOW *3.sg.pt.*
			?<stouwe> OE *stōw*
			?<touward> TOWARD
Worcestershire	2	1275–99	<wude> OE *wōd*
	3	1275–99	<luste> LOSE *3.sg.ps.*
Cambridgeshire	137	1275–99	<blud> BLOOD
			<bludi> BLOODY
			<gud> GOOD
			<must> MUST *2.sg.ps.*
			<mud> MOOD
			<suth> SOOTH
			<wud> *OE wōd*

County	No.	Date	Spellings
Herefordshire	246	1275–99	<for-soit> FORSOOTH
	247	1275–99	<(un)goid/gohid> GOOD
	248	1275–99	<in-teo> INTO
	249	1275–99	<rouf> ROOF
	1100	1275–99	<stoit> STAND *pt.*
			<stoir> OE *stōr*
			<-fungen> OE *underfōn*
			?<wou> OE *wōh*
			<roust> OE *rōs*
			<for-sout> FORSOOTH
			<dus> DO *2.sg.ps.*
			<goed> GOOD
			?<wou> OE *wōh*
			<lust> LOSE *3.sg.ps.*
			?<wouh> OE *wōh*
Gloucestershire	2002	1275–99	<goed/goet> GOOD
			<ged-/goed-> GOOD-
			<roed> ROOD
			<woed> OE *wōd*
			?<wou> OE *wōh*
			?<wowers> WOOER
			?<wouing> WOO *vn.*
Norfolk	1700	1284–1289	?<vntoun> OE *untōhen aj.*
Ely	282	1275–1324	<bi-dun> DO *ppl.*
			<guod> GOOD
Oxfordshire	1600	1275–1324	<guod/guode> GOOD
			<guod-> GOOD-
Wiltshire	140	1300–24	<dov> DO *2.sg.ps.*
			<rute> ROOT
			<lus(test)> LOOSE *imp.* & *2.sg.pt.*
Durham	188	1300–49	<soech> SOOTH *aj.*
			<south> SOOTH *n.*
Lincolnshire	169	1325–49	?<sowfast> SOOTHFAST

One might expect forms with <oi> to be northern, but that is not the case. They are confined to one text from Herefordshire, no. 246 (1275–99). There is more than just one form, so <oi> can certainly not be dismissed as a misspelling. The <i> may indicate either length or raising; diphthongisation seems rather unlikely. However, use of <u> rather than <i> would be expected to indicate raising of a back vowel. The same text has a single <ou> (for ROOF) and a single <u> (for OE *underfōn*) for etymological *ō*, which strengthens the raising hypothesis.[6] The text has <u> regularly for OE *ȳ*, though also <fuir> FIRE. More to the point, it has numerous <ei>

forms in words with OE ē, as well as <heit> HEATH once. Hence, it does not use <i> *regularly* as a marker of length, but that is not to say that <i> after <o> or <e> may not indicate length; hence, it is still uncertain whether <oi> in for example, GOOD (or <ei> in BE or THIEF) just indicates a long vowel or points to raising of the vowel. The former is more plausible.

On <gohid> GOOD and <fehit>/<fehid> FEET in *LAEME* source 246 from Herefordshire, Lass and Laing (2010) point out that the <-ehi-> and <-ohi-> spellings co-vary with <ei> and <oi>, and they conclude that 'None of the digraph spellings represent sequences longer than one syllable. The intercalation of "h" between the vowels cannot represent syllable junctions in historically monosyllabic words. Therefore, in these cases, too, we take it that "h" is a null character' (2010: 365). It is nevertheless possible that there is more to it than that, and that the insertion of <h> between two vowels suggests a diphthongal pronunciation. Pope (1934: §1237) notes in her chapter on AN orthography that 'As in Continental French […], but rather more extensively, "h" was employed to indicate hiatus between vowels, e.g. […] "pohoms"'. The difference seems to be that Pope's cited examples may show <h> at syllabic junctions, but since she does not give all the etyma, it is not clear that such is the case. Comparable, though much later, examples are found in the *Cely Letters 1472–88* (Hanham 1975), where there are several <grehyt(e)> GREAT (86/5,[7] 108/2, 126/1) in addition to <brohut> BROUGHT (117/12), <abohut> ABOUT (117/29), and also <fayȝeyr> FAIR (108/4), <towllyd> TOLD (108/14), and <plesehyd> PLEASED (117/39), all in letters by Richard Cely the younger. In <grehyt>, <brohut>, and <abohut> the 'h' seems to have been inserted to indicate hiatus between the two morae of a long vowel, whether historically diphthongal (BROUGHT) or not (GREAT, ABOUT); <fayȝeyr> and <towllyd> similarly suggest an overly careful rendering of the diphthongs [æi]/[ei] and [ou]. Taken together, Cely's <VhV>-forms seem to correspond to diphthongs in the words in question.

Forms with <ou>/<ow>/<ouw>, <ov> are recorded first in Suffolk and Worcestershire from the latter half of the twelfth century onwards; they appear in Gloucestershire and Wiltshire from the mid-thirteenth century onwards; then in Herefordshire and Norfolk in the late thirteenth century, and finally in Durham and Lincolnshire in the first half of the fourteenth century. However, in many of these cases, the vowel is followed by the labial consonants <w> or <f>, or – at least historically – by <g> or <h>, for example, in BLOW, TOWARDS, OE *wōh*, so the <w> [w] may be in anticipation of the following labial or velar/glottal consonant. For this reason, such forms have been preceded by a question mark in Table 6.1. The form <sowfast> *sōþfast* in no. 169 from Lincolnshire is difficult to explain; it may depend on a misreading of <þ> as the 'wynn', and then normal <w>-wynn equivalence (cf. 'litteral substitution sets' in Laing 1999).

The remaining forms seem to indicate vowel-shift of eME *ō* to [u:], and again the W Midlands stand out as the locus of change.

<in-tou-> INTO (no. 2001, Worcesterhire, *c.* 1200)
<lowse> LOOSE (no. 119, unlocalised language, 1240–50)
<goud>, <goudne> GOOD (no. 278, Worcestershire, mid-thirteenth century)
<rouf> ROOF (no. 246, Herefordshire, late thirteenth century)
<roust> OE *rōs* (no. 247, Herefordshire, late thirteenth century)
<for-sout> FORSOOTH (no. 248, Herefordshire, late thirteenth century)
<dov> DO (no. 140, Wiltshire, early fourteenth century)
<south> SOOTH (no. 188, Durham, first half of the fourteenth century)

Forms with <u> are recorded first in Essex from the second half of the twelfth century (but here, <cumen> may be analogical), and in Worcestershire from *c.* 1200 onwards; they are attested in Herefordshire from the early thirteenth century onwards; in Gloucestershire in the mid-thirteenth century; in Cambridgeshire in the late thirteenth century; in Ely in the late thirteenth or early fourteenth century; and in Wiltshire (no. 140) in the early fourteenth century. In no. 140, <rute> ROOT rhymes with <abute> ABOUT, and thus furnishes what seems like clear evidence of the raising of eME *ō* to [u:] from the first quarter of the fourteenth century.[8] The two lines are as follows (with interlinear glosses):

me ydrechez þroe yfoon mid þroe ku*n*ne rute
(*me afflict three foes with three kinds of roots*)

þe fond and myn oȝe fleyhs and þe world al abute
(*the fiend and my own flesh and the world all about*).

Forms with <uo> appear in Ely and Oxfordshire, the latter of which has many such forms. The language of these texts has been dated to 1275–1324. Later <uo> spellings, particularly in texts from Kent, are discussed in Sections 6.2.2 and 6.2.3.

Thus, the recorded <u> and <uo> are not confined to the W Midlands, but are attested in the E Midlands as well. Source text no. 137[9] (Cambridgeshire, 1275–99) is particularly consistent in having a number of <u> for eME *ō*. Gradon (1979: 15) interprets forms like <gud> GOOD, <blud> BLOOD, <mud> MOOD, <stud> STOOD in this text as implying 'raising and shortening of long close *o* before a final dental'. This may be the case for GOOD, BLOOD, and STOOD, but not for MOOD and ROOT, in which the vowel is still long. At any rate, it seems likely that raising, if not shortening, is indicated. Given the regularity with which <u> is used for eME *ō* in this text, it is difficult to dismiss these as mere occasional spellings or misspellings – their vowel-shift status seems indisputable.

Of the spellings adduced in Table 6.1, at least <ou>/<ow>, <ov>, <u>/<v>, and <uo> indicate that the reflex of OE *ō* has been raised to [u:]. The change seems to have started in the W Midlands and may have taken place simultaneously in the E Midlands. North of the Humber, the reflex of OE *ō* started shifting to the front from around the middle of the thirteenth century, and did not generally raise. The spellings <u> and <ui> for the reflex of OE *ō* are supposedly northern spellings (cf. Jordan 1968: §54), indicating eME *ō* > *ū̆*, but this claim is hardly tenable, since <u> is not rare in southern texts. That is to say, <u> is not *exclusively* northern, although it may be *characteristically* so; thus, SME <u> and NME <u> need not imply the same corresponding sound.

6.2.2 Discussion of SMED *material*

The following potental vowel-shift spellings are recorded in *SMED* (Table 6.2).

Thus, <ou>/<ow> for eME *ō* are not exactly thin on the ground. They appear all over the North, in the W Midlands (Cheshire, Worcestershire, Warwickshire, Wiltshire, and Oxfordshire), in parts of the E Midlands (Leicestershire, Huntingdonshire, and Berkshire), and in the South (Devon, Somerset, Dorset, Hampshire, Surrey, and Sussex). They are especially frequent in Cumberland, Berkshire, Wiltshire, Dorset, Somerset, Hampshire, Sussex, and Surrey, that is, in the South, SW Midlands, and far North. To Kristensson, some of these spellings may indicate phonetic developments other than vowel-shift raising, or NF; this applies to forms for OE **bōþltūn*, OE *brōctūn*, and OE *pōl* (Kristensson 1967: 93). However, the present-day form /bautn/ for *Bolton* in Lancashire implies a back vowel which has been raised to /u:/ before diphthongising; the form <Boulton> may therefore indicate vowel shift.

In the W Midland material, <ou> appears in OE *hrōc* ROOK in Warwickshire (1327, 1332), in OE *mōtere* 'public speaker' in Worcestershire (1327), and in OE *pōl* POOL in Cheshire (1307–09). Kristensson (1987) provides no explanation for these spellings; nor is it possible to find out whether the scribe who writes <ou> here for OE *ō*, used <ou> or not

Table 6.2 *Incidence of <ou>, <ow> for eME* ō *(not followed by* g/h/w*)* (SMED)

Area	County	Year	Spellings
North	Cumberland	1332	<Boulton> *bōþltūn* 'enclosure with buildings'
			<Broughton> BROOK
		1338	<Mourland> MOOR
			?<Houton> *hō* < *hōh* 'heel, spur of land'
			<Mourland> MOOR
	Durham	1340	<Hertilpoul> POOL
		1341	<Mourdon'> MOOR
	Lancashire	1327	<Boulton> *bōþltūn* 'enclosure with buildings'
		1332	<Boulton> *bōþltūn*
	Lincolnshire	1327	<Gouse> GOOSE
		1332	<Gouse> GOOSE
	East Riding of Y	1332	<Boulton> *bōþltūn* 'enclosure with buildings'
	North Riding of Y	1301	<Broucton'> BROOK
		1332	<Estboulton> *bōþltūn* 'enclosure with buildings'
			<Westboulton> *bōþltūn*
	West Riding of Y	1327	<Boulton> *bōþltūn* 'enclosure with buildings'
		1346	<Boulton> *bōþltūn*
W Midlands	Cheshire	1307–09	<Walkemulnepoul> POOL
	Oxfordshire	1316	<Brought(h)on/Brougthon> BROOK
		1327	<Brought(h)on/Broughtone> BROOK
	Warwickshire	1327	<Rouhinton> ROOK
		1332	<Rowhynton> ROOK
	Wiltshire	1327	<Brouk'> BROOK
			<Couk'> COOK
			<Lyȝtfout>, <Wytfout> FOOT
			<Goud(e)>, <Goudchild>, <Goud(e)wyn(e)>, <Goudgrom>, <Goudȝer>, <Goudherte>, <Goudhyne>, <Goudynow> GOOD
			<Goushurde> GOOSE
			<Houd> HOOD
			<Roucle>, <Rouk'> ROOK
			<Mour(e)> MOOR
			<Poule> POOL
			<Stroud> *strōd* 'type of marshy land'
		1332	<Broughton>, <Brouk'> BROOK

(*continued*)

Table 6.2 (*cont.*)

Area	County	Year	Spellings
			<Crouk'> CROOK
			<Goud(e)>, <Goudchild>, <Goudbred>, <Goudclerk>, <Goud(e)wyn(e)>, <Goudgrom>, <Goudheued>, <Goudhyne> GOOD
			<Roucle>, <Rouk'> ROOK
			<Mour(e)> MOOR
			<Poule> POOL
	Worcestershire	1327	<Mouter> *mōtere* 'public speaker'
E Midlands	Berkshire	1327	<Brouk'> BROOK
			<Couk>, <Coukham> COOK
			<Goudingeflod> GOOD
			<Draycotemour>, <Mour'> MOOR
			<Vnd'oure> *ōra* 'border, margin'
		1332	<Brouk'>, <Westbrouc> BROOK
			<Floudyate> *flōde* 'channel of water'
			<Goude>, <Goudemã>, <Goudhyne>, <Goudwyn> GOOD
			<Gouseye> GOOSE
			<Houk> HOOK
			<Mour'> MOOR
			<Boxour'>, <Comenoure> *ōra* 'border, margin'
			<Stroude> *strōd* 'type of marshy land'
	Huntingdonshire	1327	<Broughton> BROOK (4x)
			<Toulislond> *Tōli* (2x)
		1332	<Broughton> BROOK (2x)
	Leicestershire	1327	<Broughton> BROOK (2x)
		1333	<Broughton> BROOK (2x)
			?<Crauenhow> *hō* < *hōh* 'heel, spur of land'
South	Devon	1332	<Stroude> *strōd* 'type of marshy land'
	Dorset	1327	<Brouk(e)> BROOK
			<Floude> *flōde* 'water channel'
			<Lythfout> FOOT
			<Goudhyne>, <Goudman>, <Goudwif>, <Goudwyne> GOOD
			<Houke> HOOK
			<R(h)ouk> ROOK
			<Mourcok>, <Moure> MOOR
			<Oure> *ōra* 'border, margin'
			<Poule> POOL
			<Stoudlond'> *stōd* 'stud'
		1332	<Bouclaund> *bōc* 'book' or 'beech-tree'
			<Brouk(e)>, <Holebrouk'>, <Honybrouk'> BROOK

Area	County	Year	Spellings
			<Couk> COOK
			<Crouk'> CROOK
			<Fout>, <Langfout'>, <Roȝfout> FOOT
			<Fairandgoud'>, <Goudchild'>, <Goude>, <Goudgrom>, <Goudȝer>, <Goudhyne>, <Goudman>, <Goudtyd'> GOOD
			<Houke> HOOK
			<Bloucchehoud'>, <Bolthoud'>, <Greyhoud>, <Houd'>, <Ridhoud'> HOOD
			<Houperere> HOOP
			<R(h)ouk> ROOK
			<Mourcok>, <Mourton'> MOOR
			<Stoudlond'> *stōd* 'stud'
			<Stroudman> *strōd* 'type of marshy land'
	Hampshire	1327	<Bouklande> *bōc* 'book' or 'beech-tree'
			<Brouk(e)>, <Northbrouk> BROOK
			<Couk> COOK
			<Floude> *flōde* 'water channel'
			<Foude> FOOD
			<Fout>, <Lightefout> FOOT
			<Goude>, <Goudegrom>, <Goudehyne>, <Goudeknyght>, <Goudeyer'>, <Goudman> GOOD
			<Houke> HOOK
			<Rouk> ROOK
			<Mourcok>, <Moure> MOOR
			<Oure> *ōra* 'border, margin'
		1333	<Stroude> *strōd* 'type of marshy land'
			<Bouklande> *bōc*
			<Bouklonde> *bōc*
			<Brouk(e)> BROOK
			<Couk> COOK
			<Floude>, <Floudere> *flōde* 'water channel'
			<Goude> GOOD
			<Gous> GOOSE
			<Houke> HOOK
			<Rouk> ROOK
			<Mourcok>, <Moure>, <Mourstede> MOOR
			<Hour'> *ōra* 'border, margin'
			<Poule> POOL
			<Stroude> *strōd* 'type of marshy land'

(*continued*)

Table 6.2 (*cont.*)

Area	County	Year	Spellings
	Somerset	1327	<Bouke> *bōc* 'book' or 'beech-tree'
			<Brouke> BROOK
			<Couk>, <Kouk> COOK
			<Goude>, <Goudhert(e)> GOOD
			?<Huttone> *hō* < *hōh* 'heel, spur of land'
			<Houk(e)> HOOK
			<Houper> HOOP
			<Rouke> ROOK
			<Poule> POOL
			<Stroude> *strōd* 'type of marshy land'
		1333	<Bouke> *bōc*
			<Bouklonde> *bōc*
			<Bethebrouk/Bythebrouk>, <Brouke> BROOK
			<Couk> COOK
			<Lughtefout/Lyghtfout> FOOT
			<Goudhert(e)>, <Goudhyne>, <Goudman> GOOD
			<Gous> GOOSE
			?<Huttone> *hō* < *hōh* 'heel, spur of land'
			<Houk(e)> HOOK
			<Mour'> MOOR
			<Poule> POOL
	Surrey	1332	<Broukare> BROOK
			<Couk> COOK
			<Goudewyne> GOOD
			<Houke> HOOK
			<Houpere> HOOP
	Sussex	1327	<Brouk(e)>, <Brouker> BROOK
			<Couk> COOK
			<Floude> *flōde* 'water channel'
			<Goude>, <Goudegrom>, <Goud(e)wyne>, <Goudhier>, <Goudhyne> GOOD
		1332	<Houk(e)> HOOK
			<Brouk(e)>, <Hambrouk> BROOK
			<Couk> COOK
			<Fout>, <Sikelfout/Sykelfout> FOOT
			<Goude>, <Goudefeyre>, <Goudegrom>, <Goudesone>, <Goudhyne>, <Goudhywe>, <Goudwyne> GOOD
			?<Hou> *hō* < *hōh* 'heel, spur of land'
			<Houk(e)>, <Houker> HOOK
			<Mour(e)>, <Mowr'> MOOR
			<Scoulmaystr'> SCHOOL
			<Stroude> *strōd* 'type of marshy land'

for OE *ū* also, as one cannot get at *systems* (of (non-)co-occurrence) in Kristensson's material.

The form <Gouse> GOOSE from Lincolnshire (1327, 1332) indicates either raising or NF, although Lincolnshire seems too far south for NF to have taken place, and <ou> is generally not found for fronted *ō*. However, Britton (2002) finds that NF did originally affect Lincolnshire too; cf. Section 6.2.5.

Table 6.3 shows that there are numerous <u> for eME *ō* in the northern material. Some of the <u> forms seem to indicate raising and subsequent shortening, but not fronting, for example, those containing OE *brōm*, <Pulton> with OE *pōl* POOL, and <Ruddstan> with OE **rōdestān* ROOD STONE. Others, like <Crukdaik'> in Cumberland (1338), which probably corresponds to present-day *Crookdake* /kriukdeik/, testify to fronting and raising. In the material for the South, three forms are recorded with <u> for eME *ō*: <Munday> MONDAY in Dorset (1332); <Mustowe> for OE *gemōtstōw* 'meeting-place' in Sussex (1327); <Strude> for OE *strōd* in Somerset (1333). The two E Midlands forms <Rukke> and <Buk> are found in Essex (1327) and Suffolk (1327). Kristensson offers the following interpretation of these (1995: 51):

> In the present material <u> denotes /u/ whereas /u:/ is generally written <ou><ow>, rarely <u> or <o>. The forms *atte Buk* and *le Rukke* are therefore not likely to be forerunners of the Great Vowel shift. Probably the vowel had been shortened in *Buk* and *Rukke*.

Several forms with <uo> appear for the vowel of OE *gōd* GOOD in Kent (LSR for 1327); these are all in personal names. It is tacitly assumed that <uo>/<wo> for OE *ō* in Middle Kentish are too early for the vowel shift to have begun; therefore, <uo>/<wo> in Kentish texts are generally interpreted as implying a separate sound change, that is, either the development of an initial glide, or diphthongisation. However, such spellings could also indicate tensing/raising of the first mora of [o:], and such tensing/raising may have been part of the 'GVS' or an independent Kentish development. Samuels (1971) argues convincingly that <uo>/<wo> for OE *ō* in ME texts from Kent may indicate a diphthong [wo] or [wɔ]. Samuels thinks these were 'new parallel rising diphthongs in the back series' of vowels, the parallel being the front rising diphthongs *ia, ea, y(e)a, ie, ye*, with a 'palatal on-glide', which developed from the OE centring diphthongs (1971: 9). Still, [uo], [wo], and [wɔ] presuppose raising of the first mora from [oo] to [uo]. Further, there is another difference between the front rising diphthongs and [uo] etc. from OE *ō*: the front rising

Table 6.3 *Incidence of <u>, <uo> for eME* ō *(not followed by* g/h/w*)* (SMED)

Area	County	Year	Spellings
North	Cumberland	1332	<Prestebruther> BROTHER
		1338	<Crukdaik'> CROOKED
			<Guday>, <Gudhyne> GOOD
			<Red(e)hud(e)> HOOD
			<Mudy> *mōdig* 'brave'
			<Murthuait> MOOR
			<Muthyrby> ODan *Mōthir*
			<Studhird>, <Studholm> *stōd* 'stud'
	Durham	1296	<Redhude> HOOD
		1331	<Milnecruk'> CROOK
			<Grenehud> HOOD
		1332	<Kilnecruk> CROOK
		1335	<Kilnecruk> CROOK
		1341	<Murhows> MOOR
		1342	<Mudy> *mōdig* 'brave'
	Lancashire	1327	<Pulton> POOL
		1332	<Pulton> POOL
	Northumberland	1296	<Crucum> CROOK
			<Gudeknaue> GOOD
			<Murgref'> MOOR
			<Studherd> *stōd* 'stud'
		1312	<Crucũ/Crucum> CROOK
		1316	<Gudlad> GOOD
		1338	<Crukbayne>, <Crukwath> CROOK
	North Riding of Y	1301	<Brumpton/Brũpton'> BROOM
		1332	<Brumpton/Brũpton> BROOM
	East Riding of Y	1297	<Brumtona> BROOM
		1332	<Grauncemur> MOOR
			<Ruddstan> ROOD
W Midlands	Wiltshire	1332	<Pulton> POOL
E Midlands	Essex	1327	<Rukke> ROOK
	Suffolk	1327	<Buk> BŌC 'book' or 'beech-tree'
South	Dorset	1327	<Pulham> POOL
		1332	<Munday> MONDAY
	Kent	1327	<Guodhert>, <Guodhew(e)>, <Guodman>, <Guodson>, <Guodwyne> GOOD
	Somerset	1333	<Strude> *strōd* 'type of marshy land'
	Sussex	1327	<Mustowe> *mōtstōwe* 'meeting-place'

diphthongs developed from (falling) *diphthongs*, whereas [uo] or [wo] developed from an etymological *monophthong*. The question then arises how a rising diphthong could develop from a monophthong. Tensing or raising of the first mora, or over-rounding (cf. Wyld 1936: 235) are all possible paths of development. Data from the modern dialects might resolve the issue. Wright (1905) records [uo] for the reflex of *ō* only in E Wiltshire; [uə] is found in Buckinghamshire, Bedfordshire, N Cumberland, Dorset, N Durham, SW Devon, Essex, Kent (E and N), S Lincolnshire, Oxfordshire, Sussex, and W Wiltshire, which may simply come from [u:] by laxing of the second mora. Forms with [woə] are recorded in Dorset, and [wʌ] in Herefordshire, Gloucestershire, Oxfordshire, and Berkshire. That is, Kentish may have seen the development of new rising diphthongs in the back vowel series in ME, but such diphthongs had become rare by the beginning of the twentieth century. This is not to say that they did not exist in ME – the available ME evidence suggests that they did.

Gradon (1979), in her introduction to the re-edition of the canonical Middle Kentish text, the *Ayenbite of Inwyt* (1340), examines these matters in great detail, and systematically. So also, though not structurally, does Wallenberg in his monographs on Kentish place-names (Wallenberg 1931, 1934). Gradon, after discussing the phonetic and phonological status of <ie>/<ye> for eME *ē* in the *Ayenbite*, finds that the parallel spelling <uo> for OE *ō* in the same source supports their interpretation as indicating a 'sporadic glide development' of eME *ē* (Gradon 1979: 27). Assessing the various hypotheses put forward regarding the phonetic implications of <uo> in Kentish texts, she concludes that there is 'no doubt that the language of the *Ayenbite* shows both palatal and labial glides before the vowels *ē* and *ǭ*' (1979: 29), especially since such glides have been recorded in modern dialects, for example, in Dorset (as reported by Widén 1949: 54–5, 77).[10] It would have been useful to compare the personal names with <uo> for OE *ō* in *SMED* against the forms recorded by Wallenberg (1931, 1934), but since Wallenberg records Kentish *place*-names only, there is no basis for direct comparison.[11]

Other southern <u> forms are <Huttone> in Somerset (1327 and 1333), and <Pulton> and <Pulham> in Wiltshire (1332), and Dorset (1327) respectively; here we may be dealing with a shortened vowel, but that still does not explain the use of <u>; that is, they are most likely vowel-shift spellings.

It will be evident from the preceding tables and discussion that <ou>/<ow and <u> for OE *ō* are very numerous indeed in the South. It is likewise striking that, apart from <uo> spellings in OE *gōd* GOOD, there are no irregular forms for OE ō in Kent, and very few in Devon. Kristensson (2001) finds that Dorset has the highest percentage of <ou> forms (at 50%), followed by Hampshire, Sussex, Berkshire, and Wiltshire (with 33.1–44.5%), then by Somerset (at 18.5%) and Surrey (at 11.2%) (Kristensson 2001: 77). Kristensson now disagrees with Dobson (1968), who claimed that <ou> indicated shortened /u/ in the fifteenth and sixteenth centuries: 'the majority of forms presented here have a long vowel' (2001: 78). Kristensson argues as follows (2001: 78):

> In the late ME period <ou> was consistently used for /u:/. It is in itself unlikely that <ou> was employed for /o:/ at the same time as the old <ou> spelling for /u:/ was preserved. Further, the <ou> forms are found in a restricted area. It is conspicuous that 84 out of the 96 <ou> forms in Sx occur in the western half of the county which thus goes with Ha. Had the <ou> forms been only graphic variants of <o>, we should not have expected such a distribution of forms. When a phoneme gets a new spelling, we must assume, unless the spelling is due to foreign influence, that the phoneme is realized in a phonetically 'new' form. In my opinion, there is no doubt that <ou> stands for /u:/, i.e. that ME /o:/ had been, or was being, raised to /u:/, cf. *atte Strude* (p) So[m] 1333.

Kristensson thus seems to have been convinced[12] by the material that the changes subsumed under the 'Great Vowel Shift' were indeed earlier than most scholars will have it (although the second sentence in the quote is somewhat confusing: whether or not <ou> was used for ō is open to empirical test – the *SMED* material shows that it was). It is noteworthy that spellings with <ei>/<ey> for OE ē are found in much the same area as we find <ou>/<ow> and <u> for OE ō. Kristensson therefore draws the conclusion that at the beginning of the fourteenth century, the etymological half-close vowels ē and ō were in the process of being, or had already been, raised to their present close position (Kristensson 2001: 78–9). He finds support for this deduction in the fact that ME [ø:] from OE *ēo* had also been raised, to [y:], in the same area at about the same time.

His new position notwithstanding, Kristensson fails to realise the consequences of early vowel-shifting, for he claims that the forms <Munday> and <Mustowe> 'are due to shortening of /o:/ and subsequent raising of /o/ to /u/ after a labial [...] or to shortening of /o:/ to /u/, after /o:/, and /u/ had become partners in a quantitative correlation' (Kristensson 2001: 80). If raising of eME /o:/ to [u:] was early, shortening may have taken place *after* raising, and there is no 'quantitative correlation' between /o:/ and /u/, and no 'ME opening of short vowels'. Rather, there is raising of /o:/ to [u:] and subsequent – and completely predictable – shortening of [u:] to [u]. That raising of *ō* to [u:] was influenced and indeed speeded up by a bilabial consonant is very likely. This raises an important issue: traditionally, the 'GVS' involves sound changes which are effectively isolative from a *post facto* perspective, but the evidence suggests that they may have started out as allophonic variants, that is, occurring in certain phonetic contexts.

SMED reports numerous <ou>, <oy>, <u> for eME *ō* before *g/h/w*. These have not been included, since in these phonetic surroundings, any <u>/<w> between the etymological vowel and the following consonant may indicate either (a) the development of a glide in anticipation of the final labial or velar consonant, or (b) the vocalisation of these fricatives and of /w/, producing diphthongs with the preceding vowel. Nor have I included forms with <oo> for eME *ō*, as they are very rare and probably simply indicate length.[13]

Some of the forms with <ou> and <u> for eME *ō* in the northern area are obviously testimony to NF, that is, the fronting and raising of eME *ō* which took place in the thirteenth century, 'in Scotland and northern England, except in south Cu, La, and south-western WR[Y]' (Kristensson 1967: 91). In Kristensson's view, some of the <u> spellings may appear in shortened syllables, but raising may still have happened prior to shortening. For some counties, <o> and <u> co-vary in names that certainly refer to the same persons, so it is evident that the conventional <o> spellings continued to be used even after NF had started. Kristensson therefore rightly concludes that the 'geographical range of the fronting cannot [...] be fully ascertained, but we are justified in assuming that in the areas where *u*-forms are found, the fronted vowel was well established' (1967: 91). Hence, NF must have taken place in Northumberland, Cumberland, and Durham. In fact, the *SMED1* material indicates that NF had taken place in all of Yorkshire and Lancashire as well, but Kristensson concludes differently, due particularly to his interpretation of the <u> in names with OE *brōm*, in the East and North Ridings of Yorkshire: their occurrence 'runs counter' to the evidence for the other words with OE *ō* (Kristensson 1967: 92). Even the earliest records from the East and North Ridings apparently show <u> in names with OE *brōm*, so Kristensson infers that these forms 'belong to an earlier period than the ME fronting of *ọ̄* [...] and are in all probability the result of early shortening of *ō* and a subsequent change *o* > *u*' (1967: 92). Since the dates of these 'earliest records' are not revealed, it is difficult to assess the arguments, but the change of eME *ō* to *ǖ* is believed to have started in the thirteenth century, so it should not come as a surprise that some northern sources have spellings that indicate this change from the last decade of the thirteenth century onwards. Besides, it seems difficult to dismiss the form <Grauncemur> with OE *mōr* MOOR from the East Riding of Yorkshire (1332) as anything other than indicative of NF.

6.2.3 Discussion of LALME *material*

LALME reports many <ou>/<ow> and <u>, <v>, <w>, as well as less frequent <ov>, <oi>/<oy>, <uo>, <ui>/<uy>, <y>, <wo>, for the reflex of eME *ō*. The <u>/<v> in NME of course imply *ō* > *ǖ*, not *ū*. It is apparent from the *LALME* data, however, that many northern texts show conservative <o(o)> spellings and not <u(i)>, even in lME, whereas many southern texts have <u> for the reflex of eME *ō*. The interpretation and status of <u> in terms of implied sound value and (type of) sound change should therefore be reconsidered. That is, spellings have to be interpreted according to the systems in which they appear, namely how the writer who uses them uses the *other* letters. Also, the nature of NF may be different from that outlined in the handbooks; this is discussed in Section 6.2.5. Forms with <ou>/<ow> and <u> in *LALME* sources are recorded in Table 6.4 (words other than GOOD); forms with <ou>/<ow> for GOOD, which are very frequent, appear in Table 6.5.

In the *Appendix of Southern Forms*, the following counties are reported to have <ou> etc. for eME *ō* in words other than GOOD (individual words are unspecified in the LPs): Berkshire, Devon, Dorset, Gloucestershire, Herefordshire, Kent, Somerset, Surrey, Sussex, Wiltshire, and Worcestershire. They appear to be especially frequent in Wiltshire, Gloucestershire, and Somerset, that is, in the South-West.

In words other than GOOD, forms with <ou>/<ow> thus appear in the South (Cornwall, Somerset, Hampshire, Devon, Dorset, Kent, Surrey, and Sussex), the (S)W Midlands (Wiltshire (which also has <ov> once), Gloucestershire, Herefordshire, and Worcestershire), the E Midlands (Buckinghamshire, Berkshire, Essex, Suffolk, Norfolk, and Lincolnshire), and the North (Lancashire, the East and North Ridings of Yorkshire).

Forms with <u> are found in the NE Midlands (Lincolnshire, Norfolk, and Suffolk), the W Midlands (Warwickshire and Worcestershire), and the North (Durham, Lancashire, Westmorland, the East and West Ridings of Yorkshire, Yorkshire, and NME). Forms with <v> are almost exclusively northern: they appear in Cumberland, the East and West Ridings of Yorkshire, Northumberland, Westmorland, and in Lincolnshire. Forms with <w> appear in Westmorland.

Table 6.4 *Incidence of <ou>/<ow>, <u> etc. for eME* ō (LALME)

County	LPs	Spellings
Buckinghamshire	6630	<douþ> DO *3.sg.*
Cornwall	5010	<dowst> DO *2.sg.*
Cumberland	1182	<vd*er*> OTHER
	1035, 1170	<vther> OTHER
	1105	<vthere> OTHER
	1143	<vthir> OTHER
	452	<vthire> OTHER
Durham	388	<bus> BEHOVES
	13	<buse> BEHOVES
Essex	6280	<tougadres> TOGETHER
Hampshire	5530	<doust> DO *2.sg.*
Lancashire	595	<bus> BEHOVES; <mydir> MOTHER
	466	<mowne> MOON
	365	<outhir> OTHER
Lincolnshire	16, 194, 210, 222, 491, 508	<bus> BEHOVES
	198	<-dou*m*> *-dōm*
	180, 510	<outher> OTHER
	106	<vthir> OTHER
	213	<tu> *infinitive marker*
Norfolk	4633	<mu*n*th-> MONTH
	4670	<owther> OTHER
Northumberland	765	<vy*er*> OTHER
Somerset	5210	<douste> DO *2.sg.*
Suffolk	6161	<dowth> DO *3.sg.*
	639	<-du*m*> *-dōm*
Warwickshire	4689	<duste> DO *2.sg.*
	517	<uþ*er*> OTHER
Worcestershire	7610	<duse> DO *3.sg.*
Westmorland	389	<bus> BEHOVES; <-dwme> *-dōm*
	1236	<vther> OTHER
Wiltshire	5300	<doust> DO *2.sg.*
	5380	<dov> DO *imp.sg.*
	5361	<moudyr(e)> MOTHER
	WLTN.CT.	<ouþer> OTHER
	5371	<souþ(e)> *sōþ*
East Riding, Yks	228, 361, 362	<bus> BEHOVES
	361	<buse> BEHOVES
	1130	<howd*er*> OTHER
	576	<vther> OTHER; <anowder> ANOTHER
	362	<vth*er*/vthir/vthyr> OTHER
North Riding, Yks	412	<outhir> OTHER

(*continued*)

Table 6.4 (*cont.*)

County	LPs	Spellings
West Riding, Yks	358	<be-hufes> BEHOVES
	30, 410, 1349	<bus> BEHOVES
	410, 488, 497, 598	<buse> BEHOVES
	175	<bruther> BROTHER
	479	<-dum> *-dōm*
	53	<vther/vthir> OTHER
Yks	28	<-du*m*> *-dōm*
NME	205, 599	<buse> BEHOVES
	481	<muder> MOTHER

Table 6.5 *Incidence of <ou>, <ow>, <u>, etc. for* GOOD (LALME)

Spelling	Counties and LPs
ADJECTIVE	
<goud>	Brk 6761 6770, Chs 26, Dor 5350 9500, DTSY., Ex 6010 6340, Gl 7070 7220 7230, Ha 5480 5511 5530, Hrf 7300 7310 7320, Kt 5960, Li 910, Sal 4239, Som 5200 5210 5250 5270, Stf 729, Sur 5810, Sx 5680 5690 5840 9300 9310, Wlt 5314 5320 5361 5420 5430
<go^{u}d>	Gl 7230, Kt 5960, Wlt 5420
<goude>	Brk 6761, Chs 26, Dor 9500, Ex 6010 6340, Gl 7040 7070 7220, Ha 5480, Hrf 7260, Nt 503, Som 5200 5220 5250 5270, Sur 5810, Wrk 1306, Wlt 5300 5313 5320 5411 5420 5430, NME 590
<go^{u}de>	WRY 115
<govd>	Li 62
<gowd>	Som 5210, Sur 5651, Sx 5670, NRY 483
<gowde>	Brk 6761, Nfk 4570, Sx 5660
<gud>	Brk 6800, Cam 64, Chs 322 750, Cu 1111, Dby 1287, Dur 13 386 388, Ha 5530, La 25 154 365 404 545 764 1205, Lei 1, Li 106 206 213 491 492 587 588 901 910, Nfk 626 4564 4571 8680, Nbld 338 372 765 1218, Nt 507 514, Sal 4239, Stf 94 715 726 729, Sur 5620, Sx 5710, Wmld 389, Wlt 5420, Yk 1352, Yks 28 199, NRY 174 190 203 483, ERY 228 361 362 476 576 1126, WRY 29 30 53 115 168 234 358 398 406 454 474 496 598 605 608 611 732 1102 1248, NME 22 383 465 471 478 484 521
<gud->	Dby 257, Lei 560, ERY 472 1125
<gudd>	NME 465
<gude>	Chs 17 322, Cu 547 1038 1170, Dby 105, Dur 13 147 371 388 1005 1351, Gl 7040, Ha 5480, La 154 167 172 259 365 404 595 1198 1285 1366, Lei 560, Li 16 38 45 75 206 212 213 220 277 491 492 501 508 587 901 908, Mx 6470, Nht 9340, Nbld 156 765, Nt 164 202 278 417 503 514, Stf 726, Wmld 389 1234, Yk 145 1002 1348 1352, Yks 28 199, NWY 381 596 610, NRY 7 126 190 197 203 457 483 487 1031 1034 1211, ERY 362 366 380 472 476 576 1125 1126 1133, WRY 30 115 168 175 200 217 240 349 377 398 406 410 454 473 474 479 488 497 526 591 598 1102 1349, NME 22 205 392 465 467 471 478 481 484 521 525

Spelling	Counties and LPs
<gude->	Li 181
<guod>	Chs 26, Kt 5881 5890, Sx 5850 5920
<guode>	Kt 5890, Ox 6920, Sx 5850
<gu°de>	NRY 203
<guyd>	Li 587, WRY 175
<guyde>	Li 587
<gwod>	Kt 5900 9380
<gwode>	Kt 5870
NOUN	
<goud>	Chs 26
<gowdeȝ>	Chs 26
<gud>	WRY 605, NME 22
<gud->	Yk 1002
<guddes>	La 545
<gude>	Yk 1002
<gudes>	La 545, Yk 1352, NRY 1031, ERY 1123 1259
<gudis>	NRY 1214
<gudys>	Wlmd 1234
<gudȝ>	Cu 543
<guid>	NRY 1214
<guodys>	Kt 9380
<gwodys>	Kt 9380

The irregular spellings are particularly frequent in Cumberland, Yorkshire, Lincolnshire, and Wiltshire. Therefore, Cumberland and Yorkshire may have been the locus of NF, which goes against Kristensson's explicit claims (1967: 91); Wiltshire and the adjoining areas may have had a head start in the shift eME *ō* > [u:].

Due to the sheer number of irregular spellings for GOOD, it is examined separately. Forms with <ou>/<ow> appear in texts localised to the South, the W Midlands, the E Midlands, and parts of the North (the North and West Ridings of Yorkshire, NME). One <ov> is found in Lincolnshire; <oe> has been recorded in Gloucestershire, and Worcestershire, which ties up with the *LAEME* evidence.

Forms with <u> for the vowel in GOOD appear all over the country. Forms with <ui> appear in the North Riding of Yorkshire; <uy> occurs in Lincolnshire and the West Riding of Yorkshire; <uo> is found in Cheshire, Kent, the North Riding of Yorkshire, Oxfordshire, and Sussex; <wo> appears in Kent. In Kentish texts, Samuels (1971) believes <uo>/<wo> indicate a rising diphthong; the same may be true of the <uo> found in Sussex, but it is hardly the case for <uo> from Cheshire, the North Riding of Yorkshire, and Oxfordshire. Interestingly, *LAEME* also has some <uo>

for eME ō in a text localised to Oxfordshire. Whether this implies independent diphthongisation or raising of the long vowel remains undetermined. If the Midland and Southern <u> for the vowel of GOOD (in any of the sources examined) is indeed for [u], they corroborate Stockwell's view about the early shift of eME ō > [u:]: the shortening of ME ō is [u], which means that ME ō must have shifted to [u:], otherwise the shortened vowel would have been still spelt <o>, contrasting (perhaps) with <o>+C+<e> or <oo> for ME ō [o:].[14]

LALME (IV: *County Dictionary* and p. 318c) records <oi>/<oy> for ō in the North (the East and West Ridings of Yorkshire, Lancashire, and NME[15]), as well as in Buckinghamshire, Berkshire, Cornwall, Devon, Essex, Hertfordshire, Kent, Lincolnshire, Nottinghamshire, Suffolk, Warwickshire, and Worcestershire. The significance of <i>/<y> here is uncertain, and may be irrelevant to the vowel shift; in NME it may imply NF. Samuels (in Benskin and Samuels 1981: 53, n.12) cites <moyst> MOST and <goys> GOOSE in a text by John Wykes; these forms, in combination with other features characteristic of the South-West, are found only in SW Devon and in Cornwall in his experience. The *LALME* material demonstrates a wider area of attestation.

The *County Dictionary* also reports numerous <o(o)> for eME ō in NME; these may imply that eME ō had not shifted to ME ū̆ yet, or that the change was not yet complete, or that the change just was not 'recorded' in the spelling, as it was a realisational change only. For instance, for BROTHER, there are numerous conventional spellings, for example, <broder>, <brother>, <broþer>; there are very few <u> for the stressed vowel, and no <ou>/<ow>. For GOOD, there are also numerous spellings with <o(o)>, for example, <god(e)>, <good(e)>; the fact that GOOD is far and away the most frequently used of the ō-words in *LALME's* list may be relevant. As for OTHER, <o> spellings are literally legion. The implications are discussed in Section 6.2.5.

Such forms as <noo> NOW (Staffordshire, LP 515) and <ooure> OUR (Nottinghamshire, LP 593), suggest that the spelling <oo> had come to correspond to [u:] at this stage, and thus furnish indirect evidence that eME ō had already been raised to [u:] (cf. Section 7.2.5). Such spellings go with non-NME forms like <gud>.

6.2.4 Discussion of material from additional sources

The additional sources yield some interesting forms; some of them give evidence of NF, whereas MS Cambridge, Corpus Christi College 388

(Hunt and Benskin 2001) has forms with <u> and <ou> for the reflex of eME *ō*, testifying to the southern raising to [u:].

<doun> DO inf. (*HB2*, *HB3*)
<doun> DO past ppl. (*HB3*)
<g*ru*et> GROW (*HB2*)
<soun> SOON (*HB3*)
<spou*n*ful> SPOONFUL (*HB3*)

The language of the English portions of these texts has been localised to Ely/W Norfolk, and the hand appears to be from *c.* 1320–30 (Hunt and Benskin 2001: 193, 207). The forms listed thus seem to testify to southern-type raising of eME *ō* to [u:].

A hitherto unpublished verse charm against thieves in MS, Northamptonshire Record Office, Finch-Hatton 3047 (Benskin forthcoming), whose language probably belongs to W Lincolnshire or E Leicestershire, has the form <gude> GOOD. The hand is dated to the 'middle to later fourteenth century'; cf. Section 4.2.4.

Zachrisson reports a number of <u> and <ou>/<ow> for eME *ō* in fifteenth-century documents and private letters. Zachrisson draws the conclusion that 'the forms in question indicate that ME *ǭ* had been turned into (u.)' (1913: 77, 131, 223). Further support for this interpretation is found in the spelling of certain words which had eME *ū*, but which remained unaffected by the general diphthongisation of the reflex of eME *ū*, for example, ROOM, STOOP, WOUND; these are also frequently spelt with <ou> in Zachrisson's sources, and therefore <ou> is taken to correspond to [u:] (1913: 78). The following list is not exhaustive.

<gude> GOOD (State Papers, London)
<du> DO (Paston Letters, Norfolk)
<tuk> TAKE pt. (Parmenter, Essex)
<doune> DO past ppl. (Rotuli Parliamentorum, London)
<owdyr> OTHER (Paston Letters)
<goude> GOOD (Paston Letters)

Whitehall (1935: 69–70) documents the following spellings in *The Records of the Borough of Nottingham*[16] (cf. Section 4.3.4).

<tuke> presumably for TAKE pt. (Vol.II, no. 1, dated 1435)
<glufers> perhaps for GLOVES (Vol.II, no. 1, 1435)
<fute> presumably for FOOT (Vol.II, no. 1, 1435)
<gudes> presumably for GOOD (Vol.III, no. 20, 1496–98)

<fowte> for FOOT (Vol.II, no. 1, 1435)
<doure> for DOOR (Vol.II, no. 1, 1435)

Of the first four, Whitehall says that they 'may indicate the raising of ME *ō* (tense) to [u:], but they agree quite well with the quasi-Northern spellings found elsewhere' (1935: 69). Of the last two, he says that they are equally 'ambiguous [...] although they certainly suggest confusion with the *ou* for ME *ū*' (1935: 69–70).[17] Thus, they seem to imply change of the reflex of eME *ō*: either southern raising to [u:], or NF. Given the solidly local language, and the origins in Nottinghamshire, change of the southern type seems more likely.[18]

Wyld (1936: 234–9) also quotes a number of <ou>/<ow> and <u> for eME *ō* from the fourteenth and fifteenth centuries; he concludes that 'old tense *ō* had either developed completely its present sound [ū], or progressed far in this direction' in the fourteenth century in 'widely separated areas of England' (1936: 234).

Prins (1942a: 137) adduces several rhymes involving OE *ō* from *The Poems of William of Shoreham* (Kent, *c.* 1350).

<goud> GOOD (I: ll. 1701, 1760, 2040)
<floude> FLOOD (rhymes with <blode>, <rode>, <fode>, <gode>; III: ll. 337ff.)
<onder-stoude> UNDERSTAND pt. (rhymes with <gode>, <blode>, <forbroude>; III: ll. 130ff.)
<touke> TAKE pt. (rhymes with <bode>, <for-soke>, <loke>; III: ll. 250ff.)
<a foul> FOOL (rhymes with <coul>; IV: ll. 114 and 116)
<souþe> SOOTH (rhymes with <doþ>; VII: ll. 69 and 72)
<route> possibly ROOT (rhymes with <doute>; VII: ll. 7 and 8)

Prins (1942b) explains the 'GVS' as being 'due to a general tendency to front and incidentally narrow the main vowels' in lME (1942b: 162). Prins seeks to refute Jespersen's drag-chain theory, and to 'vindicate Luick's assumption' that eME *ē* and *ō* moved first (1942b: 162). Hence, he wants to find spellings and rhymes implying *ō* > [u:] and *ē* > [i:]. In the earlier article, such evidence was found in some fourteenth-century poems, whereas in the later article, Prins adduces spellings found in Brunne's *Handling Synne*, from the first half of the fourteenth century. A number of <ou> for etymological *ō* are cited, even ones that rhyme with etymological *ū*-words; some of the rhymes are between two *ō*-words, which is not conclusive as *rhyming* evidence, although the spellings in themselves are still innovative and indicative of vowel raising. Prins therefore concludes that 'the pronunciation of *o:* had become *u:* in the beginning of the 14th century in the N.E. Midlands, at least in some words' (1942b: 163).

After examining the contexts of the innovative spellings, Prins concludes that they are found especially in the vicinity of dental, alveolar, and labial consonants (i.e. not velar ones), and he therefore suggests that the raising of the half-close vowels may have started as an assimilatory process (1942b: 163) 'by which *o:* was adapted to the fronted and narrowed resonance chamber conditioned by the surrounding dental, alveolar, or labial consonants', and that 'This modified pronunciation might subsequently have spread to other positions, thus creating the impression of a spontaneous change'.

However, Prins finds this suggestion so untraditional that he immediately retracts it, since it would have 'serious consequences with regard to our so-called sound-laws and upset all theories of "drift" and tendencies in language' (1942b: 163). But Prins does suggest that the individual changes in the shift may have been allophonic in their early stages, an observation I have made independently regarding the developments of OE *ā* and *ȳ*, *ē*, and *ō*. If Stockwell and Minkova's hypothesis is correct, namely, that it was the vocalisation of postvocalic fricatives which set the 'GVS' in motion, all the individual changes of the shift could be allophonically triggered. Since Prins discards the assimilatory explanation, he suggests other causes, which nevertheless imply that the change in question was combinative. Prins expresses doubt that simple analogy could be so powerful a process as to make assimilation spread to *all* words of a class (1942b: 163–4). When the article was written, the idea and nature of lexical diffusion had not been worked out: lexical diffusion (cp. Phillips 2006a; McMahon 1994: 47–55) describes how an originally combinative change could spread through the lexicon and become a so-called 'exceptionless sound law'.

Black (1998) adduces <fute> FOOT and <souþe> OE *sōþ* 'true'. The documents in which these appear have been described in Section 4.2.4. Suffice it to say that they are dated to *c.* 1390–1, and that the language is mixed, with some SW Midland (Herefordshire) forms and some NE Midland (Nottinghamshire-Lincolnshire) forms, and some forms apparently written according to Welsh spelling conventions. These documents show irregular spellings for other long vowels too, and they seem to indicate vowel shift in the late fourteenth century in whatever English informed the scribe.

6.2.5 Discussion of northern fronting and southern raising

According to conventional accounts, ME <u>, <ui>/<uy> for the reflex of eME *ō* are believed to be distinctively northern spellings testifying to NF. However, as the extracted material demonstrates, many northern texts do not show <u> or <ui>/<uy> for eME *ō*. On the contrary, numerous northern texts have conservative <o(o)> for OE *ō*.

In SME, the reflex of OE *ō* underwent vowel shift to [u:], which is generally not reflected in spelling, as it (and most of the vowel-shift changes) was purely realisational and did not result in merger between distinctive phonemes. Besides, early shortening and raising is believed to have taken place in closed monosyllables, especially those ending in /d/, and this process is thought to be responsible for early <u> in texts from the south; an example is <gud> GOOD. However, as pointed out in Section 5.2.3, it is unclear why such raising and shortening of half-close vowels in closed syllables would appear only before /d/; the modern language shows a short vowel also before /t/ and /k/, for example, in FOOT, SOOT; BOOK, COOK, CROOK, HOOK, NOOK, LOOK, TOOK. Besides, <u>, <uo>, <ou>/<ow> are found in SME in words where shortening never occurred, as the material demonstrates. This poses a problem for the traditional view that <u>-type spellings are distinctly northern and must indicate NF. The traditional view may be inadequately informed: <u> is only distinctly northern if one has not seen much southern ME. The issue is rather the interpretation of <u>: it is the phonetic correlates that have been held to be distinctively northern.

In essence, it is difficult to draw the line between 'southern' and 'northern' dialects: north of the Humber, fronted eME *ō* is often reflected in the spelling as <u>, <ui>/<uy>; south of the Humber, vowel-shifted eME *ō* is sometimes spelt <u>, <ou>/<ow>, <uo>, or less frequently <eo>, <oe>, <oi> from quite an early date. Thus, there is overlap between innovative <u> for SME *ō* > [u:] and for NME *ō* > [ü:], and it is consequently hard to distinguish the two changes, since the spelling evidence for both is identical. The fact that these changes must have started at about the same time further complicates the situation.

However, <u> traditionally implied [u:], and since <u> for the reflex of OE *ū, ug*, etc. is retained far into the ME period, <u> for *ō* in southern texts may simply indicate raising to [u:], that is, vowel shift of the southern kind. Also, scribes may have kept spellings for the raised reflex of eME *ō* (<u>) apart from spellings for the reflex of eME *ū* (<ou>/<ow>) for reasons of lexical distribution.[19] From the standpoint of the participants, the issue may be logographic rather than segmental phonetics. At any rate, it does not seem too problematic to take <u> for the reflex of eME *ō* in southern texts as indicating vowel shift. Still, a detailed examination of NF, southern vowel shift, and the spellings for both, is clearly in order.

Relatively little has been written about NF; a list of relevant works is given by Britton (2002), who examines NF, which is traditionally dated to the thirteenth century. NF must have taken place after MEOSL, Britton points out, since the MEOSL product of eME *u* is *ō*, which participated in NF (2002: 221). In the conventional account, eME *ō* was first simply fronted to [ø:], which remains in some Scots dialects, whereas in northern England, the fronted vowel subsequently raised to [y:]. However, Britton believes the raising could have been not to [y:] but to lax [ʏ:], because 'the lax constituents of the diphthong [ɪʊ] that subsequently emerged in northern English dialects are best explained as deriving from a lax monophthong' (2002: 222).

For mediaeval English, NF as a process is largely inferred from modern pronunciation, that is, [ɪʊ], [ɪɤ], [ɪə], [jʊ], [jɤ], and [i:] in words containing the reflex of eME *ō*. In Scots dialects, the modern reflexes are '[ɛ], [e(:)], [ø(:)], [i(:)], and [ɪ]' (2002: 222). However, there is additional evidence for NF which is not always included in discussions of this process, but which provides important insights, for instance regarding the Lincolnshire reflexes of NF and later changes.

The following chronology is established by Britton (2002: 222; the internal chronology of stages 1. and 2. is not determined):

1. OE [o:w] > [ɔu][20] (before NF, since the reflex of this does not participate in NF)
2. MEOSL of OE *u* > [o:] (participates in NF)
3. NF: all [o:] > [ø:]
4. New [ø:w] from vocalisation of [ɣ] in [ø:ɣ], where [ɣ] > [w]
   ↳ [øu][21] > [eu] (ME) > lME [iu] (merger with etym. [iu]) > PDE [iu]/[ɪu(:)]/[ju:]

Stage 4 is seen in for example, ENOUGH and PLOUGH. ME spellings and modern pronunciation show vowel variation, due to morphophonemic 'alternation between the final [x] of uninflected forms and the intervocalic [ɣ] of inflected forms' (2002: 222), where the latter vocalised to [w] to form the diphthongal variant. Paradigmatic levelling in ME generalised one or the other vowel, resulting in the PDE dialects having either a front monophthong or the earlier [iu]/[ɪu(:)]/[ju:] in words with eME *ō*. Britton's account seems not to square entirely with, for example, *Redheugh* /redhju:f/ in Durham, where [eu] has developed seemingly without vocalisation of [ɣ]; nor does it square with <of> from NME [o:w], for example, in GROW in *LALME* (in Nottinghamshire, the North and West Ridings of Yorkshire). However, although the development of a diphthong often entails loss of the etymological velar fricative, this is not always the case, cf. Scots /pljʌx/ PLOUGH. The diphthong may arise from the development of an [u]-glide between [øː ~ yː] and /x/, and the post-vocalic /x/ may be retained or lost. Williamson assumes the development /y^{u}x/ > /yux/ > /iux/ > /jux/ > /jʌx/ in /pljʌx/ PLOUGH (pers. comm.).

Luick was among the first to propose a correlation in the geographical distribution of fronted ME *ō* and undiphthongised ME *ū*, which made him believe that the diphthongisation of the high vowels was triggered by the raising of the half-close vowels in a push-chain, 'as a strategy to resist merger' (Britton 2002: 222). Since the half-close back vowel was not raised in NME, there was no need for the high back vowel to diphthongise, as there was no danger of merger. However, and this is Britton's main point, the fact that the reflexes of eME *ō* and eME *ū* have indeed merged at /uː/ in modern N Lincolnshire dialects constitutes an embarrassment to the 'no-collapse output condition' for the 'GVS', as postulated by Lass (1976: 71). Nevertheless, this merger may not be entirely incompatible with a push-chain hypothesis – Luick himself attributed the merger to dialect contact (Britton 2002: 223):

> To the north of the area, beyond the Humber estuary, lay the East Riding of Yorkshire, where ME /uː/ remained at that value and the reflex of ME /oː/ had [ɪə] realisations. Luick therefore concluded that the source of the north Lincolnshire merger was the southward spread of /uː/ forms of the HOUSE set. […] But, in fact, Luick was wrong – not in turning to dialect contact to explain the merger, but in assuming that the source of the merger was a southward diffusion of the monophthongal forms of ME /uː/. […] I shall argue that merger of the HOUSE and GOOSE sets in that area resulted from the northward diffusion of /uː/ variants of raised ME /oː/, with consequent disappearance of most traces of the forms descended from the northern fronting of eME /oː/.

Linguists have commonly appealed to evidence from modern dialects to track the diffusion and geographical distribution of NF, but this method is fraught with difficulty, since hundreds of years have elapsed since the change took place, and subsequent changes may obscure the initial output and spread of NF. *LALME*, however, provides ME material available from 'a period much closer in time to that of Northern Fronting' (2002: 223). Apart from words where eME *ō* preceded /w/ < OE [ɣ], the spellings <u>, <ui>/<uy> for eME /oː/ words are taken to indicate a fronted vowel (which spellings are due to 'French orthographic practices'), whereas <eu>/<ew> are thought to imply the merger of [øu] with ME /eu/ (2002: 223). But as NF was a realisational change which did not cause any phonemic merger, there really was no need for scribes to change the spelling of its reflexes. 'For this reason northern scribes typically show a variation between 'o' and 'u' types of spellings for eME /oː/ that is of no phonological significance' (2002: 224). This statement seems to run counter to the claim made on the previous page, namely, that <u>, <ui>/<uy> (= <u>-type spellings) are taken to indicate a fronted reflex of eME *ō*, but Britton probably uses the term 'phonological' as he ought to, and his statement means that <u>-type spellings have *phonetic* but not *phonemic* significance. Also, <o> might have been preferred before minim clusters and in final position; these may be reasons why *LALME* does not provide as many innovative spellings as Britton might have hoped. Still, BEHOVES and POOR do provide some <u> for eME *ō* in Lincolnshire, and indeed they are dominant in some LPs. As for /øu/ (which later merged with ME *eu*), FOWL and ENOUGH are found by Britton to be the only relevant items in *LALME*; for both, <eu>/<ew> occur in Lincolnshire. However, even though OE *fugol* FOWL meets the requirements for MEOSL, it is usually grouped with those words whose postvocalic fricative vocalised in lOE, and whose assumed long vowel merged with etymological *ū*. The PDE form /faʊl/ certainly proves that the output merged with etymological *ū*, not *ō*, at least in southern English, so it is uncertain whether spellings for it ought to be included in a discussion of NF. The same could be said for BOUGH and PLOUGH, which both have /aʊ/ in PDE (RP), although in these cases, the OE etymon had *ō*.

Britton concludes from the lME spellings that NF was 'well established in parts of Lincolnshire' (2002: 226), since the *LALME* evidence clusters in the north, in the south, and in the mid-western parts of the county. However, by the late nineteenth century, 'all traces of Northern Fronting in its context-free development had vanished from' Lincolnshire (2002: 226), but traces of its contextual development remained in the mid-twentieth century; that is, the reflexes of /øu/ (< *ō* fronted before *w*) were recorded as /ɪu/, /ɪuː/, and /juː/ in northern and southern Lincolnshire. Dialect contact is behind the 'elimination of fronted reflexes of eME /oː/, in their context-free development, as a result of the spread of /uː/ reflexes of ME /oː/' (2002: 227) from the south. In other words, southern vowel-shifted [uː] for eME *ō* ousted fronted variants. The part of N Lincolnshire which has an undiphthongised reflex of eME *ū* has retained a native feature,

Britton states, basing his claim on the strong correlation in the modern dialects of northern England and of Scotland between application of NF and lack of vowel shift of eME *ū*.

Britton next deals with the origin of that vowel-shifted [u:] for eME *ō* which eventually eliminated the indigenous fronted reflexes. He suggests that it came from 'areas south and south-west of Lincolnshire, with a possibility, also, of a northward and westward spread of /u:/ from that substantial area of east and central Lincolnshire that showed no spelling evidence' of NF (2002: 227). Supporting evidence for such a diffusion of a southerly form is found in the development of OE *ā*, which was fronted to ME [a:] in the north, including Lincolnshire. This fronted reflex was however ousted by [ɔ:] variants in Lincolnshire, starting relatively early in the ME period (2002: 227). Forms with <a> for OE *ā*, indicating fronted [a:], are, in Britton's view, rare by lME in Lincolnshire, except in the northern part, where <a> and <o> co-vary. Only a 'few residual lexical traces' (2002: 228) of a fronted reflex of OE *ā* are found in NW Lincolnshire in the late nineteenth century, and in the mid-twentieth century, a fronted reflex of OE/ON *ā* was found only in the preposition *fra* FROM. Thus, the fronted reflexes of the two perhaps most typically northern eME long-vowel changes have been almost completely eliminated from the dialects of N Lincolnshire.

It would seem that Britton's chronology (MEOSL happening before NF) might destroy Stockwell's explanation of the assumed lowered output of MEOSL in terms of early vowel shift. The OSL product of eME *u* must have fallen in with etymological *ō*, since it participates in NF; therefore, Britton's chronology appears sound. But this chronology need not destroy Stockwell's early vowel-shift hypothesis for two reasons. First, Stockwell mostly deals with the 'GVS' in *southern* ME. Second, Stockwell's hypothesis may still hold if eME *ō* was raised (even in the north) *before* it was fronted, and if Ritt's hypotheses (1994) are correct. Such a raising-then-fronting hypothesis is corroborated by spellings and by suggestions made by Britton (2002: 222) and by Britton and Williamson (2002) that the immediate output of NF was a *close* front *lax* rounded vowel.

Britton's chronology:

1. OE *ōw* > [ɔʊ]
2. MEOSL: OE *u* > [o:]
3. NF: all [o:] > [ø:] or [y:] or [ʏ:]
4. ME [ø:ɣ] > [ø:w] > [øu] > [eu] > [iu] > [iu]/[ɪu(:)]/[ju:]

(Britton is non-committal with regard to the dating of the GVS)

Stockwell's chronology:

1. GVS
2. MEOSL
3. NF

Stockwell's early vowel-shift hypothesis seems logical, as it accounts for <o(o)> and <e(e)> for the MEOSL products of OE *u* and *i*, as well as for <i> and <u> for the shortened product of eME *ē* and *ō*, which most authorities hold to be later than MEOSL of *e* and *o*. The crucial issue is the relative ordering of these processes rather than any absolute date for them. I therefore suggest the following chronology and sound-values for the development of eME *ō*.

1. OE *ōw* > [ɔʊ] (cf. Jordan 1968: §106)
2. GVS (early stages): eME *ō* > [ʊ:]/[uʊ]; eME *ū* > [ɨu] (South) or [u:] (North)
3. MEOSL: OE *u* > [ʊ:] <o(o)>
4. NF: all [ʊ:] > [ʏ:]

The stage [ʊ:] or [uʊ] (or some other intermediate sound) is necessary to avoid merger with [u:] from unchanged eME *ū* in the north; otherwise, [u:] from both sources (vowel-shifted eME *ō* and unchanged eME *ū*) would have merged, and then fronted, which did not happen. Stockwell and Minkova (1988a: 363) also believe [u:] and [uw]/[ʊu] would be sufficiently dissimilar to prevent merger between raised eME *ō* and unchanged eME *ū*. Further, an [ʊ:] stage agrees better with Britton's claim that the immediate output of NF was lax [ʏ:], which again agrees better with the modern dialectal *lax* reflexes of eME *ō* (listed earlier). It also agrees well with Ritt's hypothesis (1994) regarding the rise of a tense-lax distinction in ME. Subsequently, in the south, [ʊ:] was raised (and backed) to its present value [u:]; alternatively, the reflex of eME *ō* could have been raised to [u:] immediately (in the 'GVS') in the south, at least if the reflex of eME *ū* had already diphthongised there.[22]

LAEME has no attestations of <eu>/<ew> in the relevant lexis;[23] nor any <u> for the reflex of *ō* in POOR or BROTHER. There are two cases of simplex <u> in BOUGH (< OE *bōg/bōh*): <buges> in no. 155 (Norfolk), and <buh> in no. 297 (not examined for the present work). *SMED* records not a single <eu>/<ew> for the reflex of OE *og/ug/ōg/ōh*. *LALME*, on the other hand, reports a number of <eu>/<ew> for ENOUGH and <u> etc. for POOR, as shown in Table 6.6 and Table 6.7.

Table 6.6 *Incidence of <ew>, <u> for* ENOUGH *(< OE* genōg*)* (LALME)

County	LPs	Spellings
Lancashire	23	<ynugh>
	25	<enughe>, <e-nuʒhe>, <i-nuʒhe>, <y-nuʒhe>
	365	<ynewe>
Leicestershire	560	<e-newgh>
Lincolnshire	220, 277, 492, 905, 908, 912	<enewgh>, <enewghe>, <enewyghe>, <I-newgh>, <ynew>, <y-new>, <ynewe>, <ynewgh>, <y-newʒe>
	501	<enwgh>
East Riding, Yks	576	<in-newght>
North Riding, Yks	457	<ynew>
West Riding, Yks	211, 1349	<enew>, <enewe>

For <ew> in OE *fugol* FOWL, see Section 7.2.5 Other spellings potentially indicating NF in the reflex of OE *fugol* are: <fuel> and <fules> in LP 375 (Yorkshire), and <fuxol> and <fuxul> in LP 18 (West Riding of Yorkshire).

Britton and Williamson (2002) seek to establish the dating and chronology of NF and other relevant changes, such as MEOSL, the diphthongisation of the sequence [o:ɣ] > [o:w], and the development of early loans with OFr *ü*. They base their claims on spelling evidence, even though such evidence post-dates the inception of the change, chiefly because the output would have been a realisational variant, not a phoneme, and there would thus have been no need to indicate the change in spelling. Britton and Williamson follow Jordan (1968: §39) in seeing MEOSL as having a distinct Southern and a distinct Northern variant, the Northern OSL being earlier (thirteenth century) than that affecting SME (fourteenth century); the high vowels were affected later than the mid vowels. In the traditional view, the lengthened reflex of ME *u* merged with ME *ō* at [o:]. However, Luick (1914–40: §393) suggests that when *i* and *u* were lengthened, they were lengthened to [i̞:] and [ų:], and that the historical *ē* and *ō* moved up to merge with these. Britton and Williamson also propose that ME *u* was not only lower than its long counterparts, but also less peripheral, allotting it the value [ṳ̈]; after OSL, the output was [ṳ̈:]. In addition, there was [ÿ:] in French loans, a high round frontish long vowel. Each vowel would have 'a range of phonetic realizations with (at least peripheral) intersection of areas of the vowel space in the high area' (Britton

Table 6.7 *Incidence of <u>, <uy>, <w> for* POOR *(LALME, northern area of survey)*

County	LPs	Spellings
Derbyshire	3	<pure>
Durham	13	<pure>
Lincolnshire	38, 45, 220	<pur>
	38, 220, 908	<pure>
	587	<puyr>
Nottinghamshire	202	<pure>
Northumberland	329	<pur>
Rutland	553	<pure>
Westmorland	389	<pure/pur*e*>
East Riding, Yks	361	<pur>
	576	<pure/pur*e*>
North Riding, Yks	190, 486	<pur>
	174, 197, 468, 486	<pure>
West Riding, Yks	415	<pur>
	454	<pure>
	406	<pur*e*>
NME	471, 484, 521	<pur>
	205, 471, 481, 484, 521	<pure>
	599	<pwre>

and Williamson 2002: 2); the range of each vowel is marked as an ellipse in the vowel space (cf. Labov 1994). Such ranges are called 'ambits' by Williamson (2006: 1–3), and change is a result of changes in ambits: merger, for instance, would be the result of dimensional overlap between the ambits of two phonemes. This does not, however, explain why previously separate ambits come to overlap, but it is reasonable to suppose that allophonic variation may 'push' the limits of an ambit up or down, or more to the front or back, in the vowel space. Britton and Williamson see NF as a four-stage process (2006: 1–3):

> Stage 1 represents overlapping pronunciations in members of the sets of words whose vowels are derived from OE u and OE o:. This resolves itself in a merger (Stage 2), but with the resulting vowel ṳ̟:, rather than o: (in contrast to the conventional view). Stage 3 represents an overlap between the merged (or even partially merged) ṳ̟: and o: sets with words whose vowel is a reflex of words of Old French or Anglo-French origin. This set is characterized by a high, front-to-centralized rounded vowel, which we symbolize as ÿ:. The outcome of this is Stage 4, merger into a set where the vowel in words from OE u, OE o:, and OF/AF ü is ÿ:.

Thus, Britton Williamson do not believe that OSL of *u* resulted in 'immediate merger, but [was] rather a step in a process of staged fronting by coalescence of lexical sets, enabled by the results of the lengthening of the reflexes of OE *u*' (2002: 1). Their conclusion, that the result of NF was a close front *tense* rounded vowel, /y:/, goes against Britton's claim (2002) that the NF output was [ʏ:]. In fact, a lax output accounts better for those reflexes in modern dialects which have /i(:)/ or /ø(:)/ or mid-centralised variants.

Williamson (2006) elaborates on his and Britton's claim that the Early Scots output of NF was indeed close. For support, Williamson draws on evidence of various kinds: the modern Scots reflexes of eME *ō*, French loans with *ü* (which merged with eME *ō*), and rhymes between words with OFr *ü* and the reflex of OE *ō*; such rhymes are attested from the late fourteenth century onwards (2006: 5). Williamson argues that northern OSL played a crucial role in the inception and output of NF. Essentially, /ʊ/ was lower than its historically long counterpart /u:/, and when it lengthened, it was already closer to the long monophthong which was 'one step lower in the system, [. . .] /o:/, and in lengthening encroached on [its] phonetic ambit' (Williamson 2006: 10). Subsequently, the lengthened [ʊ:] tensed (became more peripheral), and 'the process of merger was a result of the long vowels *raising* – being drawn (re-interpreted by speakers as belonging) to the ambit of the new long vowels; the new long vowels "captured" the long vowels below them' (2006: 10). What triggered the upward pressure was, in Williamson's opinion, the northern OSL of *o*, which produced [o:] and therefore 'encroached on the ambit of' historical *ō* (2006: 11). Etymological *ō* therefore moved up and merged with the output of Northern Fronted and tensed [ʊ], that is, [ʊ̈:], and as the last stage in the process of NF, this [ʊ̈:] merged with the vowel of OFr loans 'with a high front or high central vowel – [y: ~ ʉ:]' (2006: 11).[24]

6.3 Summary and conclusions

6.3.1 The southern shift ō > [u:]

It is clear that there is much less written evidence for early shifting of the back vowels than for the front. Even so, <ou>/<ow>, <u>/<v>, <ui>, <w> for eME *ō* are not infrequent. The <u>, <ui>/<uy> spellings are supposed to indicate NF when they appear in the North, but they are quite numerous in southern texts as well, in which correspondence to [ü:] is unlikely. Since OE/ME *ō* are regularly spelt <o>, all of these spellings are innovations, requiring some explanation. Given the known subsequent history of the pronunciation of eME *ō*, it seems safe to assume that the new, aberrant spellings are indications of raising and/or fronting of eME *ō*. Although such a conclusion appears to be almost surprisingly unproblematic, there is scope for even more detailed analysis of the aberrant spellings: neither the *LAEME* nor the *LALME* material was collected primarily for phonological purposes, so a close look at the entire orthography of selected texts may prove necessary before any phonological inferences may be made which are not radically removed from what one might regard as reliable. For example, if any given source has <ou>/<ow> and <u> for the reflexes of eME *ū*, and the same source has <o(o)> for eME *ọ̄*, though with occasional <ou>/<ow>, <u> for the same, the case for reading these irregular spellings as evidence for vowel shift is strengthened. It may be less straightforward to assess SME sources where eME *ū* is consistently represented by, for example, <ou>/<ow>, and eME *ō* is consistently represented by, for eaxmple, <u>/<w>, such that the spellings are in fact in complementary distribution. However, as noted before, <ou>/<ow> are equally well suited to represent [u:] as [ʊu], [əu], and [ʌu]; additionally, <u>/<w> and the like for eME *ō* are such clear innovations that I am inclined to take them at face value, that is, as indications of vowel shift or shift of phonemic class. If the foregoing premisses be admitted, the following conclusions may be drawn regarding eME *ō*.

Innovative *LAEME* forms indicate that eME *ō* had begun to raise to [u:] in Worcestershire by *c.* 1200, in Herefordshire in the early thirteenth century, in Gloucestershire (and perhaps Wiltshire) *c.* 1250, in Cambridgeshire *c.* 1275–99, in Oxfordshire, and Ely between 1275 and 1325, and in Wiltshire (and perhaps Lincolnshire) in the first half of the fourteenth century. The W Midlands report the earliest – and the highest number of – irregular spellings, but the E Midlands are also strongly represented from the mid-thirteenth century onwards. The loci of change must be sought in these areas. Innovative spellings from Durham and the North Riding of Yorkshire probably indicate NF, although the spellings are <ou> and <oe>, not the expected <u> or <ui>; similarly, <ow> in Lincolnshire sources may indicate NF.

In *SMED*, innovative spellings are numerous, and are clearly most frequent in the South (except in Devon, where they are infrequent), in Wiltshire, Berkshire, and the North (Cumberland and Yorkshire); in the North, NF is indicated rather than the 'GVS'. They also appear in Essex, Suffolk, Huntingdonshire, Leicestershire, Lincolnshire, Oxfordshire, Warwickshire, Worcestershire, Cheshire, and Lancashire. The spelling

<uo>, which is found in some quantity in a *LAEME* source entered in Oxfordshire, is found exclusively in Kent in *SMED*.

In *LALME*, innovative spellings indicative of the 'GVS' are found all over the country, particulary in the South, the SW Midlands, and the E Midlands. They are most numerous in Lincolnshire and Wiltshire, that is, in the NE Midlands and the SW Midlands. Besides, numerous innovative spellings for GOOD are found all over the country, indicating either that it is the best-attested of *LALME*'s *ō*-words,[25] or that this word may have been (among) the first to develop a raised vowel (which subsequently shortened in the case of GOOD and similar words).

In the additional sources, spellings which indicate raising are found in texts from probably Ely/W Norfolk (dated to *c.* 1320–30), and W Lincolnshire/E Leicestershire (*c.* 1350–1400).

Taken together, the irregular spellings for eME *ō* imply that the raising of the vowel began in the early thirteenth century, and that the loci of change are to be found in the (S)W Midlands (Worcestershire, Herefordshire, Gloucestershire, and Wiltshire) and in the East (Cambridgeshire, Ely, Norfolk, and Lincolnshire). In the *SMED* material, the South also stands out, and the absence of early vowel-shift spellings from this area may simply be due to the paucity of early texts from the South. Wyld (1936: 238) states quite conclusively that

> Probably further investigation of fourteenth-century texts would show that during the first half of this century old *ō* became, in the Eastern dialects, from Lincolnshire to Kent and Essex, a sound approximating to if it not quite attained the character of [ū]. From thence it passed into the London dialect.

Wyld also offers an explanation for the shift of [o:] > [u:], drawing on a similar process in modern Swedish, where the old [o:] is 'strongly over-rounded, so that to unaccustomed ears it sounds rather like some kind of [ū]' (1936: 235). Wyld may have been ignorant of the vowel shift in Swedish (and Norwegian), whereby the open and mid back vowels were raised and the close back vowel fronted, in a process very similar to the English 'GVS'. Still, over-rounding may be as likely a process as raising of the tongue position, or tensing of the tongue muscle. In fact, all three processes may have been involved in the shifting of eME *ō*.

6.3.2 The northern shift ō > [ü:]

NF is relatively well attested in both *SMED* and *LALME*; there is only one form in *LAEME*, <south> SOOTH from the first half of the fourteenth century, in no. 188 (Durham). The earliest indications of NF are <u> spellings found in *SMED*, in rolls from Durham (dated 1296), Northumberland (1296), and the East Riding of Yorkshire (1297). In the first half of the fourteenth century, forms with <u>/<w> and <ou> are found in all the northern counties (except Westmorland), as well as in Cheshire. NF may therefore have started in the northernmost counties of England in the late thirteenth century, which confirms the traditional account. Conservative <o> is dominant by far; this state of affairs may imply change in progress, or simply demonstrate the power of convention with respect to orthography.

In *LALME*, <u>, <ou> are found all over the north, especially in Cumberland and Yorkshire, but texts with northern language also show conventional <o> spellings in abundance. In some sources, <u> and <o> co-vary; examples are found in texts from Durham (LP 147), Northumberland (LP 765), the North Riding of Yorkshire (LPs 7, 197 and 483), the East Riding of Yorkshire (LPs 361 and 472), and the West Riding of Yorkshire (LPs 53 and 115). Thus, the adoption of <u>, <ui>/<uy> for the reflex of ME *ō* had not been effected over the whole area by the late fifteenth century; but whether the conventional spellings suggest that the *change* had not been completed by *c.* 1450, or whether the conventional *spellings* just lingered on for some time, is hard to determine. Sources with mixed spellings (i.e. both conventional and innovative spellings) for eME *ō* may in fact testify to change in progress. If so, NF may have taken much longer to diffuse through the lexicon than has been assumed. Hence, although NF is well attested, the assumption that this change had been completed in all NME by *c.* 1400 may not withstand close scrutiny. On the other hand, as NF was a purely realisational change, there was no need for the scribes to indicate it in spelling, cf. Britton (2002). Hence, conservative <o(o)> for *ō* need not entail 'no Northern Fronting'.

Evidence from modern northern dialects shows that eventually *ō* was fronted (Dieth 1932; Orton 1933). The ME documentary material is, however, inconclusive as evidence: it either shows no change in spelling, or mixed spellings. This may or may not imply that NF was still going on by the time that the 'GVS' had begun. Justification for viewing the change of *ọ̄* to *ǖ* as totally independent of the vowel shift thus seems hard to find. Also, the nature and 'pace' of the northern change may have been different from what the handbooks indicate. It certainly seems that the case that *ō* > *ǖ* should be treated as part of the 'GVS' would be strengthened by reviewing its relation to the 'GVS'-*type* changes of the other NME long vowels, that is, raising and fronting, but no shifting front-to-back (which excludes SME *ā* > *ǭ*, though that change is of course assumed to be too early to count anyway, in the traditional account). From the discussion in this and other chapters, the following relative chronology of NME long-vowel change may be tentatively established.

(1) Although there is not much eME material from the North, unrounding of OE *ȳ* seems to have taken place in lOE or eME in the northern counties (cf. Chapter 7), even though a rounded vowel may have been retained in certain words until the late thirteenth century in S Lancashire and perhaps in the West Riding of Yorkshire (Luick 1914–40: §287; Jordan 1968: §41; Cubbin 1981; cf. Benskin 1994). Indeed, *SMED1* records <uy> in Lancashire as late as 1332, and sporadic <u> or <o> in for example, Northumberland in 1296, the West Riding of Yorkshire in 1346, and Durham in 1342 (Kristensson 1967: 102 ff.). Unless these NME <u(y)> for OE *ȳ* are merely conventional, the unrounding of *ȳ* therefore seems to have been a long process, starting in lOE and ending in the early fourteenth century.

(2) The inception of NF is generally dated to the thirteenth century, and post-dates MEOSL, since the lengthened output of OE *u* shares the subsequent development of eME *ō* (Luick 1914–40: §406; Jordan 1968: §54; Britton 2002: 221). Since this change did not result in merger or a different distribution of phonemes, there was no need to indicate it in spelling, which is probably why, for example, <u>, <ui> are not as frequent in NME sources as one might expect. However, spellings which do indicate NF are recorded in Durham, the East Riding of Yorkshire, and Northumberland from the late thirteenth century, and in Cumberland, Lancashire, and the North and West Ridings of Yorkshire from the early fourteenth century onwards (*SMED1*).

(3) OE *ā* was not backed and rounded in NME (with the exception of S Lancashire and the southern part of the West Riding of Yorkshire, cf. Kristensson 1967: Maps 10–18), but remained as [ɑ:], and was fronted and raised to [a:], later [æ:], [ɛ:] (cf. Chapter 2). There is no agreement on the dating of the initial stages of this fronting.[26] Wyld claims that rhymes in fourteenth-century Scotch sources give evidence of fronting and raising to a half-close front sound (Wyld 1927: §157); Dobson (1968: §98) states that [ɛ:] had been reached before 1400. As the reflexes of OE *ā*, Norman French *ā* and the MEOSL output of *a* merge in northern dialects, the fronting can be safely dated after MEOSL (mid-thirteenth century). This is in agreement with Wright and Wright (1928: §51), who claim that ME *ā* was fronted to *ę̄* in the

> late thirteenth century (cf. Smith 1994: 434). *LAEME* reports forms with <ea>, <e>, etc. for OE *ā* in Cheshire in the mid-thirteenth century and in Cumberland in the thirteenth century; such forms never become frequent, but there is a peak in the period 1175–1274. *SMED* records <e>, <ae>, etc. for OE *ā* in Lincolnshire, Somerset, and Gloucestershire in the early fourteenth century; no such spellings are recorded in northern sources. *LALME* records <æ> and <e> for OE *ā* in the West Riding of Yorkshire, Yorkshire (and also in Norfolk and Warwickshire). Summing up, OE *ȳ* was unrounded to [i:] in NME, starting in lOE and reaching completion in the fourteenth century. NF of eME *ō* started in the late thirteenth century; it is unclear when it was completed. OE *ā* (along with the reflex of OE *ǣ*^{2}, which is *ā* in non-WS) was fronted to [a:] and gradually raised; the stage [ɛ:] had almost certainly been reached before 1400, and the stage [e:] may have been reached as early as the fourteenth century.
>
> With respect to the other OE long vowels, the following developments are assumed for NME. Etymological *ū* traditionally remained; eME *ī* (including the unrounded reflex of OE *ȳ*) was diphthongised in the 'GVS'; OE *ēo* was first monophthongised to [ø:] in lOE and then unrounded to [e:] in the twelfth century, merging with the reflex of eME *ē*, which was raised to [i:] in the 'GVS'; OE *ǣ*^{1} (< WGmc *ai+i*) was generally raised to [ɛ:], spelt <e(e)>, starting in the twelfth century. Evidence for vowel shift of eME *ē* and *ī* is recorded from the thirteenth century in northern sources.

Thus, it is clear that the northern long-vowel changes overlap with the 'GVS'. *Fronting* and *raising* are the two main processes involved in the northern vowel shift; besides, *diphthongisation* is seen in the development of eME *ī* (and plays an important role in the later history of long vowels in the northern dialects). Due to the early fronting of the reflexes of both OE *ā* and eME *ō*, there is later vowel shift in the *front* series of vowels only in NME; it still qualifies as a vowel shift. Some of the long-vowel changes took a long time to reach completion (certainly those involving OE *ā* and *ȳ*, and possibly that involving eME *ō*), which means that the presumably earlier changes (*ȳ* > *ī* and *ō* > *ǖ*) and specifically northern changes (*ō* > *ǖ* and *ā* > *ǣ*) overlapped with the constituent 'GVS' changes. It therefore makes no sense to distinguish between the vowel shift 'proper' and other long-vowel changes in NME. Williamson (2006: 10) states explicitly that the 'series of changes subsumed under MEOSL may be intimately connected temporally and causally to the subsequent series subsumed under the Great Vowel Shift'.

Notes

1 In MEOSL, OE *o* was lengthened to a more open ǭ in all dialects before 1250 (Wright and Wright 1928: §78; Minkova 1982 1985); that is, if one accepts the conventional view that OE *e* and *o* were [e] and [o] – Stockwell and others maintain they were [ɛ] and [ɔ]. At any rate, the MEOSL product of OE *o* did not merge with the reflex of OE *ō*, and so will not be dealt with here.

2 Since the late 1960s, some phonologists have preferred the term 'open syllable *tensing*' (cf. Anderson 1966; Malsch and Fulcher 1975), but the post-MEOSL spellings may be interpreted in different ways: if e.g. lax *u* was tensed in an open syllable, the tensed (and thus more peripheral) product ought to be spelt <u> or <ou>/<ow>, unless lax [ʊ] was half-close rather than close, in which case tense [o:] may have been closer to [ʊ] in terms of articulation than [u:] was. In other words, laxness and tenseness must be seen in correlation with vowel-height.

3 The same view is expressed by Wyld (1936: 236 ff.), who claims that etymological *ō* must have raised to [u:] first, and that there was an early shortening of this new [u:] (the product of which merged with etymological [u]). The FOOT-STRUT split occurred after the early shortening, anytime between *c.* 1450 and 1580 (1936: 232). Further, Wyld states (1936: 236) that the first orthographic evidence of the early shortening of eME *ō* is found in Brunne's *Handlyng Sinne* (Lincolnshire, 1301). Spellings in other texts, whose language has been located to Essex (*c.* 1420) and Wiltshire (*c.* 1420), also indicate shortening, for example, <sonner> SOONER and <flodde> FLOOD. Wyld concludes that vowel-shifted [u:] < eME *ō* 'was shortened by the first quarter of the fifteenth century at any rate, if we disregard the somewhat doubtful evidence from Robt. of Brunne, or if we accept it, more than a century earlier' (1936: 237). Indeed, this is the best explanation why some words underwent the FOOT-STRUT split, and some did not, giving three different reflexes of eME *ō* in PDE: [u:], [ʊ], and [ʌ].

4 Margaret Laing informs me that in no. 2002 from Gloucestershire, the majority of the <oe>-spellings 'are in original <eo> words, and they are found beside spellings implying monophthongisation mostly to E and occasionally to O. The spelling is obviously explicable in various ways by litteral substitution', though she leaves open the possibility that <oe> might correspond to a front rounded vowel (e-mail, dated 6 October 2010).

5 In Margaret Laing's view, the <e> in <ged-> could 'be an error either anticipating the ED in DEDE or a simple miswriting by a scribe whose "e" and "o" are very similar, the "e" sometimes almost lacking a tail when the body of it is made particularly fully, and the "o" sometimes gaining a tail when the second bowed stroke hits the first "c" shaped stroke too high. In this particular case, the letter seems to have been shaped deliberately as an "e", hence my reading of it thus' (e-mail, dated 25 October 2010).

6 However, in this text, the digraph <ou> is used in other contexts too, e.g. in words with OE *ū* (<flour> FLOWER, <nou> NOW), OE *ā* (<soule> SOUL, <louer> LORD), OE *ēo* (<ou> YOU < OE *ēow*); thus, one has 'to address the possibility

(if not likelihood) in this scribe's system of litteral substitution sets that may not have simple phonological equivalences' (Margaret Laing, e-mail, dated 4 November 2010).

7 The numbers refer to letter and line numbers in Hanham's edition.

8 MS Cambridge, Emmanuel College 27. *LAEME* identifies the word as ROOT, but it could also be *rout* 'company, body of men, (armed) force' (< OFr *route*), in which case the form is conventional.

9 MS British Library, Arundel 248.

10 Dobson's view that a glide developed after [ɡ] due to its high tongue position is favoured by Kristensson (2004: 80), but is *ad hoc*: the tongue position is equally high for [k t d] (Dobson 1968: §431, n.2); moreover, it is far more likely that a glide should develop between a *non*-velar consonant and a velar vowel. Jordan (1968: §46) adduces Kentish <uo>/<wo> for the reflex of ME *ǭ* after *b, p*, and *g* in lME, which may imply that a rising diphthong developed after bilabials. Alternatively, since <uo>/<wo> are found for the reflexes of both eME *ō* and *ǭ* (and <ie>/<ye> are found for the reflexes of both OE *ē* and *ēo/īo*), glides may have developed before all the mid long vowels in Kentish, or the mid long vowels may all have developed into rising diphthongs.

11 However, a quick scan of his 1934 monograph reveals the following <u>, <uo>/<wo> for the reflex of OE *ō*: <Gusselm'e> in 1327 (present-day Gushmere), and <Gussem'> in 1346, 1347, and 1348 (present-day Gosmere; both farms are in the parish of Selling), probably derived from OE *gōs* 'goose' + *sol* 'muddy pool' + *mere* 'mere, pool' (Wallenberg 1934: 305); <Gwosole> in 1334 and 1338 (present-day Little Gussels in the parish of Molash, which is adjacent to Selling), from OE *gōs* 'goose' + *sol* 'muddy pool' (1934: 379); <Guodwyne> in 1327 (personal/farm name recorded in the parish of Aldington; 1934: 464).

12 A point which is also noticed by Dance (2002).

13 Such spellings are found for the vowel of GOOSE in Lincolnshire (1332), Durham (1342 *RPD*), and the West Riding of Yorkshire (1346); for the vowel of ROOK in the West Riding of Yorkshire (1346), Gloucestershire (1327), Oxfordshire (1327), and Warwickshire (1332); for the vowel of OE *hō(h)* 'heel, spur of land' in Warwickshire (1327 and 1332).

14 Britton (2002 and pers. comm.) thinks <u> in GOOD reflects shortening before [d] in monosyllables, but such shortening seems curiously *ad hoc* and strangely confined in its lexical range, since it is unclear why such shortening should not have occurred regularly before [t] as well (it actually did in *foot* and *soot*). Vowel shortening before *voiceless* consonants is well-evidenced, but vowels tend to *lengthen* before voiced consonants, cf. the Scottish Vowel Length Rule (Aitken 1981) and the PDE allophonic difference in vowel length in e.g. *bat* vs *bad*. At any rate, a putative shortening would have to have happened after the 'GVS' in order to give [ʊ], as pointed out before. This issue is discussed in more detail in Section 6.2.5.

15 Forms like <broyer> BROTHER have not been included, since the <y> here is likely for <þ>.

16 Stevenson, W.H. (ed.). 1883. *The Records of the Borough of Nottingham. Vol. II.* London.

17 On DOOR, see Dobson (1968: §155).

18 The documents examined by Whitehall are part of *LALME* LP 96; they also feature <au>/<aw> for the reflex of eME *ū*, <ay> for the reflex of eME *ī*, and <y(e)> for the reflex of eME *ē*. Clearly, the language of this scribe shows advanced vowel shift, and the orthography and language of the original documents deserve an even more thorough examination.

19 Although this may imply a level of sophistication beyond that thought to be found in ME scribes, Orm proves otherwise, even if he is by any measure highly atypical, and hence a bad warrant for 'scribes'.

20 It seems, however, that [ɔ:u] may have been an intermediate stage between [o:w] and [ɔu].

21 Again, [ø:w] may have been an intermediate stage between [ø:w] and [øu].

22 A third alternative is a diagonal path of change (in terms of the vowel space) in the north, in which the reflex of eME *ō* was simultaneously raised and fronted to [ʏ:], which has been reported in PDE; cf. Britton (2002) and Britton and Williamson (2002).

23 ENOUGH, FOWL, BOUGH, OE *lōg* (3.sing.pret. of OE *lēan* 'to blame'), OE *lōgian* 'to lodge', OE *lōh* 'place', or OE *slōg(on)* (pret. of OE *slēan* SLAY).

24 The motivation for this merger may in Williamson's opinion have been 'a kind of hypercorrection, i.e. words with OF[r] /u/ had a certain prestige and the pronunciation of words with [ö̆:] from NF was then "pushed" in that direction with subsequent merger and exaggerated fronting' (pers. comm.). This is of course not demonstrable, but is quite possible. Williamson also puts forth a hypothesis regarding the lowering of this close vowel to close-mid in Middle Scots. As many present-day Scots dialects have a front mid reflex (rounded as well as unrounded) of eME *ō* (2006: 3–4), lowering must have taken place at some stage if the output of NF was a close vowel. After the Scottish Vowel Length Rule had taken effect, the fronted reflex of ME *ō*, [ÿ:], had a long and a short allophone. The short allophone became laxer than its long counterpart, with a range between [ʏ] and [ø], and 'its ambit came to overlap in height and backness with the ambit of V16 [= ɛ]. The main difference acoustically came to be the effect of the rounding' (2006: 17).

25 Its only competitor is OTHER, which is not listed for the southern area of survey.

26 In the South, fronting of ME *ā* < MEOSL of ME *a* had started in the fifteenth century, according to Zachrisson (1913: 56). French orthoepists equate the pronunciation of English *ā* with French [ɛ:] from the 1520s onwards (1913: 120).

CHAPTER 7

The development of ME ū

7.1 Introduction

The handbooks state that eME *ū* from various sources developed along the following lines. OE *u* was lengthened to [u:] before certain voiced homorganic consonant clusters in lOE, and thus fell in with original OE *ū*, for example, OE *pund* – later OE *pūnd* POUND, OE *hund* – later OE *hūnd* HOUND (Wright and Wright 1928: §§68–76; Campbell 1959: §§283–4; Jordan 1968: §22; Ekwall 1975: §17). In eME, the new long vowels were shortened again before some of the consonant combinations, but mostly remained before [ld, mb, nd, ng]; in PDE, the vowel has remained long before [nd], for example, in POUND, FOUND, GROUND. Jordan (1968: §22) dates this lengthening to the second half of the eighth or possibly the early ninth century; Wright and Wright (1928: §68) date it to the late ninth century. Lengthening is also seen in French loans where [u(:)] appears before the cluster [nt], for example, *munt* > *mount*, *bunté* > *bounty*, *cuntesse* > *countess* (cf. Pope 1934).[1]

The *g, h, w* after OE *ū/u* were vocalised in lOE or in ME. In the second part of the twelfth century, intervocalic and final velar *g* [ɣ] vocalised (probably to [w]) and formed a *u*-diphthong. In the thirteenth century, a glide developed between a vowel and a following palatal or velar *h* [ç x] to form *i*-diphthongs and *u*-diphthongs respectively. The *u*-diphthongs are thought to have monophthongised to [u:] (Sweet 1888: §§696–722; Luick 1914–40: §§372–3, 407–8; Wright and Wright 1928: §§104–16). Thus, according to the traditional interpretation, lOE *ū/u+g/w+V* were 'absorbed' by etymological *ū* and the output was a long monophthong [u:], which fell in with the /u:/ phoneme.

This eME /u:/ diphthongised to [ʊu] or [uw] around 1400. It became [əu] around 1500, [ʌʊ] in the seventeenth century, whence [aʊ] in the eighteenth century (Jespersen 1909: §§8.12–22; Luick 1914–40: §483; Wright 1924: §§73, 77; Dobson 1968: 685). This sound remains in many

PDE dialects, but the first element has become fronted in, for example, Cockney. ME /u:/ did not diphthongise in the mediaeval and early modern dialects north of the Humber, although the modern dialects often show a diphthongised vowel; nor did diphthongisation take place after [w] or [j], or before [p] or [m] in the vernaculars south of the Humber (Jespersen 1909: §8.23; Dobson 1968: §§162–7; Prins 1972: §4.6.1); examples include *wound, youth, droop, stoop, and room.*

In MEOSL, it is believed that the lengthening of etymological *i* and *u* was both more limited than that of *e o a* and also somewhat later, taking place in the second half of the thirteenth century in parts of the country, a century later in East Anglia (Wright and Wright 1928: §§77–85; Luick 1914–40: §392). As established in earlier chapters, MEOSL is also thought to have entailed the lowering of the affected short vowels (Wright and Wright 1928: §§84–5), but such lowering is rendered unnecessary under Stockwell's early vowel-shift hypothesis. Ritt (1994), on the other hand, argues that all ME quantitative vowel changes are related processes, due to one tendency termed 'eME quantity adjustment'. Ritt's account rests on the assumption that a tense-lax distinction arose between long and short vowels in ME, long vowels being tense and short vowels lax. Thus, when the lax [ʊ] lengthened, the product was [ʊ:], which was re-interpreted – since all long vowels were tense – as [o:], to which it was closer in quality than [u:] (1994: 79). Ritt's scenario therefore explains the apparent lowering of short close vowels when lengthened without having to postulate an extremely early (pre-MEOSL) 'GVS'.

Written evidence for the diphthongisation of *ū* is hard to come by, mostly because <ou>/<ow> had been adopted from French practice, in which they corresponded to [u] as the sole reflex of a merger between [u] and two earlier diphthongs [ɔu] and [ou].[2] According to Pope (1934: §§547–9, 698), the monophthongisation of older *ọu* to [u] took place in the late twelfth and thirteenth centuries;[3] however, in western OFr, where the origins of AN must be sought, *ọu* was levelled to [u] 'in the course of the eleventh century' (1934: §1085). AN also saw the change *ọu* to [u] 'as in Continental French' (1934: §1167).[4] In Continental French, use of <ou> for [u] 'began in the late twelfth century [...] and was adopted, though tardily, by Anglo-Norman scribes' (1934: §1220), and its 'use is occasional in the early thirteenth century' in Continental French (1934: §698). However, the 'tardiness' alluded to may be exaggerated, as analysis of a very high number of *LAEME* spellings for eME *ū* shows that <ou>/<ow> were used from the late twelfth century onwards in southern texts, but that the digraphs did not become common, or indeed dominant, until the last quarter of the thirteenth century. It appears that the use of <ou> for [u] on the Continent was triggered both by the ambiguity of <u> (which was used for etymological [u] as well as for [y] and early OFr *ọ*), and by sound changes, namely, early OFr *ọ* > *u*, and *ǫu/ọu* > *u*, and *ǫ* > *ọ* (Pope 1934: §698). The digraph <ou> was thus a back-spelling in French. Because, however, <ou>/<ow> may equally well represent a monophthong [u:] and a diphthong [ʊu]/[əu], linguists generally hesitate to use such spellings as evidence for the 'GVS'. There are a few notable exceptions: the 'Hymn to the Virgin' equates the sound value of English etymological *ū* to Welsh *ow*, which is unambiguously a diphthong (Dobson 1968: §160).

Due consideration ought also to be given to the ME 'breaking diphthong' <ou>: the entry of <ou> for a diphthong conditioned on a monophthong [o]+[x] disrupted the system, that is, the distribution of graph/digraph/trigraph for certain vowels. In OE, [u:] corresponded to <u>, [w] to <w>, [ow] and [o:w] to <ow>, and [aw] and [a:w] to <aw>. After the backing, rounding and raising of OE *ā* south of the Humber, the digraphs <ou>/<ow> were used for the reflex of OE *ā+w* also, that is, the digraph was ambiguous regarding etymology, but not regarding sound correspondence (since the root vowels of the CROW and BLOW sets have subsequently had the same development). With the adoption of <ow>/<ou> for the reflex of OE *ū*, however, the digraphs became ambiguous in terms of their implied sound value also. In ME, the reflex of OE *oht/ōht* [o(:)xt] underwent vocalisation of the postvocalic glide and simultaneous diphthongisation of the root vowel to [o(:)u], spelt <ou>. Thus, <ou>/<ow> now corresponded to three vowel phonemes: [ɔ(:)u] for OE *aw/ow/āw/ōw*, [u:] for ME *ū*, and [o(:)u]+[x] for OE *oht/ōht*. The distribution of the diphthong [o(:)u], conditioned at first, ceased to be transparent when the postvocalic glide disappeared completely. When the reflex of ME *ū* started to diphthongise, the <ou>/<ow> may have been felt to sufficiently represent this diphthong (since the digraphs already corresponded to diphthongs in the GROW/CROW and SOUGHT sets). If further orthographic differentiation was needed, this may have been achieved by the use of digraphs like <eu>/<ew> or <au>/<aw>, or trigraphs like <eou>, <oou>, all of which are found in the extracted material.

However, in contrast with the traditional view, which claims that OE *ūg/ug* were absorbed by OE *ū*, giving [u:], Stockwell (1960, 1978) and Stockwell and Minkova (1988a, 1988b) claim that the result of the vocalisation of *ug/ūg* was the minimal diphthong [uw]/[ʊu], which never monophthongised, and that it was this diphthong that caused a destabilisation of the high back vowel phoneme /u:/, which in turn opened up for the further diphthongisation of this phoneme. In other words, /u:/ would have had monophthongal as well as diphthongal allophones for several centuries, and it was only a question of time before the diphthongal variants would be generalised. Thus, Stockwell and Minkova argue for a very early stage of vowel shift in the phonemic merger of OE *ū* with the reflexes of OE *ūg/ug, ūw/uw*.

This chapter presents anomalous spellings for eME *ū* from the entire ME period, with a view to establishing whether they support the idea of an early vowel shift.

7.2 Discussion of ME spellings

7.2.1 Discussion of LAEME *material*

First, some words on the displacement of <u> by <ou>/<ow> for eME *ū* (cf. Table 7.4[5] at the end of this chapter). Forms with <ou>/<ow> appear from the latter half of the twelfth century, but they do not become common until a century later, and then mostly in the South and the W Midlands. Traditional <u> remains the most common spelling for the reflexes of eME *ū* even as late as the fourteenth century in certain areas. That is, <u> for OE/eME *ū* does not quickly disappear in favour of <ou>/<ow>. In addition, even though the postvocalic consonant of OE *ug* vocalised in lOE or eME, the majority of *LAEME* spellings for, for example, OE *fugol* FOWL still have a consonant letter after the vowel, as in <foȝel> (no. 10 from Gloucestershire) or <foweles> (no. 8 from Kent). Vocalisation of [ɣ] may still leave a disyllable, and orthographically, hiatus could hardly remain unmarked; <fowel> is transparently disyllabic, but it is still an innovation, and <foȝel> might well persist as a traditional spelling.[6] Thus, if the retention of the consonant has any significance whatever, it may be that it indicates non-identity with the etymological long vowel. That is, Stockwell (1961, 1978) and Stockwell and Minkova (1988a, 1988b) may be right that the vocalisation of *g* in *ug/ūg* never produced a long monophthong, but that the cluster was always pronounced as a minimal diphthong. However, there are a few forms with an unetymological consonant used in combination with OE *ū*. These are: <druð> OE *drū* in no. 122 (Cheshire, 1240–50; 3 occurrences); <fouvel> FOUL (< OE *fūl*) in no. 2002 (Gloucestershire, 1275–99); <fuweles> FOUL in no. 1900 (Worcestershire, 1200–49; <fuwel> for FOWL); <nuge> NOW in no. 155 (Norfolk, 1300–24).[7] The implication is that the ME reflex of OE *ug/ūg* may have been pronounced the same as

Table 7.1 *Irregular spellings for eME* ū *in* LAEME

County	No.	Date	Spellings
Worcestershire	1900	1200–49	<sceoue> SHOVE
Worcestershire	278	1250–74	<abeoten> ABOUT
			<beote/beoton> *būtan*
			<heose> HOUSE
			<heo/heou> HOW
			<þeo/þeou/þeu> THOU
			?<tuones> TOWN *pl.*
Herefordshire	246	1275–99	<beo*n*den> BIND *pt.pl.*
			<breþe> BROW
			?<coiþe> *cūþ*
			?<soint> SOUND *aj.*
Herefordshire	1100	1275–99	<breye> BROW
			<howelynge> HOWL *vn.*
			?<fuoel> FOWL
Gloucestershire	2002	1275–99	<-brei-> BROW
			?<fouvel> FOWL
			<oout> OUT
Cheshire	136	1275–99	<breyes> BROW
Unlocalised	242	1275–99	<brewe> BROW
Ely	282	1275–1324	<clouȝt> CLOUT
			<ouȝt> OUT
			<touȝ/þouȝ> THOU
East Riding, Yks	230	1300–49	<thowen> TOWN

that of OE *ū*, though whether that pronunciation took the form of a long monophthong or a minimal diphthong is an open question. At any rate, if the two reflexes had become identical, the final consonant could be used as a marker of length or be rationally extended for all /u:/ (cf. Section 7.2.5). That is, <fouvel> FOUL could be a back-spelling: if <fouvel> = FOWL, with a minimal diphthong not phonemically distinct from [u:], then <fouvel> could be extended by analogy to FOUL, either with [u:], or with *ū* already become the minimal diphthong.

Irregular *LAEME* spellings for eME *ū* which most likely indicate vowel-shift diphthongisation are recorded in Table 7.1. The following discussion is limited to the forms which probably indicate vowel shift; words which had variant forms have been left out.

As to BROW, it should be noted that OE *brū* BROW had the form *brū(w)a* in the nominative/accusative plural, and *brūna* in the genitive plural. Spellings with <u> or <o> and with <ew> or <ey> appear for this word, the latter two being innovative; that is, the irregular <ew> and <ey> in BROW could point to diphthongisation. Such spellings appear in Cheshire, Herefordshire, Gloucestershire, and an unlocalised source, in texts which are all dated to the period 1275–99.

A few *LAEME* spellings seem to indicate a glide plus a nucleus for the reflex of eME *ū*, that is, a diphthong of some kind. Source text no. 1900 (Worcestershire, 1200–49) has <fuwel-> FOUL, and <sceoue> SHOVE 1.sg. pres.ind. Analysis of the scribe's orthographic system does not disambiguate the latter form.

Text no. 246 (Herefordshire, 1275–99) has <beo*n*den> BIND pt.pl.; the same text also has <soint> SOUND and an array of different spellings for the reflex(es) of eME *ū*, although <u> is dominant. No. 278 (Worcestershire, 1250–74) likewise has regular <u>, but also a number of <eo>/<eu>, <eou>, which seem almost certainly to indicate a diphthong. No. 1100 (Herefordshire, 1275–99) has <fuoel> FOWL and <howelynge> HOWL vn.; again, <u> dominates.

No. 2002 (Gloucestershire, 1275–99) shows <fouvel> FOUL and <oout> OUT. An unlocalised text, no. 174 (*c.* 1300), reports <howele> OWL. No. 282 (Ely, 1275–1324) has some remarkable spellings with <ȝ>: <touȝ>, <þouȝ> THOU, <ouȝt> OUT, and <clouȝt> CLOUT; these appear to indicate a minimal diphthong. If ME 'breaking' of *o, a* was early, and (as appears over much of East Anglia and its fringes) [x] was lost early (especially in [xt]), then <touȝ> could be a mere back-spelling: *ohte/oȝte* > *ouhte/ouȝte*> *out* OUGHT.[8] However, <ouȝ(t)> would still indicate a diphthong. The form <thowen> TOWN in no. 230 (East Riding of Yorkshire, 1300–49) implies a glide plus nucleus, and thus almost certainly indicates early diphthongisation of *ū*.

That is, to judge by the *LAEME* material, the exact phonetic make-up of the reflex of eME *ū* is still quite elusive, but it seems likely that some of the above spellings indicate diphthongisation, as they appear to imply a glide plus a nucleus. Again, the W Midlands (Worcestershire, Herefordshire, and Gloucestershire) stand out as a possible locus of change, as does Cheshire, and – a little later – Ely and Yorkshire. The majority of such spellings appear from the late thirteenth century onwards, but the ones in no. 278 from Worcestershire are dated to 1250–74. The spellings presented earlier are hardly compelling as evidence of early vowel shift of eME *ū*, but since the evidence for the thirteenth-century raising of ME *ō* is both more extensive and less controversial, one must assume that the reflex of ME *ū* must have started to diphthongise as well, since the reflexes of the two vowels did not merge.

7.2.2 Discussion of SMED material

General

There are few irregular spellings to be extracted from *SMED*, mostly because Kristensson did not systematically record forms for eME *ū* for all areas, on the grounds that an overwhelming majority of them have the traditional <u> or <ou>/<ow>. Still, spellings for OE *u* in lengthening contexts were indeed recorded, and those with <ou>/<ow> have been analysed, since they at least imply lengthening. Although such <ou>/<ow> occur across the country, they seem most frequent in the South.

Inverted <ug> and similar spellings for eME *ū* were not recorded for *SMED*, but many attested forms imply complete vocalisation of post-vocalic <g> from *c.* 1316 onwards. Examples from *SMED5* for FOWL are <Foul> in Dorset (1327), <Fouler> (Wiltshire 1327), <Fowel> (Berkshire 1327, Hampshire 1333, Somerset 1333, and Wiltshire 1327); examples for OE *rūgan* in componds are also found in some quantity. Thus, there can be little doubt that the reflex of OE post-vocalic <g> had been completely vocalised by at least the beginning of the fourteenth century, which is unsurprising, given that a thorough assessment of all *LAEME* spellings for back vowels *+g/ht* indicates that the post-vocalic velar fricatives started to vocalise in the twelfth century; see the discussion of the vocalisation of post-vocalic [j], [ç], [ɣ], and [x] in Chapter 4.

Although <ou>/<ow> are most frequent for eME *ū* in *SMED*, there is also a scattering of <u>. Kristensson (2001) presents a different view of the phonetic implications of conventional <ou>, <u> for OE *ū* in the South. It was pointed out in Chapters 4 and 6 that the central southern counties show numerous <ou>/<ow> and also <u> for the reflexes of OE *ō*; that the same area features <ei>/<ey> for OE *ē*; and that Kristensson therefore draws the conclusion that OE *ē* and *ō* were being, or had been, raised to [iː] and [uː] respectively in the early fourteenth century. Now, <ou>/<ow> were the traditional spellings for eME *ū*; the reflexes of eME *ō* and eME *ū* are thus spelt alike in some of the southern counties in the early decades of the fourteenth century, but the reflexes of these two sounds are still kept apart in the modern language. Therefore, 'we must assume that ME /iː/ and /uː/ had developed, or were developing, into diphthongs at the time when ME /eː/ and /oː/ were raised' (Kristensson 2001: 79–80). Kristensson later confirms his new position that OE *ū* had become [ʊu] in at least parts of the South at the time when the LSRs were registered (Kristensson 2001: 91).

OE u in lengthening contexts

For *u* in lengthening context, <ou>/<ow> are dominant in the North, W Midlands, and E Midlands. These spellings imply that the vowel has been lengthened in these words, though they cannot be used as evidence of vowel-shifting. Such spellings are quite numerous in the South too, despite Kristensson's claim that they are 'occasional' and 'rare' (Kristensson 2001: 90–1).

Forms with <ou>/<ow> for OE *u* in lengthening environments appear all over the country, so Kristensson is most probably right in asserting that such spellings in the South have 'nothing to do with the <ou> forms for OE *ō* in the Central Southern counties', which indicate vowel shift (Kristensson 2001: 91). It seems strange, however, to claim that '[i]n some cases <ou> may be an inverted spelling, reflecting shortening of /u:/ (spelt <ou>) in compounds or before certain consonants', since we are here dealing with words with OE short *u*. If anything, <ou> in such cases demonstrate lengthening of OE *u*, (1) because it is known *post facto* that OE *u* did lengthen before certain consonant clusters, and (2) because <ou> is the conventional spelling for the *long* vowel. Considering that words with OE *u+nd* fell in with the reflex of OE *ū* to give PDE /aʊ/, it seems fairly safe to assume that the <ou> spellings in these cases imply a long vowel.

7.2.3 *Discussion of* LALME *material*

The irregular spellings from *LALME* appear in Table 7.2; they likely indicate diphthongisation of eME /u:/.

Forms with <eu>/<ew> are thus restricted to the North, which is interesting, since eME /u:/ supposedly never diphthongised in this area. The implied sound value of these spellings therefore remains uncertain; see Section 7.2.4 for further notes on <eu> for eME *ū* in NME. However, the forms from Lincolnshire certainly might suggest diphthongisation, as do other occasional spellings, such as <fouul> in LP 18 (West Riding of Yorkshire) and <fuel> in LP 375 (Yorkshire). Britton (2002) interprets <eu>/<ew> in FOWL and ENOUGH as evidence of NF, which is treated exhaustively in Section 6.2.5.[9] In the form <foyheles>, found in three LPs from the West Riding of Yorkshire (LPs 191, 589, 603), the <y> may be used as a length marker. However, in all the three LPs, <yh> is commonly used for [j], in YET, YE, YOU, YOUR, YEAR, YOUNG, so the claim for a length diacritic is not sustainable; <oy> therefore seems to imply some kind of diphthong (a vowel plus glide).

Table 7.2 *Irregular spellings for eME* ū (LALME)

County	LP	Spellings
Cheshire	322	<aboyte> about
East Riding, Yks	554	<new> now
Huntingdonshire	427	<dooun> down
Lancashire	25	?<ȝaw> you
	154	<haw> how
		<thawȝand> thousand
Lincolnshire	180	<new> now
Nottinghamshire		<bawndes> bounds
		<graund/graundes> ground
	96	<tawne> town
	593	<ooure> our
Wiltshire	DTSY	<thowisond> thousand
	5372	<by-þaute> without

In the form <thowisond> THOUSAND (Wiltshire, 1390), <ow> is unremarkable, but the <i> is best interpreted as indicating a diphthong consisting of a glide plus nucleus, just like similar forms found in *LAEME*. Other spellings also indicating a minimal diphthong are <dooun> DOWN in LP 427 (Huntingdonshire), <ooure> OUR in 593 (Nottinhamshire), and possibly <noo> now in LP 515 (Staffordshire). These suggest that the spelling <oo> had come to be associated with [u:] and thus provide indirect evidence that eME *ǭ* had already been raised at this stage.

LALME records numerous back spellings with unetymological <ȝ> following the reflex of OE *ū*, for example, <nowȝ> NOW in LP 673 (Ely), <oght> OUT in LP 210 (Lincolnshire), <outȝ> OUT in LP 642 (Norfolk); these will be discussed in Section 7.2.5.

Forms with <au>/<aw> are found in *LALME* sources entered in Lancashire, Nottinghamshire, and Wiltshire. In the source texts for LP 96 from Nottinghamshire and LPs 5371 (Wiltshire) and 5372 (mix between E Midlands and Wiltshire), these spellings are more frequent than the limited range of the LPs suggests.[10] However, in LP 96, <ow> is the conventional spelling for the reflex of ME *ū*, and <aw> for the reflex of OE *ā+w/g*; thus it has <owt> OUT (6x); <awe> OWN v.pl. (33x); <awne> OWN sb. (3x); <rawe> ROW sb. In other words, <au>/<aw> for OE *ū* are unconventional and indicate advanced diphthongisation. In Wlt 5371/5372, <by-þaute> is confined to Hand B (properly LP 5372), who *teste* Benskin is apparently a scribe whose own linguistic habits were acquired in the

NE Midlands (probably the Nottinghamshire-Lincolnshire border); <au> therefore seems to correspond to a maximal diphthong.[11]

Whitehall (1935) draws attention to exactly the same spellings as are found in *LALME* LP 96, from *The Records of The Borough of Nottingham.*[12] In the 'Rental of the Common Lands of the Town'[13] (dated 1435) are found: <tawn> TOWN (x6), <rawme> ROOM, <graund> GROUND (x3), <bawndes> BOUNDS, <abawyn> ABOVE. In a petition of John Mapperley[14] (dated 1483) are found: <naw> NOW, <tawn> TOWN.

Such spellings have been dismissed by Wyld (1927: 182) as evidence for the diphthongisation of ME *ū* on the grounds that the etymological diphthong *au* was beginning to be pronounced [ɔ:] at the time, and it therefore seems odd that the digraph should be used to indicate a diphthong. But in Whitehall's opinion, when the earlier mentioned fourteen spellings are added to the lists of forms cited by, for example, Wyld, there is now (1936: 66)

> a body of evidence which is too extensive to be dismissed as mere carelessness of spelling. Whether the *au*-spellings indicate a diphthong or not, they obviously conceal a linguistic or spelling phenomenon which requires elucidation. The question is necessarily reopened.

Whitehall believes it may not be possible to prove that <au>/<aw> imply a diphthong, especially since <aw> is also found in the first text mentioned earlier ('Rental of the Common Lands of the Town') for the reflex of OE *ā* (e.g. <awe> OWE, <awne> OWN). However, he thinks such spelling confusion is 'most likely to take place if the original *ū* [...] had developed to a point where confusion in sound as well as in spelling was easily possible' (1936: 983). Whitehall's reasons for taking these spellings at face value are worth reproducing in full (1936: 983, my emphasis):

> In other words, of all explanations that can be suggested for the *au*-spellings, the explanation that they represent diphthongization of ME *ū* is the simplest and the most satisfactory; and this holds good in spite of the crucial difficulty raised by Wyld's question. We know that ME *ū* was either already diphthongized or about to be diphthongized at the period of our text, and though signs of the change have not hitherto been discovered until a later period, it is the generally accepted view that it commenced at a date much earlier than our earliest spelling evidence. Furthermore, while it is perfectly true that *au* eventually came to be regarded as a way of expressing the sound [ɔ:], **it is not clear what other symbol could possibly be used as an unconscious semiphonetic spelling for the stages of the diphthongization of *ū*** that involved a back vowel as the first element of the diphthong.

Besides, <au> could equally well have corresponded to the diphthong [ɔu] at this period, which entails that <au> could imply the monophthong [ɔ:] as well as the diphthong [ɔu] (1936: 983). Whitehall thinks that the earlier statement gives the most 'satisfactory interpretation of the *au*-spellings', but admits that 'the relationship between ME *au* and ME *ou* in their Early Modern developments could profitably be linked with this problem on a more extensive scale' (1936: 983), with which one must concur.[15]

7.2.4 Discussion of material from additional sources

The irregular spellings for eME *ū* in MS Cambridge, Corpus Christi College 388 (Hunt and Benskin 2001) are remarkable (Table 7.3).

The language has been localised to Ely/W Norfolk and the hand of the MS appears to be from *c.* 1320–30 (2001: 193, 207). Like the form <thowen> TOWN found in *LAEME* text no. 230, and <thowisond> THOUSAND in 'Will of Sir John Dauntsey', these forms appear to indicate a diphthong; otherwise, it is difficult to account for the unhistorical <i>. But in contrast with the *LAEME* form <thowen>, the forms with <-owit(h)> in these texts are very numerous (cf. their LPs in Hunt and Benskin 2001: 222–8). However, they are dismissed as 'decisively analogical spellings' (2001: 202) based on the simultaneous existence of (new) monosyllabic and (traditional) disyllabic forms for NOT (< OE *nāwiht*). The analogy is as follows: since NOT may be spelt <nowit>/<nouit> as well as <nowt>, then OUT – traditionally spelt <owt> or <out> – may also be spelt <owit> or <ouit>. Although this may be the rationale behind <owit(h)> for the reflex of ME *ūt/ūþ* in these texts, it is at least possible that they

Table 7.3 *Irregular spellings for eME* ū *in MS Cambridge, Corpus Christi College 388*

Lexeme	Spellings (text: recipe no.)
ON *klút*	<clowit> (III: 39)
MOUTH	<mowit> (III: 26, 27, 36, 40)
	<mowith> (III: 6)
OUT	<houit> (II: 466, 548, 553, 592, 612, 619; III: 13)
	<howit> (II: 54, 55, 322, 401, 422, 554, 556; III: 158)
	<ouit> (II: 547, 548
	<owit> (II: 51, 105, 175, 360, 610, 615, 641, 697; III: index
WITHOUT	<wit-oweten> (III: 129)

indicate a diphthong, since <nowit> for NOT hardly implies [nu:t], but [nɔ:t], [nɔ:ɪt] or [nɔ:ət] (with hiatus). If so, diphthongisation of ME *ū* is indicated in Ely/W Norfolk around 1320–30. Incidentally, such a conclusion would support the interpretation of the irregular spellings found in *LAEME* source no. 282 (Ely) as suggesting diphthongisation, since the scribal languages are from roughly the same area, and the dates are similar. Still, analogy may certainly not be ruled out. The systems in which these spellings appear are examined in the concluding section.

Zachrisson (1913: 78–9) quotes a handful of <au>/<aw> for ME *ū*.
<mawe> OE *muȝon* (Rymer's Fœdora)
<abaught> ABOUT (Paston Letters, Norfolk)
<cawe> COW (Paston Letters)
<faunde> FIND *pt.* (Paston Letters)
<withawth/withaught> WITHOUT (Paston Letters)
<aur> OUR (Cely Papers, Essex)

Zachrisson concludes that there can be no doubt that <au>/<aw> here 'denotes a diphthongic pronunciation of ME *ū*. Indeed *au* cannot possibly be due to analogical transference, for I know of no instances where it was a traditional or regular symbol of ME *ū*' (1913: 79).

Wyld (1936: 230–2) also adduces <au>/<aw> for the reflex of ME *ū* from for example, the *Paston Letters* (Norfolk, 1440–70) and the *Cely Papers* (Essex, 1475–88). Although Wyld admits that the phonetic interpretation of these spellings remains uncertain, and that this uncertainty is compounded by their being so rare, he states that 'if the sound was still [ū] *au* would be the very worst way of expressing it' (1936: 230). Further, on the reasons why they are so rare, he says (1936: 231),

> The answer [...] is not far to seek. The traditional spelling *ou*, if taken literally to mean *o+u*, was by no means a bad representation of the pronunciation of the diphthong as it probably was during perhaps the greater part of the sixteenth century. [...] The French grammarian Mason (1622) transcribes *how* as *haow*, which certainly suggests a pronunciation not far removed from our own. Diphthongs are always difficult to analyse exactly.

Besides, since Wyld draws the conclusion that the raising of the reflex of OE *ō* to [u:] was 'probably completed during the fourteenth century at the latest', and since the reflexes of OE *ō* and old *ū* did not merge, the diphthongisation of the reflex of ME *ū* must have at least started then as well (1936: 231). In his opinion, the 'full-blown' [au] stage may have been reached in the fifteenth century in eastern parts of the country (1936: 231).

7.2.5 *Discussion of inverted <ug>/<uw> spellings for OE* ū

The fact that *u+C* (e.g. <ug>, <uh>) remains the dominant spelling for the reflexes of OE *uw/ūw, ug/ūg* up until lME indicates that these reflexes did *not* completely merge with the reflex of OE *ū* until quite late in the period; otherwise, inverted <uw>/<ug> for OE *ū* should be far more frequent in *early* ME. This suggests that the phonetic outcome of the vocalisation of the glides was a minimal diphthong, which remained, and which may have reinforced any new diphthongal allophones of /u:/ (cf. Stockwell and Minkova's hypothesis). However, as is well-known, spelling need not change as soon as the sound does, nor is phonology the sole motive for spelling innovations, or lack of such. There is thus a danger of reading too much phonology into both irregular spellings and conservative spellings.

On the other hand, there is one <uw> besides one <ug> and a few <ouȝt>, for the reflex of OE *ū not* before a velar fricative in *LAEME*, which suggests some confusion between the reflexes of OE *ū* and OE *ūg/ug* (perhaps phonemic sameness but sub-phonemic difference), although such spellings do not really become common until lME. (*SMED* does not record inverted <ug> for eME *ū*, but there are many forms that suggest complete vocalisation of OE post-vocalic *g*.) In *LALME*, such back spellings appear to cluster regionally: Apart from a few recorded forms in the South-West (Somerset, Dorset) and the South-East (Surrey, Sussex), they appear most frequently in East Anglia, the E Midlands, and in the North Central Midlands; there are also some occurrences in the W Midlands. The fact that such unetymological <ȝ>/<gh> are much more frequent in the *LALME* material than in the early material suggests that the reflexes of OE *ū* and OE *ug/ūg* had indeed merged by later ME, at least to the extent that they were no longer phonemically distinct. But the phonetic realisation of /u:/ could just as well have been a minimal diphthong as a long monophthong, and the spellings could indicate either.

These findings imply that Stockwell (1978) and Stockwell and Minkova (1988a) may very well be right in proposing that the phonetic outcome of the supposed merger between the reflexes of OE *u+w/g+V* and OE *ū* was a minimal diphthong rather than a long monophthong. Alternatively, the result may have been co-varying monophthongal (< OE *ū*) and diphthongal (< OE *ug/uw*) allophones for /u:/. A similar situation can be seen today in various accents of English, where, for example, /u:/ has allophonic [u:] besides [ʊu], or even [əu].

7.3 Summary and conclusions

The material suggests that eME *ū* may have had both monophthongal and diphthongal allophones, from when the reflexes of OE *ug/ūg, uw/ūw* were identified with the reflex of OE *ū*.

It was noted in the introductory section that historical linguists generally hesitate to use <ou>/<ow> as evidence of the diphthongisation of etymological *ū*, given the history of these digraphs. In this regard, it is interesting to note that when a vowel is inserted before <h> in the fourteenth century (e.g. <soughte>), it is described as a glide vowel, and the resulting digraphs <ou>/<ow> are always, without reservation, taken to indicate a diphthong (e.g. in Wełna 1988; Steponavičius 1997: 568; Steponavičius 2005: 313); but when the same digraphs appear for the reflex of eME *ū*, the idea that it could indicate a diphthongised reflex is always rejected with the same ease. In principle, it remains indeterminable whether <ou>/<ow> could represent a phonetic diphthong, particularly since ME <ou> is also used for an etymological diphthong in the BLOW and SOUGHT sets. Hence, <ou> for ME *ū* may equally represent a conservative [u:], or a minimal diphthong [ʊu], or an advanced [əu], [ʌu], or [au]. Appeal to such forms may thus be neither here nor there in linguistic argumentation, but it needs to be stated that such 'conservative' spellings are not in themselves sufficient proof of no change: there are some <aw> spellings co-varying with <ow>/<ou> in *LALME* sources, for example, <haw>/<how> HOW and <thawȝand> THOUSAND in LP 154 (Lancashire), and <by-þaute> and <w^t^oute> WITHOUT in LP 5372. These confirm one important assumption: lack of irregular spellings need not imply a standstill in pronunciation.

It is nonetheless curious, at least from a *post facto* perspective, that <au>/<aw> for ME *ū* are so rare. However, and I owe the following line of argumentation to Benskin (pers. comm.), [au] is the maximal diphthong for the reflex of *ū*, and the early stages were probably [ʊu], [əu]. Therefore, it is only in areas where the GVS began early that ME *ū* can have shifted to [au] in time for this to be represented in local spelling: the standardisation of English started, generally speaking, *c.* 1430, and on the basis of SE Midland, not northern, English. Local written language was obsolete by *c.* 1460–70 in most parts of southern England, but persisted in other parts of the country until the early sixteenth century, for example, in the North, and also in Exeter to *c.* 1530–40 (Benskin 1989). The GVS is assumed to have begun early in the North, but in most of the North, *ū* did not diphthongise, and in some areas remain as /u:/ to the present day. It is therefore only in those areas where (i) the GVS was early, and (ii) *ū* diphthongised at all, that <au>/<aw> should be expected. This claim is confirmed by the ME material analysed: <au>/<aw> for eME *ū* is found in, for example, Nottinghamshire, Lancashire, and the W Midlands, cf. Hand B of *LALME* LP 5372 (Wiltshire). Such <au> spellings as are known, are from lME; the *SMED* and *LAEME* material is generally too early to show them. *LALME*, however, did not record ME *ū* systematically, and its analyses must be supplemented: clearly, a more thorough and systematic investigation of material from counties showing <au>/<aw> spellings would be worthwhile, though beyond the scope of the present work. The use of <eu>/<ew> for the early stages of diphthongised *ū* is generally not a likely innovation, given the existence of the older diphthong [eu], with which the reflex of *ū* did not merge. Still, such spellings are occasionally found and appear to suggest diphthongisation: so <new> NOW in Lincolnshire and the East Riding of Yorkshire, and <feule> and similar forms for FOWL in the North. Britton (2002), however, interprets such spellings as indicative of NF (cf. Chapter 6).

Analysis of the separate spelling systems in which irregular forms appear seems in order at this stage. The following texts from *LAEME* have irregular spellings for the reflex of ME *ū*. Source no. 230 (East Riding of Yorkshire, 1300–24) has <thowen> TOWN. It also reports <fonden> FIND past ppl., <now> NOW, <plowgh> PLOUGH, <wit-outen> WITHOUT, <laghes> LAW, <noght> NOT, <agh(en)> OWN adj., <thought> THINK past ppl. The idiosyncratic spelling for TOWN is thus not an analogical spelling.

Source no. 278 (Worcestershire, 1250–74) has numerous <eo> for ME *ū*, in ABOUT, OE *būtan* 'but, without', HOUSE, HOW and THOU; it has <eou> in HOW and THOU; <eu> in THOU; <uo> in TOWN. For NOT, there are spellings indicating both monosyllabic and disyllabic forms: <noht> (x10), <na(-)wiht> (x5), <no(-)wiht> (x4), <nowhit> (once), <nowit> (once). However, the irregular spellings for the reflex of ME *ū* are very different from the disyllabic spellings for NOT. Other words with ME *ū* have <u>, <ou> or <o> for the vowel (e.g. NOW, ADOWN, HOUSE, HOW); in fact, <u> is the dominant spelling for the reflex of ME *ū*. Other words with <eo> for the root vowel are SELF (< OE *self*, but also *seolf*) and THIS fem. (< OE *þēos*), HER (< OE *hiere*), and SHE (< OE *hēo*), but also for BROTHER (< OE *brōþor*), SOON (< OE *sōna*) and SOOTH (< OE *sōþ*). For SELF, <u> is also found for the vowel, so it is possible that <eo> for ME *ū* is a back-spelling.

However, analogy does not account for the trigraphs <eou> in HOW and THOU; this trigraph is otherwise found in YOU (< OE *ēow*(*er*)), FOUR (< OE *fēower*), and *Lo!*, so it seems to correspond to a diphthong. This text also has <hire> HERE and <fliȝ> FLEE imp., as well as <goud(ne)> GOOD, suggesting vowel shift of the reflexes of ME *ē* and ME *ō*. Hence, this scribe's orthographic system is truly idiosyncratic and seems to indicate vowel shift of two back vowels and at least one front vowel, but even close analysis does not provide definite answers.

The source text for no. 1900 (Worcestershire, 1200–49) has <sceoue> SHOVE; and <grigcis> GREEK and <twinunge> OE *twēonian* vn., which may suggest raising of OE *ē*. For the reflex of OE *ō*, <touwar> and <touwarde> TOWARD are recorded, but it is uncertain whether this testifies to raising of OE *tō-* or anticipation of the following *w*.

Text no. 1100 (Herefordshire, 1275–99) has <howelynge> HOWL vn., and <fuoel> FOWL; <steo> OE *stīgan* 'to move, go, reach' inf.; <bi-syh> BE-SEE imp.; <lust> LOSE 3.sing.pres. Thus the source text for no. 1100 shows potential vowel-shift spellings for both the two long close vowels and the two long close-mid vowels.

Text no. 2002 (Gloucestershire, 1275–99) has <fouvel> FOUL, and <oout> OUT; <goed> GOOD, <roed> ROOD, <woed> OE *wōd* 'senseless, mad'; <beye> BUY inf. and <forbeyen> FOR-BUY inf., along with <-drei> OE *drī*/*drȳge* DRY. Hence, the scribe's system appears to indicate vowel shift of at least the two long back vowels, and possibly also of eME *ī*.

Source no. 282 from Ely (1275–1324) has <þouȝ> THOU, <ouȝt> OUT, and <clouȝt> ON *klūt* 'cloth'; <bi-dun> DO past ppl. and <guod> GOOD; <pleyt> PLIGHT. The orthographical system of this scribe may indicate vowel shift of the two long back vowels as well as of the long close front vowel.

In summary, a closer examination of the spelling systems of a handful of *LAEME* texts confirms the hypothesis that at least some of the early irregular spellings for eME *ū* may indicate incipient diphthongisation. This hypothesis is strengthened by the fact that the scribal systems analysed appear to be truly idiosyncratic and show potential vowel-shift forms for other ME long vowels also. These texts cluster in the SW Midlands, but Ely and the East Riding of Yorkshire are also represented.

In *LALME*, the source text for LP 154 from Lancashire has <haw> (and <how>) HOW, and <thawȝand> THOUSAND. It has <noght>/<not> NOT; <knaw>/<know> KNOW; <lagh(e)> LAW; <law>/<low> LOW;

<awen>/<awne>/<aun> and <owen> OWN adj.; <saule> SOUL sing., <saul(e)s>/<sawles> SOUL pl. It has regular <ou>/<ow> for the reflex of eME *ū*, apart from the <aw> for the root vowel of HOW and THOUSAND. It also has <neynte> NINE ord., which may indicate vowel shift of ME *ī*, and <gud(e)> GOOD, beside <god(e)>. NF of the reflex of ME *ō* is indicated by the forms with <u> for the root vowel of GOOD. The <aw>/<ow> for etymological diphthongs strengthens the vowel-shift interpretation of <haw> and <thawȝand>. LP 96 (Nottinghamshire) has been examined earlier (Section 7.2.3): it has numerous <aw>/<au> for the reflex of ME *ū*, and also a few <ay> for ME *ī*, indicating advanced vowel shift of the two close ME vowels.

'Will of Sir John Dauntsey' (Wiltshire, 1390) has <thowisond> THOUSAND; LP 5372 has <by-þaute> WITHOUT. The details of the rest of their orthographic systems are not known to me.

The two texts in MS Cambridge, Corpus Christi College 388 (Hunt and Benskin 2001) that show <-owit(h)> and <-ouit(h)> for the reflex of ME *ū+t* also have <nowit>, <nouit>, <now^{i}t> and <nowt> NOT. Other words with ME *ū* have <u> (ABOUT), <oy> (WITHOUT), or <ou>/<ow> (DOWN, HOW, WITHOUT, THOU). ME *ou* (in e.g. OWN, GROW, KNOW) is also <ow>/<ou>. Some <ei> and <ey> appear for ME *ī* (GRIND, THY). The reflex of ME *ō*, though usually <o>, is spelt <ou> a few times (DO, SOON, SPOONFUL), and <oi> in GOOD (besides <o>). Thus, although the <-owi-> etc. for ME *ū* may be back spellings, the E Midland language of these texts seems to imply an advanced pronunciation for at least eME *ī* and *ō*; the early vowel-shift interpretation of <-owi-> for ME *ū* is therefore strengthened.

Additionally, <dooun> DOWN in LP 427 (Huntingdonshire), and <ooure> OUR in LP 593 (Nottinghamshire; both *LALME*) may indicate minimal diphthongs: if <ou> implies [u:], then the preceding <o> may indicate a half-close diphthongal onset; <oout> OUT is recorded in *LAEME* text 2002 (whose language is entered in Gloucestershire, 1275–99). A near-parallel is found in MS Northamptonshire Record Office Finch-Hatton 3047 (a verse charm against thieves), in which ME *ē* is <ei>, and where ME *ei* is <eii> (Benskin forthcoming, MS: 4):

> the composition of *eii* may be *ei+i* rather than *e+ii*. [...] In *ei*, therefore, *i* may be a diacritic for vowel length. [...] If *ei* is the scribe's accustomed spelling for non-final [e:], his trigraph *eii* could then consist of *ei* corresponding to [e:], with only the second *i* corresponding to the second element of the diphthong.

The difference between the spelling <eii> for [ei], and <oou> for etymological [u:], possibly vowel-shifted [ʊu] or [əu], is that the 'diacritic' <o> comes *before* the etymological monophthong. That is, however, to be expected, given the development of an *on*-glide *before* the nucleus during the diphthongisation of ME *ū*.

The spellings discussed are somewhat incohesive in terms of their geographical distribution. However, some of them appear to cluster in the Huntingdonshire/Ely/SW Norfolk area, and in the SE Staffordshire/Nottinghamshire/E Lincolnshire area. The others may be *ad hoc* (even idiosyncratic) independent inventions, whereas those which cluster may be signs of incipient regional sound change.

In summary, the relatively high number of unorthodox <eo> for OE *ū* in *LAEME* text no. 278 (Worcestershire, 1250–74) seems to indicate diphthongisation rather decisively at an early stage, as do other irregular spellings from Herefordshire, Gloucestershire, Ely, and the East Riding of Yorkshire from roughly the same time period (*c.* 1275–1324). Later forms in *LALME* with <au>/<aw>, as well as a couple of forms with <oou>, support this notion of early vowel shift: they appear to indicate that the on-glide had gone well beyond the [ʊ] stage to [ə] or even further. The forms with <au>/<aw> are found in some quantity in the later period in Lancashire, Nottinghamshire, Wiltshire, and Huntingdonshire, that is, in the NW Midlands, SW Midlands, as well as in the northern part of the E Midlands. Wyld, adducing <au>/<aw> for eME *ū* in texts from Norfolk and Essex, from the mid-to-late fifteenth century), believes the 'full-blown' [au] stage may have been reached in the fifteenth century in eastern parts of the country (1936: 231). Ogura (1990: 30–34) finds that, for example, Norfolk, Northamptonshire, Oxfordshire, and the Cheshire-Staffordshire area are 'focal areas'; no mention is made of Cornwall and Devon, which also seem to have radical PDE reflexes for ME *ū*. From all of the above it follows that the diphthongisation of eME /u:/ may have started in the SW Midlands (Worcestershire, Wiltshire, and Gloucestershire), and independently in the East (particularly in Nottinghamshire and the Ely-Huntingdonshire area, but also in Norfolk), as well as in Lancashire and the East Riding of Yorkshire. That is, the diphthongisation of the reflex of ME *ū* may have started simultaneously in various localities, beginning in the mid-to-late thirteenth century.

Table 7.4 *Spellings for eME* ū *in* LAEME

County	No.	Date	Spellings
Peterborough	149	1154	u
Essex	4	1150–99	u
Berkshire	63	1150–99	u, ou
Essex	1200	1150–99	u
Suffolk	1300	1150–99	u ((o, ow, e))
Hampshire	143	1175–99	u
Worcestershire	170	1175–99	u ((o))
Worcestershire	5	c.1200	u
Worcestershire	2000	c.1200	u ((o, ow, v))
Worcestershire	2001	c.1200	u ((o))
Oxfordshire	232	1175–1224	u
Essex	64	1200–24	u ((v, ow))
Essex	65	1200–24	u ((e, iw))
Herefordshire	189	1200–24	u ((o))
Gloucestershire	234	1200–24	u, ou, o
Unlocalised	236	1200–24	u ((ou, o))
Shropshire	260	1200–24	u
Shropshire	261	1200–24	u ((v, e))
Shropshire	262	1200–24	u
Shropshire	1000	1200–24	u ((v))
Worcestershire	6	1200–49	u
Worcestershire	7	1200–49	u ((v))
Kent	8	1200–49	u ((o, v))
Northamptonshire	66	1200–49	u ((v))
Sussex	67	1200–49	u
Unlocalised	237	1200–49	u
Worcestershire	1900	1200–49	u ((v, o,?eo))
London	138	1225–49	u (v)
Staffordshire	146	1225–49	u
Worcestershire	245	1225–49	u ((v, o, uu))
Shropshire	272	1225–49	u ((v, o, uu))
Herefordshire	273	1225–49	u (v) ((o, uu))
Shropshire	275	1225–49	u ((v))
Worcestershire	1800	1225–49	u ((w))
Somerset	156	c.1240	u, ou
Somerset	157	c.1240	u, ou, þ
Cheshire	118	1240–50	u ((v, o))
Unlocalised	119	1240–50	u ((o, v))
Unlocalised	120	1240–50	u
Unlocalised	121	1240–50	u
Cheshire	122	1240–50	u
Unlocalised	123	1240–50	u ((o))
Unlocalised	139	13th c.	ou
Surrey	184	13th c.	u

(*continued*)

Table 7.4 (*cont.*)

County	No.	Date	Spellings
Unlocalised	265	13th c.	u
Huntingdonshire	266	13th c.	u
Unlocalised	267	13th c.	u
Unlocalised	268	13th c.	u
Unlocalised	17	1225–74	u, w, o
Unlocalised	127	1225–74	uiu
Berkshire	144	1225–74	u
Unlocalised	176	1225–74	ow, o
West Riding, Yks	231	1225–74	u
Unlocalised	235	1225–74	ou, u, o
Essex	11	1258	u
London	12	1258	u
Cheshire	124	1250–74	ou, u
Gloucestershire	158	1250–74	ou ((u, o, ow))
Worcestershire	276	1250–74	u ((v, i, o))
Worcestershire	277	1250–74	u ((v, ou, o))
Worcestershire	278	1250–74	u ((ou, eo, o, v, eou, eu, uo, e, u-u))
Wiltshire	280	1250–74	ou, u ((v, o, ow))
Lincolnshire	130	1270	u
Lincolnshire	15	1250–99	u
Unlocalised	228	1250–99	u ((ou))
Wiltshire	258	1250–99	u, v
Gloucestershire	271	1250–99	ou (u) ((o, ow))
Dorset	279	1250–99	u (v)
Worcestershire	2	1275–99	u ((o, v, w))
Worcestershire	3	1275–99	u ((ou, o, uu))
Norfolk	131	1275–99	u
Cheshire	136	1275–99	u, ou, ow, ey
Cambridgeshire	137	1275–99	u ((o))
Unlocalised	141	1275–99	u
Kent	142	1275–99	u ((o))
Devon	147	1275–99	ou, u
Devon	148	1275–99	u, o
Norfolk	150	1275–99	u ((o, v))
Lancashire	151	1275–99	ou (u)
Essex	160	1275–99	u (ou) ((o))
Gloucestershire	161	1275–99	ou ((o, u))
Norfolk	175	1275–99	u
Unlocalised	178	1275–99	u (ue, w)
Unlocalised	179	1275–99	u (o)
Unlocalised	180	1275–99	ou
Unlocalised	181	1275–99	u
Unlocalised	227	1275–99	u
Gloucestershire	229	1275–99	u ((o))
Unlocalised	233	1275–99	u (v, o)

County	No.	Date	Spellings
Unlocalised	238	1275–99	u ((o))
Unlocalised	239	1275–99	u
Unlocalised	240	1275–99	o
Unlocalised	241	1275–99	u (o)
Unlocalised	242	1275–99	u ((v, o, ew))
Unlocalised	243	1275–99	u
Unlocalised	244	1275–99	u
Herefordshire	246	1275–99	u ((ou, o, v, oi, uu, w, eo, eþ))
Herefordshire	247	1275–99	ou ((ov, o, u))
Herefordshire	248	1275–99	u ((ou, o))
Herefordshire	249	1275–99	u ((o, ou, e))
Wiltshire	263	1275–99	ov, v (u, o)
Unlocalised	274	1275–99	u
Herefordshire	1100	1275–99	u ((v, w, ow, ou, o, uo, uw, e, ey))
Norfolk	1400	1275–99	u ((v, o))
Gloucestershire	2002	1275–99	ou ((o, ow, u, e, ei))
Norfolk	1700	1284–89	u, ou ((o, v))
Lincolnshire	128	c.1300	ou, o
Lincolnshire	129	1300	u
Lincolnshire	159	c.1300	u ((o, ou, v))
Unlocalised	174	c.1300	u, ou, ow
Leicestershire	177	c.1300	u
Lincolnshire	182	c.1300	ou, u ((v, o, ouu))
Worcestershire	187	c.1300	ou
Gloucestershire	10	1275–1324	u ((o))
Unlocalised	18	1275–1324	u
Warwickshire	126	1275–1324	ou
Essex	162	1275–1324	ou, o, ow
Somerset	163	1275–1324	ou, u
West Riding, Yks	256	1275–1324	ou, u, o
West Riding, Yks	257	1275–1324	ou ((u))
Unlocalised	259	1275–1324	u
Gloucestershire	264	1275–1324	u, ou
Norfolk	269	1275–1324	u
Norfolk	270	1275–1324	u, ou, v
Ely	282	1275–1324	ou ((o, v, i, ow))
Oxfordshire	1600	1275–1324	ou (o) ((u, ov, ow, v, uy))
Unlocalised	19	1300–24	u, w, ow
Herefordshire	125	1300–24	ou, o
Wiltshire	140	1300–24	ov ((u, v, o))
Norfolk	155	1300–24	u ((v, o, ou, ow, ov))
Durham	188	1300–50	ou ((u, o))
East Riding, Yks	230	1300–50	ow, ou, o
Huntingdonshire	1500	1300–50	ou, u (v)
Ely	2003	1300–50	u
Lincolnshire	169	1325–50	ow (o) ((u, v))

Notes

1 According to Pope (1934: §§459–60), Latin *o+n* became *u+n* before the end of the Gallo-Roman period (from the late fifth to the mid-ninth century AD); *u+n* then underwent gradual nasalisation to *ũ+n*, which was retained through the Middle French period, whereupon the nasal was completely absorbed into the preceding vowel and the vowel lowered to *ǭ̃*. The absorption of the nasal was not complete until the mid-sixteenth century, and lengthening of the preceding nasalised vowel was noted at the same time (1934: §§436–7). It seems, therefore, that the loss of the nasal and the compensatory lengthening of the nasalised vowel were long-term processes, and that French loans with the relevant sounds were borrowed into English at a time when the *n* was still pronounced, but the vowel had started to lengthen.

2 Pope states that in 'Early Old French quantitative differences appear to have played no part in the differentiation of any vowels except the **e**-*sounds* [...] but in the course of Later Old and Middle French vowels appear to have been lengthened by the effacement of following consonants [...] In Middle English most vowels were differentiated by length [...] and quantitative differences appear to have been gradually established in Later Anglo-Norman' (Pope 1934: §1170). Thus, early loans with [u] may have been neutral with regard to length, but their later development shows that the vowel was either perceived as long, or lengthened at some point.

3 Such a date seems a little late, but there was contact between England and the Continent, and 'thus Continental French, written and spoken, the speech of Paris and of the northern region, as well as the whole of the western region, exercised a continuous but variable influence on insular French' (Pope 1934: §1079). Further, Pope comments that 'it is striking how often the modifications attested in Anglo-Norman find parallels either in continental dialects or in later francien' (1934: §1077).

4 In north-western Gallo-Roman, both *ǫu* and *ọu* became *eu*, which later monophthongised to [ø]; in the remainder of the northern region, Gallo-Roman and early OFr *ǫu* became *au* (Pope 1934: §549). Gallo-Roman *ǫu* was itself the product of earlier Gallo-Roman *au* or *aw+u* or *a+ww* (1934: §547).

5 Spellings for a number of lexemes were collected for this table; a list of all the lexemes is given in Stenbrenden (2010). Spellings for OE *ū* and for lengthened OE *u* of various kinds were all counted.

6 Note present standard Danish, in which the old disyllable is still (almost) residually so, with the *stød* marking the old syllable boundary: *fugl* 'fowl, bird' is [fu'ul] not [fu:l] (*Store norske leksikon*, Skautrup 1944–70).

7 There is also <muht> MOUTH in no. 182 (Lincolnshire, *c.* 1300), though in this case, <ht> is probably used for <th>.

8 The form <houȝ> HOW is found in Trevisa's translation of Higden's *Polychronicon* (Sisam 1962: 146, l. 13).

9 The form <beuch> BOUGH in Burrow (1992) may indicate a minimal diphthong, and is rather similar to <feule> and <fewel> in *LALME*; like the forms in *LALME*, <beuch> is found in NME.

10 See Chapter 1, Section 1.4.3.

11 The copy is substantially in Salisbury language, but there is a certain scattering of probably NE Midland spellings, e.g. <qwor> WHERE, <quat> WHAT, <efter> AFTER, <fro> FROM, occasional <–yn> and also <–is> in the pl.pres. ind., <has> HAS. Since Hand A, copying from the same exemplar, shows only older and later forms of Salisbury language, these NE Midland forms can hardly be attributed to the exemplar; they are likewise absent from Hand C. Therefore, as LP 5372 is in mixed language, it should be cleared off the *LALME* maps; it is a thorough *Mischsprache*, possibly idiolectal rather than textual (Benskin, pers. comm.). This will be treated by Benskin in a forthcoming paper: 'Middle English from Salisbury and Wilton'.

12 Stevenson, W.H. (ed.). 1883. *The Records of the Borough of Nottingham. Vol. II.* London. Whitehall's general observations on the nature of the irregular spellings in these documents have been quoted in Section 6.3.4.

13 Stevenson 1883 (Vol. II), no. 1.

14 Stevenson 1883 (Vol. II), no. 16.

15 These texts also have irregular spellings for the reflex of ME *ī*, which have been discussed in Section 5.3.

CHAPTER 8

The development of OE ȳ

8.1 Introduction

According to the standard accounts, OE *ȳ* was unrounded to [iː] in lOE or eME all over the North, in parts of the E Midlands, 'including Lincolnshire, Norfolk, and the districts bordering on these counties', and in parts of the South-West, 'especially Devonshire, Dorsetshire, and Wiltshire' (Wright and Wright 1928: §57 1.). It became [eː] 'in Kent and parts of Middlesex, Sussex, Essex, and Suffolk' in the course of the OE period (1928: §57 2.), whence [iː] after the 'GVS'. In the remaining parts of the country, that is, the W Midlands and parts of the South, the *ȳ* remained until the late fourteenth century, spelt <u(i)>, when it was unrounded (1928: §57 3.; cf. Jordan 1968: §39; Luick 1914–40: §§287–8). Hence, the value [iː] is supposed to have supplanted [yː] in ME, and the changes to OE *ȳ* are even by traditional accounts believed to span a period of at least three hundred years. According to Kitson, the 'most problematic element of this geography has been the eastward spread of the *u*-region in the Thames Valley, leading to serious debate whether certain literary texts should be placed in areas as far apart as' Worcestershire and Middlesex (Kitson 1998: 170).

The lOE and ME changes in the phonetic realisation of *ȳ* are not regarded as part of the 'GVS'. Even so, the dialectal reflexes of OE *ȳ* provided input to the 'GVS', either as [iː] or as [eː], the post-vowel-shift realisations being PDE /aɪ/ and /iː/ respectively.

OE *y* lengthened in the same environments as did OE *i*: before a homorganic voiced consonant cluster, especially OE *–ynd* (e.g. OE *cynd* KIND); before the digraph <cg> (e.g. OE *bycgan* BUY vb.); and before OE *–ht* (e.g. OE *flyht* FLIGHT). In Chapter 5 it was pointed out that Wright and Wright (1928: §46) claim that eME *iht* (of various origins, including OE *yht*) remained in the North and North Midlands, whereas in the South and South Midlands it was lengthened to *ī* with subsequent loss of the postvocalic fricative. It is my contention that this change contributed to the initial stages of the vowel shift, that is, the diphthongisation of the long close front phoneme /iː/. Consequently, spellings for OE *yht* have been extracted and will be analysed with this in mind.

The present chapter seeks to determine whether the collected ME material supports the traditional account of the various regional development of eME *ȳ*.

Since the sources of spellings contain material from the early, middle, and late ME period, analysis of their data presents a cross-section of ME at three periods in time. Therefore, it should be possible to observe change in progress with regard to eME *ȳ*. Further, if it can be established what regional varieties had which phonetic realisation(s) of *ȳ* at given points in time, it should be possible to determine whether any of the extracted ME spellings can be used as evidence of vowel shift.

How are various ME spellings for OE *y*/*ȳ* to be interpreted in terms of vowel change? They fall into three major groups: <i>/<y> etc. are taken to imply unrounding; <e>/<ee> and similar forms are believed to indicate lowering and unrounding; and <u> and <ui>/<uy> are supposed to imply retained [yː]. The following paragraphs discuss the three groups of spellings and their phonetic correspondences.

Forms with <e>/<ee> etc. for eME *ȳ* are usually taken to indicate lowering and unrounding to [eː]. However, the internal chronology of the lowering and unrounding involved in this process is unclear: eME *ȳ* could have (a) been lowered to [øː] before unrounding to [eː], or (b) been unrounded to [iː] first, before being lowered to [eː]. When (b) seems to be the more likely chain of events, it is probably due to the fact that if (a) were the case, the vowels would have merged with the reflexes of OE *ēo*, which monophthongised and rounded to [øː] in lOE, before unrounding to [eː] in the twelfth century all over the country except in certain parts of the W Midlands, where the rounded vowels remained until the late fourteenth century, when they unrounded there also. When such a merger between the reflexes of OE *ēo* and OE *ȳ* did not generally take place, it has been tacitly assumed that the reflexes of OE *ȳ* unrounded before being lowered. However, the chronology of these stages is obviously crucial and deserves attention, as it bears on the interpretation of <eo> and <y> for OE *ȳ*. For instance, a dialect where the reflexes of OE *ēo* had monophthongised as [øː], and where OE *ȳ* had been lowered to [øː], might produce eME <eo>/<y> for a rounded vowel of dual origin. Hence, neither <eo> nor <y> need imply unrounding of the reflexes of OE *ȳ* in such a dialect.

Anderson (1988) attempts to determine the phonetic stages of the SE change OE *ȳ* > [e:], examining the development of OE *ȳ* in Kentish, and OE <e>/<eo> for all the front vowels. In Kentish, all front vowels except OE *ī* merge, the resulting vowel being [e(:)]; this is referred to as 'The Great Kentish Collapse' (GKC). Judging by the spellings found in a ninth-century charter, and tenth-century glosses to Proverbs, Kentish underwent a series of 'developments usually regarded as quite disparate' (1988: 99). These are as follows (1988: 99–100): (1) WGmc /a/ and /a:/ appear as /e(:)/, not as /æ:/ (/a:/ > WS ǣ^1); (2) WGmc *i*-mutated /ai/ appears as /e:/, not /æ:/ (WS ǣ^2). These two changes are in evidence in both the ninth-century and the tenth-century texts, whereas the following are found in the tenth-century texts. (3) Analogically restored /ɑ/ from the first fronting of WGmc /a/, when *i*-mutated, appears as /e/, not /æ/; (4) PrOE /o/ and /o:/, *i*-mutated, appear as /e(:)/ (spelt <ę> and <y>); (5) PrOE /u/ and /u:/, *i*-mutated, appear as /e(:)/ rather than /y(:)/; (6) PrOE /i/, immediately preceded by /w/, *i*-mutated, appears as /e/.

Anderson postulates for Kentish that *i*-mutation took place before the collapse of the two *ǣ*'s, and 'that the loss of /ø(:)/ and /y(:)/ is earlier than elsewhere' (1988: 101). Chronologically, the spellings in early Kentish charters indicate that *e* and *æ* merged first at /e/, then *ø* merged with *e*, and finally *y* merged with the rest. From this Anderson concludes that it is apparent (1988: 105)

> that one traditional view, viz. that /y(:)/ unrounded first to [i(:)] before merging with /e(:)/, is untenable. If /y(:)/ had simply unrounded to [i(:)], they would have collapsed with original /i(:)/ [...] rather than with [e(:)].

The implication is that the reflex of OE *y/ȳ* in Kentish first lowered to [ø(:)] after etymological /ø(:)/ had unrounded, then was unrounded to [e(:)] and thus merged with /e(:)/ from different sources.

The spellings <u> and <ui>/<uy> imply retained [y:]. The reason why <u> could be used for this purpose is that etymological *ū*, originally spelt <u>, came to be spelt <ou>/<ow> with increasing frequency in ME, due to French scribal practice (cf. Chapter 7). However, use of <u> continued far into the period. The letter <u> alone became increasingly rare for OE *ū*, at least in some orthographies, and was available to the scribe as a means of indicating the roundedness of [y:]. According to Wright and Wright (1928: §9), use of <u> for retained [y] and <ui>/<uy> for retained [y:] was introduced by AN scribes.

Traditionally, lOE and ME <i>/<y> are regarded as both indicating unrounded [i:]. However, it seems paradoxical that <y>, which originally corresponded to [y(:)], should always be assumed to stand for a ME unrounded vowel, even in areas where the original front rounded vowel is believed to have remained: In those areas, <y> may still have corresponded to [y(:)]. Instead, individual orthographies should be submitted to analysis: If <y> is also used in words with etymological *ī/i*, that is, as back spellings, the view that <y> is a mere spelling variant for [i(:)] is justified; if, however, the scribal dialect is believed to have had retained [y:] *and* the orthography shows <y> for etymological *ȳ/y* only (and possibly for the 'unstable *īe*'), <y> could be interpreted as denoting [y:], though it does not follow that it must be.

Late standard WS <y> for etymological *ī* are analogical spellings and indicate unrounding to [i:]. For instance, the latter part of the account of Ohthere's voyage in the OE *Orosius*[1] (which is found only in the later, eleventh-century MS Cotton Tiberius B.I), has a number of <y> for OE *ī*, suggesting that etymological *y/ȳ* had already been unrounded in late WS.[2] Such back spellings are absent from the earlier Lauderdale MS, which is dated to the first half of the tenth century. Gradon (1962) adduces spellings indicating lOE unrounding of OE *y*; thus, <y> for OE *i* in certain Exeter documents 'are probably to be regarded merely as back-spellings' (1962: 66), based on OE *y* > [i]. However, some similar spellings in ten Winchester texts cannot be explained this way (1962: 67); rather, they demonstrate combinative rounding of OE *ī* after *w*. This claim is based on (a) lOE forms such as <swyþe> OE *swīþe* 'very', <ydel> OE *īdel* IDLE, and on (b) such ME forms as <hwule> OE *hwīle* WHILE and <s(w)uþe> OE *swīþe* 'very', clearly implying a rounded vowel (1962: 71). Besides, there is evidence that OE *y* > [i] before palatals, even in the SW Midlands, whereas it was retained in other positions (1962: 72).

8.2 Discussion of ME spellings

8.2.1 Discussion of LAEME *material*

OE ȳ

LAEME reports a range of spellings for the reflex of OE *ȳ*, among them <e>, <éé>, <i>, <ie>, <u>, <ui>, <y>, cf. Table 8.13 at the end of this chapter.[3]

It should be noted that a great number of texts show mixed spellings, but use particular spellings for particular words (e.g. nos. 1800 and 2000 from Worcestershire, no. 1100 from Herefordshire, no. 2002 from Gloucestershire): WHY and OE *bȳsen* 'example, model' appear mostly with

<i>/<y> throughout, even in texts with dominant <u>.[4] Thus, if unrounding of ȳ started in particular words, those words are likely to have been WHY, *Dryhten*, and possibly *bȳsen* (but note the *caveat* earlier). These words are among the commonest words recorded. It should be noted, therefore, that numbers, with regard to dominant vs. less dominant spellings, may be skewed, due to the high frequency of occurrence of the word WHY; a case in point is no. 123 (unlocalised, dated to 1240–50), which shows 12 <u> and 7 <i> for OE ȳ: the <u> forms occur in 6 different lexemes, whereas all of the <i> appear in forms for WHY. A simple count of *tokens* therefore indicates that <i> is twice as frequent as <u> in this scribal text; a count of *types*, however, suggests otherwise.

Table 8.1 shows a number of <i> for OE ȳ. However, many of these sources show consistent <u>, <ui>/<uy>, <e> or other spellings for the reflex of OE ȳ, and use <i> only for WHY and/or OE *bȳsen*. When these are excluded, the list of texts with <i> for OE ȳ is as shown in Table 8.2.[5]

Thus, OE ȳ seems to have started unrounding very early, probably in lOE, and apparently all over the country. The unrounding was clearly in progress in the latter half of the twelfth century as far south as Essex and Suffolk; unrounding seems complete in the North and the E Midlands in the late period covered by *LAEME*, at least in parts of Lincolnshire, Norfolk, Oxfordshire, and Huntingdonshire. More surprisingly, unrounding must have started quite early in the W Midlands and the South also.

Forms with <ie> (except in OE *þēostor/þȳster*) appear in Essex (nos. 64 and 65, both 1200–24), Kent (no. 142, 1275–99), Lincolnshire (no. 15, 1250–99), and Norfolk (no. 150, 1275–99; and no. 155, 1300–24). As for nos. 64 and 65, <ie> is the dominant form in both, and in no. 64, <i> is also dominant. The <ie> here may be an AN spelling, denoting unrounding to [i:], although a diphthongal pronunciation cannot be ruled out. The lexical yield for no. 65 is small, whereas that for no. 64 is quite high, and the source shows a mixture of forms: dominant <ie> and <i>, and minor variants <e> and <y>. The <i> and <y> spellings indicate unrounding, whereas <e> points to lowering, so it is possible that the <ie> spellings imply some sound in between [i:] and [e:]. No. 142 has dominant <e> and minor variants <ie> and <éé>, which clearly points to lowering and unrounding. In this source, <ie> is found only once for the vowel of HIRE (preterit), whereas there are three forms with <e> for the same, so it is possible that the <i> represents vowel shift of ē to [i:], or is an AN <ie> for [e:]; the former solution seems more probable. As pointed out in Chapter 4, however, <ie>/<ye> for etymological ē are recorded in Middle Kentish texts, which Gradon (1979: 29) interprets as indicating a

Table 8.1 *Incidence of <i> for OE* ȳ (LAEME)

Area	County	No.	Date
North	Durham	188	1300–49
E Midlands	Cambridgeshire	137	1275–99
	Ely	282	1275–1324
	Essex	4, 1200	1150–99
		64	1200–24
	Huntingdonshire	1500	1300–49
	Lincolnshire	128, 182	*c.* 1300
	Norfolk	150, 1400	1275–99
		1700	1284–89
		155	1300–24
	Northamptonshire	66	1200–49
	Suffolk	1300	1150–99
W Midlands	Cheshire	118	1240–50
	Gloucestershire	158	1250–74
		271	1250–99
		2002	1275–99
		10, 264	1275–1324
	Herefordshire	189	1200–24
		273	1225–49
		246, 247, 248, 1100	1275–99
	Oxfordshire	232	1175–1224
		1600	1275–1324
	Shropshire	260, 261, 262, 1000	1200–24
		275	1200–49
		272	1225–49
	Wiltshire	280	1250–74
	Worcestershire	5, 2000	*c.* 1200
		6, 7, 1900	1200–49
		245, 1800	1225–49
		276, 277, 278	1250–74
		2, 3	1275–99
South	Devon	147, 148	1275–99
	Kent	8	1200–49
		142	1275–99
	Surrey	184	13th century
	Sussex	67	1200–49
Unlocalised	*Unlocalised*	119, 120, 121, 123, 141, 228, 238, 241, 242	

palatal glide. Since $\bar{y} > \bar{e}$ early in Kentish, the <ie> forms referred to earlier may indicate the same development. No. 15 shows dominant <y> alongside <ie>, and has <y> in WHITE, so it seems relatively certain that the $\bar{y}$ had been unrounded to [i:] in this scribal dialect. No. 150 has dominant

Table 8.2 LAEME *incidence of* <i> *for OE* ȳ, *excluding* WHY *and* bȳsen (LAEME)

Area	County	No.	Spg proportions	Date
North	Durham	188	i	1300–49
E Midlands	Ely	282	i ((u, y))	1275–1324
	Essex	1200	u (i, e) ((eo))	1150–99
	Huntingdonshire	1500	i (y) ((u))	1300–49
	Lincolnshire	182	i	*c.* 1300
	Norfolk	150	i (ie)	1275–99
		1400	i ((y))	1275–99
		1700	i	1284–89
		155	i, ie	1300–24
	Northamptonshire	66	u, i	1200–49
	Suffolk	1300	i	1150–99
W Midlands	Cheshire	118	u ((i, ui, eo))	1240–50
	Gloucestershire	10	u, i (e)	1275–1324
		264	i	1275–1324
	Herefordshire	248	i (u, e)	1275–99
	Oxfordshire	232	i	1175–1224
		1600	u, uy ((i, y, yu))	1275–1324
	Worcestershire	1900	u ((i, ui, eo, e))	1200–49
		278	u ((i, v, eo))	1250–74
South	Devon	147	i	1275–99
		148	i	1275–99
	Kent	8	e, ie (i)	1200–49
	Surrey	184	u (i, y)	13th century

<i>, and shows <ie> in DRY only; no. 155 has dominant <i> and <ie>; thus, Norfolk also seems to have undergone unrounding of [y:] to [i:].

Continued use of <y> for OE *ȳ* is attested in Cumberland, Ely, Essex, Gloucestershire, Hampshire, Herefordshire, Huntingdonshire, Lincolnshire, Norfolk, Oxfordshire, Somerset, and Surrey. In order to establish whether <y> here corresponds to retained [y:] and not to unrounded [i:], one has to examine the entire orthographic systems of these sources: for instance, if <y> is never used for the reflex of OE *ī*, that would strengthen the case for viewing <y> as indicating a retained front round vowel. Of the texts listed earlier, only the source text for no. 2003 (1300–50) seems **not** to use <y> for OE *i/ī*, except for a single remarkable <yt> for the 2. plural pronoun; as the scribal dialect is entered in Ely, however, it seems unlikely that <y> for OE *ȳ* here should correspond to [y:].

Table 8.3 *Incidence of <u> for OE* (LAEME)

Area	County	No.	Date
E Midlands	Ely	282	1275–1324
	Essex	4, 1200	1150–99
	Huntingdonshire	1500	1300–49
	Northamptonshire	66	1200–49
	Suffolk	1300	1150–99
W Midlands	Cheshire	118, 122	1240–50
	Gloucestershire	158	1250–74
		271	1250–99
		229, 2002	1275–99
		10	1275–1324
	Herefordshire	189	1200–24
		246, 247, 248, 249, 1100	1275–99
	Oxfordshire	1600	1275–1324
	Shropshire	260, 261, 262, 1000	1200–24
		275	1200–49
	Warwickshire	126	1275–1324
	Wiltshire	280	1250–74
	Worcestershire	170	1175–99
		5, 2000, 2001	*c.* 1200
		6, 7, 1900	1200–49
		245, 1800	1225–49
		276, 277, 278	1250–74
		2	1275–99
South	Berkshire	63	1150–99
	Surrey	184	13th century
Unlocalised	*Unlocalised*	119, 120, 121, 123	1240–50
		235	1225–74
		241, 242	1275–99

Table 8.3 shows that <u> for OE *ȳ* first appears in the Essex-Suffolk area and in Worcestershire in the late twelfth century, whence they spread to adjacent areas in the course of the next one hundred and fifty years, though independent origins cannot be ruled out.

As Table 8.4 demonstrates, <ui>/<uy> are found first in Suffolk in the second half of the twelfth century; in Shropshire and Worcestershire in the first half of the thirteenth century; in Cheshire in the mid-thirteenth century; in Gloucestershire, Herefordshire, and Oxfordshire in the latter half of the thirteenth century; and in Norfolk in the first half of the fourteenth century. They are particularly frequent in no. 1600 from Oxfordshire.

Table 8.4 *Incidence of <ui>/<uy> for OE* ȳ (LAEME)

Area	County	No.	Date
E Midlands	Norfolk	155	1300–24
	Suffolk	1300	1150–99
W Midlands	Cheshire	118, 122	1240–50
	Gloucestershire	271	1250–99
		2002	1275–99
	Herefordshire	246, 247	1275–99
	Oxfordshire	1600	1275–1324
	Shropshire	261	1200–24
	Worcestershire	1900	1200–49
		245, 1800	1225–49
		187	*c.* 1300
Unlocalised	*Unlocalised*	119, 120, 121	1240–50

If <u> and <ui>/<uy> indicate retention of [y:], the extracted spellings suggest that OE *ȳ* remained rounded not only in the W Midlands and Wiltshire to at least the end of the thirteenth century, but also in Huntingdonshire, Norfolk, Oxfordshire, and Warwickshire into the fourteenth century; no. 282 (Ely, 1275–1324) also has a few <u> forms, but the rest of the spellings suggest unrounding. And although nos. 118 and 122 from Cheshire show a mixture of forms for the reflexes of OE *ȳ* (<u>, <ui>, <i>, <eo>), <u> is dominant, implying that the unrounding was not complete in the NW Midlands even in the mid-thirteenth century. The <u> forms from Berkshire, Essex, Suffolk, and Surrey are early, but they also seem to indicate that Wright and Wright (1928: §57) are wrong in stating that the reflex of OE *ȳ* had become [e:] in Essex and Suffolk in lOE, as laid out in the introductory section to this chapter: <e> spellings do indeed occur in Essex (nos. 4, 64, and 1200) and Suffolk (no. 1300), but they are not dominant. Sussex is poorly represented in the eME material, but no. 67 (E Sussex, 1200–49) has <i>, not <e>, for OE *ȳ*. The <u> forms from Wiltshire (no. 280, 1250–74) suggest that unrounding had not taken place there, certainly not in OE, despite Wright and Wright's explicit claim for Wiltshire.

Lass and Laing (2005) assert that the ME dialects of the W Midlands in fact did *not* have front rounded vowels, that is, [y(:)] and [ø(:)] from OE *y*/*ȳ* and *eo*/*ēo*, respectively. In their opinion, *ȳ* became [i:] or [e:], as traditionally claimed, or merged with the reflex of OE *ū*, in different areas. Additionally, they claim that <y> for OE *ȳ* is not reported in the SW

Midlands, which is not entirely true. Analysis of all *LAEME* sources entered in the W Midlands reveals that the following texts do have <y> for OE *ȳ*, though admittedly only for WHY: nos. 246 and 1100 (Herefordshire), no. 2002 (Gloucestershire), and arguably no. 1600 (Oxfordshire). To support their claims, Lass and Laing use spellings for ȳ from *LAEME* text nos. 277 (Worcestershire), 272 (Shropshire), and 280 (Wiltshire); these sources will therefore be examined in detail in the following.

No. 272 has dominant <u>, with a variant <v>, for OE *ū*; and <i> for OE *ȳ*. Likewise, no. 277 shows dominant <u>, with secondary variants <ou>, <v>, <o> for OE *ū*; and dominant <u>, with minor variant <i> for OE *ȳ*. No. 280 has dominant <ou> and <u>, with minor variants <v>, <o>, <ow> for OE *ū*; and dominant <u>, with minor variants <ou>, <i>, <eo> for OE *ȳ*; cf. Table 8.13. Close analysis of all W Midlands texts in *LAEME* reveals that although many of them show <u> for both OE *ȳ* and OE *ū*, the majority also show different minor variants for each reflex. For example, <ou>/<ow>, <o>, <uu>, <v>/<w>, <ov> are quite common as minor variants for OE *ū*, whereas such spellings are rare for OE *ȳ*; for OE *ȳ*, secondary and minor variants like <ui>/<uy>, <i>, <e>, <eo> are more common. Some W Midland sources keep the two reflexes apart orthographically: In these, the recorded forms indicate unrounding (and sometimes lowering) of OE *ȳ*.[6] However, most of the W Midland sources have mixed spellings, which often 'contradict' each other in terms of implied sound value; a case in point is no. 246 from Herefordshire (1275–99), which shows dominant <u> for OE *ȳ*, suggesting a retained rounded vowel, but also minor variants <y>/<i>, indicating unrounding. The same source shows dominant <u>, with minor variants <ou>, <o>, <v>, <oi>, <uu>, <w>, <eo>, <eþ> for the reflex of OE *ū*. In other words, it is difficult indeed to draw any decisive conclusions about the precise phonetic nature of the reflexes of OE *ȳ* (and *ū*) in these scribal dialects.

LAEME also reports a few <o> and <ou> for OE ȳ. Forms with <o> are found in Worcestershire (nos. 5 and 2001, both dated to *c.* 1200), but only for OE *þȳster* and cognates; <ou> appears in no. 125[7] (Herefordshire, 1300–24), as well as in no. 280[8] (Wiltshire, 1250–74). These could be interpreted as supporting Lass Laing's claim that the reflex of OE *ȳ* was in the process of merging with the reflex of OE *ū*, since <ou>/<ow> virtually always correspond to OE *ū*.

In this context, eME spellings for lengthened OE *y* may shed light on the problem. Most of the W Midlands texts have dominant <u> for OE *y* in lengthening contexts, though occasional <i> is not infrequent, particularly for OE *yht*, and particularly towards later ME. That is, OE *y* in lengthening environments seems to have remained rounded in the greater part of the W Midlands. Exceptions are indeed found, in no. 260 from Shropshire (1200–24), which has dominant <ey> for lengthened OE *y* other than for *yht*, for which <uht>/<uh> are found; no. 158 from Gloucestershire (1250–74), which has <e> as well as <u>; no. 161 from Gloucestershire (1275–99), which reports <ey> only for lengthened OE *y*; no. 10 (Gloucestershire, 1275–1324), which has <u> and <ei>. All the forms referred to in the preceding may suggest lowering and unrounding to [e:]. Nevertheless, the reflex of OE *yht* appears to have generally merged with the reflex of OE *iht* quite early; cf. Chapter 5.

Two of Lass and Laing's assertions have therefore been proven correct: there is no 'neat geographical tri-partition for /y/', and 'Not only are the symbol-to-sound mappings more multiplex than is suggested, but there is a strong element of lexical specificity in the set of reflexes' (Lass and Laing 2005: 281). Put differently, the orthographic rendering of a given OE vowel varies from word to word. This in fact agrees with the tenets of lexical diffusion: Sound-change starts in very frequent words, or in certain phonetic environments, whence it spreads to less frequent words, or other (eventually all) phonetic contexts. The third claim, that no 'particular spellings [are] uniquely associated with OE /y(:)/' (2005: 281), is not correct: <ui>/<uy> are used for OE *ȳ* only (for OE *ū*, <uy> is found only in no. 1600 from Oxfordshire). As for their claim that the reflex of OE *ȳ* merged with that of OE *ī* in some places, and with that of OE *ē* in others, it is no more than the traditional, and correct, account. It is their belief that the reflex of OE *ȳ* fell in with OE *ū* in the SW Midlands which is the most interesting, and the hardest to prove.

Evidence from the modern SW Midlands dialects may be used to resolve the case: If the modern accents have one identical reflex for OE *ū* and OE *ȳ*, the ME spellings may be taken to indicate merger; if not, ME sources from the area simply show lack of distinct orthographic representations, but not merger. The modern pronunciations of words with OE *ū* and OE *ȳ* were extracted from the *SED* (Orton and Dieth 1962) for the W Midland counties, including Wiltshire, and Berkshire. This evidence suggests strongly that there was no merger between the reflexes of OE *ū* and OE *ȳ* in the area in question, since there are predominantly unrounded off-glides for the OE *ȳ*, and clearly rounded off-glides for OE *ū*. However, there are exceptions, found in certain places in the NW Midlands, that is, Cheshire and Staffordshire.[9] In these localities, there is sometimes a diphthong with an *unrounded* off-glide for COWS/KYES (<OE *cȳ*), MOUSE, HOUSE, MOUTH, DROUGHT, THOUSAND, CLOUDS (OE *ū*), as

well as for DRY, HIDE, FIRE, WRIGHT, WHY (OE *ȳ*). It should be noted, then, that these have converged on the 'normal' reflex for eME *ȳ* and not for eME *ū*, as Lass and Laing claim.

Thus, the SW Midlands spellings for OE ȳ and OE *ū* in *LAEME* imply merger of *figurae*, but not of *potestates*, as otherwise it would have been impossible for the reflexes of the two sounds to unmerge later. However, variationist linguistics (e.g. Weinreich, Labov and Herzog 1968; Kytö and Rissanen 1997: 9–10) opens up for the possibility of the reversal of sound-change when different phonemic systems come into contact. Such contact would indeed be the only way in which a true merger could be undone, cf. Stenroos (2005: 304). Although the modern evidence shows that OE *ū* and OE *ȳ* did not merge in ME, at least not at /u:/, that does not preclude merger at an earlier stage, if different phonemic systems came into contact later, and resulted in the reversal of the merger. However, the sheer number of <u> and <ui>/<uy> from the W Midlands, not only in *LAEME*, but also in the later material, suggests that a front rounded [y:] was indeed retained in at least parts of that area until lME.

Table 8.5 indicates that <e> and <eo> are most numerous in Essex, Herefordshire, and Worcestershire. However, most of the texts reporting <e>/<eo> show mixed spellings for OE *ȳ/y*; the majority of the texts which use <e(o)> do so only for OE *þēostor/þȳster* and cognates, for OE *ālȳfedlīc*, OE *ālȳse(n)dnes*, or OE *gȳmelēast(līce)*.[10] Sources with <e(o)>, etc. for lexical items other than these are nos. 4, 64, 160, 1200 from Essex, no. 161 from Gloucestershire, nos. 8 and 142 from Kent, no. 169 from Lincolnshire, no. 1300 from Suffolk, no. 156 from Somerset, and no. 280 from Wiltshire.

Thus, <e> and <eo> for OE ȳ start appearing in the second half of the twelfth century in Essex and Suffolk; they are reported in Kent *c.* 1200–24; then in Somerset around 1240; in Gloucestershire and Wiltshire *c.* 1250–99; and finally in Lincolnshire in the early fourteenth century. There can be little doubt that *ȳ* > [e:] must have started in the SE Midlands, and that the change was native to Kent as well as to parts of the E Midlands and parts of the South-West. Gradon (1962: 74–5) points out that <e> 'appears as a spelling for Old English *y* in many parts of the country where Kentish influence can hardly be assumed', although she does not elaborate. Forms with <e(o)> are dominant in no. 160 from Essex, no. 161 from Gloucestershire, nos. 8 and 142 from Kent, no. 169 from Lincolnshire, and no. 156 from Somerset.

The form <dreie> OE *drȳge* DRY is recorded once in an unlocalised text, no. 19 (1300–24), and indicates vowel shift. A single <flei>

Table 8.5 *Incidence of <e>, <éé>, <eo>, etc. for OE* ȳ (LAEME)

Area	County	No.	Date
E Midlands	Essex	4, 1200	1150–99
		64	1200–24
		160	1275–99
	Lincolnshire	169	1325–49
	Peterborough	149	1154
	Suffolk	1300	1150–99
W Midlands	Cheshire	118	1240–50
	Gloucestershire	158	1250–74
		161, 2002	1275–99
		10	1275–1324
	Herefordshire	189	1200–24
		246, 247, 248, 1100	1275–99
	Shropshire	260, 261, 1000	1200–24
	Wiltshire	280	1250–74
	Worcestershire	170	1175–99
		5, 2000, 2001	*c.* 1200
		1900	1200–49
		1800	1225–49
		276, 277, 278	1250–74
		3	1275–99
South	Kent	8	1200–49
		142	1275–99
	Somerset	156	*c.* 1240
Unlocalised	*Unlocalised*	120, 121	1240–50
		242	1275–99

OE *flȳge* FLY n., as well as one <fleye> FLY inf., are reported in no. 2002 from Gloucestershire (1275–99), but it is possible that the etymon here is OE *flēoge*, since both forms are attested in OE. These two forms are hence uncertain evidence and should be used with caution with regard to vowel-shifting.

OE y *in lengthening contexts*

The material extracted and analysed includes the reflexes of OE *y* before (a) voiced homorganic consonant clusters (e.g. KIND, MIND); (b) the OE digraph *cg* (e.g. BUY); and (c) OE –(*r*)*ht* (e.g. FLIGHT, WRIGHT); cf. Table 8.6.

These spellings indicate unrounding to [i:], since <y> is found for etymological *ī*. Still, many of the texts show either different or co-varying

Table 8.6 *Incidence of <i>, <y>, <ie> for lengthened OE* y (LAEME)

Area	County	No.	Date
North	West Riding, Yks	256	1275–1324
E Midlands	Ely	282	1275–1324
	Essex	1200	1150–99
		64	1200–24
	Lincolnshire	169	1325–49
		182	*c.* 1300
	Norfolk	150	1275–99
		155	1300–24
	Suffolk	1300	1150–99
W Midlands	Cheshire	118	1240–50
		136	1275–99
	Gloucestershire	2002	1275–99
	Herefordshire	246, 247, 1100	1275–99
	Oxfordshire	1600	1275–1324
	Wiltshire	280	1250–74
	Worcestershire	2001	*c.* 1200
		6, 7, 1900	1200–49
		277, 278	1250–74
		2	1275–99
Unlocalised	*Unlocalised*	119, 121, 122	1240–50
		179, 180	1275–99

dominant forms: generally the reflexes for categories (a) and (b) are the same, whereas those for (c) are different. Examples are: no. 282 (Ely), which has <i>/<y>, <u> for categories (a) and (b), <iȝt(h)> for category (c); no. 64 (Essex), which has <e> for categories (a) and (b), <iht> and <uht> for (c); no. 2002 (Gloucestershire), which has <ui>, <u>, <ey> for (a) and (b), <iȝt> and <uiȝt> for (c). In other words, unrounding may not have been complete in these scribal dialects. However, unrounding seems to have been complete in the language which informed source no. 136 (Cheshire), no. 282 (Ely), no. 1200 (Essex), no. 182 (Lincolnshire), nos. 150 and 155 (Norfolk), no. 2 (Worcestershire), and no. 256 (the West Riding of Yorkshire). In no. 1200, unrounding seems to have been accompanied by lowering to [e:]. It should be noted that of these, the following show dominant <i>/<y> for the long vowel as well: nos. 282, 182, 150, 155; in nos. 136 and 256, reflexes of OE *ȳ* are lacking. Thus, in the eME dialects of Ely, Lincolnshire, and Norfolk, lengthened OE *y* certainly appears to have undergone unrounding. The reflex of OE *yht* seems to have fallen in with OE *iht* before lengthened *y* was unrounded in other environments.

Table 8.7 *Incidence of <e> for lengthened OE* y (LAEME)

Area	County	No.	Date
E Midlands	Cambridgeshire	137	1275–99
	Essex	4, 1200	1150–99
		64	1200–24
	Lincolnshire	169	1325–49
W Midlands	Gloucestershire	158	1250–74
		161	1275–99
		10	1275–1324
	Worcestershire	2000	*c.* 1200
South	Kent	8	1200–49
		142	1275–99
		291	1325–49
Unlocalised	*Unlocalised*	233	1275–99

The <e>-type forms for lengthened OE *y* in Table 8.7 indicate early lowering and unrounding to [e:] in Essex, Kent, and Worcestershire, a little later in NE Gloucestershire, and later still in the NE Midlands, that is, Cambridgeshire and Lincolnshire. Close analysis of dominant, secondary, and minor spelling variants in these sources suggests that lowering to [e:] was taking place in Essex, Kent, Gloucestershire in the early period covered by *LAEME*; the process appears to have been complete in Kent by the early thirteenth century. This is not surprising, given the fact that late Old Kentish shows [y(:)] > [e(:)] (cf. Anderson 1988). The scattered <e> forms in the NE Midlands and Worcestershire are a little more surprising.

A few more forms with <ei>/<ey> are recorded for the lengthened OE *y* than for the etymologically long vowel, cf. Table 8.8.

Close analysis of the spelling systems of these sources still leaves open the question whether all the <ei>/<ey> for OE *ycg* imply diphthongisation to [ɪi] or [əi], but the ones in no. 65 from Essex and no. 2002 from Gloucestershire may do so, and the forms in no. 137 from Cambridgeshire and nos. 269 and 285 from Norfolk are almost certainly evidence of vowel shift. The form <ley> in nos. 260 from Shropshire and 159 from Lincolnshire likely also implies diphthongisation. Forms with <ey> for OE *yht* are recorded in nos. 161 from Gloucestershire and 169 from Lincolnshire. The spelling systems of these texts are as follows. In no. 161, whose spelling system is truly idiosyncratic, <ey> is actually the dominant spelling for the reflex of OE *y*(*r*)*ht*, as well as for OE *eaht, eoht, iht*. However, as <e> is the only spelling found for the reflex

Table 8.8 *Incidence of <ei>/<ey> for lengthened OE* y (LAEME)

County	No.	Date	Spellings
Cambridgeshire	137	1275–99	<bein> BUY *inf.*
Essex	65	1200–24	<beið> BUY *3.sg.pres.*
	160	1275–99	<for-beyen> FOR-BUY
Gloucestershire	161	1275–99	<dreyte> *dryhten*; <fleyt> FLIGHT; <vreyte> FRIGHT;
	2002	1275–99	<man-keyne> MANKIND
	10	1275–1324	<beye> BUY *inf.*; <forbeyen> FOR-BUY <beiþ> BUY *3.sg.pres.*
Kent	8	1200–49	<beið> BUY *3.sg.pres.*
Lincolnshire	159	*c.* 1300	<ley> LIE *n.*
	169	1325–49	<fleyt> FLIGHT
Norfolk	269	1275–1324	<beyn> BUY *inf.*
	285	1300–24	<beye> buy *inf.*; <beyes> buy *3.sg.pres.*
Shropshire	260	1200–24	<ley> LIE *n.*

of OE *ȳ*, it may be that the <y> in, for example, <dreyte> OE *dryhten* or <vreyte> FRIGHT may symbolise a vocalised intervocalic fricative and not the off-glide of a diphthong. The difference may seem historical rather than phonetic, but a diphthong forms one unit, whereas a vocalised fricative may be considered part of the syllabic coda, especially if the vocalisation has not gone beyond [ç] or [ʝ]. Indeed, the same scribe once writes <fleȝt> FLIGHT, besides <fleyt>. On the other hand, the form <man-keyne> MANKIND may make such an interpretation less likely, considering the absence of a palatal fricative in OE *cynd*. It could be argued, however, that if <ey> co-occurs with <y> before [ç], their interchange could be extended to non-[ç] contexts by analogy. It is nevertheless tempting to take these <ey> forms, and at the very least the one for MANKIND, at face value as representing a diphthong. No. 169 has <y> as well as <e> for the reflex of OE *ȳ*, though only <y> for OE *y*. The form <fleyt> FLIGHT in this text thus may either imply diphthongisation, or the <y> merely symbolises a vocalised glide. However, no. 169 also has <byer> BUYER, which suggests complete vocalisation of the intervocalic consonant. The interpretation of this spelling therefore remains uncertain, though it should be noted that all other *LAEME* texts whose language has been localised to Lincolnshire show <i>/<y> for eME *ȳ*.

In conclusion, if the <ei>/<ey> spellings discussed indicate that OE *y* has been unrounded, lengthened, and diphthongised, this diphthongisation apparently started in the East (Essex) and W Midlands (Shropshire) in the early thirteenth century; it then seems to have spread to, or started independently in, other parts of the East (Cambridgeshire, Norfolk, and Lincolnshire) and West (Gloucestershire) in the course of a hundred years or so.

Forms with <ui>/<uy> are found in Cheshire (no. 124, 1250–74), in Essex (no. 4, 1150–99), in Gloucestershire (no. 2002, 1275–99), in Herefordshire (no. 247, 1275–99), in Oxfordshire (no. 1600, 1275–1324), and in Suffolk (no. 1300, 1150–99), as well as in no. 119 (unlocalised, 1240–50). Such spellings would be expected in W Midlands texts, since retention of a rounded vowel is well-attested in this area; however, <ui>/<uy> are also found in Essex and Suffolk, and suggest that unrounding was not complete there in the late twelfth century. Forms with <u> are frequent, and are found in texts from all over the country. These spellings are conventionally interpreted as indicating the retention of front rounded [y:], but see the discussion earlier.

8.2.2 Discussion of SMED *material*

OE ȳ

The material for the North indicates that Cumberland, Northumberland, Westmorland, Durham, the North and East Ridings of Yorkshire, and Lincolnshire had [i:] for OE ȳ. Some 'deviating' <u> spellings are explained by Kristensson as 'due to scribal influence' (Kristensson 1967: 117). As for the West Riding of Yorkshire, the majority of names with OE *y/ȳ* have <i>, though there are some <u>. Kristensson concludes that the normal reflex of OE *ȳ* in the West Riding is *ī* 'in all positions except after [ʃ], sporadically before *l*' (1967: 118). The case is less straightforward for Lancashire, since spellings are mixed; Kristensson finds that S Lancashire, that is, south of the Ribble, may have had both [y:] and [i:], whereas N Lancashire had [i:] (1967: 119). There are also two forms with <uy> for OE *ȳ* in Lancashire (1327, 1332).

From spellings for the W Midlands, Cheshire, Gloucestershire, Herefordshire, Oxfordshire, Shropshire, Staffordshire, Warwickshire, and Worcestershire all still seem to have had [y:] in the early fourteenth century (Kristensson 1987: 95). Derbyshire also seems to have had [y:], except in the easternmost tip, which had [i:]; Leicestershire had [y:] in the west, [i:] in the east and south; Nottinghamshire had /i:/. Kristensson assumes that there will have been 'a fairly wide transition territory between /y(:)/ and /i(:)/ areas' (1987: 96). Names with OE *hyll* form a slightly different pattern, with Nottinghamshire emerging as a transition area, with <i> and <u> equally dominant.

In the early fourteenth century, material for the E Midlands suggests that Rutland, Huntingdonshire, Norfolk, and N Cambridgeshire had [i:]; Bedfordshire, Hertfordshire, Middlesex, and Buckinghamshire had [y:]; Suffolk and Essex had [e:]. N Northamptonshire had [i:], S Northamptonshire had [y:]. Cambridgeshire had [i:] north of the city of Cambridge; south of it, it had [e:] to the east and [y:] to the west.

OE *ȳ* is spelt variously <i>/<y> (indicating [i:]), <e> (implying [e:]), and <u> (indicating [y:]) in the material for the South. In the material for Kent, <e> is dominant; <e> and <u> are found in all of Sussex, though <e> is dominant in the east and <u> in the west; <u> is dominant for Surrey (except in the easternmost tip, which has <e>), Berkshire, Hampshire, Wiltshire, Dorset, and Somerset; and both <i> and <u> are found in Devon. Thus, Kent, the eastern half of Sussex, and the easternmost tip of Surrey probably had [e:] at the beginning of the fourteenth century, whereas Devon probably had both [i:] and [y:], and the remaining area had [y:]. The case may be a little different for OE *ȳ* + palatal consonant, 'in that /y(:)/ has been unrounded in an area which had its core in Ha and Do[r] but also covered Berkshire, W[lt] and So[m]' (2001: 118), and Surrey, though not Sussex or Kent. In Devon, there seems to have been a tendency to unround *ȳ* regardless of phonetic context (cf. Kristensson 2001: 118; Gradon 1962).

Regarding vowel shift, only two <ey> for OE *ȳ* are recorded in the E Midlands (Table 8.9). They are found in the Cambridgeshire Roll for 1330 and the Essex Roll for 1327. Kristensson believes (1995: 141) that these forms originate in OE *drēge*, since OE *ȳ* gives either ME /i:/ (spelt <i>/<y>) or ME /y:/ (spelt <ui>/<uy>). This argument is tautological. *SMED1* does not record <ey> for OE *ȳ*. Material from the South yields two forms with <ey> for DRY, one from Berkshire and one from Sussex. As for comments on the development of OE *ȳ* before ȝ, *SMED5* claims that it results in /i:/ or /y:/, therefore <Dreye> 'goes back to OE *drēge*' (Kristensson 2002: 257). Kristensson notes also that <u> for *i*-mutated *eaht* implies lOE *ȳ* from earlier *īe* (Kristensson 2002: 221); such forms are 'found in the whole area except in Kent, eastern Sx, eastern S[u]r, Devon, and Berkshire' (2002: 221).[11]

Cubbin (1981) also treats <u> and <i>/<y> for OE *ȳ* in a variety of ME onomastic sources, including the LSR; his findings are therefore discussed here. Cubbin is concerned with the reflexes of OE *ȳ* in Lancashire, especially the problematic southern part, and he tries to determine whether it

Table 8.9 *Incidence of <ey> for OE* ȳ (SMED)

Area	County	Roll	Spelling
E Midlands	Cambridgeshire	1330	<Dreye-> DRY
	Essex	1327	<Dreye> DRY
South	Berkshire	1327	<Dreye> DRY
	Sussex	1332	<Dreye> DRY

was an [y:] area or an [i:] area. He seems predisposed, however, to discard all <i>/<y> spellings as unreliable and suspicious. He is right in treating the sources with caution, and he is certainly justified when he concludes that some of the material was recorded by non-local scribes, and that the spellings contained therein therefore ought not to be taken as incontrovertible proof of vowel-change. But the notions of change in progress and lexical diffusion seem at first entirely unknown to him: He discards all documents as 'unreliable' if they show mixed <i>/<y> and <u> for the reflex of OE *ȳ*; and unfortunately, this approach makes him dismiss local spellings which seem to indicate unrounding to [i:] in S Lancashire at an early date.[12] He thus concludes, with apparent relief, that the evidence extracted from the Coucher Book of Whalley Abbey 'finally establishes the whole of South Lancashire as a solid *u*-county' (1981: 89), as if it were the conclusion he had anticipated. Unfortunately, his conclusion cannot be taken seriously.

Even the Coucher Book contains some <i> spellings for the reflex of OE *ȳ*, however, and these are dealt with in some detail as they 'fall into [...] a small number of extremely significant groups' (1981: 90), but their presence does not change Cubbin's opinion of Lancashire as a *u*-county. Benskin, also criticising Cubbin's methods and conclusions, points out that in the material from the Coucher Book, the (Benskin 1994: 184, n. 6)

> *i*-forms do appear to pattern coherently, and it is possible that the local and chronological variations were as Dr Cubbin represents them. It is accordingly hard to see why other sources containing *i*-forms were dismissed out of hand, instead of being subjected to similarly close analysis.

The coherent pattern referred to is found for the reflexes of OE *kylen* KILN, OE *myln* 'mill', OE *mycel* 'big, much', and partly OE *wyrhta* WRIGHT. The dates of the deeds in which they occur are examined carefully, revealing that <u> is always earlier than <i>. Thus, Cubbin states that we are 'able to date sound changes not just in general terms in this hitherto totally obscure period, but also for individual words. We can establish the very decade in which individual words capitulated to the prevailing phonological tide' (Cubbin 1981: 96). On this evidence, the vowel of *kylen* seems to have unrounded between 1220–50; that of *myln* sometime after 1260; that of *mycel* in the late thirteenth century. The date for *wyrhta* is not given, but Cubbin states that it 'is clear from previous research' (1981: 100) that it was one of the first words to show <i>, which agrees with my own findings. Cubbin's adduced evidence therefore indicates lexical diffusion (cp. Phillips 2006a; McMahon 1994: 47–55) and change in progress in S Lancashire in the thirteenth century. Moreover, it seems Kristensson is right in stating that the reflex of OE *ȳ* was in the process of unrounding to [i:] in S Lancashire in the period investigated.

OE y *in lengthening contexts*

There are a few <uy> for OE *y* in an open syllable in the North (Table 8.13); the items in question are OE **ryding* 'clearing' and OE *ryge* RYE. The forms all occur in Lancashire (1327, 1332). There are also four <uy> for OE *–yht* in the W Midlands, in Gloucestershire (1327), Oxfordshire (1327), and Staffordshire (1327, twice), in addition to the one for OE *drȳge* in Oxfordshire (1327). It is Kristensson's contention that in these forms, '<y> denotes a glide developed before [ç], but otherwise <uy> is a spelling for /y:/' (Kristensson 1987: 99). For the reflex of OE *y+g*, there are a few <uy> in the W Midlands, in OE *ryge* RYE. These spellings appear in Warwickshire (1327, 1332), Gloucestershire (1327), and Oxfordshire (1327), and probably indicate [y(:)].

With reference to vowel-shifting, forms with <ey> for OE *y/ȳ* are recorded in Table 8.10.

Kristensson does not discuss the Lincolnshire and Staffordshire spellings, but refers the reader to the work of Sundby (1963), who notes the following on the forms <Whelwreyth'> and <Whelwreyt'>: 'We may be concerned with analogical forms suggested by the ME interchange of *e, ei, i* as rendering the high front vowels in front of /ht/' (Sundby 1963: 124–5). This 'interchange' has been discussed in detail in Chapter 5 on eME *ī*. On <Beythe> in the Sussex Roll for 1327, Kristensson concludes that OE *y+ȝ* resulted in /i:/, spelt <y(e)> (Kristensson 2002: 257), although the spelling here is <ey>, not <ye>.

There are eight forms with <ey> for OE *yg* in the E Midlands: in Essex (1327, 1332), in Norfolk (1332), and in Suffolk (1327). In addition, there are four <ey> for the vowel in OE *slyht* 'slaughter', all in Essex (1327). There are also four <ey> for the stressed vowel in OE *wyrhta*, in Cambridgeshire

Table 8.10 *Incidence of <ey> for OE* y (SMED)

Area	County	Roll	Spelling
North	Lincolnshire	1327	<Whelwreyt'/Whelwreyth> WRIGHT
E Midlands	Cambridgeshire	1330	<Wreyth> WRIGHT
	Essex	1327	<Reydon> *rygen* (< RYE)
			<Sleyter(e)> SLYHT
		1332	<Reydon> *rygen* (< RYE)
	Norfolk	1332	<Reydon> RYE
			<wreythe> WRIGHT
	Suffolk	1327	<Reydone> RYE
W Midlands	Staffordshire	1332	<Wreyte> WRIGHT
South	Sussex	1327	<Beythe> *byht* BIGHT

(1330), in Norfolk (1332), and in Staffordshire (1332). In these, <ey> is a secondary variant, with dominant <i>/<y> in Cambridgeshire (1330) and Staffordshire (1332), whereas <ey> is a minor variant in Norfolk (1332). On <Sleyter(e)> from OE *slyht*, Kristensson comments that the '<y> denotes a glide developed before [ç] which later disappeared' (1995: 75). It is unclear whether Kristensson refers to the disappearance of the glide or [ç], but it is presumably the latter. In my view, <Sleyter(e)> for OE *slyht* is an exact parallel to, for example, <fleyt> for OE *flyht* FLIGHT (recorded in *LAEME*), and could be an indication of vowel-shifting. However, the same counter-arguments apply as for all <ey> for the reflexes of OE *ī* and of OE front vowels followed by <ht>. They therefore cannot be used as evidence for vowel-shifting, unless one believes, and the present writer does, that the interchange of diphthong and monophthong before [ç] was contributory to the initiation of the 'GVS'.[13]

8.2.3 Discussion of LALME *material*

OE ȳ

The following *LALME* items were examined for the purpose of this chapter: for OE *ȳ*, the items FIRE, 'PRIDE etc.' (from which were extracted forms for BRIDE, HIDE, and PRIDE), and WHY; for OE *y* in lengthening context, the item 'KIND etc.' (from which were collected forms for KIND and MIND).

Indicating an unrounded and lowered [e:] for the reflex of OE ȳ, <e(e)> is found in lME in parts of the East (Buckinghamshire, Cambridgeshire,

Ely, Norfolk, Suffolk, Essex, Middlesex, Hertfordshire, Leicestershire, and Lincolnshire), parts of the South (Kent, Surrey, Sussex, Hampshire, Wiltshire, Dorset, and Devon), and in parts of the West (Gloucestershire, Worcestershire, and Oxfordshire).

Forms with <ei>/<ey> appear in the East: Ely (LP 552), Cambridgeshire (LP 291), Northamptonshire (LP 705), Norfolk (LPs 642, 669, 4280, 4564, 4569, 4647, 4662, 4665, 4570), Suffolk (LPs 4635, 8450), Essex (LP 6040); in the South: Surrey (LP 5651), Sussex (LP 5680), Dorset (LP 5350), Devon (LPs 5120, 9400); and in the West: Shropshire (LP 4239), Worcestershire (LP 7761).

At least some of these may indicate vowel shift, but not in areas where OE *ȳ* > [e:]. Thus, the forms found in Northamptonshire (<feir> FIRE) and Shropshire (<heyden> HIDE) may be the only ones which are safe to use as evidence of diphthongisation of a high front vowel ([i:] or [y:]). Additionally, FIRE is commonly out of line with other words having OE *ȳ*; diphthongisation before [r] is possible, as it is more widely attested in eModE (Dobson 1968: §218). The scribal systems of these two texts need closer examination.

LP 705 (Northamptonshire) shows <feir>, but also <fir(e)> FIRE; it has <ei>/<ey> in THEY, <ey>/<ay> for the stressed vowel of AWAY, <ai>/<ay> in DAY, but also <ei> besides <e> for the vowel of FLESH. Thus, the scribe usually writes a digraph for the etymological diphthongs *ei* and *ai*. For the vowel of WAY, the scribe writes <ei>/<ey>, <ai>/<ay> as well as <eyȝ>; the latter suggests the loss of post-vocalic [ç] or [j] in the HIGH set. The text shows variation between <i>-type and <ei>-type spellings for EYE and HIGH, but only <niȝ> for NIGH. It has <how(e)> as well as <howȝ> for HOW, which implies identity between the reflexes of *ū* and *ug/ūg*.

LP 4239 (Shropshire) has <neynne> NINE and <heyden> HIDE, but <pryde> PRIDE. The reflex of *ī* is generally spelt <y>, although <ye> is found in LIFE; <y> and <I> both appear for I (1st pers.pron.). The reflex of *ȳ* appears once as <ey> in LITTLE, but it is generally spelt <uy>, <y(e)>; lengthened OE *y* is <u(y)>, <y(e)>, suggesting a retained close front rounded vowel. In words with OE or eME *ei* or *ai*, the scribe generally writes <ay>, <ei>/<ey>. For the vowel of the HIGH set, this text has <eȝ>, <e>, <ye>, <yeȝ>, <yȝ>, indicating variation between [i:(j)]/[i:(ç)] and [e:(j)]/[e:(ç)]. EYE is spelt <ey>, and the vowel of DIE <ye>/<yȝe> in the infinitive, and <eye>, <ye>, <yeu> in the preterit, which again suggests variation in the pronunciation of the reflex of ME *eġ*. Thus, it must be concluded that the case for viewing <feir> and <heyden> as indicating vowel shift is neither strengthened nor weakened, although the presence of <neynne> and <leytel> beside <heyden> in LP 4239 seems to favour the vowel-shift explanation for <ey> for historical *ȳ* and *ī*.

There are enough <u>, <ui>/<uy> spellings for OE *ȳ* to suggest that the retained front rounded vowel was not unrounded in 'the rest of the country' in the late fourteenth century (Wright and Wright 1928: §57). Such spellings are found in great quantity, especially – but not exclusively – in texts from the W Midlands and the South; they are rare in texts from the East and North-East, which suggests that the vowel had unrounded in these areas by late ME. Some tokens with <uy> are reported in S Lancashire, and seem to indicate retained [y:] (Kristensson 1967: 118–9).

In addition to the two forms discussed earlier, vowel shift may also be indicated by the form <fouyre> FIRE in LP 189 (Staffordshire): <uy> is common for the reflex of OE *ȳ*, but the <o> before it suggests an on-glide; alternatively <ou> could suggest [u:], and the <y> could imply [i]. With both these interpretations, there is a diphthong for the reflex of *ȳ*. Other interesting forms in this context are <fyier> in LP 5970 (Kent), <fyȝer> in LP 4665 (Norfolk), and <feore> in LP 4686 (Warwickshire), since they indicate a diphthongal pronunciation of the vowel. The forms <fier>/<fyer> are well attested, and seem to imply a diphthong too, and they seem a little late to be dismissed as AN spellings. LP 6110 (Essex) has <pryȝde> for PRIDE; this spelling is discussed later.

OE y *lengthened*

Forms with <e> for lengthened OE *y* are found in the South (Berkshire, Cornwall, Devon, Somerset, Dorset, Wiltshire, Hampshire, Surrey, and Sussex (numerous), Kent); in the East (Lincolnshire, Cambridgeshire, Norfolk (numerous), Suffolk (numerous), Essex (numerous), and London); and in the West (Gloucestershire, Worcestershire, Oxfordshire, and Warwickshire). In other words, the development of OE *y* in lengthening environments seems to be roughly the same as that of OE *ȳ*, as far as the lowering and unrounding are concerned.

Forms with <u>, <ui>/<uy> are recorded in the South (Somerset, Berkshire, Hampshire, Wiltshire, and Sussex) and in the West (Shropshire (frequent), Gloucestershire (numerous), Herefordshire (numerous), Worcestershire (frequent), and Warwickshire). They are most numerous in the West, and do not appear at all in texts which have been localised to the East or the North. This suggests that the lengthened vowel, just like the etymologically long vowel, had been unrounded to [i:] in these areas. A front rounded vowel seems, however, to have been retained in the South-West and the West.

Vowel shift may be indicated in <moynde> MIND in LP 6761 (Berkshire) and LP 7670 (Worcestershire), as <oy> is not traditionally used for OE *ȳ*, but for the diphthong [ɔɪ]. Likewise, <keynde> KIND in LP 5210 (Somerset), and <meynde> MIND in LP 5190 (Somerset) and LP 7660 (Worcestershire) suggest diphthongisation.

The forms <myȝnd> MIND and <fyȝnd> FIND in LP 9580 (Gloucestershire), and <kyȝnde> KIND and <pryȝde> PRIDE in LP 6110 (Essex) are odd, and indicate that <ȝ> is used as a marker of length, since there is no etymological postvocalic fricative in these words; the <ȝ> could also represent the tenser second element of a minimal diphthong [ɪi]. However, <yȝ> is frequent for HIGH and NIGH also, so it may be a back-spelling, as discussed earlier and in Chapter 5.

A more thorough examination of the use of <ȝ> in LP 9580 (Gloucestershire) and LP 6110 (Essex) reveals the following. In LP 6110, <ȝ> is recorded in initial position in <ȝyt>/<ȝit> YET, <ȝatys> GATE pl., <ȝaf> (but also <gaf>) GIVE pt., <ȝeldynge> YIELD pres.ppl.; in syllable-initial position in <byȝou*n*de> BEYOND; in other positions, it is attested in <dyȝe> DIE, <eyȝen>/<yȝen> EYES pl., <hyȝe>/<hyȝ>/<heyȝ>/<hey> HIGH, <seyȝe>/<sey-> SAY, <seyȝ> SEE sg.pt., and <þorghȝ>/<þorȝhȝ> THROUGH. It is possible that <ȝ> corresponds to a final fricative in THROUGH and to a plosive before *a* in GATE and GAVE (but the past ppl. is <ygyue>/<gyue>, so <g> may imply [j]), but elsewhere it seems to indicate [j]. If so, the digraph <yȝ> in <kyȝnde> and <pryȝde> may correspond either to [ij] (or some such diphthong) or to [i:].

In LP 9580, <ȝ> is recorded in (syllable-)initial position in <aȝens>/<ayens> AGAINST, <a-ȝeyn>/<agayne> AGAIN, <ȝitt>/<ȝit> YET, <ȝaf> GIVE sg.pt., <ȝede> WENT; in other positions in <þeyȝ> THOUGH, <noȝt> NOT, <myȝt> MIGHT, and <þoruȝ> THROUGH. At least in initial position before a front vowel, <ȝ> is likely to correspond to [j] here, and it may imply a fricative in final position and before [t]; indeed, the use of <ȝ> in MIGHT – in which it may correspond to variant pronunciations [mi:t] and [mɪçt] in the scribal dialect – may provide the analogy whereby it has come to be used in unhistorical positions in <fyȝnd> and <myȝnd> also.

8.2.4 Discussion of material from additional sources

The only form which might indicate vowel-shifting of OE *ȳ* in the additional material is <feyr> in MS Cambridge, Corpus Christi College 388 (Hunt and Benskin 2001; recipes 322 and 466), whose language has been placed in Ely/W Norfolk; the hand has been dated to *c*. 1320–30. These texts also show digraphs for the reflexes of eME *ī*; cf. section 5.4.4. However, the counter-arguments regarding the use of <ei>/<ey> for vowel-shift of eME *ī* apply here also.

The findings of Wyld (1913–14a, 1913–14b) may be worth noting here. Wyld investigates the development of OE *ȳ* in ME. He also makes use of onomastic material, such as Hundred Rolls and Feudal Aids, covering the thirteenth, fourteenth, and fifteenth centuries. He thus exploits the same kind of material as Kristensson and Ek, and the same arguments may therefore be levelled against his inferences. Nevertheless, Table 8.11 gives a summary of Wyld's conclusions regarding the reflexes of OE *ȳ* in ME.[14]

As Wyld rightly notes, 'Very few areas are perfectly clear-cut' (1913–14a: 45). Wyld admits that he has not placed the names or spellings accurately within each county. If he had, he would probably have divided, for example, Surrey and Sussex into *u*-areas in the west and *e*/*i*-areas in the east, thus more or less agreeing with Kristensson's conclusions in *SMED*. Likewise, Cambridgeshire (which is not divided into Cambridgeshire and Ely) would probably have been sectioned into different parts, Ely certainly being an *i*-area. Similarly, NW Leicestershire and Northamptonshire would have been assigned to the *i*-area (although Wyld finds more <e> than <i> in the latter).

Wyld considers Lancashire to be an *u*-area, and the West Riding of Yorkshire an *i*-area, although <u> (and indeed <e>) is found in some quantity in texts from the West Riding. Thus, the northernmost counties (which are not investigated), along with the West Riding, Nottinghamshire, Lincolnshire, Rutland, Huntingdonshire (and Peterborough), Cambridgeshire, and Norfolk are assigned to the *i*-area; Suffolk, Essex, Kent, and seemingly Sussex (with twice as many <u> as <e>) are assigned to the *e*-area; the remaining counties, except Devon, are *u*-counties. Devon has a few more <i> than <u>, so Wyld draws the conclusion that unrounding probably took place independently there in eME (Wyld 1913–14b: 149–50).

Given the existence of pronunciations with /iː/ for OE *ȳ* in the modern dialects of the South-West, for example, /miːs/ for 'mice', Wyld tries to determine whether OE *ȳ* > *ē* in the South-East could have spread to the South-West. He concludes from the material that such influence would be unlikely; nor does he find that there was any independent southern/south-western eME *ȳ* > *ē*, although he considers the possibility of a development *ȳ* > *ī* > *ē* in Devon (1913–14b: 151–3). In the South-East, Wyld believes that Kent was the locus of the change OE *ȳ* > [eː], but that the

Table 8.11 *ME spelling reflexes of OE ȳ (Wyld 1913–14)*

County	Spellings
Lancashire	u ((i, e))
Cheshire	u ((i))
Shropshire	u ((i, e))
Herefordshire	u ((i, e))
Derbyshire	u (i) ((e))
Staffordshire	u
Worcestershire	u ((i))
Leicestershire	u (i, e)
Warwickshire	u ((i, e))
Oxfordshire	u (i) ((e))
Northamptonshire	u ((e, i))
Bedfordshire	u ((i, e))
Buckinghamshire	u ((i))
Hertfordshire	u ((i, e))
Middlesex/London	i (u, e)
Surrey	u ((i))
West Riding, Yks	i ((e, u))
Nottinghamshire	i (u) ((e))
Lincolnshire	i ((u, e))
Rutland	i
Huntingdonshire	i ((u))
Cambridgeshire	i (e)
Norfolk	i ((u))
Suffolk	i, e ((u))
Essex	e, u ((i))
Kent	e ((u, i))
Sussex	u (e) ((i))
Devon	i, u (e)
Somerset	u ((i, e))
Dorset	u (i) ((e))
Wiltshire	u ((i, e))
Gloucestershire	u ((i, e))
Berkshire	u (i) ((e))
Hampshire	u ((i, e))

change spread to the adjoining areas and was thus native to Essex, Suffolk, and parts of Surrey, and Cambridgeshire as well (Wyld 1913–14a: 52). He therefore dismisses the view that ME <e> for OE *ȳ* in these areas could be the result of Kentish 'loans'. Some of the <e> spellings could be due to the W Midland distinction between common OE *ȳ*, for which all W Midland texts write <u>, <ui>/<uy>, and late WS *ȳ* (< *īe*, and mutated *io*, *ea*), for which genuinely southern texts also write <u>, etc., but for which W Midland texts typically write Mercian <e>. However, when texts from the W Midlands show <u> for the reflex of OE *īe*, this is not due to southern influence, in Wyld's opinion (Wyld 1913–14a: 47–8).

Finally, Wyld notes that <y> in those areas where [y(:)] was retained, could indicate a still rounded front vowel (Wyld 1913–14a: 51), which agrees with my own observations. He observes (1913–14a: 51):

> If the latter possibility existed, many of the difficulties would disappear, since a large number of forms which I assume to be *i*-forms, both in Pl[ace] N[ame]s and in texts, altho' spelt *y* would have to be put among the *u*-forms, and would thus reduce the inconsistencies.

8.3 Summary and conclusions

8.3.1 The general development of OE ȳ *and lengthened OE* y

According to the traditional accounts, OE *ȳ* was unrounded to [i:] in lOE or eME in the North, in parts of the E Midlands (Lincolnshire and Norfolk), and in parts of the South-West (Devon, Dorset, and Wiltshire); became [e:] in Kent, and in parts of Middlesex, Sussex, Essex, and Suffolk; remained in the rest of the country and was unrounded to /i:/ in the late fourteenth century.

Most *LAEME* texts show mixed spellings for OE *ȳ* and lengthened OE *y*, and these spellings often imply 'competing' phonetic correspondences, so it is difficult to draw any definite conclusions for eME. Unrounding had started in the West-Saxon area in lOE, as is evidenced by <i> for OE *ȳ*, and analogical <y> for OE *ī*. In eME, <i> forms in WHY and OE *bȳsen* are particularly common, even in texts with dominant <u>, <ui>/<uy>. Forms with <i> start appearing in Essex, Suffolk, and Hampshire in the late twelfth century; in Worcestershire, Oxfordshire, Kent, and Northamptonshire in the early thirteenth century; in Cumberland, Cheshire, Somerset, and Surrey in the mid-thirteenth century; in Lincolnshire, Norfolk, Devon, Gloucestershire, and Herefordshire in the late thirteenth century; and finally in Ely, Huntingdonshire. and NRY in the early fourteenth century. By the end of the period covered by *LAEME*, unrounding seems to have been complete in the North, and in Lincolnshire, Norfolk, Oxfordshire, Huntingdonshire, and Devon. Unrounding and lowering to [e:] is indicated in the East (Essex and Suffolk) from the late twelfth century, in Kent from the early thirteenth century onwards, and in the South-West (Somerset, Wiltshire, and Gloucestershire) from the mid-to-late thirteenth century; forms with <e> are also found in Lincolnshire in the early fourteenth century. A front rounded [y:] seems to have been preserved in large parts of the country, and in some areas as late as the early fourteenth century: <u> and <ui>/<uy> are reported in texts from Berkshire, Essex, Suffolk, and Worcestershire dated to 1150–1200; in texts entered in Northamptonshire, Herefordshire, and Shropshire dated to the early thirteenth century; in texts from Cheshire, Gloucestershire, Oxfordshire, Wiltshire, and Surrey dated to the mid-to-late thirteenth century; and in text from Ely, Huntingdonshire, and Norfolk dated to the early fourteenth century.

In *SMED*, we find that, in the early fourteenth century, all of the North and Lincolnshire had [i:], with the possible exception of the West Riding of Yorkshire and Lancashire. Kristensson concludes that both were [i:]-areas, but that [y:] was also used in Lancashire south of the Ribble. In the W Midlands, Cheshire, Staffordshire, Shropshire, Herefordshire, Worcestershire, Warwickshire, Gloucestershire, and Oxfordshire had [y:]; Derbyshire also had [y:], except in the easternmost tip, which had [i:]; Leicestershire had [y:] in the west and [i:] in the east and south; Nottinghamshire had [i:]. In the E Midlands, Rutland, Huntingdonshire, and Norfolk had [i:]; Bedfordshire, Hertfordshire, Middlesex, and Buckinghamshire had [y:]; Suffolk and Essex had [e:]; Northamptonshire had [i:] in the northern half, [y:] in the southern half. Cambridgeshire had [i:] north of the city of Cambridge (including Ely); south of it, it had [e:] to the east and [y:] to the west. In the South, Devon seems to have had [i:] and [y:]; Somerset, Dorset, Wiltshire, Hampshire, Berkshire, Surrey had [y:] (Surrey may have had [e:] in the easternmost tip), Sussex had [e:] in the east, [y:] in the west; Kent had [e:]. OE *ȳ* before palatals appears to have developed differently: in this context, *ȳ* > [i:] in the South-West; there are traces of such a development also in Surrey, but not in Sussex or Kent; Devon showed a tendency to unround regardless of context.

Ek (1972) examines the development of OE *ēo* and *ȳ* in south-eastern ME, using onomastic material which at least partly overlaps with the *SMED* material, although much of it is earlier. He draws the following conclusions concerning the reflex of OE *ȳ* in the South-East (1972: 122):

> The centres of the *e*-development are Kent, Essex, and Suffolk. East Sussex, East Surrey, Middlesex, and London City, Hertfordshire and Cambridgeshire may be called border areas where the *e*-development, however, is the commonest type.
>
> Norfolk no doubt originally belonged to the *e*-area. Even in late OE, however, *i*-forms spread form the neighbouring Midland *i*-area.

Table 8.12 *Summary of ME spellings for OE y̌ (Ek 1972)*

County\Spgs	<e>	<i>	<y>	<u>	Total
Kt	831	143	30	268	1272
	65.33%	11.24%	2.36%	21.07%	
Mx	109	47	12	80	248
	43.95%	18.95%	4.84%	32.26%	
Ex	486	180	42	117	825
	58.91%	21.82%	5.09%	14.18%	
Htf	121	49	16	102	288
	42.01%	17.01%	5.55%	35.42%	
Cam	187	144	42	45	418
	44.74%	34.45%	10.05%	10.77%	
Suffolk	610	105	44	78	837
	72.88%	12.55%	5.26%	9.32%	
Norfolk	48	281	42	27	398
	12.06%	70.6%	10.55%	6.78%	

That is, from his material it appears that Norfolk, N Ely, Huntingdonshire, and the western-most tip of Hertfordshire were *i*-areas in the early fourteenth century. The 'border areas' E Sussex, E Surrey, Middlesex, London, the greater part of Hertfordshire, and Cambridgeshire show a mixture of spellings. Table 8.12 summarises Ek's tables of tokens and percentages in each county (1972: 55–9).

It is clear that Kent, Essex, and Suffolk were indeed [e(:)] areas, and that Norfolk was an [i(:)] area in the period investigated by Ek. Middlesex seems genuinely mixed, with dominant <e>, but with quite frequent <u> and <i>/<y> also. Hertfordshire likewise has dominant <e>, but <u> forms are very frequent. As for Cambridgeshire, if <i> and <y> are combined, spellings indicating unrounding to [i(:)] are just as frequent as <e>. Thus, Kristensson and Ek disagree on the status of the reflex of OE ȳ in S Ely, Cambridgeshire, Hertfordshire, Middlesex, and London: Ek thinks these areas all had [e(:)]; Kristensson thinks they had retained [y(:)] (Middlesex, Hertfordshire, and SW Cambridgeshire), or [i(:)] (N Cambridgeshire and Ely), or [e(:)] (SE Cambridgeshire); the dividing line between [e(:)] and [y(:)] cuts London in half, according to *SMED*.

Regarding the development of OE ȳ in the dialects of ME, Kitson (reviewing Kristensson 2002) observes the following (1998: 170):

> Part of the difference [between Ek and Kristensson] is one of date. Kristensson's rolls for these counties are mostly from 1327 and 1332/4, all

> from the fourteenth century [...] Ek used evidence from the twelfth century onward where available. So what the two investigations show between them is a retreat of the *e*-reflex in favour of the *u*-reflex as well as, further north, the *i*-reflex. Anglo-Saxon charter boundaries, which have *e* sporadically as far west as Dorset and as far north-west as Northamptonshire, go to confirm this. LALME I map 408 shows a slightly smaller area again.

The *LALME* material for OE *ȳ* and lengthened *y* suggests that [e:] < OE *ȳ* remained in parts of the East, parts of the West, and parts of the South in lME; retained [y:] is indicated by spellings from the West and the South (and from the West Riding of Yorkshire), but the vowel seems to have been unrounded in the East and North.

Wyld (1913–14a: 49–51) addresses the questions, what sound was implied by <u>, and why are there so many 'conflicting' spellings for it? He points out that the reflex of OE *ȳ* must have been, or become, different from French [y(:)] in both *i*-areas and *u*-areas; otherwise words with French [y(:)] would have unrounded also. Spellings for OE *ēo* may shed light on this issue, since the reflex of this sound is supposed to have monophthongised to [ø:], also spelt <u>, <ui>/<uy> in the W Midlands. Wyld suggests two possible lines of development in this area (1913–14a: 50):

(a) OE *ēo* > ME [ø:] > [y:], merging with old *ȳ*,
(b) OE *ȳ* > [ø:], merging with or becoming similar to [ø:] < OE *ēo*.

Wyld favours alternative (b), not least because of occasional <e> for OE *ȳ*. Further, he states that (1913–14a: 50)

> I cannot regard this spelling as indicating an ordinary [ĕ] sound, as it unquestionably did in the Eastern *e*-group. It appears not improbable that in some parts of the Midl. area, OE *y̆* had been lowered, and partially un-rounded. The degree of un-rounding no doubt varied in different areas, so that the scribes were at a loss how to express the sound. In some districts it may have had a fair degree of rounding, in others, so little, that *e* seemed not an unsuitable symbol to express it. At any rate one can understand that in spite of the traditional spelling with *u, ui*, this seemed an inapt way of writing two sounds so unlike as French *u* in *fruit*, and OE. *ȳ* in *huiden* 'hide', must have become by the end of the 14th century. The sound had no doubt developed innumerable shades of pronunciation throughout the huge area of the W. and Central Midlands, and may have ranged from something very like the old sound in the extreme South West of the area where this merges into Southern, to a vaguish mid-front vowel, with hardly any rounding, in other parts.

Wyld seems absolutely right in this, and one can only speculate as to the implied phonetic value(s) of <e>, <u>, <ui>/<uy> for OE *ȳ*, and of similar spellings for OE *ēo*. Present-Day Norwegian has a phonemic difference between two high front rounded vowels, [y(:)] (< ON *ȳ*) with in-rounding, and [ʉ(:)] (< ON *ū*) with out-rounding. That is, despite Wyld, one need not resort to partial unrounding, as there are different ways of producing rounded vowels. Additionally, there is lax [ʏ], which lies between [y/i] and [e] in phonetic space.

Another interesting and important fact emerges from analysis of the *LAEME* material for eME *ȳ*, namely, that the sound change does not take effect in all words of a given word class at the same time, but is implemented slowly throughout the lexicon, affecting word by word. Ek also concludes that certain spellings seem particularly frequent for certain words (e.g. 1972: 62). Likewise, Cubbin (1981) finds that the first words with OE *y* to show <i>, implying unrounding, were WRIGHT, KILN, MILL, and *mycel* 'big, much'. Such lexical patterning suggests that *at the outset*, sound change may always be conditioned by the phonetic environment, but that it gathers momentum by analogy or generalisation, and eventually ends up as a more or less 'exceptionless sound-law'. Thus, Neogrammarians and proponents of lexical phonology may both be right: the latter look at the *mechanisms* of change, whereas the former focus on the end *result* of change.

8.3.2 Diphthongisation and raising of eME ȳ

As far as vowel-shift diphthongisation of eME *ȳ* is concerned, the following may be noted. Some *LAEME* spellings indicate diphthongisation: for OE *ȳ*, <dreie> DRY in an unlocalised source (1300–24); for lengthened *y*, <beið> BUY in Essex (1200–24), <bein> BUY in Cambridgeshire (1275–99), <man-keyne> MANKIND in Gloucestershire (1275–99), <beye> and <forbeyen> BUY in Gloucestershire (1275–99); <beyn> BUY in Norfolk (1275–1324). Diphthongisation is likewise suggested by the form <ley> LIE n. (<OE *lyge/lige*, *lygen*), which appears in two sources from Shropshire (1200–24) and Lincolnshire (*c.* 1300). Raising of /e:/ to [i:] is indicated by <i-hierde> HIRE 3.sg.pt. in no. 142 from Kent (1275–99), which otherwise shows dominant <e>.

SMED reports <Dreye> DRY in sources from Cambridgeshire, Essex, Sussex, and Berkshire; their vowel-shift status is unclear.

Some *LALME* spellings indicate vowel-shift diphthongisation: <keynde>, <meynde>, <moynde> for KIND and MIND in Berkshire, Somerset, and Worcestershire; <feir> FIRE in Northamptonshire; <heyden>

Table 8.13 *Spellings for eME* ȳ *in* LAEME[a]

County	No.	Date	OE *ȳ*	OE *y*[b]
Essex	4	1150–99	u ((e, i*, ie))	u,?ui
Berkshire	63	1150–99	u	Ø
Essex	1200	1150–99	u (i) ((eo))	e, i; i
Suffolk	1300	1150–99	i (u) ((e, eo, ui))	i, ui; i, u
Hampshire	143	1175–99	y	Ø
Worcestershire	170	1175–99	u	Ø
Worcestershire	5	c.1200	u ((i*))	u
Worcestershire	2000	c.1200	u (i*)	u; u
Worcestershire	2001	c.1200	u	Ø; u, i
Oxfordshire	232	1175–1224	i	Ø
Essex	64	1200–24	ie, i (e, y)	e; i, u
Essex	65	1200–24	ie	ei
Herefordshire	189	1200–24	i* ((u))	u
Shropshire	260	1200–24	u (i*)	Ø; u
Shropshire	261	1200–24	u ((i*, ui))	Ø; u
Shropshire	262	1200–24	u ((i*))	Ø; u
Shropshire	1000	1200–24	u ((i*))	u; u
Worcestershire	6	1200–49	u (i)	i
Worcestershire	7	1200–49	u ((i*))	i, u
Kent	8	1200–49	e (i)	e, ei
Northamptonshire	66	1200–49	u, i	Ø
Sussex	67	1200–49	i*	Ø
Worcestershire	1900	1200–49	u ((i, ui))	u; u, i
Worcestershire	245	1225–49	u (i*) ((ui))	u; u
Shropshire	272	1225–49	i*	Ø
Herefordshire	273	1225–49	i*	Ø
Shropshire	275	1200–49	u (i*)	u
Worcestershire	1800	1225–49	i* (u) ((ui, ei))	u; u
Somerset	156	c.1240	y, e	Ø
Somerset	157	c.1240	y	Ø
Cheshire	118	1240–50	u ((i, ui))	Ø; i, u
Unlocalised	119	1240–50	u, i, ui	i, ui
Unlocalised	120	1240–50	u (ui, i*)	Ø; u
Unlocalised	121	1240–50	u ((ui, i*))	u; u, i
Cheshire	122	1240–50	u, ui	u; u, i
Unlocalised	123	1240–50	u, i*	u; u
Cumberland	132	13th c.	y	Ø
Surrey	184	13th c.	u (i, y)	Ø
Unlocalised	235	1225–74	u	Ø
Cheshire	124	1250–74	Ø	ui
Gloucestershire	158	1250–74	u, i*	e, u
Worcestershire	276	1250–74	u ((i*))	u; u
Worcestershire	277	1250–74	u ((i*))	u; i, u
Worcestershire	278	1250–74	u ((i, v))	u, i; i (u)

(*continued*)

Table 8.13 (*cont.*)

County	No.	Date	OE $\bar{y}$	OE y^b
Wiltshire	280	1250–74	u ((ou, i*, eo))	u, i; i
Lincolnshire	15	1250–99	y, ie	Ø
Unlocalised	228	1250–99	i*, y*	u
Gloucestershire	271	1250–99	u, ui, i*	Ø
Worcestershire	2	1275–99	u (i*)	Ø; i
Worcestershire	3	1275–99	i*	u
Cheshire	136	1275–99	Ø	Ø; i
Cambridgeshire	137	1275–99	i*	ei
Unlocalised	141	1275–99	i*	Ø
Kent	142	1275–99	e ((ie, éé))	Ø
Devon	147	1275–99	i	Ø
Devon	148	1275–99	i	Ø
Norfolk	150	1275–99	i (ie)	Ø; i
Essex	160	1275–99	e	ey
Gloucestershire	161	1275–99	e	ey; ey, eȝ
Unlocalised	179	1275–99	Ø	i
Unlocalised	180	1275–99	Ø	ie
Gloucestershire	229	1275–99	u	Ø
Unlocalised	238	1275–99	i*	Ø
Unlocalised	241	1275–99	u, i	Ø
Unlocalised	242	1275–99	u (i*)	u
Herefordshire	246	1275–99	u (ui, y*, i*)	u, i
Herefordshire	247	1275–99	u, ui, i*	u, uy; i
Herefordshire	248	1275–99	i (u)	Ø
Herefordshire	249	1275–99	u	Ø
Herefordshire	1100	1275–99	u (i*) ((y*))	u; i, y, u
Norfolk	1400	1275–99	i ((y))	Ø
Gloucestershire	2002	1275–99	ui (i*) ((y*, u))	ui, u, ey; i, ui
Norfolk	1700	1284–89	i	Ø
Lincolnshire	128	c.1300	i*	Ø
Lincolnshire	182	c.1300	i	Ø; i
Worcestershire	187	c.1300	uy	Ø
Gloucestershire	10	1275–1324	u, i	u, ei
Warwickshisre	126	1275–1324	u	Ø
Somerset	163	1275–1324	Ø	Ø; u
West Riding, Yks	256	1275–1324	Ø	Ø; i
Gloucestershire	264	1275–1324	i	Ø
Norfolk	269	1275–1324	Ø	ey
Ely	282	1275–1324	i ((u, y))	y, i, u; i
Oxfordshire	1600	1275–1324	u, uy ((i, y, yu))	u, uy (ui); i
Unlocalised	19	1300–24	ei	Ø
Herefordshire	125	1300–24	ou	Ø
Wiltshire	140	1300–24	u	Ø

County	No.	Date	OE *ȳ*	OE *y*[b]
Norfolk	155	1300–24	i, ie	Ø; i
Durham	188	1300–49	i	Ø
Huntingdonshire	1500	1300–49	i (y) ((u))	Ø
Ely	2003	1300–49	y	Ø
Lincolnshire	169	1325–49	y, e	y; ey

[a] Tokens for OE *þȳster* and cognates, OE *ālȳman, ālȳsednes, gȳmelēast* have been excluded. Only texts with any tokens for OE *ȳ/y* have been included in the table. Asterisked spellings appear for WHY and OE *bȳsen* only.

[b] In this column the forms before the semi-colon are for OE *y* before *cg* or a voiced homorganic consonant cluster; the forms after the semi-colon are for OE *yht*.

HIDE and <neynne> NINE in Shropshire; <fouyre> FIRE in Staffordshire. The forms <fyier>, <fyȝer>, <feore> (in Kent, Norfolk, and Warwickshire) imply a bimoric vowel, and may thus also indicate diphthongisation. One additional source has <feyr> FIRE (Ely or W Norfolk, *c.* 1320–30).

That is, the loci of the diphthongisation of eME ȳ in the 'GVS' are found in the E Midlands (Lincolnshire, Cambridgeshire, Ely, Norfolk, Northamptonshire, and Essex), the W Midlands (Gloucestershire, Worcestershire, Shropshire, and Staffordshire), and the South-West (Somerset and Berkshire); Sussex may also have been affected early. Kent shows raising of eME *ē* (< OE ȳ) to [iː] in the late thirteenth century.

Notes

1 Bately, J. (ed.). 1980. *The Old English Orosius*. Early English Text Society, Supplementary Series 6. London: Oxford University Press.

2 Examples of back spellings are <swȳþe> OE *swīþe* 'very', <scypa> OE *scipu* SHIP gen.pl., <swȳna> OE *swīna* SWINE gen.pl.

3 The *LAEME* items *dryht* 'multitude, army, company', *dryhten* 'lord, ruler' and cognates, as well as *tyht* 'instruction, training', and *tyhtan* 'to stretch, draw' were inadvertently overlooked when the tables of proportions were made. However, it is unlikely that the exclusion of *tyht/tyhtan/dryht* has skewed the proportions of spellings; *dryhten*, on the other hand, is a very frequent word (531 tokens in *LAEME*), and the overwhelming majority of the tokens have <i> for the stressed vowel. Thus, along with *why* and *bȳsen*, *dryhten* may be one of the earliest words in which OE *y/ȳ* was unrounded.

4 However, OE had *bīsen* besides *bȳsen*, and a minor form *hwiȝ* besides *hwȳ* for WHY (Clark Hall 1962). OE *þȳster* 'dark, gloomy' and cognates are frequently spelt with <e(o)>, though all other words with etymological *ȳ* may be spelt with <u>, <ui>/<uy> etc. in the same texts; however, this is most likely due

to the fact that OE had *pēostor* besides *pȳster*, and that the <e(o)> forms in *LAEME* are derived from the former. The spellings extracted indicate that $\bar{y}$ in OE *pēostor* seems to have been native only to the W Midlands (Worcestershire, Gloucestershire, and Herefordshire) and perhaps to Essex; elsewhere, this word seems to have had OE *ēo*. It appears, therefore, that it should be left out of the list of words with OE $\bar{y}$ which formed the basis for the count of dominant and non-dominant forms in Table 8.13. Likewise, OE *ālȳfednes* (from OE *ālīefan* 'to allow, give leave to, grant'), *ālȳse(n)d(nes)* (from OE *ālīesan* 'to loosen, let loose, redeem'), *gȳmelēast(nes)* (from OE *gīemelēas* 'careless, negligent') show patterns different from other OE $\bar{y}$ words; Clark Hall (1962) cites these as having mainly OE *īe*. For this reason, all of the earlier words have been excluded in the count of spellings.

5 In the following texts, WHY is the only lexical item with OE $\bar{y}$ that occurs: nos. 137 (Cambridgeshire), 273 (Herefordshire), 128 (Lincolnshire), 272 (Shropshire), 67 (Sussex), and unlocalised texts (nos. 141, 228, 238).

6 Such texts are nos. 232 from Oxfordshire (1175–1224), 189 from Herefordshire, (1200–24), 273 from Herefordshire (1225–49), 3 from Worcestershire (1275–99), 161 from Gloucestershire (1275–99), and 248 from Herefordshire (1275–99).

7 In <couþe> 1.sg.pres.ind. of OE *cȳþan* 'to proclaim, utter, make known'.

8 In <fousde> from OE *fȳs(e)de*, 1/3 sg.pret. of *fȳsan* 'to send forth; drive away, banish; hasten, prepare oneself'.

9 **Cheshire**: Locality 1: merger in [aɪ] or [ɑɪ]; Locality 2: merger in [æɪ] for some words; Locality 3: merger in [ɛɪ] for some words; Locality 4: merger in [aɪ]; Locality 5: merger in [ɛɪ] or [aɪ]. **Staffordshire**: Locality 2: merger in [ɛɪ]; Localities 7–9: merger in [ɒɪ]; Locality 10: minimal distinction between [ɑːɪ] and [aːɪ]; Locality 11: merger in [aɪ].

10 Clark Hall (1962) cites forms with OE *īe* as the main form for the last three.

11 As discussed in the introductory chapter, the main problem with the *SMED* forms and their interpretation is Kristensson's belief that all LSR spellings indicate strictly local pronunciations and are unaffected by the transmitting scribes – unless they do not square with Kristensson's preconceived ideas about regional distribution, in which case 'scribal influence' is invoked, but not explained. Given the presentation of material in *SMED*, one cannot know how many scribes even in the LSR material wrote e.g. <e> for the reflex of OE $\bar{y}$ in Kent, to take one example.

12 Indeed, when some scribes use a mixture of <i>/<y> and <u>, his interpretation is that 'We may be dealing with a very complex set of dialect boundaries, or we may be dealing with confused scribes. In these circumstances we reject the testimony of the scribes' (1981: 74), even when the material seems to be genuinely local.

13 Regarding <Reydon> in Norfolk (1332), Kristensson points out that the place referred to 'is just on the Sf[k] boundary, and [the form] is due to influence from Sf[k]' (1995: 75). There are similar forms in Suffolk (<Reydone>) and Essex (<Reyndon>), but no mention is made of them here. Later, however,

Kristensson claims that the '[f]orms in <ey> go back to OE **rege*, **regen*' (1995: 141), thus again having recourse to unattested OE forms. It is interesting that all the places with a *ryge* or *rygen* component, for which the Middle English E Midland material gives diphthongal spellings, also have diphthongal spellings in PDE. Thus, Norfolk (1332) has <Reydon>, and the place referred to is now called *Roydon* (not found in Forster 1981; the *Domesday Gazetteer* (Darby and Versey 1975) cites two places called *Roydon* in Norfolk, one called *Regadona/Regedona* in *Domesday Book*, the other *Reiduna*); Suffolk (1327) has <Reydone>, and the places referred to are now called *Raydon* and *Reydon* (modern pronunciation /reɪd(ə)n/, Forster 1981; the places are called *Reinduna/-dune* and *Rienduna* in *Domesday Book*, cf. Darby and Versey 1975); Essex (1327) has <Reydon>, and the place referred to is now called *Roydon* (not found in Forster 1981; the place is called *Ruindune* in *Domesday Book*, cf. Darby and Versey 1975). The ME forms with <Ri–> or <Ry–>, however, all have PDE *Ry-*.

14 Wyld uses his own system of showing whether a spelling is dominant or not; this has been converted into *LALME* usage, with single and double round brackets enclosing secondary and minor forms (based on Wyld's adduced material and his tables). There are, however, a very few mistakes in his tables: Buckinghamshire, for instance, is labelled an '*u-(i-e)* ' county (Wyld 1913–14a: Table I, p. 6), but the adduced spellings for Buckinghamshire do not contain a single form with <e> (1913–14a: 21–2), nor does Table II (starting opposite p. 32). Moreover, his notation does not always include very infrequent spellings; Table 8.11 does.

CHAPTER 9

Summary and conclusions

> It is absurd to dogmatize where, at the best, intelligent speculation must take the place of certainty.
>
> H.C. Wyld (1936: 232)

9.1 Summaries of long-vowel shifts

The irregular spellings extracted and analysed in the preceding chapters are generally occasional; that is, they are usually rare and aberrant even in the texts in which they are found. Additionally, the material is complex and the spellings point in different directions with respect to their phonetic correspondences. Therefore, it is worth repeating Curzan and Palmer's caution that the linguist must avoid the temptation 'to extrapolate too far from the particular database/genre under analysis, since its examples tell us not about language generally and entirely but about language in that specific discourse or genre, in those available texts' (2006: 21). Texts from early ME are particularly rare, at least from the North and the Central Midlands; thus, one should refrain from generalising on the basis of irregular spellings recorded in these areas. The analysis of the corpus material has therefore been 'a synthesis of introspective and observational procedures' (McEnery and Wilson 2001: 19). However, certain patterns have emerged in the available material, as described in the preceding chapters and as summarised in the following.

9.1.1 The development of OE ȳ

The reflexes of OE *ȳ* and lengthened OE *y* unrounded first in the North and parts of the E Midlands; by *c.* 1300, unrounding appears to have been completed in the North, in the NE Midlands, and in Devon. However, a retained [y:] may have co-varied with [i:] in S Lancashire until the early fourteenth century. There is of course much earlier evidence from lOE, even from the West-Saxon area, testifying to the unrounding of lOE *ȳ*, as reported by Gradon (1962). Spellings suggesting the development *ȳ* > [e:] are attested in *LAEME* sources entered in Essex and Suffolk from the late twelfth century, in Kent from the early thirteenth century onwards, and in the South-West from the mid-to-late thirteenth century. A front close rounded vowel was retained in large parts of the country until late ME, and they are not confined to the W Midlands: <u>, <ui>/<uy> start to appear in Berkshire, Essex, Suffolk, and Worcestershire from the late twelfth century, in Northamptonshire, Herefordshire, and Shropshire in the early thirteenth century, in Cheshire, Gloucestershire, Oxfordshire, Wiltshire, and Surrey in the mid-to-late thirteenth century, and also in the NE Midlands in the early fourteenth century. However, given that <i> is dominant in the E Midlands, it is difficult to believe that [y:] was retained in this area at such a late date.

The later material from *SMED* and *LALME* generally confirms the traditional tripartite division: unrounding of *ȳ* to [i:] took place in the North and East, lowering and unrounding to [e:] was a feature of Eastern and South-Eastern dialects, and retention of [y:] was a characteristic of the W Midlands. However, lowering and unrounding to [e:] is also suggested by eME <e>-type spellings in parts of the South-West. Additionally, the border areas are fuzzy, and the authorities disagree on the details, for which the reader is referred to Chapter 8.

There is, however, general consensus (Wyld 1913–14a, 1913–14b; Ek 1972; *SMED*) that in the early 1300s, the *i* area comprised all the six northern counties, except perhaps S Lancashire, as well as Lincolnshire, Nottinghamshire, Rutland, Peterborough, Huntingdonshire, and Norfolk. There is also mostly agreement that the *e* area included all of Suffolk, Essex, Kent, E Sussex, and E Surrey, and that the W Midlands and the South still had [y:], although Devon may have been an [i:]-area. Minor <i> and <e> variants are found all over the South and SW Midlands.

Vowel-shift raising of the reflex of eME *ȳ* > [e:] to [i:] is indicated in a late thirteenth-century *LAEME* source entered in Kent. Vowel-shift diphthongisation of /i:/ (< eME *ȳ*) is indicated in the early 1200s in Essex and Shropshire, and in the late 1200s in Cambridgeshire, Gloucestershire, Norfolk, and Lincolnshire. *SMED* sources from the early fourteenth century report potential vowel-shift spellings in Cambridgeshire, Essex, Sussex, and Berkshire, thus corroborating the *LAEME* material. *LALME* has vowel-shift spellings in texts localised to Berkshire, Somerset, Worcestershire, Shropshire, and Northamptonshire, and the additional sources indicate vowel shift in the Ely/W Norfolk area *c.* 1320–30. Hence, the loci of the diphthongisation of eME *ȳ* must be sought in the E Midlands, the W Midlands, and the South-West.

9.1.2 The development of OE ā

The backing and rounding of the reflex of OE *ā* seems to have started simultaneously in the (S)W Midlands, the SE Midlands, and the South-East, as *LAEME* sources entered in these areas show dominant <o> at an early stage (1150–1225). Kitson (pers. comm.) has found <o> in a Dorset source from the latter half of the eleventh century, and Liebl (2006) believes the change started in the eleventh century, based on analysis of lOE and eME place-name material. Liebl concludes that the change of OE *ā* > /ɔ:/ 'might have started in Late Old English more or less simultaneously in several counties in the South as well as the East and West Midlands and radiated from there' (2006: 30). This agrees well with my own findings. The change *ā* > *ǭ* appears *not* to have been complete by 1225 in all SME, however, but may have been a slow process which did not reach completion until lME.

Kristensson (1967) concludes from the *SMED* material that in the early 1300s, the divide between SME *ǭ* and NME *ā* cut across the middle of Lancashire, the middle of the West Riding of Yorkshire, and the middle of Lincolnshire, from the Ribble in the west to the North Sea in the east. Isophones change over time, so the *ā*/*ǭ*–divide may have been slightly different in the fifteenth century, as indicated by the *LALME* material, in which <a> is attested also in the NE Midlands and North Central Midlands. The recorded spellings in *SMED* and *LALME* demonstrate continued use of <a> even in lME, even in the far south. But as the bulk of the evidence suggests backing and rounding of OE *ā* from at least the eleventh century in SME, such late <a> spellings in possibly all cases reflect early shortening, whether in compounds or habitually unstressed position; certainly from the evidence as presented in *LALME*, no clear cases have been noted of <a> for OE *ā* in free position, though it is a question whether recourse to the texts themselves would alter this view.

The *LAEME* material surprisingly shows less frequent <o> for OE *ā* in the vicinity of <w>. It is possible that if the change *w*+*ā* > [wɔ:] was early, <o> needed to be used only in contexts where it was not predictable, for Liebl finds that the presence of /w/ was 'highly conducive to the raising and rounding' of *ā* (2006: 24), which is what one would expect (simple progressive assimilation). However, Benskin (1982b), examining texts which form part of *LALME* LP 472 (East Riding of Yorkshire), finds that OE *ā* is variously spelt with <a> or <o>, but that OE *ā+w* is regularly <aw> in, for example, KNOW and OWN. Thus, the distribution of <a> vs. <o> is clearly conditioned before *w*, whereas it is hard to find any conditions when *ā* is in free position. Retention of <a> before *w* is in fact a characteristic of late NME semi-standardised texts. Forms with <o> are, however, common for OE *swā* from an early date, which implies that this very frequent word was a leader in the lexical diffusion of [ɔ:].

In NME, OE *ā* remained, and was eventually fronted and raised. Use of <æ>, <ea>, <eo>, <ei>, etc. is attested in *LAEME* sources entered in the South, SE Midlands, and the W Midlands from the late twelfth century onwards, and is not recorded in Northern texts until the mid-thirteenth century. This may be a corollary of the fact that Northern texts from the eME period are scarce, but <e>-type spellings are also extremely infrequent in *SMED*, and are found only in Gloucestershire, Somerset, and Lincolnshire; they are likewise uncommon in *LALME*, but a very few such forms are recorded in texts entered in Yorkshire. The paucity of <e>-type spellings for OE *ā* in the North suggests either that the fronting and raising of *ā* was later than we are led to believe, or that traditional spellings were retained regardless of sound-change. Smith (1994: 436) concludes from occasional <ee> in Chaucerian MSS that [ɛ:] or even [e:] had been reached in NME by Chaucer's time. Smith regards the Northern change *ā* > [æ:] > [ɛ:] as part of the Northern Great Vowel Shift (Smith 1994: 434–6).

Liebl agrees with Lutz (2004) that SME OE *ā* > [ɔ:] and OE *ǣ* > [ɛ:] were roughly simultaneous and may have been early instances of long-vowel raising. Lutz believes the latter could have been a prelude to the 'GVS', which is possible. However, if the changes affecting the two low vowels OE *ā* and *ǣ* were simultaneous, and one of them is interpreted as a prelude to the 'GVS', there is no reason to deny the same status to the other change. If this be permitted, the raising of the two open vowels may have been the trigger that set the vowel shift in motion; Lutz regards this as evidence that the shift was a push-chain in conventional terms. As is clear from the foregoing discussion, the metaphor is not regarded as useful in the present work. In fact, these changes underline my own conviction that treating only some vowel-changes as part of a shift is arbitrary.

9.1.3 The development of OE ǣ

It is difficult to use spellings to determine the course of change of OE *ǣ* in ME, as use of <æ> was slowly discontinued after the Norman Conquest, and <e> may equally correspond to [æ:], [ɛ:], and [e:]. Besides, non-Saxon OE had *ē* for WS *ǣ*^{2}, so there is considerable uncertainty as to the phonetic correspondences of <e>. Still, the authorities agree that the spellings for the shortened products of OE *ǣ* are useful, in that [æ:] was shortened to <a>, and [e:] was shortened to <e>; indeed, analysis of shortened forms for *strǣt* STREET is behind the traditional identification of the [e:] vs. [æ:] domains for *ǣ*^{2}. However, the three corpora exploited do not contain (potential) shortened forms in such quantity that they were deemed worth using.

The material extracted does not contradict the conventional account that all OE dialects had [æ:] for *ǣ*^{1} (<WGmc *ai+i*), and that *ǣ*^{2} (<WGmc *ā*) was reflected as Saxon [æ:], and Anglian and Kentish [e:]. Certainly, the two reflexes are not kept apart in any of the corpora, but there are higher numbers of <a>/<æ>/<ea> for *ǣ*^{2} than for *ǣ*^{1} in the W Midlands sources in *LAEME*, which is as expected. The high frequency of <a>-type spellings in the E Midlands probably indicates, at least partly, the East Saxon development *ǣ*^{2} > [a:]. The digraph <ea> is a W Midland innovation; it is possible that it arose as a means of distinguishing the two *e*'s ([e:] and [ɛ:]/[æ:]) orthographically.

Lutz (2004) believes the raising of OE *ǣ* to [ɛ:] started in the eleventh century, which seems reasonable, given the high number of <e> even in the earliest *LAEME* sources; see the preceding section for Lutz's interpretation of the early raising of the two open long monophthongs. Further raising to [e:] may be in evidence from the mid-thirteenth century. If so, etymological *ē* must have started to raise also by this date, since the two reflexes were kept apart far into the eModE period. Forms with <i>/<y> in both *LAEME* and *SMED* are indicative of raising all the way to [i:]; they are recorded in WRY, the NE Midlands, the South-West, and Worcestershire in the period 1250–1330. Such spellings are exceedingly rare in later ME and eModE, which suggests that the variants [e:] and [i:] co-existed for a lengthy period of time, and that the latter was rare, both regionally and lexically. The lexical leader in this change may have been SILLY, for which there are a few very early <i> forms. Zachrisson (1913) and Dobson (1968) agree that the orthoepistical evidence suggests [i:] from the sixteenth century, although [i:] for OE *ǣ* was not adopted into the standard language until the seventeenth or eighteenth century.

9.1.4 The development of OE ē and ēo

Old English ē

Early <i(e)> and <y(e)> which are not AN spellings for [e:] are recorded from the late twelfth century in *LAEME* sources: eME *ē* > [i:] is thus indicated in Hampshire, and possibly Oxfordshire, Essex, Suffolk, and Worcestershire, in the period 1150–1200; in Kent and possibly Sussex in the period 1200–49; in Wiltshire 1250–74; in Gloucestershire, Cambridgeshire, and Norfolk in the period 1275–99; and in Lincolnshire and Oxfordshire *c.* 1275–1324. That is, the South-East, the E Midlands, and the SW Midlands are likely loci of the change.

Wełna (2004) adduces forms with <i>/<y> for *ē* from Gloucestershire, Shropshire, Oxfordshire, Lancashire, Yorkshire, London, and Norfolk, from *c.* 1290 onwards, which in large part agrees with my own findings. However, some of the *ē*-words cited by Wełna must have raised *ē* to [i:] early, since they participate in the (presumably later) vowel shift of ME *ī* > PDE /aɪ/. For this reason, the raising of ME *ē* is sensibly divided into two stages: an early one affecting words, mainly of French origins (e.g. FRIAR, DICE, but also BRIAR), and a later one, affecting the remaining *ē*. Still, the surviving evidence is not much earlier for the presumed earlier change than for the later change, so such a division remains – at this stage – a theoretical possibility more than an empirical certainty. There is the added problem of explaining why some ME *ē*-words participated in the earlier change, while the majority of *ē*-words did not. The preponderance of French words subject to the earlier change suggests that the tense [e:] of OFr or AN was identified with English /i:/ in the course of borrowing (cf. Dobson 1968: 655).

In *SMED*, a few <i>/<y> for OE *ē* seem to imply vowel shift, in the North Riding of Yorkshire, Lincolnshire, Huntingdonshire, Norfolk, Warwickshire, and Somerset. Thus, they are scattered across the country, but seem to cluster in the NE Midlands and possibly in the South-West. Vowel-shift spellings in *LALME* are reported in the West Riding, Norfolk, the South-East, and in the SW Midlands. The additional sources give evidence of raising in S Yorkshire/N Lincolnshire (*c.* 1300), Kent (*c.* 1350), W Lincolnshire/E Leicestershire (*c.* 1350–1400), Devon (*c.* 1380), Herefordshire (1390s), and Nottinghamshire (1435 and 1483). Thus, the area around Lincolnshire stands out as a locus of change, which is corroborated by the late forms from Nottinghamshire. Together, the ME evidence implies that ME *ē* > [i:] started independently in the SW Midlands, the E Midlands, and Yorkshire. Wyld

(1936: 206–7) believes that the present value [i:] had been reached 'before the end of the fourteenth century', a view borne out by the present investigation.

Old English ēo

OE *ēo* > [ø:] in the eleventh century, and was unrounded to [e:] in the course of the ME period. *SMED* material suggests that all of the North had [e:] in the first half of the fourteenth century, even the southern part of Lancashire; so did the E Midlands. In the W Midlands in the early fourteenth century, Derbyshire, Nottinghamshire, Leicestershire, and probably Cheshire, had [e:]; Shropshire, Staffordshire, Herefordshire, Worcestershire, Warwickshire, Gloucestershire, and Oxfordshire probably still had [ø:] or raised [y:], though this [ø:]/[y:] may have begun to unround to [e:]. It seems likely that [ø:]/[y:] and [e:] were used side by side for some time. The same is true for at least parts of the South, where <e> is dominant in the early fourteenth century, but where rounded reflexes still linger on (except in Sussex and Kent). Ek (1972) believes that not only Kent, but also London, Middlesex, Essex, Hertfordshire, and S Cambridgeshire had *īe* (< *īo*) for the reflex of OE *ēo* *c.* 1300. Numerous <ie> in *LAEME* may support this claim, but they may equally be interpreted as AN spellings for [e:]; Kristensson (1995: 123, n.92) dismisses Ek's claim on grounds of frequency. At any rate, collation of Ek's and Kristensson's materials shows that by 1300, <ie> was indeed recessive and its domain considerably smaller than Ek suggests.[1]

Judging by the *LAEME* material, OE *ēo* > [i:] early in Suffolk, Essex, and Lancashire in the late twelfth and early thirteenth centuries, and in the NW Midlands and Kent in the period 1200–50; raising may be in evidence in Norfolk in the period 1275–1325. *SMED* has a few <i>/<y> in the early 1300s. Here, the E Midlands, the South-East, and the South-West stand out. *LALME* spellings indicating vowel shift cluster in the North, the NW Midlands, and the NE Midlands.

9.1.5 The development of eME ō

The SME shift ō > [u:]

Innovative spellings in *LAEME* indicate that eME *ō* had begun to raise to [u:] in the (S)W Midlands (Worcestershire, Herefordshire, Gloucestershire, and perhaps Wiltshire) in the period *c.* 1175–1250, in Cambridgeshire *c.* 1275–99, in Oxfordshire and Ely between 1275 and

1325, and in Wiltshire (and possibly Lincolnshire) in the early fourteenth century.

In *SMED*, innovative spellings appear all over the North, in parts of the E Midlands (Huntingdonshire and Berkshire), and across the W Midlands and the South. They are especially frequent in the South, SW Midlands, and far North. Forms with <u> are clearly most frequent in the North, but are also recorded in the South-East and South-West. The spelling <uo> for ME *ō*, which is found in some quantity in a *LAEME* source entered in Oxfordshire, is found almost exclusively in Kent in *SMED*. Samuels (1971: 9) believes such <uo> forms in Kentish sources may indicate a rising diphthong [wo] or [wɔ].

In *LALME*, innovative spellings are found in most of the South and the Midlands; they are most numerous in Wiltshire and Lincolnshire. In the additional sources, spellings which indicate raising are found in texts entered in Ely/W Norfolk (*c.* 1320–30) and W Lincolnshire/E Leicestershire (*c.* 1350–1400).

Taken together, the irregular spellings for eME *ō* imply that the raising of the vowel began in the early thirteenth century, and that it started in the (S)W Midlands and in the (N)E Midlands. In the *SMED* corpus, the South also stands out, and the absence of vowel-shift forms from the South in the earlier material is probably due to the scarcity of early ME texts from this area. Wyld (1936: 238) is confident that

> Probably further investigation of fourteenth-century texts would show that during the first half of this century old *ō* became, in the Eastern dialects [...] a sound approximating to if it not quite attained the character of [ū]. From thence it passed into the London dialect.

The NME shift ME ō > [ü:]

Only one *LAEME* form may indicate NF, in a source from Durham, no. 188 (1300–50); <ow> in Lincolnshire sources may indicate NF or raising to [u:]. The earliest indications of NF are in fact <u> forms found in *SMED*, in rolls from Durham, Northumberland, and the East Riding of Yorkshire (all 1290s). In the first half of the fourteenth century, forms with <u>/<w> and <ou> are found in all the northern counties (except Westmorland), as well as in Cheshire. NF may therefore have started in the northernmost counties of England in the mid-to-late thirteenth century, which confirms the traditional account. Conservative <o> is dominant by far in *SMED*. In *LALME*, forms with <u>, <ou> are found all over the northern area of survey, but texts with northern language also use conventional <o> spellings in abundance. In many northern sources, <u> and <o> co-vary.

Thus, the adoption of <u>, <ui>/<uy> for the reflex of ME *ō* had not been effected over the whole northern area by the late fifteenth century; but whether the conventional spellings suggest that the *change* had not been completed in all NME by *c.* 1450, or whether the conventional *spellings* just lingered on for some time, is difficult to determine. Sources with mixed spellings may in fact testify to change in progress. If so, NF may have taken much longer to diffuse through the lexicon than has been assumed, and NF may consequently have been going on at the time when the 'GVS' started. On the other hand, as NF was a purely realisational change, there was no need for the scribes to indicate it in spelling, cf. Britton (2002). Hence, conservative <o(o)> for *ō* need not entail 'no Northern Fronting'.

9.1.6 The development of ME ī

In *LAEME*, incipient diphthongisation of OE *ī* seems to be in evidence in texts entered in Essex, Shropshire, Worcestershire, and Gloucestershire. For OE *i* in lengthening contexts, diphthongisation is implied in Essex, Ely, Cumberland, Durham, Herefordshire, besides Gloucestershire. The status of <ei>/<ey> for the reflexes of OE *eaht* and *eoht* remains uncertain,[2] but they are found in Essex, Norfolk, Worcestershire, and Gloucestershire. The digraphs <ei>/<ey> for eME *ī* are attested in *LAEME* from the first half of the thirteenth century onwards. Analogical <awi> AWAY is found in Worcestershire (no. 278, 1250–74), and strongly suggests an [əi]-like diphthong for ME *ī* in the W Midlands.

In *SMED*, diphthongisation of ME *ī* is indicated as follows. For OE *ī*, <ey> is found in Northumberland, Staffordshire, Warwickshire, Cambridgeshire, Hertfordshire, and Kent, in the period 1307 to 1330; the earliest spellings are attested in Hertfordshire and Northumberland. A few <ei>/<ey> for OE *–ig-* are recorded in Essex, Lincolnshire, and Norfolk. For late OE *–iht*, some <ey> are reported in Leicestershire, Bedfordshire, and Cambridgeshire. Analogical <y> for etymological *ei* appears in Hampshire and Somerset. Diphthongisation of ME *ī* is therefore indicated in the E Midlands and the South in the early 1300s.

In *LALME*, forms with <ay>, etc. for ME *ī* are found in Cornwall, Norfolk, and Staffordshire. For the reflex of OE *ī*, numerous <ey> are found in Wlt 5371; other forms with <ei>/<ey> are recorded in sources entered in Cumberland, Ely, Leicestershire, Lincolnshire, and Norfolk, pointing to the NE Midlands as a locus of change. For OE *i* in lengthening environments, <ei>/<ey> appear across the country. For OE *ēah*, one <ay> is attested in Norfolk. Analogical <i>/<y> for etymological *ei, ai* is found all over the country.

Material from additional sources indicates vowel shift in Ely/W Norfolk around 1320–30 (Hunt and Benskin 2001), and in Nottinghamshire or Herefordshire *c.* 1390 (Black 1998). The <ay> forms from Nottinghamshire (*c.* 1496) adduced by Whitehall (1935) certainly suggest advanced diphthongisation of the reflex of ME *ī* in the NE Midlands in the late 1400s. So also do <ay>/<ai> in Norfolk and Essex sources from the latter half of the fifteenth century (Zachrisson 1913).

Clearly, the Midlands, both East and West, stand out as possible loci of change. Stockwell concludes from ME as well as modern dialectal evidence that 'the vowel shift *must* have gotten a head start in this part of the country' (2006: 179; his emphasis), referring to the W Midlands in general, and to Gloucestershire in particular. However, vowel-shift spellings are found all over the country, although in smaller numbers in the North and the South. Ogura (1985, 1990) has found that the most advanced PDE pronunciations of the reflex of ME *ī* are found in Essex and Oxfordshire, and that these hence were likely loci of change in ME, at least with respect to the 'GVS'.

9.1.7 The development of eME ū

The dating of the diphthongisation of the reflex of ME *ū* is difficult, mostly because <ou>/<ow>, adopted after the Norman Conquest, may equally correspond to [u:] and to [ʊu]/[əu]. Conclusive evidence is thin on the ground before *c.* 1450, but detailed examination of the orthographic systems of some of the *LAEME* texts with early irregular spellings has revealed that vowel shift likely started in the SW Midlands (Worcestershire, Herefordshire, and Gloucestershire) in the mid-to-late thirteenth century, in Ely in the period 1275–1324, and in the East Riding of Yorkshire in the early fourteenth century. In *LALME*, <au>/<aw> are found in Nottinghamshire, Lancashire, and Wiltshire, and <oou> for OE *ū* is attested in Huntingdonshire and Nottinghamshire. One additional source reports other anomalous forms in Ely/W Norfolk *c.* 1320–30 (Hunt and Benskin 2001). Clearly, at least some of the aberrant spellings cluster in the NE Midlands and the W Midlands, and may be signs of incipient regional sound-change. The other anomalous spellings, for example in Lancashire and the East Riding of Yorkshire, may be independent inventions, but are likewise indicative of vowel shift. Statistical analyses of the proportions of <u>-type vs. <ou>/<ow>-type spellings for ME *ū* in ME might reveal lexical and regional preferences. For instance, it is reasonable to assume that <ou>/<ow> were first used in French loans and in the London/Westminster area, and close analysis of the available material might support or disprove this assumption.

9.1.8 Conclusion

In conclusion, the (S)W Midlands and the E Midlands stand out as loci of long-vowel changes in ME. This could simply be a corollary of the fact there is more surviving eME material from these areas than from the North, the South and the Central Midlands, but as the findings for early ME are in fact supported by the later material, the likelihood of such an explanation is diminished. Irregular spellings indicating early vowel shift are quite numerous, as the present work has shown, and they suggest that the changes conventionally subsumed under the 'GVS' started in the mid-to-late thirteenth century. If the changes to OE *ȳ*, OE *ēo*, OE *ǣ*, the SME change to OE *ā*, and NF are also included, an even earlier date must be assumed for this putative 'ME long-vowel shift'; more on the dating of ME long-vowel changes is found in Section 9.3.

9.2 Isolative vs. combinative change, and lexical diffusion

Spellings which imply early vowel shift have often been dismissed as showing exceptional developments in certain phonetic environments; so, for instance, early <i>/<y> for etymological *ē* before [r] (Section 4.2.4). This view is probably informed by the *a priori* assumption that the 'GVS' was an isolative change. However, such 'exceptional' changes could *be* the early stages of the 'GVS': it has been concluded in previous chapters – and this might be the most unexpected finding of this work – that nearly all the long-vowel changes examined seem to have started as combinative sound-changes, whose outputs were subsequently extended by analogy to other (and eventually all) phonetic environments.

For instance, OE *ā* seems to have been backed and rounded first in the vicinity of [w] and/or [n], more specifically in the words *swā* SO, *nāwiht* NOT and *ān* ONE (cf. Liebl 2006). In this context, the vacillation between *a* and *o* before nasals in (non-Mercian) OE should be borne in mind, as should the effect of lengthening before homorganic consonant clusters (which critically includes a nasal plus another consonant), which may well have destabilised the old *ā* vs. *ō* contrast. After Anglo-Frisian fronting, there seems to have been genuine uncertainty as to whether the vowel was *a*-like or *o*-like before a nasal. Acoustic analyses of PDE [ɑ:] and [ɔ:], especially in the vicinity of [w] and [n], might prove fruitful, in that they may elucidate which phonetic environments are most favourable for rounding of open central/back vowels.

Likewise in seemingly combinative change, the reflex of ME *ē* appears to have raised first before [r] in words of French origin (cf. Wełna 2004). ME *ī* may have diphthongised first before dental, dentalveolar and alveolar consonants (due to co-articulation); besides, the digraphs <ei>/<ey> are more frequent before voiced consonants than before voiceless ones (Maci 2006). The lexical range and degree of attestation are very high indeed for OE *ȳ*, and on the evidence of the spellings, OE *ȳ* may have unrounded to [i:] first in the words WHY, *dryhten* 'lord, ruler' and *bȳsen* 'example', as <i> greatly preponderates in these words from an early date. A leader in the raising of OE *ō* may have been GOOD, and Prins (1942b) finds that raising took place in the vicinity of non-velars first.

Similar conclusions have been reached for, for example, the deveopment of /æ/ in the Northern Cities Shift in present-day AmE (Labov 1994: 180–193). These findings are in agreement with the principles of lexical phonology, which state that sound-changes usually take place in very frequent words first, whence they spread by analogy to other words of the same set. Bybee (2001: 1) states that her work

> introduces into the traditional study of phonology the notion that language use plays a role in shaping the form and content of sound systems. In particular, the frequency with which individual words or sequences of words are used and the frequency with which certain patterns recur in a language affects the nature of mental representation and in some cases the actual phonetic shape of words.

Therefore, the Neogrammarians and the proponents of lexical phonology may both be right with respect to theories of sound-change. That is, they have simply looked at different stages of change: The Neogrammarians formulated 'exceptionless sound-laws' because they looked at the result of a change *after* its completion, whereas lexical phonologists look at the *mechanisms* of change, especially the initial stages of a change and the phase during which the change is being implemented.

9.3 The dating of the 'GVS'

It is often claimed that <ei>/<ey> for eME *ī* cannot be used as evidence for the diphthongisation of *ī* because the product never merged with original *ei*. In that case, <i>/<y> cannot be used as evidence for the raising of eME *ē* either, since the raised product never merged with original *ī*. Similarly, <u> and <ou>/<ow> cannot be used as evidence for the raising of eME *ō* because the raised product never merged with original *ū*. Finally, <au>/<aw> cannot be used as evidence for the diphthongisation of eME *ū* because the diphthongised product never merged with original *au*. In short, no irregular spellings are admissible as evidence for sound-change at all if the new sound did not merge with the historical sound traditionally spelt the same way as the irregular spellings. Clearly, such a view fails to consider the status of irregular spellings: They are by definition outside the normal orthographic system, and they may represent subconscious interference from speech habits (cf. Chapter 1). Interference from speech is not the only source or irregular spellings, however: Other sources could be eye rhymes and analogy. Orthography is a visual medium, and there are various reasons why a particular scribe would write a word anomalously.

Perhaps the most compelling reason for interpreting some of the disputed spellings as evidence for diphthongisation of ME *ī* and *ū* may be the evidence for the other constituent changes, by logical inferences *post facto*: If the reflexes of ME *ē* and *ō* had started to raise, the reflexes of ME *ī* and *ū* must have started to diphthongise, as merger would otherwise have ensued. Therefore, even if the evidence for the diphthongisation of *ī* and *ū* is inconclusive in itself (due to the ambivalence of the phonetic correspondences of <ei> and <ou>), and circumstantial at best, the less controversial evidence for the raising of ME *ē* and *ō* necessarily implies the simultaneous diphthongisation of *ī* and *ū*. If, therefore, the adduced spellings for ME *ē* and *ō* are accepted, raising of ME *ē* and *ō* and diphthongisation of ME *ī* and *ū* appear to have started in parts of the E Midlands and W Midlands in the course of the thirteenth century.

Wyld (1927, 1936) and Kökeritz (1954) postulate a relatively early date for the initial stages of the shift. Kökeritz remarks that it was then common to date the early stages of the vowel shift to the very early fifteenth century (1954: 9). But by then, he says, ME *ē* and *ō* had begun to be pronounced [i:] and [u:], respectively, and ME *ī* and *ū* had started to diphthongise. It is conventional when reading Chaucer's poetry aloud to (1954: 9)

> use a kind of standardized ME that supposedly was current in London [...] from, say, 1200–1400. Since language is never static, such a pronunciation would probably sound old-fashioned to Chaucer, could he hear it, perhaps reminding him of the speech of his grandparents. Late 14th-century speakers undoubtedly used very close variants of *ẹ̄* [e:] and *ọ̄* [o:] verging on [i:]

> and [u:], and they must already have been diphthongizing *ī* [i:] in *like* and *ū* [u:] in *house* to a certain extent.

Wyld similarly maintains that ME *ē* must have reached its present [i:] stage before the end of the fourteenth century, and that ME *ō* may very well have approximated [u:] in the early fourteenth century in the East (1936: 238). Wyld's work remains curiously ignored, perhaps due to Dobson's dismissal of much of Wyld's evidence or hypotheses (Dobson 1968: *passim*, e.g. §§107, 115 (Notes 2 and 4), 116, 132 Note). Dobson's reasons for rejecting Wyld's evidence and hypotheses are based on (1) the orthoepists' statements, (2) Dobson's own theories, and (3) Dobson's differing interpretations of the adduced spellings as being either analogical, or conventional, or showing quantity variation, or demonstrating shortening under weak stress, etc. However, many of the orthoepists' statements must be taken with a pinch of salt, and it is unclear why Dobson's theories are superior to Wyld's. Analogical and conventional spellings must of course be reckoned with, but Dobson's insistence that the majority of <i> for ME *ē* are due to shortening under weak stress or quantity variation seems *ad hoc*.

The dating of the initial stages of the 'GVS' depends on which changes are regarded as part of the shift. It is evident from the conclusions drawn in preceding chapters that there is a considerable temporal overlap between the supposedly early changes affecting OE *ȳ*, OE *ēo*, OE *ǣ*, OE *ā* (in SME), and OE *ō* (in NME) on the one hand, and the 'GVS' on the other (Table 9.1). Consequently, justification for treating them as separate changes is hard to find. Rather, long-vowel raising, diphthongisation, and fronting have been, and are, recurring processes in the history of English, and the ME period simply appears to be a particularly intensive period of such vowel-shifting.

Since the individual etymological long vowels did not generally merge, except in the close and close-mid front vowel area, it is obvious that many of the changes in question must have been roughly simultaneous. Otherwise, a series of mergers would have taken place. However, since the reflex of OE *ȳ* generally *did* merge with that of eME *ī*, the unrounding of [y:] to [i:] must have been earlier than the other changes. The backing and rounding of the reflex of OE *ā* did not result in merger, as there was no open back rounded long vowel prior to this change. Thus, [ɑ:] > [ɔ:] may have taken place either before or after the changes affecting the mid and close vowels. There is considerable vacillation between conservative <a> and innovative <o> for OE *ā* for a lengthy period of time; so also the replacement of

Table 9.1 *The dating of ME and eModE long-vowel shifts*

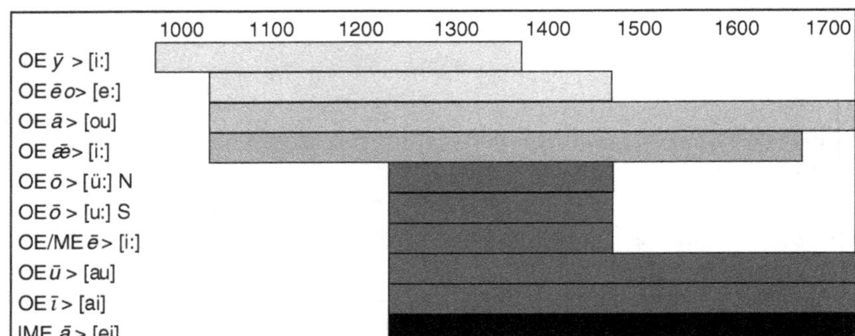

etymological <o> by <u> for NME *ō* was still not fully worked out by 1500. This lag in orthography shows either the power of spelling tradition, or else shows that the changes took longer to reach completion than the received wisdom will have it. It is of course possible that these explanations both hold, but in different areas. Conservative spellings are to be expected, however, as NF did not produce a new phoneme, only a new realisation of the pre-existing phoneme, and there was consequently no reason for changing the orthography (Black 1998; Britton 2002). Nevertheless, subconscious interference from pronunciation may produce unconventional spellings, and such spellings are not really rare even in eME. If my interpretation of these be permitted, the vowel shift may well have started in the thirteenth century; certainly, in the fourteenth century, the shift was well on its way. If the changes to OE *ǣ* and OE *ā*, and the vocalisation of post-vocalic OE *g*, are included, this comprehensive ME long-vowel shift started in the eleventh century at the latest, and did not come to a halt (if indeed it did) until perhaps the mid-eighteenth century.

9.4 The 'GVS' in a wider perspective

The findings summarised in 9.1 indicate clearly that the traditional 'GVS' is only one part of some long-term drift in English (and other Gmc languages), and that the conventional definition of the shift is untenable.

9.4.1 The inception of sound-change

Stockwell and Minkova (1988a, 1988b, 1997), Wełna (1988), Pilch (1997), Ritt (1994) and Stepanovicius (1997, 2005) all point to other systemic changes as either triggering the shift, or lending support to its effectuation and outcome. Such systemic changes include the vocalisation of post-vocalic consonants producing new diphthongs, homorganic lengthening, SHOCC, MEOSL, TRISH, etc. Ultimately, such quantitative changes are probably due to the Gmc stress accent and to the formation of 'ideal syllables' (Ritt 1994), or 'the introduction of strict bimoraicity in stressed syllables' (Lorentz 1996: 113); Prokosch (1939: §50) asserts that the Gmc stress accent is responsible for the 'standardization of the quantity of accented syllables that took place in all Germanic languages during the 13th and 14th centuries' (cf. Antonsen 1965: 23–25; Árnason 1980: 86ff.; but see Bermúdez-Otero 1998). Crucially, such quantitative changes could have played a more prominent role in the inception of the 'GVS' than has been traditionally assumed. Williamson claims explicitly that the 'GVS' and OSL 'may be intimately connected temporally and causally' (2006: 10–11), in that the upward pressure in NF was triggered by the northern OSL of *o*, whose output [o:] 'encroached on the ambit of' historical *ō* (2006: 11). Pelt (1980) similarly sees a connexion between the Dutch vowel shift and open syllable lengthening, and Eliasson (2010) maintains that quantitative changes triggered the Swedish back-vowel shift. Indeed, Sweet (1888) stated that 'The influence of quantity on other changes is very marked, especially as regards vowels' (1888: 30). Clearly, the relationship between lOE/eME quantitative changes and ME long-vowel changes ought to be properly assessed, so as to confirm or refute the various hypotheses that they are all related – changes in quantity still constitute largely unexamined, and perhaps undecidable, parts of English language history. Essentially, lOE and eME vowel lengthenings and shortenings should all be included in a proper assessment of long-vowel changes. Abstracting only *some* of these changes and labelling them 'the Great Vowel Shift' fails to recognise the phonological history as a whole and how sub-parts of phonological systems are interconnected.

The present work has been concerned with *when* and *where* questions regarding ME long-vowel changes, but it does not seem out of place to ask at this point *why* there is phonetic change in the first place. Indeed, if phonemes are viewed as occupying small, fixed points in the vowel space, sound-change poses a vexing problem; in the Jonesian vowel chart of cardinal vowels, sounds do seem to occupy small and fixed points, but Jones was of course concerned with specific phones, not phonemes. However, at least since Weinreich, Labov and Herzog (1968), there has been increased awareness of inherent variation and variability in all areas of language. Further, 'decades of empirical observation demonstrate conclusively that [variation is not purely random and idiosyncratic]: linguistic variation turns out to be patterned and orderly' (Guy 1994: 133); there is 'orderly heterogeneity' to use Weinreich, Labov and Herzog's term. To be sure, some idea of variation must have been present in the Neogrammarians' notion of sounds too, as they clearly distinguish between isolative changes and combinative changes, and the latter take place exactly because of the influence of neighbouring sounds on the affected phone. Yet it is implicit in their 'exceptionless sound laws' that sounds are particle-like entities which either do or do not undergo a given change. Labov (1994: *passim*, e.g. p. 99), on the other hand, shows explicitly how phonemes occupy larger areas in the articulatory-acoustic space by virtue of their range of allophones, and the limits of the range of each phoneme is shown schematically as an ellipse. That is, 'the units in a system are realized variably. Their realizations are presumed to scatter (within limits) in articulatory-acoustic space' (Williamson 2006: 2). For instance, the allophones of PDE /e/ are generally lower before /l/ than before /t/ in RP, and so its articulatory-acoustic range covers the close-mid to open-mid front area. It only takes a gradual shifting of the (frequencies of) realisations and limits of a phoneme for it to change. For example, ME *ē* would have occupied a certain area in the vowel space, with possibly closer allophones realised before alveolars, and with less close allophones before velars, due to co-articulation or anticipation. If the closer allophones were generalised by analogy, the 'GVS' would have been on its way. The articulatory range of a phoneme, represented schematically as an ellipse, is called an 'ambit' by Williamson (2006: 3; cf. Section 6.2.5):[3]

> the spatial dimensions of different, but "neighbouring" vowels may overlap in realization. Processes of change, such as merger and split, can be conceived in terms [of] how ambits change. For example, the development of a significant degree of dimensional overlap between the phonetic ambits of two phonemes may lead to merger.

Such 'dimensional overlap' between ambits could be caused by allophonic variation and allophonic change; speech habits change over time (Smith 2007: 77–8). For example, in GA, acoustic analysis of some informants' speech (Labov 1994: 98–101) reveals dimensional overlap between the ambits of /æ/ (the closer allophones) and /e/ (the more open allophones), but as long as the phonetic contexts in which the overlapping allophones occur are different, there is no danger of merger; when allophones of separate phonemes overlap in the *same* contexts, however, merger ensues.

Hajek (1997) makes interesting observations regarding the reasons for sound-change. Admittedly, he is concerned with nasalization, but the reasons he postulates seem equally plausible for other types of sound-change: In essence, there is a mismatch between Speaker A's production (articulation) of a sound, and Speaker B's perception, and subsequent production, of the same sound. Speaker B (in learning the language) tries to emulate by articulatory means the perceptual stimulus he receives from Speaker A's production, and may be only partly successful. Bybee expresses the same view when, after identifying muscular gestures as the mechanisms 'responsible for the majority of attested sound changes' (2001: 200), she stresses that (2001: 200)

> it is important to bear in mind that the articulatory changes they handle all must also have an acoustic-perceptual component, as such changes in articulation cannot be transmitted across speakers except via the acoustic dimension. Thus, no study of articulatory mechanisms is complete without an associated study of the acoustic-perceptual mechanisms of transmission.[4]

Another issue is the shape of the vowel space and the consequences of our visual representation of this space for our perception of vowel change. This is best illustrated by MEOSL and the supposed attendant raising of short vowels when lengthened (and supposed lowering of long vowels when shortened, cf. Section 4.1). Thus, handbooks traditionally insist that ME /e/ was raised when lengthened, as the lengthened product is spelt <i>; ME /i:/, when shortened, on the other hand, is spelt <e>, suggesting lowering. Kristensson hence dismisses <u> for ME /o:/ as evidence of vowel-shift, because lME /o:/ and /u/ are said to be partners in a 'quantitative correlation' (2001: 80). It seems, however, that lME /o:/ and /u/ can only be *perceived* partners in a quantitative correlation if it can be shown that eME *ō* had shifted to /u:/ already. One would think that the long vowels would have to be at least slightly raised for there to be a quantitative correlation between /u/ and /o:/ (unless the correlation is purely etymological), at least if one believes in the trapezoid diagram of the vowel space, which is in fact anatomically misleading: Prokosch (1939: 97–8) uses the shape of a somewhat distorted ellipse or ovoid for the articulatory vowel space (with especially the high back corner knocked off), as do Labov (1994: 256–60) and Labov, Ash and Boberg (2006), in which [ʊ] and [o:], and [ɪ] and [e:], are much closer than they appear to be in the standard Jonesian diagram.[5] Articulatorily, [ɪ] and [ʊ] are half-close rather than close, and they 'are acoustically and perceptually much more like [e, o] than [i, u]' (Lass 1992: 3). Besides, shortened [e:] and [o:] 'tend to be perceived as /ɪ, ʊ/' by speakers of German (1992: 3). Schane (1990) explains these facts in terms of phonological aperture: the three phonetic

Table 9.2 *ME and eModE long-vowel shifts*

OE vowel, PDE reflex	Type of change	Date of beginning of change
ȳ > *ī* > /aɪ/	unrounding	950
	diphthongisation	1250
ēo > *ø̄* > *ē* > /iː/	monophthongisation	11th century
	unrounding	12th–15th centuries
	raising	1250
ā > *ǭ* > *ō* > [ou] > /əʊ/	rounding	11th century
	raising	16th century
	diphthongisation	16th century
ǣ > *ę̄* > *ē* > /iː/ or /eɪ/	raising	/ɛː/ 11th c.; /eː/ 15th c.; /iː/ 16th c.
	(diphthongisation)	(16th–17th centuries)
ē > /iː/	raising	1225
ō > */uː/ or /ʊ/ ~ /ʌ/*	raising	1225
	shortening; unrounding	14th–15th centuries; 15th–16th centuries
NF: ō > [üː]	(often fronted in PDE)	
	NF: fronting and raising	(late) 13th century
ī > /aɪ/	diphthongisation	1250
ū > /aʊ/	diphthongisation	1250

features of vowel height, laxness, and retracted tongue root are related, both acoustically and articulatorily. Acoustically, '[ɪ] and [eː] have nearly identical formant values', but 'they will be perceived differently *because of the length of the vowel*' (1990: 11, his emphasis). In fact, all the three phonetic features are characterised by a higher F1. Articulatorily, the three features involve varying degrees of openness, centrality, and pharyngeal narrowing (1990: 13). In essence, the issues surrounding MEOSL and its output may in fact be *caused* by our representing the vowel-space as a trapezoid; that is, they are pseudo-problems. Representing the articulatory vowel-space in a more realistic way, and combining acoustic and articulatory approaches, might prove fruitful for the entire discipline of historical phonology.

With respect to the changes analysed here, it is possible to break down all ME long-vowel changes into a small number of recurring phonetic processes, that is, raising, fronting, diphthongisation, monophthongisation (of a nucleus plus identical off-glide), new diphthongisation (from vowel plus vocalised off-glide), etc., as indicated in Table 9.2.

This reveals the cyclical nature of vowel systems and raises the question, *Are these types of changes somehow related?* Such a view seems to go counter to what I have claimed earlier, that systemic considerations only do not explain the 'GVS'. I do not believe in the 'GVS' (or any other vowel or consonant shift) as a *Ding an sich*, but it seems clear that they are somehow *systemic* in nature, although this system would probably be much bigger than that consisting of long monophthongs only. In fact, vowel-shifts of the type witnessed in ME are attested in most other Gmc languages also, along with quantitative changes similar to MEOSL, SHOCC, and TRISH. Again, this raises questions like, *How is Gmc different from other IE languages, and how may this difference cause the changes considered here?* The one thing that makes early Gmc stand out from its IE relatives is the fixing of the stress on the root-syllable of all lexemes, and the development of stress-timing. This, then, is where the source of a large number of qualitative and quantitative Gmc sound-changes must be sought.

To give a measure of credence to such a statement, it is necessary to identify the phonetic correlates of stress. Stress may involve pitch prominence (accent), intensity (perceptual loudness, muscular effort, and greater expiration of air), duration, and any combination of these (Ladefoged 1962; Gimson 1970; Sweet 1888: 33; Versloot 2008: 239). Research on prelinguistic infants by Davis *et al.* (2000) suggests that prosodic features like respiratory force are acquired before words: 'At a pre-lexical stage these infants are producing acoustic correlates of adult stress to some degree independent of the linguistic details of the adult lexicon' (2000: 1264). Further, Grossman *et al.* (2010: 778) state that 'Despite its complexity, typically developing [...] children and adults are able to preceive and comprehend this prosody automatically' from an early age, and they find that the same applies generally to high-functioning autistic children. These findings seem to indicate that humans are wired to perceive, understand, and make use of prosodic cues prior to lexical learning.

Astruc and Prieto (2006) conclude that vowel quality, spectral balance, and longer duration are acoustic correlates of stress, while correlates for accent are pitch and overall spectral intensity. The fundamental frequency is also believed to correlate systematically with stress in stress-timed languages, but Ortega-Llebaria and Prieto find that duration effects are the more consistent result of stress. Interestingly (2010: 91),

> the largest duration differences between stressed and unstressed syllables are found in the [a]-[ə] alternation, showing that the changes in vowel quality between corresponding vowels not only provide a spectral correlate to the stress contrast, but they also have the effect of amplifying the duration differences that were triggered by stress.

Vowel reduction, on the other hand, has been found to correlate with formant frequency differences (Ortega-Llebaria and Prieto 2010: 91, and references there cited). As a consequence, stressed syllables and vowels behave differently from unstressed syllables and vowels. Since stress in Gmc involves intensity (perceptual loudness and more muscular and respiratory force) in addition to pitch prominence, various articulatory features are a consequence of stress: stressed vowels are longer and usually more peripheral (in terms of the vowel space), fortis plosives have more aspiration, etc. Lack of stress, on the other hand, involves little muscular effort and perceptual 'softness', and often low/level pitch; unstress therefore has articulatory consequences like shorter and more centralised vowels (or at least loss of vowel contrasts, cf. Lass 2009), vowel reduction, vowel and consonant elision, and little to no aspiration of fortis plosives, etc. Thus, what is known as the 'syncopation period' in early Gmc may be interpreted as only the beginning of a long process involving the gradual reduction and loss of unstressed vowels and syllables, the last major instance of which is witnessed (in English) in the loss of final schwa. Related to this reduction process are the lOE and ME processes that lengthen vowels in open syllables and shorten vowels in words of two or more syllables. Clearly, metrical considerations play a crucial role here, as indeed pointed out by Ritt (1994).

So what could cause such large-scale changes in both vocalic quality and quantity? To answer this question, historical linguists have often resorted to phonemic considerations and metaphors like 'push-chains' and 'drag-chains', which labels are believed not only to capture the phonetic reality of the sound-changes they describe, but also to *explain* them (cf. Section 1.1). Phonologists often lose sight of the phonetic bases of phonology, simply because chain-shifts do seem to happen in order to uphold phonological systems. However, to account for sound-changes in a phonetically responsible manner, I believe we must return to phonetics: (1) one must break down systemic sound-changes into their constituent phonetic parts (as in Table 9.2), and (2) one must find empirical evidence from synchronic articulatory and acoustic phonetics that accounts for the processes revealed by (1). For instance, acoustic analyses of all the PDE long vowels and their range of allophones might throw light on the phonetic processes involved in the ME long-vowel shifts examined here, given the Uniformitarian Principle,[6] and may establish the phonetic contexts which are most conducive to raising, fronting, and diphthongisation. Acoustic, perceptual, and articulatory analyses of stressed vs. unstressed sounds might reveal important differences which may underlie recurring tendencies in the history of not only English but of Gmc generally. Examination of the distribution of stress and accent in disyllabic words in Gmc is likely to shed light on both segmental and supra-segmental phenomena like stress-levelling, pitch peak delay, development of contrastive tone, stress shift, vowel lengthening, etc., as argued convincingly by Versloot (2008).

Sweet (1888: 19–21) in fact formulated the basic principles of vowel-change, which by definition suggests recurrence; he states that 'Long vowels tend to narrowness, raising, and cleaving [i.e. diphthongisation]; short vowels to widening, lowering, and smoothing' (1888: 30; cf. Sievers 1850). In more recent years, Stockwell (1978) and Labov (1994) have formulated very similar principles (though couched in different terms and within different theoretical frameworks), and Labov, Ash and Boberg (2006: Chapter 3) establish a whole set of such principles, based on both acoustic and articulatory measurements. Samuels (1972: 21–5, 42, 145), in formulating similar principles, pays more attention to prosodic features (cf. Berndt 1982) like stress and unstress, forceful styles and relaxed styles of pronunciation.

Table 9.2 reveals that in English, long vowels tend to be fronted and raised, front close vowels tend to be diphthongised, back close vowels are either fronted or diphthongised, and new diphthongs tend to be produced from the vocalisation of post-vocalic liquids and semi-vowels. Research on articulatory phonetics suggests that (in Gmc), the tongue is more tense for long monophthongs (simply to keep it stable for the duration of their pronunciation), and that the tongue tends to be closer and more fronted for long monophthongs than for short/lax monophthongs (Samuels 1972: 21). This would in large part explain why long vowels are often fronted and raised in Gmc (for example in NF, the 'GVS', parts of the Dutch vowel shift, and the Norwegian/Swedish back-vowel shift), and short vowels are lowered and backed (Northern Cities Shift, Canadian Shift, parts of the New Zealand English short-vowel shift). A momentary 'under-shooting' of the target in the pronunciation of long close vowels would explain the development of onset glides, producing minimal diphthongs as allophones of /i:/ and /u:/, as witnessed in present-day Swedish [ʋijn] 'wine', in Cockney and Australian English [bɪit] or [bəit] BEAT (Wells 1982: 306; cf. Sweet 1888: 21–2). Thus, although no sound-change is ever necessary, when sounds do change, they tend to follow certain paths in Gmc. This view of (systemic) sound-changes as based in simple articulatory, acoustic, segmental, and supra-segmental phonetics is in fact supported by my empirically based conclusion that many or all of the vowel changes here considered were combinative at the outset.

In conclusion, I believe that the inception of sound-changes, as well as the paths they take, is the result of language-internal – articulatory, acoustic-perceptual and prosodic – properties, and that diachronic sound-change is best elucidated and explained by empirical phonetic research on present-day languages and ongoing processes of change.

9.4.2 The adoption and spread of sound-change

Whereas I believe the inception of sound-changes is caused by language-internal factors, their adoption and spread is properly the domain of socio-linguistics (Berndt 1982: 201). 'Typically, changes spread in two dimensions, one linguistic and one social; that is, they make their way through both the language system, spreading from [phonetic] context to [phonetic] context, as well as through the social system, moving from speaker to speaker' (Gordon 2001: 5). Raumolin-Brunberg provides interesting insights in this respect, although she is not concerned with long-vowel shifts. She adopts the model introduced by Labov (1994: 65), which divides the time taken from an innovative form is first introduced into a speech community until the change has been completed, into five distinct phases (Raumolin-Brunberg 2006: 125).

1. The 'incipient' phase, where the new form is found in less than 15% of potential cases
2. The 'new and vigorous' phase, where the frequency of the new form is 15–35%
3. The 'mid-range' phase, where the new form occurs in 36–65% of cases
4. The 'near-completion' phase, in which the frequency of the new form is 66–85%
5. The 'completed' phase, where the new form is found in more than 85% of cases.

Leaders of linguistic change are defined as those persons who use a new form in more than 30% of potential cases in the *incipient* phase, in which the *average* is below 15%; leaders in the new and vigorous phase are those individuals who use the innovative form in more than 50% of potential cases, when the average lies between 15% and 35%. Raumolin-Brunberg finds that such a distinction is valid, since the leaders of a change in an incipient phase may not be the same individuals as those that are leaders in the next phase. For three innovative forms which spread in lME and eModE,[7] she finds that the leaders were to be found in the middle classes (merchants, professionals, gentry) in the incipient stages, and that the changes spread from there to the higher and lower ranks; that the leaders in the new and vigorous phase, however, were influential people with a very high social standing (nobility and royalty); that the same individuals were not necessarily leaders in all changes, but could be innovative with respect to certain changes, and conservative with respect to others; that women were often leaders, as were 'geographically mobile people, most likely with a great many weak [social] links' (2006: 130); that regional *origins* were to be detected for certain changes, but that the changes were *spread* through the capital; and finally that for a linguistic change to catch on and be spread generally across the country and across the population, it would have to be adopted and used by people with the very high social status. Labov (1994: 78) states that 'no cases have been recorded in which the highest-status social group acts as the innovating group', which is supported by Raumolin-Brunberg's findings. Similar analysis of 'GVS' spellings might corroborate or rebut Raumolin-Brunberg's conclusions, as it seems to be generally accepted now that at least the raising of the reflex of ME *ā* to [e:], in the late stages of the 'GVS', was promoted by the 'Mopsae' (London society ladies) of the sixteenth century (Dobson 1968: §102; Smith 1993: 270). In other words, middle class 'upwardly mobile' women from London were leaders in the incipient phase of new [e:] for conservative [ɛ:] < ME *ā*.

It has also been observed that 'sound changes begin at a slow rate, progress rapidly in midcourse, and slow down in their last stages' (Labov 1994: 65), which produces a characteristic S-shaped curve for the rate of sound-change (cf. Denison 1999). This 'slowing down' in the last stages of sound-change explains (a) why, in the 'completed stage', an innovative form may not be found in 100% of the potential contexts, and (b) why there are virtually always exceptions to sound-changes. Lexical diffusion simply comes to a halt before all the eligible lexis is affected. Thus, there is always a certain amount of irregularity, obscuring what the direction of change may have been at the outset.

Notes

1 Ek may still be correct in assuming that some of the areas surrounding Kent (with both Saxon and non-Saxon reflexes) originally also saw the development OE *ēo* > *īo* > *īe*, as it would be difficult to account for the 18% <i>-forms in the period 1100–1300 otherwise.

2 The diphthongisation of ME *ī* involves not only the reflexes of OE *ī* and *i* before homorganic consonant clusters and before *g*, but also the reflexes of OE *i/eo/ea+ht*, OE *ēag/ēah*, and OE *ēog/ēoh*.

3 A 'real' ambit is shown for instance by Smith (2007: 76).

4 Similar views were expressed by Sweet, as early as in his *History of English Sounds* (1888: 15).

5 Besides, [u] can never be as back as [ɑ], because the highest point of the tongue cannot be close *and* very back, for obvious anatomical reasons, which explains the diachronic as well as synchronic tendency to front /u:/ (cf. Wells 1982: 147–8, 303). Labov, Ash and Boberg (2005) find that the acoustic vowel-space is triangular, while articulatory vowel-space is egg-shaped, with [i] and [ɑ] making up the ends of the ovoid. This discrepancy might go some way towards explaining the mismatch between production and perception.

6 For instance, Ortega-Llebaria and Prieto (2010: 92) report that in Dutch, 'stressed [a] reduced to unstressed [ɑ] by lowering F1 and F2 and raising F3, while no significant formant frequency differences were found for stressed vs. unstressed [o]'. Such or similar processes may be significant in the vowel changes examined here.

7 The three innovations are (1) the spread of the object form *you* into subject position, (2) the replacement of *–th* by *–s* for the 3.pers.sing.pres.ind., and (3) the loss of *–n* in *mine/thine* as attributive adjectives.

References

Aitken, A.J. 1981. 'The Scottish Vowel-Length Rule'. In: Benskin, M. and M.L. Samuels (eds.). *So meny people longages and tonges: philological essays in Scots and mediaeval English presented to Angus McIntosh*. Privately published; 131–157.

Aitchison, J. 1987. 'The Language Lifegame: Prediction, Explanation and Linguistic Change'. In: Koopman, W. *et al.* (eds.). *Explanation and Linguistic Change*. Amsterdam: John Benjamins; 11–32.

Aitchison, A.J. 1991. *Language Change: Progress or Decay?* Cambridge University Press.

Algeo, J. and T. Pyles. 2005 [5th ed.]. *The Origins and Development of the English Language*. Boston: Thomson Wadsworth.

Anderson, J. 1988. 'The Great Kentish Collapse'. In: Kastovsky, D. *et al.* (eds.). *Luick Revisited*. Tübingen: Gunter Narr Verlag; 97–107.

Anderson, J.M. and C.J. Ewen (eds.). 1980. *Studies in Dependency Phonology. Ludwigsburg Studies in Language and Linguistics 4*. Ludwigsburg: R.O.U. Strauch.

Anderson, S. 1966. *West Scandinavian Vowel Systems and the Ordering of Phonological Rules*. Ph.D. thesis, Illinois Institute of Technology.

Antonsen, E. 1965. 'On Defining Stages in Prehistoric Germanic'. *Language* 41/1: 19–36.

Árnason, K. 1980. *Quantity in Historical Phonology: Icelandic and Related Cases*. Cambridge University Press.

Astruc, L. and P. Prieto. 2006. 'Stress and accent: acoustic correlates of metrical prominence in Catalan'. URL: http://prosodia.upf.edu/home/arxiu/publicacions/astruc/astruc_stress-accent-metrical-prominence.pdf

Auer, P. 1993. 'Is a rhythm-based typology possible? A study of the role of prosody in phonological typology'. *KontRI Working Paper No. 21*, University Konstanz.

Bately, J. 1980. *The Old English Orosius*. Early English Text Society, Supplementary Series 6. London: Oxford University Press.

Baugh, A.C. and T. Cable. 2005. *A History of the English Language*. Oxford: Routledge.

Bazell, C.E. 1962. 'Six Questions of Old and Middle English Morphology'. In: Davis, N. and C.L. Wrenn (eds.). *English and Medieval Studies Presented to J.R.R. Tolkien on the Occasion of His Seventieth Birthday*. London: George Allen and Unwin; 51–62.

Beals, K. *et al.* (eds.). 1994. *CLS 30 (Papers from the 30th Regional Meeting of the Chicago Linguistic Society). Volume 2: The Parasession on Variation in Linguistic Theory*. Chicago: the Chicago Linguistic Society.

Benediktsson, H. (ed.). 1970a. *The Nordic Languages and Modern Linguistics*. Reykjavik: Vísindafélag Íslendinga.

Benediktsson, H. 1970b. 'Aspects of Historical Phonology'. In: Benediktsson, H. (ed.). *The Nordic Languages and Modern Linguistics*. Reykjavik: Vísindafélag Íslendinga; 87–129.

Bennett, J.A.W. and G.V. Smithers (eds.). 1966. *Early Middle English Verse and Prose*. Oxford: Clarendon Press.

Benskin, M. 1977. 'Local Archives and Middle English Dialects'. *Journal of the Society of Archivists* 5/8: 500–514.

1982a. 'The Letters <þ> and <y> in Later Middle English, and Some Related Matters'. *Journal of the Society of Archivists* 7: 13–30.

1982b. 'Marian Verses from a Hedon Manuscript: some new materials for the Middle English dialectology of the East Riding'. *Revista Canaria de Estudios Ingleses* 5: 27–58.

1989. 'Some Aspects of Cumbrian English, Mainly Medieval.' In: Breivik, L.E. *et al.* (eds.) *Essays on English Language in Honour of Bertil Sundby.* Oslo: Novus Forlag; 13–46.

1991a. 'The "Fit"-Technique Explained'. In: Riddy F. (ed.). *Regionalism in Late Medieval Manuscripts and Texts. Essays celebrating the publication of a Linguistic Atlas of Late Mediaeval English*; 9–26. Cambridge: D.S. Brewer; 9–26.

1991b. 'In Reply to Dr. Burton'. *Leeds Studies in English. New Series* XXII: 209–262.

1992. 'Some New Perspectives on the Origins of Standard Written English'. In: van Leuvensteijn, J.A. and J.B. Berns (eds.). *Dialect and Standard Language/Dialekt und Standardsprache in the English, Dutch, German and Norwegian Language Areas*. Oxford; 71–105.

1994. 'Descriptions of Dialects and Areal Distributions'. In: Laing, M. and K. Williamson (eds.). *Speaking in Our Tongues*. Cambridge: D.S. Brewer; 169–187.

2002. 'Chancery Standard'. In: Kay, C., C. Hough and I. Wotherspoon (eds.). *New Perspectives on English Historical Linguistics. Selected papers from 12 ICEHL, Glasgow, 21–26 August 2002*. Amsterdam/Philadelphia: John Benjamins; 1–40.

Forthcoming. 'A Charm Against Thieves'. Paper on MS, Northamptonshire Record Office, Finch-Hatton 3047.

Benskin, M. and M. Laing. 1981. 'Translations and *Mischsprachen* in Middle English Manuscripts'. In: Benskin, M. and M.L. Samuels (eds.). *So meny people longages and tonges*. Privately published; 55–106.

Benskin, M. and M.L. Samuels (eds.). 1981. *So meny people longages and tonges: philological essays in Scots and mediaeval English presented to Angus McIntosh*. Privately published.

Bermúdez-Otero, R. 1998. 'Prosodic Optimization: The Middle English Length Adjustment'. *English Language and Linguistics* 2/2: 169–197.
Berndt, R. 1982. *A History of the English Language*. Leipzig: Verlag Enzyklopädie.
Black, M. 1998. 'Lollardy, Language Contact and the Great Vowel Shift'. *Neuphilologische Mitteilungen 1 XCIX 1998*: 53–69.
Blair, Peter H. 1991. *An Introduction to Anglo-Saxon England*. Cambridge University Press.
Bloomfield, L. 1926. 'A Set of Postulates for the Science of Language'. *Language* 2: 153–164.
Boisson, C. 1982. 'Remarques sur la chronologie interne du grand changement vocalique en anglais'. In: *Apports français à la linguistique anglaise. Travaux 35*, CIEREC. Université de Saint-Etienne.
Brisard, F. and M. Meeuwis. 1994. 'Variability and Code Allocation in Theory Formation on Language Change'. In:Beals, K. *et al.* (eds.). *CLS 30 (Papers from the 30th Regional Meeting of the Chicago Linguistic Society). Volume 2: The Parasession on Variation in Linguistic Theory*. Chicago: The Chicago Linguistic Society;13–26.
Britton, D. 2002. 'Northern Fronting and the North Lincolnshire Merger of the Reflexes of ME /u:/ and ME /o:/'. *Language Sciences* 24: 221–229.
Britton, D. and K. Williamson. 2002 (ms.). 'A review of *Northern Fronting* and its developments in England and Scotland'. Paper read at the 12th ICEHL, Glasgow, Scotland, 23 August 2002.
Brown, C. (ed.). 1950. *English Lyrics of the XIIIth Century*. Oxford: Clarendon Press.
(ed.). 1952. *Religious Lyrics of the XIVth Century*. Oxford: Clarendon Press.
Burrow, J. (ed.). 1992. *English Verse 1300–1500*. London: Longman.
Burton, T.L. 1991. 'On the Current State of Middle English Dialectology'. *Leeds Studies in English. New Series* XXII: 167–208.
Bybee, J. 2001. *Phonology and Language Use*. Cambridge University Press.
Cabanillas, I. de la Cruz. 1999. 'Northern Features in *The Reeve's Tale*'. In: López, A.B. *et al.* (eds.). *'Woonderous Ænglissce', SELIM Studies in Medieval English Language*. Universidade de Vigo; 43–50.
Campbell, A. 1959. *Old English Grammar*. Oxford: Clarendon Press.
Catford, J.C. 1977. *Fundamental Problems in Phonetics*. Edinburgh University Press.
Clark Hall, J.R. 1960. *A Concise Anglo-Saxon Dictionary*. Cambridge University Press.
Crothers, J. 1978. 'Typology and Universals of Vowel Systems'. In: Greenberg, J. (ed.). *Universals of Human Language: Phonology*. Stanford University Press; 93–153.
Cruttenden, A. 2014. *Gimson's Pronunciation of English*. Abingdon: Routledge.
Cubbin, G.P. 1981. 'Dialect and Scribal Usage in Medieval Lancashire: A New Approach to Local Documents'. *Transactions of the Philological Society 79/1*: 67–117.
Curzan, A. and C.C. Palmer. 2006. 'The Importance of Historical Corpora, Reliability, and Reading'. In: Facchinetti, R. and M. Rissanen (eds.). *Corpus-Based Studies of Diachronic English*. Bern, New York etc.: Peter Lang; 17–34.

Dance, R. 2002. Review of Kristensson 2001. *Notes and Queries, September 2002*: 398–399.
Darby, H.C. and G.R. Versey. 1975. *Domesday Gazetteer*. Cambridge University Press.
d'Ardenne, S.R.T.O. 1961 (for 1960). *Þe liflade ant te passiun of Seinte Iuliene*. Early English Text Society, Original Series 248. London: Oxford University Press.
Dauer, R. 1983. 'Stress-timing and Syllable-timing Reanalysed'. *Journal of Phonetics* 11: 51–62.
Daunt, M. 1939. 'Old English Sound-Changes Reconsidered in Relation to Scribal Tradition and Practice'. *Transactions of the Philological Society 38/1:* 108–137.
Davidsen-Nielsen, N. 1972. *English Phonetics*. Oslo: Gyldendal.
Davis, B.L. *et al.* 2000. 'Prosodic Correlates of Stress in Babbling: An Acoustical Study'. *Child Development* 71/5: 1258–1270.
Davis, N. 1968. Review of Kristensson 1967. *Notes and Queries 1968, Vol. 15, No. 7*: 270–272.
Davis, N. and C.L. Wrenn (eds.). 1962. *English and Medieval Studies Presented to J.R.R. Tolkien on the Occasion of his Seventieth Birthday*. London: George Allen and Unwin.
Denison, D. 1999. 'Slow, Slow, Quick, Quick, Slow: The Dance of Language Change'. In: López, A.B. *et al.* (eds.). *'Woonderous Ænglissce', SELIM Studies in Medieval English Language*. Universidade de Vigo; 51–64.
Dieth, E. 1932. *A Grammar of the Buchan Dialect*. Cambridge: W. Heffer and Sons.
Dinkin, A. and W. Labov. 2007. 'Bridging the Gap: Dialect Boundaries and Regional Allegiance in Upstate New York'. Paper read at the Penn Linguistics Colloquium 31, 24 February 2007.
Dobranski, S.B. 2005. *Readers and Authorship in Early Modern England*. Cambridge University Press.
Dobson, E.J. 1955. 'Early Modern Standard English'. *Transactions of the Philological Society 54:1*: 25–54.
1961. Review of Stanley 1960. *Notes and Queries 206, Nos. 10, 11, 12.*
1968. *English Pronunciation 1500–1700, Vol. I.* Oxford: Clarendon Press.
Dobson, E. 1969. 'Notes on Sound-Change and Phoneme-Theory'. *Brno Studies in English, Volume Eight*. Brno; 43–48.
Donegan, P.J. 1985. *On the Natural Phonology of Vowels*. New York: Garland.
Unpublished conference paper. 'The English Vowel Shift: A Typological Perspective'.
Durian, D. and M.J. Gordon. 2011. 'What are we talking about when we talk about vowel shifts'. Paper presented at NWAV 40, 30 October 2011, Georgetown University.
2012. *A New Perspective on Vowel Variation across the 19th and 20th Centuries in Columbus, OH*. Ph.D. dissertation, The Ohio State University.
Eaton, R. and W. Koopman. 1987. 'Introduction'. In: Koopman *et al.* 1987; 1–10.
Eaton, R. *et al.* (eds.). 1985. *Papers from the 4th International Conference on English Historical Linguistics*. Amsterdam, Philadelphia: John Benjamins.

Ek, K-G. 1972. *The Development of OE ȳ and ēo in South-Eastern Middle English*. Lund: Gleerup.

Ekwall, E. 1975. *A History of Modern English Sounds and Morphology*. Oxford: Basil Blackwell.

Eliasson, S. 2010. 'Kedjeförskjutningen av långa bakre vokaler och svenskans «tionde» vokal'. *Studier i svenska språkets historia* 11: 127–136.

Endresen, R.T. 1988. *Fonetikk: ei elementær innføring*. Oslo: Universitetsforlaget.

Facchinetti, R. and M. Rissanen. 2006. *Corpus-Based Studies of Diachronic English*. Bern, New York etc.: Peter Lang.

Fisiak, J. (ed.) 1997. *Studies in Middle English Linguistics*. Berlin and New York: Mouton de Gruyter.

Forster, K. 1981. *A Pronouncing Dictionary of English Place-Names*. London, Boston and Henley: Routledge and Kegan Paul.

Frankis, J. 1986. 'The Great Vowel-Shift and Other Vowel-Shifts'. In: Nixon, G. and J. Honey (eds.). *An Historic Tongue: Studies in English Linguistics in Memory of Barbara Strang*. London: Routledge; 133–137.

Gimson, A.C. 1970. *An introduction to the pronunciation of English*. London: E. Arnold.

Gnanadesikan, A.E. 1997. *Phonology with ternary scales*. Ph.D. dissertation, University of Massachusetts.

Gordon, M.J. 2000. 'Tales of the Northern Cities'. *American Speech*, 75, 4: 412–414.

2001. *Small-Town Values and Big-City Vowels: A Study of the Northern Cities Shift in Michigan*. Publication of the American Dialect Society. Number 84. Durham: Duke University Press.

Gradon, P. 1962. 'Studies in Late West-Saxon Labialization and Delabialization'. In: Davis, N. and C.L. Wrenn (eds.). *English and Medieval Studies Presented to J.R.R. Tolkien on the Occasion of His Seventieth Birthday*. London: George Allen and Unwin; 63–76.

1979. *The Ayenbite of Inwyt. Vol. II*. Early English Text Society, Original Series 278. London: Oxford University Press.

Grossman, R.B. *et al.* 2010. 'Lexical and Affective Prosody in Children with High-Functioning Autism'. *Journal of Speech, Language, and Hearing Research* 53: 778–793.

Guy, G. 1994. 'The Phonology of Variation'. In: Beals, K. *et al.* (eds.). *CLS 30. Papers from the 30th Regional Meeting of the Chicago Linguistic Society. Volume 2: The Parasession on Variation in Linguistic Theory*; 133–149.

Hajek, J. 1997. *Universals of Sound Change in Nasalization*. Oxford: Blackwell.

Hanham, A. 1975. *The Cely Letters 1472–1488*. Early English Text Society, Original Series 273. London: Oxford University Press.

Hart, J. 1569. *An Orthographie, Conteyning the Due Order and Reason, Howe to Write or Paint Thimage of Mannes Voice, Most Like to the Life or Nature*. London.

Haugen, E. 1970. 'The Language History of Scandinavia: A Profile of Problems'. In: Benediktsson, H. (ed.). *The Nordic Languages and Modern Linguistics*. Reykjavik: Vísindafélag Íslendinga; 41–79.

1976. *The Scandinavian Languages. An Introduction to their History*. London: Faber and Faber.

Haugen, E. and T.L. Markey. 1972. *The Scandinavian Languages. Fifty Years of Linguistic Research (1918–1968)*. The Hague: Mouton.

Heltveit, T. 1953. *Studies in English Demonstrative Pronouns. A Contribution to the History of English Morphology*. Oslo: Akademisk Forlag.

Hickey, R., M. Kytö, I. Lancashire and M. Rissanen. 1997. *Tracing the Trail of Time. Proceedings from the Second Diachronic Corpora Workshop*. Amsterdam: Rodopi.

Hogg, R.M. 1983. 'The Sound of Words: Some Phonological Influences on English Vocabulary'. *Bulletin of the John Rylands University Library of Manchester* 66/1; 88–104.

1992. *A Grammar of Old English*. Oxford: Blackwell.

1997. 'Using the Future to Predict the Past: Old English Dialectology in the Light of Middle English Place-Names'. In: Fisiak, J. (ed.). *Studies in Middle English Linguistics*. Berlin, New York: Mouton de Gruyter; 207–220.

Holthaus, E. 1885. 'Beiträge zur Geschichte der englischen Vokale'. *Anglia* 8: 86–144.

Hudson, A. 1969. 'Review of Kristensson 1967'. *The Review of English Studies*, XX, 77: 68–69.

1989. 'Review of Kristensson 1987'. *The Review of English Studies, New Series*, XV, 157: 104–105.

Hudson, R. 1997. 'Inherent Variability and Linguistic Theory'. *Cognitive Linguistics* 8/1: 73–108.

Hunt, T. and M. Benskin (eds.). 2001. *Three Receptaria from Medieval England. The languages of medicine in the fourteenth century*. Medium Ævum Monographs, New Series XXI. Oxford: Society for the Study of Mediaeval Languages and Literature.

Jespersen, O. 1909 [4th ed. 1928]. *A Modern English Grammar, Part I*. Heidelberg: Carl Winters Universitätsbuchhandlung.

Johannessen, J. *et al.* (eds.). 2003. *På språkjakt – problemer og utfordringer i språkvitenskapelig datainnsamling*. Oslo: Unipub.

Johnston, P. A. 1980. *A Synchronic and Historical View of Border Area Bimoric Vowel Systems*. Ph.D. dissertation. University of Edinburgh.

1992. 'English Vowel Shifting: One Great Vowel Shift or Two Small Vowel Shifts?' *Diachronica* IX/2: 189–226.

Johnston, R.C. 1987. *Orthographia Gallica*. Anglo-Norman Text Society, Plain Texts Series 5. Oxford: Express Litho Service.

Jones, C. 1989. *A History of English Phonology*. London: Longman.

Jordan, R. 1968. *Handbuch der mittelenglischen Grammatik: Lautlehre*. Heidelberg: Carl Winter Universitätsverlag.

Kastovsky, D. *et al.* (eds.). 1988. *Luick Revisited*. Tübingen: Gunter Narr Verlag.

Kitson, P. 1998. 'Review Article of Kristensson 1995'. *NOMINA* 21: 169–178.

Koopman, W. *et al.* (eds.). 1987. *Explanation and Linguistic Change*. Amsterdam: John Benjamins.

Kristensson, G. 1967. *A Survey of Middle English Dialects 1290–1350. The Six Northern Counties and Lincolnshire* [SMED1]. Lund: CWK Gleerup.

1976. 'Lay Subsidy Rolls and Dialect Geography'. *English Studies* 57: 51–59.

1987. *A Survey of Middle English Dialects 1290–1350: The West Midland Counties* [SMED2]. Lund University Press.

1995. *A Survey of Middle English Dialects 1290–1350: The East Midland Counties* [SMED3]. Lund University Press.

1997. 'The Old English Anglian/Saxon Boundary Revisited'. In: Fisiak, J. (ed.) *Studies in Middle English Linguistics*. Berlin and New York: Mouton de Gruyter; 271–281.

2001. *A Survey of Middle English Dialects 1290–1350: The Southern Counties. I. Vowels (except Diphthongs)* [SMED4]. Lund University Press.

2002. *A Survey of Middle English Dialects 1290–1350: The Southern Counties. II. Diphthongs and Consonants* [SMED5]. Lund University Press.

Kuhn, S.M. and R. Quirk. 1953. 'Some recent interpretations of Old English digraph spellings', *Language 29*. Reprinted in Quirk 1968; 38–54.

Kytö, M. and M. Rissanen. 1997. 'Introduction. Language analysis and diachronic corpora'. In: Hickey, R., *et al.* (eds.). *Tracing the Trail of Time. Proceedings from the Second Diachronic Corpora Workshop*. Amsterdam: Rodopi; 9–22.

Kytö, M., M. Rissanen and S. Wright (eds.). 1994. *Corpora Across the Centuries. Proceedings of the First International Colloquium on English Diachronic Corpora*. Amsterdam: Rodopi.

Kökeritz, H. 1932. *The Phonology of the Suffolk Dialect*. Uppsala: Appelbergs Boktryckeri.

1953. *Shakespeare's Pronunciation*. New Haven: Yale University Press.

1954. *A Guide to Chaucer's Pronunciation*. Stockholm: Almqvist and Wiksell.

Labov, W. 1994. *Principles of Linguistic Change, Vol. I.* Oxford: Blackwell.

1996. 'The Organization of Dialect Diversity in North America'. Paper read at the *ICSLP4, the Fourth International Conference on Spoken Language Processing at Philadelphia, 6 October 1996.*

2002. 'West Germanic vs. North Germanic: insights from the study of chain shifts in progress'. Paper read at the annual meeting of *Norsk forening for språkvitenskap*, 7 May 2002, University of Oslo.

Labov, W., M. Yaeger, and R. Steiner. 1972. *A Quantitative Study of Sound Change in Progress*. Philadelphia: U.S. Regional Survey.

Labov, W., S. Ash and C. Boberg. 1997. 'A National Map of the Regional Dialects of American English'. URL: www.ling.upenn.edu/phono_atlas/NationalMap/NationalMap.html

Labov, W., S. Ash, and C. Boberg. 2006. *The Atlas of North American English: Phonetics, Phonology and Sound Change*. New York: Walter de Gruyter.

Ladefoged, P. 1962. *Elements of Acoustic Phonetics*. Edinburgh and London: Oliver and Boyd.

1982. *A C5b ourse in phonetics*. New York: Harcourt, Brace, Jovanovich.

2005 [2nd ed.]. *Vowels and Consonants*. Malden, Oxford and Carlton: Blackwell.

LAEME, see Laing, M. 2008.

Laing, M. (ed.). 1989. *Middle English Dialectology: essays on some principles and problems*. Aberdeen University Press.

1993. *Catalogue of Sources for a Linguistic Atlas of Early Medieval English*. Cambridge: D.S. Brewer.

1994. 'The Linguistic Analysis of Medieval Vernacular Texts: Two Projects at Edinburgh'. In: Kytö, M. *et al.* (eds.). *Corpora Across the Centuries. Proceedings of the First International Colloquium on English Diachronic Corpora*. Amsterdam: Rodopi; 121–141.

1995. 'A Linguistic Atlas of Early Middle English'. *Medieval English Studies Newsletter* 33. University of Tokyo; 1–8.

1999. 'Confusion *wrs* Confounded: Litteral Substitution Sets in Early Middle English Writing Systems'. *Neuphilologische Mitteilungen* 100: 251–270.

2000. '"Never the Twain Shall Meet": Early Middle English – the East West divide'. In: Taavitsainen, I. *et al.* (eds.). *Placing Middle English in Context. Topics in English Linguistics Series*. Berlin/New York: Mouton de Gruyter; 97–124.

2008. *A Linguistic Atlas of Early Middle English*. University of Edinburgh. www.lel.ed.ac.uk/ihd/laeme1/laeme1.html

Laing, M. and R. Lass. 2003. 'Tales of the 1001 Nists: The Phonological Implications of Litteral Substitution Sets in Some Thirteenth-Century South-West Midland Texts'. *English Language and Linguistics* 7.2: 257–278.

Laing, M. and K. Williamson. 1994. *Speaking in Our Tongues*. Cambridge: D.S. Brewer.

LALME, see McIntosh, Samuels, Benskin *et al.* 1986.

Lass, R. 1974. 'Linguistic Orthogenesis; Scots Vowel Quantity and the English Length Conspiracy'. *York Papers in Linguistics* 4: 7–26.

1976. *English Phonology and Phonological Theory*. Cambridge University Press.

(ed.). 1969. *Approaches to English Historical Linguistics. An Anthology*. New York: Holt, Rinehart and Winston.

1980. *On Explaining Language Change*. Cambridge University Press.

1987a. 'Language, Speakers, History and Drift'. In: Koopman, W. *et al.* (eds.). *Explanation and Linguistic Change*. Amsterdam: John Benjamins; 151–176.

1987b. 'On sh*tting the Door in Early Modern English: A Reply to Professor Samuels'. In: Koopman, W. *et al.* (eds.). *Explanation and Linguistic Change*. Amsterdam: John Benjamins; 251–256.

1988. 'Vowel Shifts, Great and Otherwise: Remarks on Stockwell and Minkova'. In: Kastovsky, D. *et al.* (eds.). *Luick Revisited*. Tübingen: Gunter Narr Verlag; 395–410.

1990. 'What, if anything, was the Great Vowel Shift?' Paper read at the Sixth International Conference on English Historical Linguistics; 144–155.

1992. 'The Early Modern English Short Vowels *Noch Einmal*, Again'. *Diachronica* IX/1: 1–11.

1997. *Historical Linguistics and Language Change*. Cambridge University Press.

2009. 'On Schwa: Synchronic Prelude and Historical Fugue'. In: Minkova, D. (ed.) *Phonological Weakness in English. From Old to Present-Day English*. Basingstoke: Palgrave Macmillan; 47–77.

Lass, R. and M. Laing. 2005. 'Are Front Rounded Vowels Retained in West Midland Middle English?'. In: Ritt and Schendl 2005; 280–290.

2010. 'In Celebration of eEarly Middle English "h"'. *Neuphilologische Mitteilungen* 111: 357–366.

Lass, R. and S. Wright. 1985. 'The South African Chain-Shift: Order Out of Chaos?' In: Eaton, R. *et al.* (eds.). *Papers from the 4th International Conference on English Historical Linguistics*. Amsterdam: John Benjamins; 137–161.

Liebl, C. 2006. 'The A and O of a medieval English Sound-Change: Prolegomena to a Study of the Origins and Early Geographical Diffusion of /ɑ:/ > /ɔ:/'. In: Ritt, N. *et al.* (eds.). *Medieval English and Its Heritage. Structure, Meaning and Mechanisms of Change*. Frankfurt am Main: Peter Lang; 19–35.

Liljencrants, J. and B. Lindblom. 1972. 'Numerical Simulation of Vowel Quality Systems: The Role of Perceptual Contrast'. *Language*, 48, 4: 839–862.

Lorentz, O. 1996. 'Length and Correspondence in Scandinavian'. *Nordlyd* 24: 111–128.

Łubowicz, A. 2011. 'Ch. 73. Chain Shifts'. In: van Oostendorp, M. *et al.* (eds.). *The Blackwell Companion to Phonology, Vol.* III. Oxford: Blackwell 1717–1735.

Luick, K. 1896. *Untersuchungen zur englischen Lautgeschichte*. Straßburg: Trübner.

1899. 'Über die Diphthongierung van me. *ū, ī* und verwandte deutsche Erscheinungen'. *Archiv für das Studium der neueren Sprachen und Litteraturen* 53/103: 267–277.

1901. 'Der Ursprung der neuenglischen AI- und AU-diphthonge'. *Englische Studien* 29: 405–411.

1912. 'Über die neuenglische Vokalverschiebung'. *Englische Studien* 45: 432–437.

1914–1940. *Historische Grammatik der englischen Sprache, Vol. I, Parts 1 and 2*. Oxford: Basil Blackwell.

1932. 'Zur neuenglischen Lautgeschichte'. *Archiv für das Studium der neueren Sprachen 1932*: 89–90.

Lutz, A. 2004. 'The First Push: A Prelude to the Great Vowel Shift'. *Anglia, Band 122 (2004) Heft 2*: 209–224.

Maci, S.M. 2006. 'The Phonetic Representation of ME ī in Some Norfolk Works of the Late Fifteenth Century'. *English Studies*, 87, 2, *April*: 148–168.

Majocha, E. 2005. *Some early Middle English dialect features in the South-East Midlands; an onomastic study*. Ph.D. dissertation. University of Edinburgh.

Majors, T. and M.J. Gordon. 2008. 'The [+spread] of the Northern Cities Shift'. *University of Pennsylvania Working Papers in Linguistics. Volume 14, Issue 2. Selected Papers from NWAV 36*: 111–120.

Malsch, D.L. and R. Fulcher. 1975. 'Tensing and Syllabication in Middle English'. *Language*, 51, 2: 303–314.

Markus, M. 1994. 'The concept of ICAMET (Innsbruck Computer Archive of Middle English Texts). In: Kytö, M. *et al.* (eds.). *Corpora Across the Centuries. Proceedings of the First International Colloquium on English Diachronic Corpora*. Amsterdam: Rodopi; 41–52.

Martín, M.A. 2002. 'Old English <eo> in Middle Kentish Place-Names'. In: *SELIM no. 10 2000*: 55–75.

Martinet, A. 1952. 'Function, Structure, and Sound Change'. *Word* 8: 1–32.

1955. *Économie des changements phonétiques: traité de phonologie diachronique.* Bern: A. Francke.

McCarthy, C. 2010a. 'The Northern Cities Shift in Real Time: Evidence from Chicago'. *University of Pennsylvania Working Papers in Linguistics. Volume 15, Issue 2. Selected papers from NWAV 37*: 101–110.

2010b. 'The Northern Cities Shift in Chicago'. *Journal of English Linguistics* XX*(X)*: 1–22.

McClure, P. 1973. 'Lay Subsidy Rolls and Dialect Phonology'. In: Sandgren, F. (ed.). *Otium et Negotium. Studies in Onomatology and Library Science presented to Olof von Feilitzen. Acta Bibliothecae Regiae Stockholmiensis XVI*; 188–194.

McEnery, T. and A. Wilson. 2001 [2nd ed.]. *Corpus Linguistics. An Introduction.* Edinburgh: Edinburgh University Press.

McIntosh, A. 1956. 'The Analysis of Written Middle English'. *Transactions of the Philological Society*: 26–55.

1963. 'A New Approach to Middle English Dialectology'. *English Studies* 44: 1–11.

1969. 'Review article of Kristensson 1967'. *Medium Ævum* 38/2: 210–16.

McIntosh, A., M.L. Samuels, M. Benskin *et al.* 1986. *A Linguistic Atlas of Late Mediaeval English, Vols. I-IV.* Aberdeen University Press.

McMahon, A. 1994. *Understanding Language Change.* Cambridge University Press.

2000. *Lexical Phonology and the history of English.* Cambridge University Press.

Meurman-Solin, A. 1997. 'Text Profiles in the Study of Language Variation and Change'. In: Hickey, R. *et al.* (eds.). *Tracing the Trail of Time. Proceedings from the Second Diachronic Corpora Workshop.* Amsterdam: Rodopi 199–214.

Minkova, D. 1982. 'The Environment for Open Syllable Lengthening in Middle English'. *Folia Linguistica Historica* III/1: 29–58.

1985. 'Of Rhyme and Reason: Some Foot-Governed Quantity Changes in English'. In: Eaton, R. *et al.* (eds.). *Papers from the 4th International Conference on English Historical Linguistics.* Amsterdam, Philadelphia: John Benjamins; 163–178.

1987. 'The Trajectory Constraint and "Irregular" Rhymes in Middle English'. Review article. *Folia Linguistica Historica* VIII/1–2: 481–501.

1997. 'Constraint Ranking in Middle English Stress-Shifting'. *English Language and Linguistics* 1/1: 135–175.

2014. *A Historical Phonology of English.* Edinburgh University Press.

Mitchell, A.G. and A. Delbridge. 1965. *The Pronunciation of English in Australia.* Sydney: Angus and Robertson.

Moore, S., Meech, S.B. and H. Whitehall. 1935. 'Middle English Dialect Characteristics and Dialect Boundaries'. *Essays and Studies in English and Comparative Literature, Vol. 13.* Ann Arbor: University of Michigan Press; 1–60.

Mossé, F. 1945. *Manuel de l'anglais du Moyen-Âge, I. Vieil-anglais.* Paris: Aubier.

Nevanlinna, S. 1999. Review Article of Kristensson 1995. *Studia Neophilologica* 71: 253–256.

Ogura, M., W.S-Y. Wang and L.L. Cavalli-Sforza. 1991. 'The Development of Middle English *ī* in England: a Study in Dynamic Dialectology'. In: Eckert,

P. (ed.). *New Ways of Analyzing Sound Change*. New York: Academic Press; 63–106.

Ogura, M. 1990. *Dynamic Dialectology. A Study of Language in Time and Space*. Tokyo: Kenkyusha.

1995. 'The Development of Middle English ī and ū: A reply to Labov (1992, 1994)'. *Diachronica* 12: 31–53.

Ortega-Llebaria, M. and P. Prieto. 2010. 'Acoustic Correlates of Stress in Central Catalan and Castilian Spanish'. *Language and Speech* 54/1: 73–97.

Orton, H. 1933. *The Phonology of a South Durham Dialect*. London: Kegan Paul, Trench, Trubner and Co.

Orton, H. and E. Dieth. 1962. *The Survey of English Dialects*. Leeds: Arnold.

van Oostendorp, M. *et al.* (eds.). 2011. *The Blackwell Companion to Phonology, Vol. III*. Oxford: Blackwell.

Peacock, R.B. 1869. A Glossary of the Dialect of the Hundred of Lonsdale, North and South of the Sands, in the County of Lancaster. Asher & Co. for the Philological Society.

Peeters, W.J.M. 1991. *Diphthong Dynamics*. Doctoral dissertation, the University of Utrecht. Kampen: Mondiss.

Pelt, J. 1980. 'Vowel Shift and Open Syllable Lengthening: A Length Conspiracy in Dutch'. In: Anderson, J.M. and C.J. Ewen (eds.). *Studies in Dependency Phonology. Ludwigsburg Studies in Language and Linguistics 4*. Ludwigsburg: R.O.U. Strauch; 61–101.

Penzl, H. 1957. 'The Evidence for Phonemic Change'. In: Pulgram, E. (ed.) *Studies Presented to Joshua Whatmough on His Sixtieth Birthday*. The Hague: Mouton; 193–208.

Phillips, B.S. 1997. 'The *Peterborough Chronicle* diphthongs.' In: Fisiak, J. (ed.) *Studies in Middle English Linguistics*. Berlin and New York: Mouton de Gruyter; 429–438.

Phillips, B. 2006a. *Word Frequency and Lexical Diffusion*. Basingstoke: Palgrave Macmillan.

2006b. 'Word Frequency Effects in the Great Vowel Shift'. Paper read at the 14th International Conference on English Historical Linguistics, Bergamo, Italy, 21–25 August 2006.

Pilch, H. 1997. 'Middle English Phonetics: A systematic survey including notes on Irish and Welsh Loanwords.' In: Fisiak, J. (ed.) *Studies in Middle English Linguistics*. Berlin and New York: Mouton de Gruyter; 437–467.

Pope, M.K. 1934. *From Latin to Modern French With Especial Consideration of Anglo-Norman*. Manchester University Press.

Prins, A.A. 1942a. 'A Few Early Examples of the Great Vowel Shift'. *Neophilologus* 27: 134–137.

1942b. 'The Great Vowel Shift Reconsidered'. *English Studies* 24: 161–168.

1972. *A History of English Phonemes*. Leiden University Press.

Prokosch, E. 1939. *A Comparative Germanic Grammar*. Yale University: the Linguistic Society of America.

Quirk, R. 1968. *Essays on the English Language, Medieval and Modern*. London and Harlow: Longmans.

Raumolin-Brunberg, H. 2006. 'Leaders of Linguistic Change in Early Modern England'. In: Facchinetti, R. and M. Rissanen (eds.). *Corpus-Based Studies of Diachronic English*. Bern, New York etc.: Peter Lang; 115–134.

van Reenen, P. and A. Wijnands. 1989. 'Early Diphthongizations of Palatalized West Germanic [u:]. The Spelling *uy* in Middle Dutch'. In: Aertsen, H. and R.J. Jeffers (eds.) 1993. *Papers from the 9th International Conference on Historical Linguistics*. Amsterdam: John Benjamins; 389–415.

Ringgaard, K. 1982. 'On the Problem of Merger'. In: Maher, J.P. *et al.* (eds.). *Papers from the 3rd International Conference on Historical Linguistics*. Amsterdam: John Benjamins; 387–395.

Rissanen, M. 1994. 'The Helsinki Corpus of English Texts'. In: Kytö, M. *et al.* (eds.). *Corpora Across the Centuries. Proceedings of the First International Colloquium on English Diachronic Corpora*. Amsterdam: Rodopi; 73–79.

Ritt, N. 1994. *Quantity Adjustment. Vowel Lengthening and Shortening in Early Middle English*. Cambridge University Press.

Ritt, N. and H. Schendl (eds.). 2005. *Rethinking Middle English: Linguistic and Literary Approaches*. Frankfurt am Main: Peter Lang.

Ritt, N. *et al.* (eds.). 2006. *Medieval English and Its Heritage. Structure, Meaning and Mechanisms of Change*. Frankfurt am Main: Peter Lang.

Samuels, B.D. 2006. *Nothing to Lose but Their Chains: Rethinking Vocalic Chain Shifting*. Unpublished BA thesis, Harvard University.

Samuels, M.L. 1963. 'Some Applications of Middle English Dialectology'. *English Studies* 44: 81–94. Reprinted in Lass 1969: 404–418.

1971. 'Kent and the Low Countries: Some Linguistic Evidence'. In: Aitken, A.J., A. McIntosh and H. Pálsson (eds.). *Edinburgh Studies in English and Scots*. London: Longman; 3–19.

1972. *Linguistic Evolution*. Cambridge University Press.

1985. 'The Great Scandinavian Belt'. In: Eaton, R. *et al.* (eds.). *Papers from the 4th International Conference on English Historical Linguistics, Amsterdam, 10–13 April 1985*. Amsterdam: Benjamins; 269–281. Reprinted in Laing 1989: 106–115.

1987a. 'The Status of the Functional Approach'. In: Koopman, W. *et al.* (eds.). *Explanation and Linguistic Change*. Amsterdam: John Benjamins; 239–250.

1987b. 'A Brief Rejoinder to Professor Lass'. In: Koopman, W. *et al.* (eds.). *Explanation and Linguistic Change*. Amsterdam: John Benjamins; 257–258.

Schane, S.A. 1990. 'Lowered Height, Laxness, and Retracted Tongue Root: Different Manifestations of Phonological APERTURE'. *Word* 41/1: 1–16.

Schlemilch, W. 1914. Beiträge zur Sprache und Orthographie spätaltenglischer Sprachdenkmäler der Übergangszeit. Halle: Niemeyer.

Sievers, E. 1850. *Grundzüge der Phonetik: Zur Einführung in das Studium der Lautlehre der indogermanischen Sprachen*. Leipzig: Breitkopf und Hartel.

Sievers, E. and K. Brunner (rev.). 1942. *Altenglische Grammatik*. Halle/Saale: Max Niemeyer.

Sievers, E. and A. Cook (transl. and rev.). 1968. *An Old English Grammar*. New York: Greenwood.

Sisam, K. 1962. *Fourteenth Century Verse and Prose*. Oxford: Clarendon Press.

Sivertsen, E. 1960. *Cockney Phonology*. Oslo University Press.

Skauptrup, P. 1944–70. *Det danske sprogs historie*. København: Gyldendal.

Smith, J.J. 1993. 'Dialectal Variation in Middle English and the Actuation of the Great Vowel Shift'. *Neuphilologische Mitteilungen* XCIV/3–4: 259–277.

1994. 'The Great Vowel Shift in the North of England, and Some Spellings in Manuscripts of Chaucer's *Reeve's Tale*'. *Neuphilologische Mitteilungen* 95: 433–437.

1996. *An Historical Study of English*. London: Routledge.

2006. 'Phonaesthesia, *Ablaut* and the history of the English demonstratives'. In: Ritt *et al.* 2006: 1–17.

2007. *Sound Change and the History of English*. Oxford University Press.

Smithers, G.V. 1952 and 1957. *Kyng Alisaunder*. Early English Text Society, Original Series 227 and 237. London: Oxford University Press.

Stanley, E.G. 1960. *The Owl and the Nightingale*. Nelson's Medieval and Renaissance Library. London.

1972. *The Owl and the Nightingale*. Manchester University Press.

Stenbrenden, G.F. 1996. *The Great Vowel Shift: Problems of Reification and Analysis*. Unpublished *Cand.Philol.* thesis. University of Oslo.

1999. 'A Reassessment of the Chronology and Regional Spread of Certain English Long-Vowel Changes, ca. 1250–1500'. In: López, A.B. *et al.* (eds.). *'Woonderous Ænglissce'. SELIM Studies in Medieval English Language*. Universidade de Vigo: Servicio de Publicacións; 161–174.

2003a. 'On the Interpretion of Early Evidence for ME Vowel-Change'. In: Blake, B. and K. Burridge (eds.). *Historical Linguistics 2001. Selected papers from the 15th International Conference on Historical Linguistics, Melbourne, 13–17 August 2001*. John Benjamins; 403–415.

2003b. 'On the inception and spread of early ME *ā* > *ǭ* – some observations'. Paper read at the 1st International Conference on English Historical Dialectology, Bergamo, 4–6 September 2003.

2009. 'An investigation into the development of OE *ȳ* and lengthened *y* in Middle English.' Paper read at the Historical Language and Literacy in the North Sea Area conference, Stavanger, 26–28 August 2009.

2010. *The Chronology and Regional Spread of Long-Vowel Changes in English, c. 1150–1500*. Ph.D. dissertation, University of Oslo.

2013. 'The Diphthongisation of ME *ū*: the Spelling Evidence'. In: Andersen, G. and Bech, K. (eds.) *English Corpus Linguistics: Variation in Time, Space and Genre: Selected Papers from Icame 32* (*Language & Computers*). Rodopi; 53–67.

Stenroos, M. 2005. 'Spelling Conventions and Rounded Front Vowels in the Poems of William Herebert.' In: Ritt, N. and H. Schendl (eds.). *Rethinking Middle English: Linguistic and Literary Approaches*. Frankfurt am Main: Peter Lang; 291–308.

Steponavičius, A. 1997. 'Middle (and Old) English Prerequisites for the Great Vowel Shift'. In: Fisiak, J. (ed.) *Studies in Middle English Linguistics*. Berlin and New York: Mouton de Gruyter; 561–572.

2005. 'The Great Vowel Shift as a Paradigmatic Restructuring of the Late ME Vowel System'. In: Ritt, N. and H. Schendl (eds.). *Rethinking Middle*

English: Linguistic and Literary Approaches. Frankfurt am Main, etc.: Peter Lang; 309–316.

Stockwell, R.P. 1952. *Chaucerian Graphemics and Phonemics: A Study in Historical Methodology*. Ph.D. dissertation. University of Virginia.

1960. 'The Middle English "Long Close" and "Long Open" Mid Vowels'. In: *University of Texas Studies in Literature and Language* 2: 529–538.

1964. 'On the Utility of an Overall Pattern in Historical English Phonology'. In: *Proceedings of the Ninth International Congress of Linguists*. The Hague: Mouton; 663–671.

1972. 'Problems in the Interpretation of the Great English Vowel Shift'. In: Smith, M.E. (ed.) 1972. *Studies in Linguistics in Honor of George L. Trager*; 344–362. The Hague: Mouton.

1978. 'Perseverance in the English Vowel Shift'. In: Fisiak, J. (ed.) 1978. *Recent Developments in Historical Phonology*. The Hague: Mouton; 337–348.

1985. 'Assessment of Alternative Explanations of the Middle English Phenomenon of High Vowel Lowering when Lengthened in the Open Syllable'. In: Eaton, R. *et al.* (eds.). *Papers from the 4th International Conference on English Historical Linguistics*. Amsterdam, Philadelphia: John Benjamins; 303–318.

2006. 'The Status of Late Middle English <*ei*> Spellings as Early Evidence of the English Vowel Shift'. In: Schaefer, U. (ed.). *The Beginnings of Standardization: Language and Culture in Fourteenth-Century England*. Frankfurt am Main: Peter Lang; 175–180.

Stockwell, R.P. and D. Minkova. 1988a. 'The English Vowel Shift: problems of coherence and explanation'. In: Kastovsky, D. *et al.* (eds.). *Luick Revisited*. Tübingen: Gunter Narr Verlag; 355–394.

1988b. 'A Rejoinder to Lass'. In: Kastovsky, D. *et al.* (eds.). *Luick Revisited*. Tübingen: Gunter Narr Verlag; 411–417.

1990. 'The Early Modern English Vowels, More o' Lass'. *Diachronica* VII/2: 199–213.

1997. 'On Drifts and Shifts'. *Studia Anglica Posnaniensia* XXXI: 283–303.

Strang, B. 1970. *A History of English*. London: Methuen.

1980. 'The ecology of the English monosyllable'. In: Greenbaum, S. *et al.* (eds.). *Studies in English linguistics for Randolph Quirk*. London: Longman; 277–293.

Stürzinger, J. 1884. *Orthographia Gallica. Ältester Traktat über französische Aussprache und Orthographie nach vier Handschriften zum ersten Mal hrsg.* Altfranzösische Bibliothek, 8. volume. Heilbronn: Henninger.

Sundby, G. 1963. *Studies in the Middle English Dialect Material of Worcestershire Records*. Bergen and Oslo: Norwegian Universities Press.

Sweet, H. 1888. *A History of English Sounds*. Oxford: Clarendon Press.

1953. *Sweet's Anglo-Saxon Primer*. Oxford: Clarendon Press.

Söderholm, T. 1970. *The End-Rhymes of Marvell, Cowley, Crashaw, Lovelace and Vaughan. Acta Academiae Aboensis, Ser. A, Vol. 39, nr. 2*. Ekenäs.

Torp, A. and L.S. Vikør. 1993. Hovuddrag i norsk språkhistorie. Ad Notam Gyldendal.

Versloot, A.P. 2008. *Mechanisms of Language Change: Vowel Reduction in 15th Century West Frisian*. Utrecht: LOT.

Wallenberg, J.K. 1931. *Kentish Place-Names. A Topographical and Etymological Study of the Place-Name Material in Kentish Charters Dated before the Conquest*. Uppsala: A.-B. Lundequistska Bokhandeln.

1934. *The Place-Names of Kent*. Uppsala: Appelbergs Boktryckeriaktiebolag.

Weinreich, U., W. Labov, and M.I. Herzog. 1968. 'Empirical Foundations for a Theory of Language Change'. In: Lehmann, W.P. and Y. Malkiel (eds.). *Directions for Historical Linguistics: A Symposium*. Austin and London: University of Texas Press; 95–195.

Wells, J.C. 1982. *Accents of English I. An Introduction*. Cambridge University Press.

Wełna, J. 1988. '*Historische Grammatik* and Middle English diphthongal systems.' In: Kastovsky, D. *et al.* (eds.). *Luick Revisited*. Tübingen: Gunter Narr Verlag; 419–433.

2004. 'Middle English *ē*-Raising: a Prelude to the Great Vowel Shift'. *Studia Anglica Posnanienska* 40: 75–83.

Western, A. 1912. 'Über die neuenglische Vokalverschiebung'. *Englische Studien* 45: 1–8.

Whitehall, H. 1935. 'Some Fifteenth-Century Spellings From the Nottingham Records'. In: *Essays and Studies in English and Comparative Literature*; 61–71. Ann Arbor: University of Michigan Press.

Widén, B. 1949. *Studies on the Dorset Dialect*. Lund: C.W.K. Gleerup.

Williamson, K. 2006 (ms.). 'Further reflections on the outcomes of Northern Fronting in Older Scots'. Paper read at 14 ICEHL, University of Bergamo, 21–25 August, 2006.

Winters, M.E. 1997. 'Kurylowicz, Analogical Change, and Cognitive Grammar'. *Cognitive Linguistics* 8/4: 359–386.

Wolfe, P.M. 1972. *Linguistic Change and the Great Vowel Shift in English*. Berkeley: University of California Press.

Wrenn, C.L. 1943. 'The Value of Spelling as Evidence'. *Transactions of the Philological Society*: 14–39.

Wright, J. 1905. *The English Dialect Grammar*. Oxford, London, Edinburgh, Glasgow, New York and Toronto: Henry Frowde.

1924. *An Elementary Historical New English Grammar*. Oxford University Press.

Wright, J. and E.M. Wright. 1925. *Old English Grammar*. Oxford University Press.

1928. *An Elementary Middle English Grammar*. Oxford University Press.

Wright, L. 1996. *Sources of London English: medieval Thames vocabulary*. Oxford: Clarendon Press.

Wyld, H.C. 1913–14a. 'The Treatment of OE. *ȳ* in the Dialects of the Midland, and SE. Counties, in ME'. *Englische Studien* 47: 1–58.

1913–14b. 'Old English *ȳ* in the Dialects of the South, and South Western Counties in Middle English.' *Englische Studien* 47: 145–166.

1927. *A Short History of English*. Third edition. London: John Murray.

1936. *A History of Modern Colloquial English*. Oxford: Basil Blackwell.

Zachrisson, R.E. 1913. *Pronunciation of English Vowels 1400–1700*. Göteborg: Wald. Zachrissons Boktryckeri.

1970. *The English Pronunciation at Shakespeare's Time as Taught by William Bullokar: With word-lists from all his works*. New York: AMS Press.

Index

CPSIA information can be obtained
at www.ICGtesting.com
Printed in the USA
LVHW042004140119
603860LV00016B/367/P